Taking SIDES

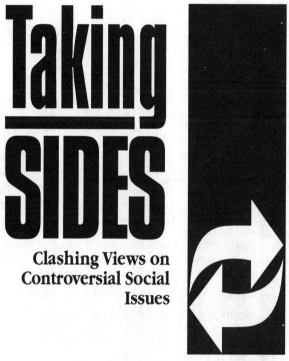

Clashing Views on Controversial Social Issues

Tenth Edition

Edited, Selected, and with Introductions by

Kurt Finsterbusch
University of Maryland

Dushkin/McGraw-Hill
A Division of The McGraw-Hill Companies

To my wife, Meredith Ramsay, who richly shares with me a life of the mind and much, much more.

Photo Acknowledgments

Cover image: © 1999 by PhotoDisc, Inc.

Cover Art Acknowledgment

Charles Vitelli

Manufactured in the United States of America

Tenth Edition

123456789BAHBAH321098

Library of Congress Cataloging-in-Publication Data

Main entry under title:
    Taking sides: clashing views on controversial social issues/edited, selected, and with introductions by Kurt Finsterbusch.—10th ed.
    Includes bibliographical references and index.
    1. Social behavior. 2. Social problems. I. Finsterbusch, Kurt, *comp.*

302

0-697-39113-2

95-83865

 Printed on Recycled Paper

PREFACE

The English word *fanatic* is derived from the Latin *fanum*, meaning temple. It refers to the kind of madmen often seen in the precincts of temples in ancient times, the kind presumed to be possessed by deities or demons. The term first came into English usage during the seventeenth century, when it was used to describe religious zealots. Soon after, its meaning was broadened to include a political and social context. We have come to associate the term *fanatic* with a person who acts as if his or her views were inspired, a person utterly incapable of appreciating opposing points of view. The nineteenth-century English novelist George Eliot put it precisely: "I call a man fanatical when ... he ... becomes unjust and unsympathetic to men who are out of his own track." A fanatic may hear but is unable to listen. Confronted with those who disagree, a fanatic immediately vilifies opponents.

Most of us would avoid the company of fanatics, but who among us is not tempted to caricature opponents instead of listening to them? Who does not put certain topics off limits for discussion? Who does not grasp at euphemisms to avoid facing inconvenient facts? Who has not, in George Eliot's language, sometimes been "unjust and unsympathetic" to those on a different track? Who is not, at least in certain very sensitive areas, a *little* fanatical? The counterweight to fanaticism is open discussion. The difficult issues that trouble us as a society have at least two sides, and we lose as a society if we hear only one side. At the individual level, the answer to fanaticism is listening. And that is the underlying purpose of this book: to encourage its readers to listen to opposing points of view.

This book contains 40 selections presented in a pro and con format. A total of 20 different controversial social issues are debated. The sociologists, political scientists, economists, and social critics whose views are debated here make their cases vigorously. In order to effectively read each selection, analyze the points raised, and debate the basic assumptions and values of each position, or, in other words, in order to think critically about what you are reading, you will first have to give each side a sympathetic hearing. John Stuart Mill, the nineteenth-century British philosopher, noted that the majority is not doing the minority a favor by listening to its views; it is doing *itself* a favor. By listening to contrasting points of view, we strengthen our own. In some cases we change our viewpoints completely. But in most cases, we either incorporate some elements of the opposing view—thus making our own richer—or else learn how to answer the objections to our viewpoints. Either way, we gain from the experience.

Organization of the book   Each issue has an issue *introduction*, which sets the stage for the debate as it is argued in the YES and NO selections. Each issue concludes with a *postscript* that makes some final observations and points the way to other questions related to the issue. In reading the issue and forming your own opinions you should not feel confined to adopt one or the other of the positions presented. There are positions in between the given views or totally outside them, and the *suggestions for further reading* that appear in each issue postscript should help you find resources to continue your study of the subject. At the back of the book is a listing of all the *contributors to this volume*, which will give you information on the social scientists whose views are debated here. Also, on the *On the Internet* page that accompanies each part opener, you will find Internet site addresses (URLs) that are relevant to the issues in that part.

Changes to this edition   This new edition has been significantly updated. There are seven completely new issues: *Are Communication Problems Between Men and Women Largely Due to Radically Different Conversation Styles?* (Issue 5); *Is Increasing Economic Inequality a Serious Problem?* (Issue 8); *Has Affirmative Action Outlived Its Usefulness?* (Issue 10); *Will Welfare Reform Benefit the Poor?* (Issue 13); *Are Vouchers the Solution to the Ills of Public Education?* (Issue 14); *Should Doctor-Assisted Suicide Be Legalized for the Terminally Ill?* (Issue 15); and *Should Drug Use Be Decriminalized?* (Issue 17). In addition, for the issues on moral decline (Issue 1), immigration (Issue 3), the decline of the traditional family (Issue 7), the poor (Issue 9), the influence of big business on government (Issue 11), and population growth (Issue 19), one or both of the selections were replaced to bring a fresh perspective to the debates. In all, there are 22 new selections. The issues that were dropped from the previous edition were done so on the recommendation of professors who let me know what worked and what could be improved. Wherever appropriate, new introductions and postscripts have been provided.

A word to the instructor   An *Instructor's Manual With Test Questions* (multiple-choice and essay) is available through the publisher for the instructor using *Taking Sides* in the classroom. A general guidebook, *Using Taking Sides in the Classroom*, which discusses methods and techniques for integrating the pro-con approach into any classroom setting, is also available. An online version of *Using Taking Sides in the Classroom* and a correspondence service for *Taking Sides* adopters can be found at www.cybsol.com/usingtakingsides/. For students, we offer a field guide to analyzing argumentative essays, *Analyzing Controversy: An Introductory Guide*, with exercises and techniques to help them to decipher genuine controversies.

   Taking Sides: Clashing Views on Controversial Social Issues is only one title in the Taking Sides series. If you are interested in seeing the table of contents for any of the other titles, please visit the Taking Sides Web site at http://www.dushkin.com/takingsides/.

Acknowledgments We received many helpful comments and suggestions from our friends and readers across the United States and Canada. Their suggestions have markedly enhanced the quality of this edition of *Taking Sides* and are reflected in the new issues and the updated selections. Our thanks go to those who responded with specific suggestions for this edition:

Bonnie Ach
Chapman University

Fasih Ahmed
North Carolina Agricultural
  and Technical State
  University

Donald Anspach
University of Southern Maine

Susanne Blieberg Seperson
Dowling College

Olga Bright
Chaffey College

Jami Brown
Riverside Community
  College

Deborah Burris-Kitch
University of La Verne

Ting-Shih Chia
Morningside College

James Crispino
University of Connecticut

Peter Heckman
Nebraska Wesleyan
  University

Antonio F. Holland
Lincoln University

Shirin Hollis
Southern Connecticut State
  University

Karen M. Jennison
University of Northern
  Colorado

Kristine Kleptach Jamieson
Ashland University

Cynthia Marconi-Hick
Richard Stockton College
  of New Jersey

Terry Mills
University of Florida

Kristin Park
Westminster College

Joann Sloan
Gordon College

I also wish to acknowledge the encouragement and support given to this project over the years by Mimi Egan, former publisher for the Taking Sides series. I am grateful as well to David Dean, list manager for the Taking Sides series, and David Brackley, senior developmental editor.

I want to thank my wife, Meredith Ramsay, for her example and support.

I also want to thank George McKenna for many years as a close colleague and through many editions of this book.

Kurt Finsterbusch
University of Maryland

CONTENTS IN BRIEF

PART 1   CULTURE AND VALUES   1

Issue 1.   Is America in Moral Decline?   2

Issue 2.   Does the News Media Have a Liberal Bias?   22

Issue 3.   Is Third World Immigration a Threat to America's Way of
            Life?   40

PART 2   SEX ROLES, GENDER, AND THE FAMILY   59

Issue 4.   Is Feminism a Harmful Ideology?   60

Issue 5.   Are Communication Problems Between Men and Women
            Largely Due to Radically Different Conversation Styles?   82

Issue 6.   Should Society Be More Accepting of Homosexuality?   100

Issue 7.   Is the Decline of the Traditional Family a National Crisis?   116

PART 3   STRATIFICATION AND INEQUALITY   137

Issue 8.   Is Increasing Economic Inequality a Serious Problem?   138

Issue 9.   Are the Poor Largely Responsible for Their Poverty?   152

Issue 10.   Has Affirmative Action Outlived Its Usefulness?   168

PART 4   POLITICAL ECONOMY AND INSTITUTIONS   187

Issue 11.   Is Government Dominated by Big Business?   188

Issue 12.   Should Government Intervene in a Capitalist Economy?   206

Issue 13.   Will Welfare Reform Benefit the Poor?   224

Issue 14.   Are Vouchers the Solution to the Ills of Public Education?   246

Issue 15.   Should Doctor-Assisted Suicide Be Legalized for the Terminally
            Ill?   262

PART 5   CRIME AND SOCIAL CONTROL   279

Issue 16.   Is Street Crime More Harmful Than White-Collar Crime?   280

Issue 17.   Should Drug Use Be Decriminalized?   298

Issue 18.   Is Incapacitation the Answer to the Crime Problem?   316

**PART 6   THE FUTURE: POPULATION/
           ENVIRONMENT/SOCIETY   337**

Issue 19.   Does Population Growth Threaten Humanity?   338

Issue 20.   Are Standards of Living in the United States Improving?   354

CONTENTS

Preface   i

Introduction: Debating Social Issues   xiv

PART 1   *CULTURE AND VALUES*   1

ISSUE 1.   **Is America in Moral Decline?**   2

YES: Gertrude Himmelfarb, from *The De-Moralization of Society: From Victorian Virtues to Modern Values*   4

NO: Everett C. Ladd, from "The Myth of Moral Decline," *The Responsive Community*   12

Gertrude Himmelfarb, a professor emeritus of history, details some of the increasing moral problems in America and interprets them as being part of a larger pattern, which she calls "the de-moralization of society." Everett C. Ladd, president of the Roper Center for Public Opinion, empirically tests the moral decline thesis and finds that, according to the indicators that he employs, it is a myth.

ISSUE 2.   **Does the News Media Have a Liberal Bias?**   22

YES: H. Joachim Maitre, from "The Tilt to the News: How American Journalism Has Swerved from the Ideal of Objectivity," *The World and I*   24

NO: Martin A. Lee and Norman Solomon, from *Unreliable Sources: A Guide to Detecting Bias in News Media*   31

Journalism professor H. Joachim Maitre argues that news reporters are liberals who allow their political views to seep into their reporting. Media critics Martin A. Lee and Norman Solomon argue that media bias in reporting is toward the conservative status quo.

ISSUE 3.   **Is Third World Immigration a Threat to America's Way of Life?**   40

YES: Peter Brimelow, from *Alien Nation: Common Sense About America's Immigration Disaster*   42

NO: John Isbister, from *The Immigration Debate: Remaking America*   48

Peter Brimelow, a writer and senior editor of *Forbes* and *National Review*, asserts that the large influx of immigrants from non-European countries threatens to undermine the cultural foundations of American unity. John Isbister, a provost at the University of California, Santa Cruz, cites research showing that immigration does not have the many negative impacts that people like Brimelow fear. He argues that immigration has a negligible effect on earnings and public finances and that its cultural impacts "will make it more obvious that the United States is a plural and not a unicultural society."

PART 2   SEX ROLES, GENDER, AND THE FAMILY   59

ISSUE 4.   Is Feminism a Harmful Ideology?   60

YES: Robert Sheaffer, from "Feminism, the Noble Lie," *Free Inquiry*   62

NO: William H. Chafe, from *The Paradox of Change: American Women in the Twentieth Century*   69

Robert Sheaffer, a consulting editor for *Skeptical Inquirer*, argues that feminists are attempting to impose an inappropriate equality on men and women that conflicts with basic biological differences between the genders. William H. Chafe, a professor at Duke University, maintains that the vast improvements that women have made and the obvious need to end continuing discrimination demonstrate the value of feminism.

ISSUE 5.   Are Communication Problems Between Men and Women Largely Due to Radically Different Conversation Styles?   82

YES: Deborah Tannen, from *You Just Don't Understand: Women and Men in Conversation*   84

NO: Mary Crawford, from *Talking Difference: On Gender and Language*   91

Deborah Tannen, a professor of sociolinguistics, argues that men and women have strikingly different communication styles, in that men's concerns about maintaining or enhancing their status greatly affects what they hear and say, while women's concern about connections and closeness greatly affects their communication. Professor of psychology Mary Crawford argues that the thesis that men and women have radically different communication styles is greatly exaggerated in the media and is based on simplistic stereotypes.

ISSUE 6.   Should Society Be More Accepting of Homosexuality?   100

YES: Richard D. Mohr, from *A More Perfect Union: Why Straight America Must Stand Up for Gay Rights*   102

NO: Carl F. Horowitz, from "Homosexuality's Legal Revolution," *The Freeman*   109

Philosophy professor Richard D. Mohr argues that homosexuality is neither immoral nor unnatural and that homosexuals should have the same rights as heterosexuals. Carl F. Horowitz, a policy analyst at the Heritage Foundation, argues that legal acceptance of homosexuality has already gone too far.

ISSUE 7.   Is the Decline of the Traditional Family a National Crisis?   116

YES: David Popenoe, from "The American Family Crisis," *National Forum: The Phi Kappa Phi Journal*   118

NO: Stephanie Coontz, from *The Way We Really Are: Coming to Terms With America's Changing Families*   125

Sociologist David Popenoe contends that families play important roles in society but how the traditional family functions in these roles has declined dramatically in the last several decades, with very adverse effects on children. Family historian Stephanie Coontz argues that current discussion of family decline includes a false idealization of the traditional family of the past and misleading interpretations of current data on families. She finds that the trends are both positive and negative.

PART 3   STRATIFICATION AND INEQUALITY   137

ISSUE 8.   Is Increasing Economic Inequality a Serious Problem?   138

YES: Paul Krugman, from "The Spiral of Inequality," *Mother Jones*   140

NO: Christopher C. DeMuth, from "The New Wealth of Nations," *Commentary*   146

Economist Paul Krugman demonstrates the dramatic increase in income inequality by comparing data on income shares for 1970 and 1994. He assesses some of the potential nightmarish impacts of increasing inequality, including societal disintegration. Christopher C. DeMuth, president of the American Enterprise Institute for Public Policy Research, argues that the "recent increase in income inequality . . . is a very small tick in the massive and unprecedented leveling of material circumstances that has been proceeding now for almost three centuries and in this century has accelerated dramatically."

ISSUE 9.   Are the Poor Largely Responsible for Their Poverty?   152

YES: Nicholas Eberstadt, from "Prosperous Paupers and Affluent Savages," *Society*   154

NO: David M. Gordon, from "Values That Work," *The Nation*   161

Nicholas Eberstadt, a researcher with the American Enterprise Institute and the Harvard University Center for Population and Development Studies, contends that poverty and numerous problems "devolve from predictably injurious patterns of individual and parental behavior." The late professor of economics David M. Gordon attacks the values explanation for poverty and other problems because they ignore the structure and behavior of the economic system. He maintains that the decline of decent paying and steady jobs for workers without college educations is the real explanation for these problems.

ISSUE 10. Has Affirmative Action Outlived Its Usefulness? 168

YES: Walter E. Williams, from "Affirmative Action Can't Be Mended," *Cato Journal* 170

NO: Clarence Page, from *Showing My Color* 177

Professor of economics Walter E. Williams asserts that "the civil rights struggle for blacks is over and won," so affirmative action policies are unjust and adversely affect society. Journalist Clarence Page argues that affirmative action has largely opened doors for blacks that they should have gone through many years earlier and that, with prejudice and discrimination still virulent, some affirmative action is still needed to equalize opportunities.

PART 4   POLITICAL ECONOMY AND INSTITUTIONS 187

ISSUE 11. Is Government Dominated by Big Business? 188

YES: G. William Domhoff, from *Who Rules America? Power and Politics in the Year 2000*, 3rd ed. 190

NO: Jeffrey M. Berry, from "Citizen Groups and the Changing Nature of Interest Group Politics in America," *The Annals of the American Academy of Political and Social Science* 196

Political sociologist G. William Domhoff argues that the "owners and top-level managers in large income-producing properties are far and away the dominant power figures in the United States" and that they have inordinate influence in the federal government. Jeffrey M. Berry, a professor of political science, contends that public interest pressure groups that have entered the political arena since the end of the 1960s have effectively challenged the political power of big business.

ISSUE 12. Should Government Intervene in a Capitalist Economy? 206

YES: Ernest Erber, from "Virtues and Vices of the Market: Balanced
Correctives to a Current Craze," *Dissent* 208

NO: Milton and Rose Friedman, from *Free to Choose: A Personal
Statement* 215

Author Ernest Erber argues that capitalism creates serious social problems
that require government intervention to correct. Economists Milton and Rose
Friedman maintain that the market operates effectively and protects citizens better when permitted to work without the interference of government
regulations.

ISSUE 13. Will Welfare Reform Benefit the Poor? 224

YES: Daniel Casse, from "Why Welfare Reform Is Working,"
Commentary 226

NO: David Stoesz, from "Welfare Behaviorism," *Society* 233

Daniel Casse, a former senior director of the White House Writers Group,
asserts that 1.2 million people came off the welfare rolls since the 1996 welfare
reform legislation was passed, without noticeable signs of increased misery
as opponents of the reform had predicted. Social work professor David Stoesz
surveys state welfare programs and sees in them little to support optimism
about the full impact of welfare reform.

**ISSUE 14. Are Vouchers the Solution to the Ills of Public
Education?** 246

YES: Kevin Walthers, from "Saying Yes to Vouchers: Perception,
Choice, and the Educational Response," *NASSP Bulletin* 248

NO: Albert Shanker, from "Privatization: The Wrong Medicine for
Public Schools" *Vital Speeches of the Day* 254

Teacher Kevin Walthers examines the criticisms of public education and argues that vouchers and choice are well suited to correct its deficiencies, which
include a lack of professionalism among teachers and low academic standards. Albert Shanker, president of the American Federation of Teachers
until his death in 1998, argues that there is no evidence that privatizing the
public schools works or that the public wants vouchers. He maintains that
the public wants discipline and academic standards, which can be provided
by public schools modeled after those of countries with better primary and
secondary education than the United States.

ISSUE 15. Should Doctor-Assisted Suicide Be Legalized for the Terminally Ill?   262

YES: Marcia Angell, from "The Supreme Court and Physician-Assisted Suicide: The Ultimate Right," *The New England Journal of Medicine*   264

NO: Paul R. McHugh, from "The Kevorkian Epidemic," *The American Scholar*   270

Marcia Angell, executive editor of *The New England Journal of Medicine*, presents medical and ethical reasons justifying doctor-assisted suicide, including that it honors the autonomy of the patient and is merciful in cases when pain cannot be adequately relieved. Paul R. McHugh, director of the Department of Psychiatry and Behavioral Sciences at the Johns Hopkins University School of Medicine, argues that sick people who wish to kill themselves suffer from verifiable mental illness and that, since they can be treated for their pain and depressed state, physicians cannot be allowed to kill them.

PART 5   CRIME AND SOCIAL CONTROL   279

ISSUE 16. Is Street Crime More Harmful Than White-Collar Crime?   280

YES: John J. DiIulio, Jr., from "The Impact of Inner-City Crime," *The Public Interest*   282

NO: Jeffrey Reiman, from *The Rich Get Richer and the Poor Get Prison: Ideology, Class, and Criminal Justice,* 5th ed.   288

John J. DiIulio, Jr., a professor of politics and public affairs, analyzes the enormous harm done—especially to the urban poor and, by extension, to all of society—by street criminals and their activities. Professor of philosophy Jeffrey Reiman argues that the dangers posed by negligent corporations and white-collar criminals are a greater menace to society than are the activities of typical street criminals.

ISSUE 17. Should Drug Use Be Decriminalized?   298

YES: Ethan A. Nadelmann, from "Commonsense Drug Policy," *Foreign Affairs*   300

NO: James A. Inciardi and Christine A. Saum, from "Legalization Madness," *The Public Interest*   308

Ethan A. Nadelmann, director of the Lindesmith Center, a drug policy research institute, argues that history shows that drug prohibition is costly and futile. Examining the drug policies in other countries, he finds that decriminalization plus sane and humane drug policies and treatment programs can greatly reduce the harms from drugs. James A. Inciardi, director of the Center for Drug and Alcohol Studies at the University of Delaware, and his associate Christine A. Saum argue that legalizing drugs would not eliminate drug-related criminal activity and would greatly increase drug use. Therefore, the government should continue the war against drugs.

ISSUE 18. Is Incapacitation the Answer to the Crime Problem?   **316**

YES: Morgan O. Reynolds, from "Crime Pays, But So Does Imprisonment," *Journal of Social, Political, and Economic Studies*   **318**

NO: D. Stanley Eitzen, from "Violent Crime: Myths, Facts, and Solutions," *Vital Speeches of the Day*   **327**

Professor of economics Morgan O. Reynolds argues that "crime pays" for most criminals but that catching, convicting, and imprisoning more criminals would greatly reduce the crime rate. Professor emeritus of sociology D. Stanley Eitzen argues that the "get tough with criminals" approach to reducing crime costs too much and does not deal with the fundamental causes of crime.

PART 6   *THE FUTURE: POPULATION/*
            ENVIRONMENT/SOCIETY   **337**

ISSUE 19. Does Population Growth Threaten Humanity?   **338**

YES: Lester Brown, from "Food Scarcity: An Environmental Wakeup Call," *The Futurist*   **340**

NO: Julian L. Simon, from "The State of Humanity: Steadily Improving," *Cato Policy Report*   **347**

Lester Brown, president of the Worldwatch Institute, argues that the environment is deteriorating and that nature's limits are being exceeded due to population growth. Julian L. Simon, a professor of economics and business administration, asserts that "all aspects of material human welfare are improving in the aggregate," so population and economic growth are benefiting, not threatening, humanity.

ISSUE 20. Are Standards of Living in the United States Improving?   **354**

YES: W. Michael Cox and Richard Alm, from "The Good Old Days Are Now," *Reason*   **356**

NO: Beth A. Rubin, from *Shifts in the Social Contract: Understanding Change in American Society* **365**

Economist and banker W. Michael Cox and business journalist Richard Alm contend that Americans consume more, live better, live longer and healthier, achieve a higher net worth, enjoy more leisure time, and have more income per capita today than in 1970. Sociology professor Beth A. Rubin claims that Americans have lost income on average over the past 25 years and have experienced instability in their family relationships.

Contributors **376**

Index **380**

INTRODUCTION

Debating Social Issues

Kurt Finsterbusch

WHAT IS SOCIOLOGY?

"I have become a problem to myself," St. Augustine said. Put into a social and secular framework, St. Augustine's concern marks the starting point of sociology. We have become a problem to ourselves, and it is sociology that seeks to understand the problem and, perhaps, to find some solutions. The subject matter of sociology, then, is ourselves—people interacting with one another in groups.

Although the subject matter of sociology is very familiar, it is often useful to look at it in an unfamiliar light, one that involves a variety of theories and perceptual frameworks. In fact, to properly understand social phenomena, it *should* be looked at from several different points of view. In practice, however, this may lead to more friction than light, especially when each view proponent says, "I am right and you are wrong," rather than, "My view adds considerably to what your view has shown."

Sociology, as a science of society, was developed in the nineteenth century. Auguste Comte (1798–1857), the French mathematician and philosopher who is considered to be the father of sociology, had a vision of a well-run society based on social science knowledge. Sociologists (Comte coined the term) would discover the laws of social life and then determine how society should be structured and run. Society would not become perfect, because some problems are intractable, but he believed that a society guided by scientists and other experts was the best possible society.

Unfortunately, Comte's vision was extremely naive. For most matters of state there is no one best way of structuring or doing things that sociologists can discover and recommend. Instead, sociologists debate more social issues than they resolve.

The purpose of sociology is to throw light on social issues and their relationship to the complex, confusing, and dynamic social world around us. It seeks to describe how society is organized and how individuals fit into it. But neither the organization of society nor the fit of individuals is perfect. Social disorganization is a fact of life—at least in modern, complex societies such as the one we live in. Here, perfect harmony continues to elude us, and "social problems" are endemic. The very institutions, laws, and policies that produce benefits also produce what sociologists call "unintended effects"— unintended and undesirable. The changes that please one sector of the society may displease another, or the changes that seem so indisputably healthy at first turn out to have a dark underside to them. The examples are end-less. Modern urban life gives people privacy and freedom from snooping neighbors that the small town never afforded; yet that very privacy seems to breed an uneasy sense of anonymity and loneliness. Take another example: Hierarchy is necessary for organizations to function efficiently, but hierarchy leads to the creation of a ruling elite. Flatten out the hierarchy and you may achieve social equality—but at the price of confusion, incompetence, and low productivity.

This is not to say that all efforts to effect social change are ultimately futile and that the only sound view is the tragic one that concludes "nothing works." We can be realistic without falling into despair. In many respects, the human condition has improved over the centuries and has improved as a result of conscious social policies. But improvements are purchased at a price—not only a monetary price but one involving human discomfort and discontent. The job of policymakers is to balance the anticipated benefits against the probable costs.

It can never hurt policymakers to know more about the society in which they work or the social issues they confront. That, broadly speaking, is the purpose of sociology. It is what this book is about. This volume examines issues that are central to the study of sociology.

CULTURE AND VALUES

A common value system is the major mechanism for integrating a society, but modern societies contain so many different groups with differing ideas and values that integration must be built as much on tolerance of differences as on common values. Furthermore, technology and social conditions change, so values must adjust to new situations, often weakening old values. Some people (often called conservatives) will defend the old values. Others (often called liberals) will make concessions to allow for change. For example, the protection of human life is a sacred value to most people, but some would compromise that value when the life involved is a 90-year-old comatose man on life-support machines who had signed a document indicating that he did not want to be kept alive under those conditions. The conservative would counter that once we make the value of human life relative, we become dangerously open to greater evils—that perhaps society will come to think it acceptable to terminate all sick, elderly people undergoing expensive treatments. This is only one example of how values are hotly debated today. Three debates on values are presented in Part 1. In Issue 1, Everett C. Ladd challenges the common perception that morals have declined in America, while Gertrude Himmelfarb provides empirical support for the declining morality thesis. In Issue 2, the news media, which is a major influence on people's values, is analyzed for its bias. H. Joachim Maitre objects to the news media for being too liberal, while Martin A. Lee and Norman Solomon maintain that it is actually too conservative. In Issue 3, Peter Brimelow argues that the current levels of immigration are too high and that the immigrant cultures are too different from American culture to be assimilated. Thus, immigration is threatening America's cultural unity. John Isbister, in opposition, argues that the cultural impacts of immigration are positive and that any of its economic harms are negligible.

SEX ROLES, GENDER, AND THE FAMILY

An area that has experienced tremendous value change in the last several decades is sex roles and the family. Women in large numbers have rejected major aspects of their traditional gender roles and family roles while remaining strongly committed to much of the mother role and to many feminine characteristics. In fact, on these issues women are deeply divided. The ones who seek the most change identify themselves as feminists, and they have been at the forefront of the modern women's movement. Now a debate is raging as to whether or not the feminist cause really helps women. In Issue 4, Robert Sheaffer attacks feminism as intellectually unsound and doomed to failure because its goals conflict with biological realities. William H. Chafe identifies many positive changes that feminists have brought about and many changes that are still needed. Issue 5 focuses on the causes of communication problems between men and women. It has recently been advanced that such problems are largely the result of radically different conversation styles between the genders. Deborah Tannen champions this view, contending that men's concerns about maintaining status and women's concerns about maintaining connections and closeness affects their interpretations of what they hear and say to each other. Mary Crawford asserts that this view has become popularized and exaggerated by the media and that the basis of the thesis is demeaning to women. Issue 6 deals with the gay rights movement and discrimination against homosexuals. Richard D. Mohr argues that homosexuals are unjustly treated. He further contends that homosexuality is neither immoral nor unnatural and that it should be tolerated and respected. Carl F. Horowitz argues that the more blatant behaviors of many homosexuals are deeply offensive to heterosexuals and that communities have the right to control the undesirable behavior of gay men and lesbians. Issue 7, which has been much debated by feminists and their critics, asks, Is the decline of the traditional family a national crisis? David Popenoe is deeply concerned about the decline of the traditional family, while Stephanie Coontz thinks that such concern amounts to little more than nostalgia for a bygone era.

STRATIFICATION AND INEQUALITY

Issue 8 centers around a sociological debate about whether or not increasing economic inequality is a serious problem. Paul Krugman claims that it is, while Christopher C. DeMuth argues that consumption patterns indicate that inequality has actually decreased in recent decades. Closely related to this debate is the issue of why the poor are poor. The "culture of poverty" thesis maintains that most long-term poverty in America is the result of a common culture among the poor. The implication is that those who always seek immediate material gratification will not climb out of poverty, even if they are helped by welfare and other social programs. Others see most of the poor as victims of adverse conditions; they consider the culture of poverty thesis a way of "blaming the victim." Issue 9 offers two very different views on this issue, with Nicholas Eberstadt arguing that lower-class culture does perpetuate poverty and David M. Gordon arguing that very adverse conditions of life and a lack of opportunities are the primary causes of poverty.

Today one of the most controversial issues regarding inequalities is affirmative action. Is equality promoted or undermined by such policies? Walter E. Williams and Clarence Page take opposing sides on this question in Issue 10.

POLITICAL ECONOMY AND INSTITUTIONS

Sociologists study not only the poor, the workers, and the victims of discrimination but also those at the top of society—those who occupy what the late sociologist C. Wright Mills used to call "the command posts." The question is whether the "pluralist" model or the "power elite" model is the one that best fits the facts in America. Does a single power elite rule the United States, or do many groups contend for power and influence so that the political process is accessible to all? In Issue 11, G. William Domhoff argues that the business elite have a dominating influence in government decisions and that no other group has nearly as much power. Jeffrey M. Berry counters that liberal citizen groups have successfully opened the policy-making process and made it more participatory. Currently, grassroots groups of all kinds have some power and influence. The question is, how much?

The United States is a capitalist welfare state, and the role of the state in capitalism (more precisely, the market) and in welfare is examined in the next two issues. Issue 12 considers whether or not the government should step in and attempt to correct for the failures of the market through regulations, policies, and programs. Ernest Erber argues that an active government is needed to protect consumers, workers, and the environment; to bring about greater equality; and to guide economic and social change. Milton and Rose Friedman argue that even well-intended state interventions in the market usually only make matters worse and that governments cannot serve the public good as effectively as competitive markets can. One way in which the government intervenes in the economy is by providing welfare to people who cannot provide for their own needs in the labor market. Issue 13 debates the wisdom of welfare reform policies. In it, Daniel Casse argues that the Work Opportunity Reconciliation Act, signed in 1996, has effectively moved over 1 million people off the welfare rolls without significant harm to them. David Stoesz argues that the welfare reform was based on faulty assumptions about welfare participants and that in the long run, the reform will turn out to be counterproductive.

Education is one of the biggest jobs of government as well as the key to individual prosperity and the success of the economy. For decades the American system of education has been severely criticized. Recently the criticism has brought education into an ideological debate over the proper role of the government, private enterprise, and markets in public education. In Issue 14, Kevin Walthers reviews common criticisms of public education, including the lack of professionalism among teachers and low academic standards. He promotes vouchers and school choice as the way to improve the schools. Albert Shanker, in reply, looks to schools in countries in which students are performing exemplarily, noting that these nations have not turned to privatization. He concludes that improvements in public education can be accomplished without resorting to vouchers, which he maintains that the public does not want anyway.

The final issue in this section—doctor-assisted suicide—is truly one of life and death. The actions of Dr. Jack Kevorkian, who has assisted in over 100 patient suicides, have brought this issue into the public light. In Issue 15, Marcia Angell presents medical and ethical reasons why she believes that doctor-assisted suicide is merciful and right. Paul R. McHugh maintains that suicidal patients suffer from depression and that they can and should be treated psychologically, not murdered.

CRIME AND SOCIAL CONTROL

Crime is interesting to sociologists because crimes are those activities that society makes illegal and will use force to stop. Why are some acts made illegal and others (even those that may be more harmful) not made illegal? Surveys indicate that concern about crime is extremely high in America. Is the fear of crime, however, rightly placed? Americans fear mainly street crime, but Jeffrey Reiman argues in Issue 16 that corporate crime—also known as "white-collar crime"—causes far more death, harm, and financial loss to Americans than street crime. In contrast, John J. DiIulio, Jr., points out the great harm done by street criminals, even to the point of social disintegration in some poor neighborhoods. Much of the harm that DiIulio describes is related to the illegal drug trade, which brings about such bad consequences that some people are seriously talking about legalizing drugs in order to kill the illegal drug business. Ethan A. Nadelmann argues this view in Issue 17, while James A. Inciardi and Christine A. Saum argue that legalization would greatly expand the use of dangerous drugs and increase the personal tragedies and social costs resulting therefrom. Finally, Issue 18 examines the extent to which deterrence or tough sentencing of criminals reduces crime. The debate is whether American society should focus on deterrence by meting out sentencing on a tougher and more uniform basis or whether the emphasis should be on rehabilitating criminals and eliminating the social conditions that breed crime. These alternatives are explored in the debate by Morgan O. Reynolds and D. Stanley Eitzen.

THE FUTURE: POPULATION/ENVIRONMENT/SOCIETY

Many social commentators speculate on "the fate of the earth." The environmentalists have their own vision of apocalypse. They see the possibility that the human race could overshoot the carrying capacity of the globe. The resulting collapse could lead to the extinction of much of the human race and the end of free societies. Population growth and increasing per capita levels of consumption, say some experts, are leading us to this catastrophe. Others believe that these fears are groundless. In Issue 19, Lester Brown and Julian L. Simon argue over whether or not the world is threatened by population growth.

The last issue in this book tries to assess the status in America of people's standards of living. In Issue 20, Beth A. Rubin presents trends showing that Americans are losing out economically, socially, and psychologically. W. Michael Cox and Richard Alm, in contrast, argue that Americans have never had it so good. Although they may not make as much money in real terms, they buy more with their money and live longer and healthier lives.

THE SOCIAL CONSTRUCTION OF REALITY

An important idea in sociology is that people construct social reality in the course of interaction by attaching social meanings to the reality they are experiencing and then responding to those meanings. Two people can walk down a city street and derive very different meanings from what they see around them. Both, for example, may see homeless people—but they may see them in different contexts. One fits them into a picture of once-vibrant cities dragged into decay and ruin because of permissive policies that have encouraged pathological types to harass citizens; the other observer fits them into a picture of an America that can no longer hide the wretchedness of its poor. Both feel that they are seeing something deplorable, but their views of what makes it deplorable are radically opposed. Their differing views of what they have seen will lead to very different prescriptions for what should be done about the problem. And their policy arguments will be based upon the pictures in their heads, or the constructions they have made of reality.

The social construction of reality is an important idea for this book because each author is socially constructing reality and working hard to persuade you to see his or her point of view; that is, to see the definition of the situation and the set of meanings he or she has assigned to the situation. In doing this, each author presents a carefully selected set of facts, arguments, and values. The arguments contain assumptions or theories, some of which are spelled out and some of which are unspoken. The critical reader has to judge the evidence for the facts, the logic and soundness of the arguments, the importance of the values, and whether or not omitted facts, theories, and values invalidate the thesis. This book facilitates this critical thinking process by placing authors in opposition. This puts the reader in the position of critically evaluating two constructions of reality for each issue instead of one.

CONCLUSION

Writing in the 1950s, a period that was in some ways like our own, the sociologist C. Wright Mills said that Americans know a lot about their "troubles" but they cannot make the connections between seemingly personal concerns and the concerns of others in the world. If they could only learn to make those connections, they could turn their concerns into *issues*. An issue transcends the realm of the personal. According to Mills, "An issue is a public matter: some value cherished by publics is felt to be threatened. Often there is a debate about what the value really is and what it is that really threatens it."

It is not primarily personal troubles but social issues that I have tried to present in this book. The variety of topics in it can be taken as an invitation to discover what Mills called "the sociological imagination." This imagination, said Mills, "is the capacity to shift from one perspective to another—from the political to the psychological; from examination of a single family to comparative assessment of the national budgets of the world.... It is the capacity to range from the most impersonal and remote transformations to the most intimate features of the human self—and to see the relations between the two." This book, with a range of issues well suited to the sociological imagination, is intended to enlarge that capacity.

On the Internet . . .

Fairness and Accuracy in Reporting (FAIR)
FAIR is a national media watch group that offers well-documented criticism of media bias and censorship. FAIR seeks to invigorate the First Amendment by advocating for greater diversity in the press. FAIR scrutinizes media practices that marginalize public interest and minority and dissenting viewpoints.
http://www.fair.org/

Freedom Forum
The Freedom Forum is a nonpartisan, international foundation dedicated to free press and free speech for all societies. Its mission is to help society and the news media understand one another better.
http://www.freedomforum.org/

The International Center for Migration, Ethnicity, and Citizenship
The center is engaged in scholarly research and public policy analysis bearing on international migration, refugees, and the incorporation of newcomers in host countries.
http://www.newschool.edu/icmec/

National Immigrant Forum
This pro-immigrant organization examines the effects of immigration on U.S. society. Click on the links for discussion of underground economies, immigrant economies, race and ethnic relations, and other topics.
http://www.immigrationforum.org/national.htm

The National Network for Immigrant and Refugee Rights (NNIRR)
The NNIRR serves as a forum to share information and analysis, to educate communities and the general public, and to develop and coordinate plans of action on important immigrant and refugee issues.
http://www.nnirr.org/

Society of Professional Journalists
At this site you will find the Electronic Journalist, the online service for the Society of Professional Journalists. This site links you to articles on media ethics, accuracy in media, media leaders, and other media and society topics.
http://www.spj.org/

PART 1

Culture and Values

Sociologists recognize that a fairly strong consensus on the basic values of a society contributes greatly to the smooth functioning of that society. The functioning of modern, complex urban societies, however, often depends on the tolerance of cultural differences and equal rights and protections for all cultural groups. In fact, such societies can be enriched by the contributions of different cultures. But at some point the cultural differences may result in a pulling apart that exceeds the pulling together. Three areas where the issue of cultural consensus or cultural clashes is prominent today are moral decline, the news media, and the immigration of peoples from different cultures. Analysis of these issues involves strongly held value differences.

■ Is America in Moral Decline?

■ Does the News Media Have a Liberal Bias?

■ Is Third World Immigration a Threat to America's Way of Life?

ISSUE 1

Is America in Moral Decline?

YES: Gertrude Himmelfarb, from *The De-Moralization of Society: From Victorian Virtues to Modern Values* (Alfred A. Knopf, 1995)

NO: Everett C. Ladd, from "The Myth of Moral Decline," *The Responsive Community* (vol. 4, no. 1, 1993/1994)

ISSUE SUMMARY

YES: Gertrude Himmelfarb, a professor emeritus of history, details some of the increasing moral problems in America and interprets them as being part of a larger pattern, which she calls "the de-moralization of society."

NO: Everett C. Ladd, president of the Roper Center for Public Opinion, empirically tests the moral decline thesis and finds that, according to the indicators that he employs, it is a myth.

Morality is the glue that holds society together. It enables people to deal with each other in relative tranquility and generally to their mutual benefit. Morality influences us both from the outside and from the inside. The morality of others affects us from outside as social pressure. Our conscience is morality affecting us from inside, even though others, especially parents, influence the formation of our conscience. Because parents, churches, schools, and peers teach us their beliefs and values (their morals) and the rules of society, most of us grow up wanting to do what is right. We also want to do things that are pleasurable. In a well-functioning society the right and the pleasurable are not too far apart, and most people lead morally respectable lives. On the other hand, no one lives up to moral standards perfectly. In fact, deviance from some moral standards is common, and when it becomes very common the standard changes. Some people interpret this as moral decline, while others interpret it as simply a change in moral standards or even as progress.

The degree of commitment to various moral precepts varies from person to person. Some people even act as moral guardians and take responsibility for encouraging others to live up to the moral standards. One of their major tactics is to cry out against the decline of morals. There are a number of such voices speaking out in public today. In fact, many politicians seem to try to outdo each other in speaking out against crime, teenage pregnancy, divorce, violence in the media, latchkey children, irresponsible parenting, etc.

Cries of moral decline have been ringing out for centuries. In earlier times the cries were against sin, debauchery, and godlessness. Today the cries are often against various aspects of individualism. Parents are condemned for sacrificing their children for their own needs, including their careers. Divorced people are condemned for discarding spouses instead of working hard to save their marriages. Children of elderly parents are condemned for putting their parents into nursing homes to avoid the inconvenience of caring for them. The general public is condemned for investing so little time in others and their communities while pursuing their own interests. These criticisms against individualism may have some validity. On the other hand, individualism has some more positive aspects, including enterprise and inventiveness, which contribute to economic growth; individual responsibility; advocacy of human rights; reduced clannishness and prejudice toward other groups; and an emphasis on self-development, which includes successful relations with others.

The morality debate is important because moral decline not only increases human suffering but also weakens society and hinders the performance of its institutions. The following selections require some deep reflection on the moral underpinnings of American society as well as other societies, and they invite the reader to strengthen those underpinnings.

Many have decried the high levels of crime, violence, divorce, and opportunism, but few argue the thesis of the moral decline of America as thoroughly and as passionately as Gertrude Himmelfarb, the author of the first selection. But is she reading the facts correctly? According to Everett C. Ladd in the second selection, the common viewpoint that a serious moral decline is in progress is a myth. He argues that numerous morality indicators do not show the decline that the decline thesis expects. Therefore, even in the face of the statistics on crime and divorce, Ladd concludes that there has not been "a deterioration of moral conduct."

YES   Gertrude Himmelfarb

A DE-MORALIZED SOCIETY

[T]he current statistics are not only more troubling than those a century ago; they constitute a trend that bodes even worse for the future than for the present. Where the Victorians had the satisfaction of witnessing a significant improvement in their condition, we are confronting a considerable deterioration in ours. . . .

In the United States, the figures are no less dramatic. Starting at 3 percent in 1920 (the first year for which there are national statistics), the illegitimacy ratio rose gradually to slightly over 5 percent by 1960, after which it grew rapidly: to almost 11 percent in 1970, over 18 percent in 1980, and 30 percent by 1991—a tenfold increase from 1920, and a sixfold increase from 1960. . . .

In teenage illegitimacy the United States has earned the dubious distinction of ranking first among all industrialized nations. The rate tripled between 1960 and 1991: for whites it increased almost fivefold; for blacks the increase was less spectacular, but the final rate was almost four times that of the whites. In 1990, one in ten teenage girls got pregnant, half of them giving birth and the other half having abortions. . . . In 1970, 5 percent of fifteen-year-old girls in the United States had had sexual intercourse; in 1988, 25 percent had. . . .

* * *

There are no national crime statistics for the United States for the nineteenth century and only partial ones (for homicides) for the early twentieth century. Local statistics, however, suggest that as in England the decrease in crime started in the latter part of the nineteenth century (except for a few years following the Civil War) and continued into the early twentieth century. There was even a decline of homicides in the larger cities, where they were most common; in Philadelphia, for example, the rate fell from 3.3 per 100,000 population in midcentury to 2.1 by the end of the century.

National crime statistics became available in 1960, when the rate was under 1,900 per 100,000 population. That figure doubled within the decade and tripled by 1980. A decline in the early 1980s, from almost 6,000 to 5,200, was followed by an increase to 5,800 in 1990; the latest figure, for 1992, is somewhat under 5,700. The rate of violent crime (murder, rape, robbery, and aggravated assault) followed a similar pattern, except that the increase after 1985 was more precipitous and continued until 1992, making for an almost fivefold rise from 1960. In 1987, the Department of Justice estimated that eight of every ten Americans would be a victim of violent crime at least once in their lives. The incidence of nonviolent crime is obviously greater; in 1992 alone, one in four households experienced such a crime.

Homicide statistics go back to the beginning of the century, when the national rate was 1.2 per 100,000 population. That figure skyrocketed during Prohibition, reaching as high as 9.7 by one account (6.5 by another) in 1933, when Prohibition was repealed. The rate dropped to between 5 and 6 during the 1940s and to under 5 in the fifties and early sixties. In the mid-sixties, it started to climb rapidly, more than doubling between 1965 and 1980. A decline in the early eighties was followed by another rise; in 1991 it was just short of its 1980 peak. . . .

There are brave souls, inveterate optimists, who try to put the best gloss on the statistics. But it is not much consolation to be told that the overall crime rate in the United States has declined slightly from its peak in the early 1980s, if the violent crime rate has risen in the same period—and increased still more among juveniles and girls (an ominous trend, since the teenage population is also growing). Nor that the divorce rate has fallen somewhat in the past decade, if it doubled in the previous two decades; if more people, including parents, are cohabiting without benefit of marriage (the rate in the United States has increased sixfold since 1970); and if more children are born out of wedlock and living with single parents. (In 1970, one out of ten families was headed by a single parent; in 1990, three out of ten were.) Nor that the white illegitimacy ratio is considerably lower than the black illegitimacy ratio, if the white ratio is rapidly approaching the black ratio of a few decades ago, when Daniel Patrick Moynihan wrote his percipient report about the breakdown of the black family. (The black ratio in 1964, when that report was issued, was 24.5 percent; the white ratio now is 22 percent. In 1964, 50 percent of black teenage mothers were single; in 1991, 55 percent of white teenage mothers were single.)

Nor is it reassuring to be told that two-thirds of new welfare recipients are off the rolls within two years, if half of those soon return, and a quarter of all recipients remain on for more than eight years. Nor that divorced mothers leave the welfare rolls after an average of five years, if never-married mothers remain for more than nine years, and unmarried mothers who bore their children as teenagers stay on for ten or more years. (Forty-three percent of the longest-term welfare recipients started their families as unwed teenagers.)

Nor is the cause of racial equality promoted by the news of an emerging "white underclass," smaller and less conspicuous than the black (partly because it is more dispersed) but rapidly increasing. If, as has been conclusively demonstrated, the single-parent family is the most important factor associated with the "pathology of poverty"—welfare dependency, crime, drugs, illiteracy, homelessness—a white illegitimacy rate of 22 percent, and twice that for white women below the poverty line, signifies a new and dangerous trend. This has already reached a "tipping point" in some working-class communities, creating a white underclass with all the characteristics of such a class. (Charles Murray finds a similar underclass developing in England, with twice the illegitimacy rate of the rest of the population; there it is a purely class rather than racial phenomenon.)

Nor can one be sanguine about statistics suggesting that drug use in the United States has fallen among casual users, if it has risen among habitual users; or that heroin addiction is decreasing, if crack-cocaine addiction is increasing (or, as more recent statistics show, both are on the rise); or that drug addiction among juveniles is lagging behind alcoholism. Nor can one take much satisfaction in the knowledge that the infant mortality rate has fallen, if it is disproportionately high in some groups, not because prenatal care is unavailable, but because single parents often do not avail themselves of it or because their drug or alcohol addiction has affected their infants....

* * *

In his essay "Defining Deviancy Down," Senator Moynihan has taken the idea of deviancy a step further by describing the downward curve of the *concept* of deviancy. What was once regarded as deviant behavior is no longer so regarded; what was once deemed abnormal has been normalized. As deviancy is defined downward, so the threshold of deviancy rises: behavior once stigmatized as deviant is now tolerated and even sanctioned. Mental patients can rarely be institutionalized or even medicated against their will; free to live on the street, they are now treated, and appear in the statistics, not as mentally incapacitated but as "homeless." Divorce and illegitimacy, once seen as betokening the breakdown of the family, are now viewed benignly as "alternative life styles"; illegitimacy has

been officially rebaptized as "nonmarital childbearing"; and divorced and unmarried mothers are lumped together in the category of "single parent families." And violent crime has become so endemic that we have practically become inured to it. The St. Valentine's Day Massacre in Chicago in 1929, when four gangsters killed seven other gangsters, shocked the nation and became legendary, immortalized in encyclopedias and history books; in Los Angeles today as many people are killed every weekend.

It is ironic to recall that only a short while ago criminologists were accounting for the rise of the crime rates in terms of our "sensitization to violence." As a result of the century-long decline of violence, they reasoned, we had become more sensitive to "residual violence"; thus more crimes were being reported and apprehended. This "residual violence" has by now become so overwhelming that, as Moynihan points out, we are being desensitized to it.

Charles Krauthammer has proposed a complementary concept: "Defining Deviancy Up." As deviancy is normalized, so the normal becomes deviant. The kind of family that has been regarded for centuries as natural and moral—the "bourgeois" family, as it is invidiously called—is now seen as pathological, concealing behind the facade of respectability the new "original sin," child abuse. While crime is underreported because we have become desensitized to it, child abuse is grossly overreported, including fantasies imagined (often inspired by therapists and social workers) long after the supposed events. Similarly, rape has been "defined up" as "date rape," to include sexual relations that the participants themselves may not have perceived as rape at the time.

The combined effect of defining deviancy up and defining it down has been to normalize and legitimize what was once regarded as abnormal and illegitimate, and, conversely, to stigmatize and discredit what was once normal and respectable. This process, too, has occurred with startling rapidity. One might expect that attitudes and values would lag behind the reality, that people would continue to pay lip service to the moral principles they were brought up with, even while violating those principles in practice. What is striking about the 1960s "sexual revolution," as it has properly been called, is how revolutionary it was, in sensibility as well as reality. In 1965, 69 percent of American women and 65 percent of men under the age of thirty said that premarital sex was always or almost always wrong; by 1972, those figures had plummeted to 24 percent and 21 percent. For women over the age of thirty, the figures dropped from 91 percent to 62 percent, and for men from 62 percent to 47 percent—this in seven short years....

Language, sensibility, and social policy conspire together to redefine deviancy. But the true effect may better be conveyed by an almost random array of facts. In his book on the underclass, Myron Magnet presents a sampling of statistics:

> By 1970 a baby born and raised in a big city had a greater chance of being murdered than a World War II GI had of dying in battle. Today, a twelve-year-old American boy has an 89% chance of becoming a victim of violent crime in his lifetime.... In mid-1989, one out of every four young black American males was either in jail or on probation—a larger proportion than was in college.

For a long time social critics and policymakers have found it hard to face up to the realities of our moral condition, in spite of the statistical evidence. They criticize the statistics themselves or try to explain them away....

* * *

These realities have been difficult to confront because they violate the dominant ethos, which assumes that moral progress is a necessary by-product of material progress. It seems incomprehensible that in this age of free, compulsory education, illiteracy should be a problem, not among immigrants but among native-born Americans; or illegitimacy, at a time when sex education, birth control, and abortion are widely available; or drug addiction, once associated with primitive cultures and bohemian individuals. We rarely question that assumption about moral progress because we are suspicious of the very idea of morality. Moral principles, still more moral judgments, are thought to be at best an intellectual embarrassment, at worst evidence of an illiberal and repressive disposition. It is this reluctance to speak the language of morality, far more than any specific values, that separates us from the Victorians.

Most of us are uncomfortable with the idea of making moral judgments even in our private lives, let alone with the "intrusion," as we say, of moral judgments into public affairs. We are uncomfortable not only because we have come to feel that we have no right to make such judgments and impose them upon others, but because we have no confidence in the judgments themselves, no assurance that our principles are true and right for us, let alone for others. We are constantly beseeched to be "nonjudgmental," to be wary of crediting our beliefs with any greater validity than anyone else's, to be conscious of how

"Eurocentric" and "culture-bound" we are. *"Chacun à son goût,"* we say of morals, as of taste; indeed, morals have become a matter of taste.

Public officials in particular shy away from the word "immoral," lest they be accused of racism, sexism, elitism, or simply a lack of compassion. When members of the president's cabinet were asked whether it is immoral for people to have children out of wedlock, they drew back from that distasteful word. The Secretary of Health and Human Services replied, "I don't like to put this in moral terms, but I do believe that having children out of wedlock is just wrong." The Surgeon General was more forthright: "No. Everyone has different moral standards.... You can't impose your standards on someone else."

It is not only our political and cultural leaders who are prone to this failure of moral nerve. Everyone has been infected by it, to one degree or another....

In Victorian England, moral principles and judgments were as much a part of social discourse as of private discourse, and as much a part of public policy as of personal life. They were not only deeply ingrained in tradition; they were also embedded in two powerful strains of Victorian thought: Utilitarianism on the one hand, Evangelicalism and Methodism on the other. These may not have been philosophically compatible, but in practice they complemented and reinforced each other, the Benthamite calculus of pleasure and pain, rewards and punishments, being the secular equivalent of the virtues and vices that Evangelicalism and Methodism derived from religion.

It was this alliance of a secular ethos and a religious one that determined social policy, so that every measure of poor relief or philanthropy, for example, had to justify itself by showing that it would promote the moral as well as the material well-being of the poor. The principle of "less eligibility," the "workhouse test," the distinction between "pauper" and "poor," the stigma attached to the "able-bodied pauper," indeed, the word "pauper" itself—all of which figured so largely in the New Poor Law—today seem invidious and inhumane. At the time, however, they were the result of a conscious moral decision: an effort to discourage dependency and preserve the respectability of the independent poor, while providing at least minimal sustenance for the indigent.

In recent decades we have so completely rejected any kind of moral calculus that we have deliberately, systematically divorced welfare—no longer called "relief"—from moral sanctions or incentives. This reflects in part the theory that society is responsible for all social problems and should therefore assume the task of solving them; and in part the prevailing spirit of relativism, which makes it difficult to pass any moral judgments or impose any moral conditions upon the recipients of relief. We are now confronting the consequences of this policy of moral neutrality. Having made the most valiant attempt to "objectify" the problem of poverty, to see it as the product of impersonal economic and social forces, we are discovering that the economic and social aspects of that problem are inseparable from the moral and personal ones. And having made the most determined effort to devise social policies that are "value-free," we find that these policies imperil both the moral and the material well-being of their intended beneficiaries.

In de-moralizing social policy—divorcing it from any moral criteria, requirements, even expectations—we have de-moralized, in the more familiar sense, both the individuals receiving relief and society as a whole. Our welfare system is counterproductive not only because it aggravates the problem of welfare, creating more incentives to enter and remain within it than to try to avoid or escape from it. It also has the effect of exacerbating other more serious social problems. Chronic dependency is an integral part of the "social pathology" that now constitutes almost a single "social problem." ...

Just as many intellectuals, social critics, and policymakers were reluctant for so long to credit the unpalatable facts about crime, illegitimacy, or dependency, so they find it difficult to appreciate the extent to which these facts themselves are a function of values—the extent to which "social pathology" is a function of "moral pathology" and social policy a function of moral principle.

* * *

The moral divide has become a class divide. The "new class," as it has been called, is not in fact all that new; it is by now firmly established in the media, the academy, the professions, and the government. In a curious way, it is the mirror image of the "underclass." One might almost say that the two have a symbiotic relationship to each other. In its denigration of "bourgeois values" and the "Puritan ethic," the new class has legitimated, as it were, the values of the underclass and illegitimated those of the working class, who are still committed to bourgeois values and the Puritan ethic. ...

By now this "liberated," anti-bourgeois ethic no longer seems so liberating. The moral and social statistics have become so egregious that it is now finally permissible to speak of the need for "family values." Under the headline "Courage to Say the Obvious," the black liberal columnist William Raspberry explained that he meant no disrespect for the many admirable single women who raise decent families, but he was worried about social policies that were likely to produce more single mothers. This column, and others like it, appeared in April 1993, soon after *The Atlantic* featured a long article by Barbara Dafoe Whitehead summarizing the recent work of social scientists about the family. The article created a sensation, partly because of the provocative title, "Dan Quayle Was Right," and partly because of the message encapsulated on the cover: "After decades of public dispute about so-called family diversity, the evidence from social-science research is coming in: The dissolution of two-parent families, though it may benefit the adults involved, is harmful to many children, and dramatically undermines our society. ...

* * *

One of the most effective weapons in the arsenal of the "counter-counterculture" is history—the memory not only of a time before the counterculture but also of the evolution of the counterculture itself. In 1968, the English playwright and member of Parliament A. P. Herbert had the satisfaction of witnessing the passage of the act he had sponsored abolishing censorship on the stage. Only two years later, he complained that what had started as a "worthy struggle for reasonable liberty for honest writers" had ended as the "right to represent copulation, veraciously, on the public stage." About the same time, a leading American civil-liberties lawyer, Morris

Ernst, was moved to protest that he had meant to ensure the publication of Joyce's *Ulysses*, not the public performance of sodomy.

In the last two decades, the movements for cultural and sexual liberation in both countries have progressed far beyond their original intentions. Yet few people are able to resist their momentum or to recall their initial principles. In an unhistorical age such as ours, even the immediate past seems so remote as to be antediluvian; thus anything short of the present state of "liberation" is regarded as illiberal. And in a thoroughly relativistic age such as ours, any assertion of value— any distinction between the publication of *Ulysses* and the public performance of sodomy—is thought to be arbitrary and authoritarian....

The main thing the Victorians can teach us is the importance of values—or, as they would have said, "virtues"—in our public as well as private lives. And not so much the specifically Victorian virtues that we may well value today, as the importance of an ethos that does not denigrate or so thoroughly relativize values as to make them ineffectual and meaningless.

* * *

The Victorians were, candidly and proudly, "moralists." In recent decades that has almost become a term of derision. Yet contemplating our own society, we may be more respectful of Victorian moralism. We may even be on the verge of assimilating some of that moralism into our own thinking. It is not only "values" that are being rediscovered, but "virtues" as well....

Industrialism and urbanism—"modernism," as it is now known—so far from contributing to the de-moralization of the

poor, seems to have had the opposite effect. At the end of the nineteenth century, England was a more civil, more pacific, more humane society than it had been in the beginning. "Middle-class" manners and morals had penetrated into large sections of the working classes. The traditional family was as firmly established as ever, even as feminist movements proliferated and women began to be liberated from their "separate spheres." Voluntary associations and public agencies mitigated some of the worst effects of industrialism and urbanism. And religion continued to thrive, in spite of the premature reports of its death. (It even managed to beget two of the most important institutions of the twentieth century, the British trade-union movement and the Labour Party, both of which were virtually born in the chapel.)

* * *

If Victorian England did not succumb to the moral and cultural anarchy that is said to be the inevitable consequence of economic individualism, it is because of a powerful ethos that kept that individualism in check, as it also kept in check the anarchic impulses in human nature. For the Victorians, the individual, or "self," was the ally rather than the adversary of society. Self-help was seen in the context of the community as well as the family; among the working classes this was reflected in the virtue of "neighbourliness," among the middle classes, of philanthropy. Self-interest stood not in opposition to the general interest but, as Adam Smith had it, as the instrument of the general interest. Self-discipline and self-control were thought of as the source of self-respect and self-betterment; and self-respect as the precondition for the respect and approbation of others. The individual, in short, was assumed to have responsibilities as well as rights, duties as well as privileges.

That Victorian "self" was very different from the "self" that is celebrated today. Unlike "self-help," "self-esteem" does not depend upon the individual's actions or achievements; it is presumed to adhere to the individual regardless of how he behaves or what he accomplishes. Moreover, it adheres to him regardless of the esteem in which he is held by others, unlike the Victorian's self-respect which always entailed the respect of others. The current notions of self-fulfillment, self-expression, and self-realization derive from a self that does not have to prove itself by reference to any values, purposes, or persons outside itself—that simply is, and by reason of that alone deserves to be fulfilled and realized. This is truly a self divorced from others, narcissistic and solipsistic. It is this self that is extolled in the movement against "codependency," which aspires to free the self from any dependency upon others and, even more, from any responsibility to others. Where the interrelationship of dependency and responsibility was once regarded as a natural human condition, the source of such virtues as love, friendship, loyalty, and sociability, "codependency" is now seen as a pathological condition, a disease requiring a radical cure.

This is the final lesson we may learn from the Victorians: that the ethos of a society, its moral and spiritual character, cannot be reduced to economic, material, political, or other factors, that values—or better yet, virtues—are a determining factor in their own right. So far from being a "reflection," as the Marxist says, of the economic realities, they are themselves, as often as not, the crucial agent in shaping those realities. If in a period of rapid economic and social change, the Victorians managed to achieve a substantial improvement in their "condition" and "disposition," it may be that economic and social change do not necessarily result in personal and public disarray. If they could retain and even strengthen an ethos that had its roots in religion and tradition, it may be that we are not as constrained by the material circumstances of our time as we have thought. A post-industrial economy, we may conclude, does not necessarily entail a postmodernist society or culture.

It is often said that there is in human beings an irrepressible need for spiritual and moral sustenance. Just as England experienced a resurgence of religion when it seemed most unlikely (the rise of Puritanism in the aftermath of the Renaissance, or of Wesleyanism in the age of deism), so there emerged, at the very height of the Enlightenment, the movement for "moral reformation." Today, confronted with an increasingly de-moralized society, we may be ready for a new reformation, which will restore not so much Victorian values as a more abiding sense of moral and civic virtues.

NO

Everett C. Ladd

THE MYTH OF MORAL DECLINE

The moral state of the United States is the subject of enormous attention and concern. Although this has been a recurring theme throughout American history, there is some indication that concern has grown in our own time. Rushworth M. Kidder, President of the Institute for Global Ethics, recently noted in *The Public Perspective* that dozens of ethics organizations are springing up across the nation, hundreds of executive ethics seminars are conducted every year, and thousands of students are participating in character education at school. The press is now full of discussions of ethics issues. Kidder cites data showing, for example, that between 1969 and 1989 the number of stories found under "ethics" in the *New York Times* index increased four-fold.

Survey data also indicate that the proportion of the public troubled by what they perceive to be serious deficiencies in the moral state of the nation is not only large but expanding. True, throughout the span of our history for which we have survey data, large majorities have expressed dissatisfaction with such matters as the honesty and standards of behavior of their fellow citizens. Nonetheless, the proportions today are at the highest levels we have seen. For instance, in 1938, when asked if the "general morals" of young unmarried people were better or worse than they had been 10 years earlier, 42 percent of those interviewed by the Roper Organization said they were worse, compared to just 13 percent who said they were better. In 1987, 60 percent of those interviewed in a Yankelovich Clancy Shulman poll said teenagers were "less moral in their behavior at present than when [the respondents] were growing up," while only 11 percent described young people as more moral. Every time we have located a pair of queries like this from the 1930s–50s span on the one hand, and from the 1980–90s on the other, we have found the same pattern: Majorities always profess to see decline in moral standards, but the majority is larger in the contemporary period than earlier.

Again and again, polls show Americans expressing this kind of values nostalgia. But has there in fact been a deterioration in moral conduct in the United States, as compared to, say, the 1950s? Ethical norms and moral conduct are of great importance to the health of the American society and polity, and it certainly matters which way the great engines of contemporary society are pulling us with regard to them. Yet for all the importance of this question and the attention it has received, the data are not as clear as the polls might suggest.

THERE'S ALWAYS SO MUCH WRONG

One obstacle standing in the way of productive analysis involves the fact that at every point in time, in the view of many thoughtful people, ethical standards and moral conduct leave much to be desired. Michael Josephson and his colleagues have attempted empirical work on Americans' moral judgments and behavior which, they say, reveals that a "disturbingly high proportion of young people regularly engage in dishonest and irresponsible behavior." What an extraordinary way to put it! It is, after all, a little late in human history to present as a finding that a disturbingly high proportion of people variously err and sin. The Josephson study documents that many young people are struggling and stumbling ethically, but it tells us nothing about whether things are actually getting better or worse.

Is the contemporary U.S. beset with moral decline? If we had a "Morality Index," on which 100 was utopia and zero the modern equivalent of Sodom and Gomorrah, and found the U.S. standing at 50, that should be cause for national concern. But it would be one thing if we also found that the country's position on this mythic measure had been 80 in 1867, 70 in 1917, and 60 in 1957, quite another if we found that it had been hovering around 50 in each of those earlier years.

We don't have such an index, nor do we have the kind of imaginative and thorough data-gathering such a measure would require. We only know that moral conduct today is "deficient." I have no intention of making light of this when I note that part of the reason we think today's problems are so pressing is that they are the ones we face. Since we can do absolutely nothing about previous sins, present problems are the "worst" in the sense that they are the ones that occupy us and require our efforts at remedy....

CHANGING STANDARDS AND PERCEPTIONS

Assessing the moral state of the union is made more difficult by the fact that our standards keep changing. Moreover, the institutions through which the public gains a sense of the moral state of the nation now tend to portray social and political institutions in a negative light.

As to changing standards, consider the area of race relations. Surely we have made enormous strides along this dimension of national moral conduct since the 1850s. We have ended slavery and, all too belatedly, we must acknowledge, eradicated the system of gross exclusion of African-Americans from various facilities and entitlements, known as "Jim Crow." Survey data on racial attitudes and various behavioral data alike attest to the spread and strengthening of public support for extending to African-Americans the Declaration's lofty insistence that all people are created equal and possess inalienable rights.

But in assessing moral conduct, we seem largely to ignore this historical perspective. Is America now living in satisfactory accord with the norm set forth in the Declaration of Independence and in other statements of national ideals? Of course not. But today's shortcomings are the ones that now occupy us—even when we recognize marked gains from times past. *We expect more of ourselves in this area than we did 50 or 150 years ago—and we come up short.*

Media studies have for some time examined the issue of political negativism or cynicism, suggesting that press bias results not so much from political preferences as from professional outlook. The press often portrays various national institutions as seamy and even unworthy of support. Austin Ranney argues that there is not so much "a political bias in favor of liberalism or conservatism, as a structural bias..." which encourages a cynical and excessively manipulative view of politics. Michael Robinson's research has supported the view that the press fosters a pervasive cynicism:

> Events are frequently conveyed by television news through an inferential structure that often injects a negativistic, contentious, or anti-institutional bias. These biases, frequently dramatized by film portrayals of violence and aggression, evoke images of American politics and social life which are inordinately sinister and despairing.

In addition to America's historic sense of creedal anxiety, then, recent factors, such as changing standards of justice and press negativism, may be encouraging an even more pessimistic view. At the very least, all these factors suggest there is reason to doubt that the apparently widespread sense of moral decline is simply a reflection of the actual progression.

WHAT THE DATA ACTUALLY SHOW

The various factors sketched above present terrible difficulties for the literature which purports to provide thoughtful guidance on the matter of which way we are headed. As a result, analysts often seem to be led to the conclusion that deterioration is occurring, even when available information is inconclusive or flat-out says otherwise.

When we look at the status of religion in America and a number of moral norms, it is not at all clear America is in moral decline. The country's religious life, for instance, is often considered a moral barometer. A decade ago, I was asked to prepare a conference paper reviewing what surveys had to say about the religious beliefs and practices of the American people. As the Reverend Richard John Neuhaus observed at the New York Conference, the conventional wisdom had it that "America is or is rapidly becoming a secular society."

I began my paper by acknowledging that on this subject, as on so many, there are severe limits as to what polls can tell us. They are blunt instruments, unable to help us much with the searching, the ambiguity, the depth and subtlety that necessarily surround any basic set of human needs and values. Nevertheless, the story told by survey research was remarkably clear and unambiguous with regard to the general character and directions of Americans' religious life: namely, the U.S. is distinguished from most other advanced industrial democracies by the persisting strength of religious beliefs and of organized religious practice. As Seymour Martin Lipset argued in *The First New Nation,* published in 1963, "the one empirical generalization which does seem justified about American religion is that from the early nineteenth century down to the present, the United States has been among the most religious countries in the Christian world." Similarly, James Reichley concluded his examination of *Religion in American Life* with the assessment that "Americans remain, despite recent incursions of civil humanism among cultural elites and relentless promotion of egoism by advertising and entertainment media, overwhelmingly, in Justice [William O.] Douglas's words, 'a religious people'."

My own assessments of available survey information have supported these observations. Americans continue, for example, in virtually unchanging proportions to describe religion as important in their own lives. The proportion describing themselves as members of a church or synagogue, while down just a bit from the levels of the 1930–50s, has, on the whole, remained both high and constant. Surveys conducted by the National Opinion Research Center have continued to find overwhelming majorities of the public describing the Bible as either "the actual word of God... to be taken literally, word for word," (the response of 33 percent in 1993); or as "the inspired word of God, but not everything in it should be taken literally, word for word" (49 percent stating this). Only 15 percent categorized the Bible as "an ancient book of fables, legends, history, and moral precepts recorded by men." Also, prayer remains integral to Americans, even among young adults and high-income citizens (65 percent and 69 percent of whom, respectively, agreed with the statement that "prayer is an important part of my daily life").

Perhaps most striking is the extent to which the U.S. differs religiously from other advanced industrial democracies.

In 1981, Gallup conducted a series of surveys cross-nationally which found 79 percent of Americans saying they gained strength from religion, compared to 46 percent in Britain, 44 percent of West Germans, and 37 percent of the French. Similarly, 84 percent of those interviewed in the U.S. said they believed in heaven, as against 57 percent in Britain, 31 percent in West Germany, 27 percent in France, and 26 percent in Sweden.

This isn't to say that there have been no changes in the structure of American religious life. We know, for example, that over the last 30 to 40 years, while the proportion of the population which is "churched" has remained basically constant, the denominational mix has changed quite strikingly. Sociologist Benton Johnson notes that American religious groups have differed greatly in terms of membership gains and losses. He points out that evangelical churches have prospered even as main-line Protestant denominations have suffered serious membership losses during this period.

Taking a longer view of American religious experience from the eighteenth century to the present, we see many substantial shifts. Interesting enough, though, these shifts are more often than not in the opposite direction from those assumed in most commentary. That is, *the long movement over time in the U.S. seems clearly to be toward religion*, not away from it. Pointing to the decline of organized atheism and church membership gains in the nineteenth century, sociologist Theodore Caplow suggested:

One concedes too much when one says we're just about as religious as we used to be. We may be a good deal more religious than we used to be.

Yet, while virtually all the scholars who have reviewed the systematic data which are available to us have reached the same conclusions on American religious experience, most of the group assembled at the New York conference strongly rejected the idea that American religious commitments are notably strong and enduring. For example, George Marsden, a leading student of evangelicalism and fundamentalism, dismissed most of the findings on religious belief as essentially meaningless because, as he saw it, they picked up only an insubstantial, superficial, essentially trivial commitment. "As you know," Marsden argued, "the common comment on fundamentalism is that it is just secularism in disguise. It is a way of endorsing a materialistic, self-centered lifestyle. And that's something that could be said about a lot of American Christianity."

Marsden brought up the often-cited remark which is attributed (perhaps entirely incorrectly, according to some historians) to Dwight Eisenhower. Ike is reputed to have said: "Our government makes no sense unless it is founded on a deeply religious faith—and I don't care what it [that faith] is." This hollow, instrumental approach to faith encapsulates, Marsden argued, what's wrong with religion in the U.S.

Political scientist Stanley Rothman had a perspective similar to Marsden's:

In a public opinion survey people are asked, "Do you believe in hard work?" Sure, everyone may mouth that. But there's a difference between saying that and actually doing it.... And I would say the same thing about religious attitudes among the population as a whole. Modernization of the west has led to the erosion of the traditional structures and beliefs...

now there is evidence that people no longer take religion so seriously, unless they redefine it in some ways. I think there has been a general redefinition, not among the whole population, but among substantial segments of the population, so as to fit religion into their own wishes and desires.... Unfortunately this cannot be proven with data.

And so it went. Most of the participants were convinced that in a deeper sense, whatever the numbers seem to show, religious belief is in precipitous decline in modern America.

Nor is religion the only area in which our perceptions of deterioration conflict with other measures of experience. While there are important areas where Americans are in deep disagreement about what constitutes the proper moral or ethical standards—the case of abortion is certainly a prime example—far more often than not the data point to broad agreement on the norm. As Table 1 shows, norms condemning various forms of cheating, lying, and stealing seem firmly entrenched across most of the population. If we are going to hell in a handbasket, it's not because the preponderance of Americans have abandoned their attachment to many of the older verities.

But does this simply suggest that hypocrisy is on the rise—that we have become more inclined to act contrary to our professed standards? Not necessarily. Take the case of cheating. A lot of people, including many educators, seem to believe that cheating is on the rise—even though young Americans continue to condemn cheating. But many of the best survey data available to us say otherwise. The Gallup Youth Surveys, for example, show that many more young people describe cheating at their own schools as *more infrequent* now than three

Table 1
Professed Norms Are Strong and Conventional

Tax Fraud	Extramarital Affairs
Question: Do you feel it is wrong if . . . a taxpayer does not report all of his income in order to pay less income taxes?	**Question:** Do you think it is always wrong or sometimes okay for . . . a married person to have sex with someone other than his/her spouse?
Wrong: 94% Not Wrong: 4%	**Always Wrong: 87% Sometimes OK: 11%**
Source: Survey by NORC for the International Social Survey Program (ISSP), Feb.–April 1991.	*Source:* Survey by Yankelovich Clancy Shulman for Time/CNN, June 4–5, 1991.
Question: Have you ever cheated on your federal income taxes, or not?	**Question:** (If ever married) Have you ever had sex with someone other than your husband or wife while you were married?
No: 95% Yes: 4%	**No: 83% Yes: 17%**
Source: Survey by the Gallup Organization, March 28–30, 1991.	*Source:* Survey by NORC-GSS, February–April 1993.

Lying	Stealing
	Question: The . . . eighth commandment is . . . Do not steal . . . Does the way you live these days completely satisfy . . . or not at all satisfy that commandment?
Question: Do you think it is sometimes justified to lie to friends or to family members or do you think lying is never justified?	
Never: 73% Depends: 10% Justified: 18%	**Completely: 86% Not at All: 2%**
Source: Survey by CBS News/New York Times, December 7–9, 1992.	*Source:* Survey by Barna Research Group, January 1992.

decades ago. The proportion saying that they themselves have cheated at some time or another, while high, seems to be decreasing.

We know that people often fail to live up to standards to which they express adherence. But we also know that norms matter—that is, they actually regulate conduct, if imperfectly—and that large changes in conduct rarely, if ever, take place without correspondingly large changes in professed norms. Consider, for example, premarital sexual relations. Behavior has clearly shifted mightily in the "sexual revolution" of the last several decades, but so too has the professed norm. When there is a problem, as in the latter area, the survey findings readily pick it up.

One of the things that seem to be bothering Americans most is the sense that the old-time standards-setting, which was centered around the institutions of family and church, is being replaced by new ones, centered in remote and morally vacuous institutions, such as popular music, TV, and movies. Data presented in Table 2 demonstrate this concern clearly. But as we see in the table, other data show that most of us say that, for us personally, the old order of standards-setting still holds. Furthermore, a Roper Organization survey for *Good Housekeeping* in 1991 found that 86 percent of women shared

Table 2
Where Do Today's Values Come From?

Question: What do you think (has/should have) the most influence on the values of young people today?

	Has	Should Have
TV & Movies	34%	1%
Parents	20	74
Young People	19	1
Musicians & Music Videos	10	0
Celebrities, Athletes	6	1
Teachers	5	9
Political Leaders	2	1
Religious Leaders	1	11
Military Leaders	1	0

Source: Survey by Mellman & Lazarus for Massachusetts Mutual Life Insurance Co., September 1991.

Question: What do you feel has been the single most important factor in influencing your beliefs about what is right or wrong?

Parents	47%
Religion	28%
Personal Experience	8%
Other	8%
Not sure	9%

Source: Survey by Yankelovich Clancy Shulman for Time, January 19–21, 1987.

the values of their parents, 10 percent had somewhat different values, and only 4 percent had very different values. In the same survey, 85 percent of the women who were mothers thought their children would have the same values.

Once again, there is a striking tension between the perceived deterioration in moral norms and conduct nationally on the one hand, and the sense of strength and continuity drawn from personal experience on the other. We see this again and again across many areas. Thus 63 percent of respondents in a Gallup survey of November 1992 said that "religion as a whole" is losing its influence on American life, while only 27 percent described religion's influence

as increasing. As we have seen, though, a great deal of the data indicates that religion in America continues to flourish.

INDIVIDUALISM: STRENGTH OR WEAKNESS?

The moral shortcomings of this society often grow out of the same elements that enhance national life. The positives and negatives are frequently but flip sides of a single structure of national values. As many analysts from Alexis de Tocqueville on down to the present have observed, the core of the sociopolitical ideology on which the U.S. was founded is a uniquely insistent and far-reaching individualism —a view of the individual person which gives unprecedented weight to his or her choices, interests, and claims. This distinctive individualism has always enriched the moral life of the country in important regards and posed serious challenges to it in yet others....

An abundance of data from our own time show that this dynamic sense of individual responsibility and capabilities has continued. Philanthropy has also increased dramatically: in 1955, individuals gave more than $5 billion to charity; this amount rose to $102 billion in 1990 (a rate of increase that outpaced inflation significantly). Surveys suggest that, in recent years, the proportion of the populace giving of its time for charitable and social service activities has actually been increasing. The moral life of the nation is thus strengthened.

Individualism has contributed much historically to the vitality of American family life and created a distinctively American type of family. Children, nineteenth century visitors often remarked, didn't occupy a subordinate place—"to be seen and not heard"—like their European counterparts, but were exuberant, vociferous, spoiled participants. Similarly, visiting commentators often remarked on the effects of America's pervasive individualism on the status of women. Bryce, for example, saw women's rights more widely recognized in the U.S. than in Europe. This had resulted, he argued, because "the root idea of democracy cannot stop at defining men as male human beings, anymore than it could ultimately stop at defining them as white human beings.... Democracy is in America more respectful of the individual... than it has shown itself in Continental Europe, and this regard for the individual enured to the benefit of women."

But just as the country's demanding individualism has liberated individuals to achieve productive lives for themselves and contribute to a dynamic public life, so it has also been a source of distinctive problems. Many analysts have argued that these problems with the American ideology are evident not so much in the fact that these ideals are sometimes unachieved, as that their achievement may create terrible difficulties....

Present-day critics of the "dark side" of individualist America charge that individualism has come to emphasize the gratification of the self over the needs of various important social institutions including, above all, the family. In *Habits of the Heart: Individualism and Commitment in American Life*, Robert Bellah and colleagues grant that "our highest and noblest aspirations, not only for ourselves, but for those we care about, for our society in the world, are closely linked to our individualism." Moreover, America cannot abandon its individualism, for "that would mean for us to abandon our deepest identity."

Still, Bellah *et al.* insist, "some of our deepest problems both as individuals and as a society are also closely linked to our individualism." It has become far too unrestrained. Historically in the U.S., the natural tendencies within individualism toward narrow self-service were mitigated by the strength of religion and the ties of the local community. No longer. In their view, individualism has been transmogrified by a radical insistence upon individual autonomy, so profoundly corrosive of the family and other collective institutions that depend upon substantial subordination of individual claims for social goods.

The recent historical record suggests that neither the boosters nor the knockers of individualism quite have it right. On the positive side, factors like the continued strength of voluntarism in America signal the degree to which individualism strengthens moral conduct by stressing individual responsibility and encouraging the view that "what I do" can really matter. Also, the individualistic ethic in America has fueled important advances for women and African-Americans under the banner of the "inalienable rights" to "Life, Liberty and the pursuit of Happiness." On the other hand, that ethic constantly runs the risk of leaving the individual far too radically autonomous. It suggests that whatever serves a person's sense of his/her rights and entitlements is, miraculously, good for the society or, at the least, something which the society may not lightly challenge.

But the down-side of contemporary individualism does not quite play itself out in the way that recent arguments suggest. Individualism does not necessarily equal "selfishness." Rather, it seems to be that Americans are construing their own self-interest too narrowly. Hence, many of the men and women implicated in the rise in divorce and single-parent households—which has posed difficulties for many children and communities—would seem to have a "narrow" sense of self-interest, which is not serving them or their children very well. They need to be reminded, as Tocqueville argued, that self-interest is only justified when it is "properly understood" in a communal context, which is to say that individuals can only flourish in robust communities....

Has there been a deterioration of moral conduct? Probably not. But we have been given ample proof that extending commitment to our national idea, which centers around a profound individualism, is by no means an unmixed blessing. As the U.S. has progressed in recognizing the worth and the claims of people previously excluded from the Declaration's promise, it has also encouraged tendencies which have destructive possibilities, liable to see the individual as too radically autonomous and leave him too narrowly self-serving. In seeking to improve the moral conduct of the nation, earlier generations of Americans have had to build on the positive elements of the country's individualist ethic, so as to curb its dark side. Ours is surely no exception.

POSTSCRIPT

Is America in Moral Decline?

Handwringing over weakening morals has long been a favorite pastime. Yet are Americans less moral today than they were a century ago? Consider that slavery has been abolished, civil rights for minorities have been won and generally accepted, tolerant attitudes have greatly increased, and genocide toward American Indians ceased a long time ago. How could Americans have made so much progress if they have been getting much worse for hundreds of years? Such reflections cast suspicion over the moral decline thesis. On the other hand, this thesis is supported by many trends, such as increasing crime and divorce. The issue is important because morality is a distinctive trait of the human species and essential to cooperative interactions. If morality declines, coercive restraint must increase to hold harmful behaviors in check, but self-restraint is much less costly than police restraint.

At the center of the issue of the trends in morality is the issue of the blessings and curses of individualism, which balance out according to Ladd. One tenet of individualism is that we should not judge each other. Though this may be kindly in the short run, according to Himmelfarb, it demoralizes social policy and weakens society in the long run. Capitalism would be another demoralizing factor because it encourages self-interest and the passion for personal gain. Higher education may be another culprit because it relativizes values. In general, the forces behind the demoralization of society as described by Himmelfarb are not likely to be reversed in the medium-term future.

Most of the relevant literature is on aspects of the moral decline. Few works challenge the decline thesis. One example is Nicholas Lemann's "It's Not as Bad as You Think It Is," *The Washington Monthly* (March 1997). On the other side, see William J. Bennett's *De-Valuing of America* (Summet Books, 1992) for an exposition of the moral decline thesis. Richard Stivers attributes the moral decline to a culture of cynicism in *The Culture of Cynicism: American Morality in Decline* (Basil Blackwell, 1994). Two strong statements on moral decline are Charles Derber's *The Wilding of America: How Greed and Violence Are Eroding Our Nation's Character* (St. Martin's Press, 1996) and Robert Bork's *Slouching Towards Gomorrah* (Regan Books, 1996).

Two highly visible public figures have recently proposed other solutions to the current moral crisis. John W. Gardner, the founder of the citizens' lobby Common Cause, proposes a large-scale mobilization for national renewal. See "National Renewal," *National Civic Review* (Fall–Winter 1994). Retiring senator Bill Bradley proposes many small actions for revitalizing civil society in "America's Challenge: Revitalizing Our National Community," *National Civic Review* (Spring 1995).

ISSUE 2

Does the News Media Have a Liberal Bias?

YES: H. Joachim Maitre, from "The Tilt to the News: How American Journalism Has Swerved from the Ideal of Objectivity," *The World and I* (December 1993)

NO: Martin A. Lee and Norman Solomon, from *Unreliable Sources: A Guide to Detecting Bias in News Media* (Carol Publishing Group, 1992)

ISSUE SUMMARY

YES: Journalism professor H. Joachim Maitre argues that news reporters are liberals who allow their political views to seep into their reporting.

NO: Media critics Martin A. Lee and Norman Solomon argue that the media are owned and operated by men and women whose bias in reporting is toward the conservative status quo.

"A small group of men, numbering perhaps no more than a dozen 'anchormen,' commentators and executive producers... decide what forty to fifty million Americans will learn of the day's events in the nation and the world." The speaker was Spiro Agnew, vice president of the United States during the Nixon administration. The thesis of Agnew's speech, delivered to an audience of midwestern Republicans in 1969, was that the television news media are controlled by a small group of liberals who foist their liberal opinions on viewers under the guise of "news." The upshot of this control, said Agnew, "is that a narrow and distorted picture of America often emerges from the televised news." Many Americans, even many of those who were later shocked by revelations that Agnew took bribes while serving in public office, agreed with Agnew's critique of the "liberal media."

Politicians' complaints about unfair news coverage go back much further than Agnew and the Nixon administration. The third president of the United States, Thomas Jefferson, was an eloquent champion of the press, but after six years as president, he could hardly contain his bitterness. "The man who never looks into a newspaper," he wrote, "is better informed than he who reads them, inasmuch as he who knows nothing is nearer to truth than he whose mind is filled with falsehoods and errors."

The press today is much different than it was in Jefferson's day. Newspapers then were pressed in hand-operated frames in many little printing shops around the country; everything was local and decentralized, and each paper averaged a few hundred subscribers. Today, newspaper chains have taken over most of the once-independent local newspapers. The remaining independents rely heavily on national and international wire services. Almost all major magazines have national circulations; some newspapers, like *USA Today* and the *Wall Street Journal*, do too. Other newspapers, like the *New York Times* and the *Washington Post*, enjoy nationwide prestige and help set the nation's news agenda. Geographical centralization is even more obvious in the case of television. About 70 percent of the national news on television comes from three networks whose programming originates in New York City.

A second important difference between the media of the eighteenth century and the media today has to do with the ideal of "objectivity." In past eras, newspapers were frankly partisan sheets, full of nasty barbs at the politicians and parties the editors did not like; they made no distinction between "news" and "editorials." The ideal of objective journalism is a relatively recent development. It traces back to the early years of the twentieth century. Disgusted with the sensationalist "yellow journalism" of the time, intellectual leaders urged that newspapers cultivate a core of professionals who would concentrate on accurate reporting and who would leave their opinions to the editorial page. Journalism schools cropped up around the country, helping to promote the ideal of objectivity. Although some journalists now openly scoff at it, the ideal still commands the respect—in theory, if not always in practice—of working reporters.

These two historical developments, news centralization and news professionalism, play off against one another in the current debate over news "bias." The question of bias was irrelevant when the press was a scatter of little independent newspapers. If you did not like the bias of one paper, you picked another one—or you started your own, which could be done with modest capital outlay. Bias started to become an important question when newspapers became dominated by chains and airwaves by networks, and when a few national press leaders like the *New York Times* and the *Washington Post* began to emerge. Although these "mainstream" news outlets have been challenged in recent years by opinions expressed in a variety of alternative media—such as cable television, talk radio, newsletters, and computer mail—they still remain powerful conveyers of news.

Is media news reporting biased? The media constitutes a major socializing institution, so this is an important question. Defenders of the media usually hold that although journalists, like all human beings, have biases, their professionalism compels them to report news with considerable objectivity. Media critics insist that journalists constantly interject their biases into their news reports. The critics, however, often disagree about whether such bias is liberal or conservative, as is the case with this issue. In the following selections, H. Joachim Maitre argues that the news media tilt to the left, while Martin A. Lee and Norman Solomon contend that the slant of the news media supports a conservative status quo.

23

YES

H. Joachim Maitre

THE TILT TO THE NEWS: HOW AMERICAN JOURNALISM HAS SWERVED FROM THE IDEAL OF OBJECTIVITY

"Mr. President," said the nation's second-ranked television news anchorman on May 27 [1993] and via satellite, "if we could be one-hundredth as great as you and Hillary Rodham Clinton have been in the White House, we would take it right now and walk away winners.... Thank you very much, and tell Mrs. Clinton we respect her and we are pulling for her."

Dan Rather's declaration of adoration and active support for the presidential couple was not meant for public viewing but—recorded through a technical glitch—caused yet another puncture in the perforated armor of American journalism. In professionally purer times, Rather's indiscretion would have destroyed what was left of his credibility as an honest news broker. He had shown his tilt.

Finally, after years of heated public debates and often tedious scholarly discourse over alleged institutional liberal bias in the American news media, there is no argument on the basics any longer. "Everyone knows," said political scientist James Q. Wilson in the June 21, 1993, edition of the *New Republic,* "that the members of the national media are well to the left of the average voter."

For those skeptics still demanding statistical evidence that journalists tend to hold liberal political views, numbers were provided in a summer 1992 survey of fourteen hundred journalists, reported in *The American Journalist in the 1990s,* published by the New York–based Freedom Forum Media Studies Center. It concluded that 44.1 percent of those polled consider themselves Democrats and only 16.3 percent Republicans. The gap had grown since 1982, when a similar survey was done, and is now far larger than among the general population.

BIAS CREEPS INTO REPORTING

These figures as such would be of limited interest if they did not strengthen the suspicion that the journalist's personal political and philosophical preferences, his system of beliefs, his world-view would—unavoidably—seep into his reporting and that the stated imbalance between liberal and conservative leanings and loyalties already is gravely affecting the ways and worth of news reporting in this country. Slant is becoming ever more visible, nowhere more so than on television "news."

Examples of liberal bias and resulting slant abound. President Clinton had been in office less than a month when megastar Dan Rather offered his helping hand: Clinton's program "will include money to put people back to work repairing this country's infrastructure, roads, bridges, and other public works" (CBS, February 17). Rather's unspoken message: The Clinton administration will rebuild the America run down through years of neglect by Clinton's Republican predecessors in the White House. Bill Clinton will create the employment lost in previous years. News, or partisan propaganda?

Soon, Dan Rather's new coanchor, Connie Chung, another Clinton fan, identified Clinton's adversary: "The Senate Republicans are threatening to block the president's $16 billion job creation program" (CBS, April 1). Or: "Held up in the Senate is President Clinton's $16 billion plan to bring unemployment down" (CBS, April 2). And: "President Clinton says the $16 billion is crucial to boosting the economy" (CBS, April 6).

But what was the opposition's line of argumentation? Neither Rather nor Chung ever addressed the conceptual base for Republican resistance to Clinton's ambitious employment program and to "Clintonomics" in general, to wit: In free societies, the creation of jobs is a central task for private enterprise, not for the government and its various bureau-cracies. This concept in its implementation resulted in the creation of millions of jobs in the 1980s, but that had been under President Reagan—anathema for the liberal mind-set.

The rule of liberal media bias starts with terminology. The term *liberal* is generally used in a positive sense in America. "Liberal social policies" are good by implication; "restrictive social policies" are bad. To be "liberal" suggests generosity and open-mindedness; to be "conservative" implies selfishness and closed-mindedness. Derived from the Latin word *liber* (free), *liberal* once stood for persons and ideas that favored freedom. In many European countries, that original meaning still prevails. Not so in America, where—in particular when applied to public policy—*liberal* has come to mean favoring government intervention and control to secure economic and social justice.

Thus, the expansion of government activities and the growth of government itself are favored by today's liberals, while liberating commerce (through deregulation) and the economy from government intervention and control has become a conservative ideal. Classic liberal spokesmen for a free economy such as Friedrich von Hayek and Milton Friedman (both recipients of the Nobel Prize in economics) have been relegated to conservative status by the liberal class dominant in the media and in politics. At the same time, contemporary America's most successful advocate of government intervention in commerce and the economy, Sen. Edward Kennedy, is also America's best-known "liberal"—or socialist, in reality.

Television news coverage of American economic affairs has been the subject of an in-depth report by Ted Smith of Virginia Commonwealth University.

The study, titled *The Vanishing Economy: Television Coverage of Economic Affairs, 1982–87*, involved systematic analysis of three full years of coverage during the Reagan presidency and found a highly consistent pattern of emphasis and omission. Smith demonstrates that network news journalists have chosen not only to stress problems and failures but to limit or eliminate coverage of gains and success. In some instances, Smith says, "those restrictions have been so extreme that it would be difficult or impossible for a person who relied exclusively on television evening news for his knowledge of the world to form an accurate understanding of the world." He concludes: "To be blunt, systematic suppression of positive information, economic or otherwise, is nothing less than systematic censorship. As such, it strikes at the foundations of the democratic process."

THE MEDIA AND THE DEMOCRATS: SUPPRESSING NEGATIVE INFORMATION

With Clinton's election and the return of the Democrats to majority rule in Congress, television's coverage of economic affairs faces the challenge of liberal economic policies and their implementation. Chances are that the "systematic suppression of positive information," as found by Smith, will be replaced by systematic suppression of negative information. Liberal policies and plans will be granted the benefit of the doubt. During the budget debates of the past summer, criticism of Reagan policies far outweighed serious analysis of Clinton's campaign platform and his economic package, advertised as seeking a "deficit reduction."

The purpose of the phrase *deficit reduction* was to avoid the more candid term *tax increase* and, at the same time, to mislead Americans into thinking "that the change has something to do with reducing the federal budget," says Tom Bethell, one of the country's few nonconforming journalists, in an article in the September 1993 issue of the *American Spectator*. Bethell reveals numbers and trends that easily could have been published in prestigious newspapers (but were not) or made public on television news programs (but were not thought newsworthy) and concludes:

The Clinton economic plan has all along been an exercise in deception, with the news media acting as collaborators or dupes.... On April 8, the Office of Management and Budget [OMB] published the 1994 federal budget. The next day, major newspapers published full-page stories on the budget, but all failed to give the outlay and revenue totals. It has become a convention among journalists that only the deficit, or "difference," should be published. The difference between what and what? We are rarely told. The failure to publish the totals, of course, disguises the extent to which they continue to rise. An uncritical Washington press corps has permitted Clinton to talk of "spending cuts" without publishing the numbers on which his claim is based.

Many ordinary citizens agree with this assessment of today's media. One man, Douglas Losordo, chastised the *Boston Globe* in a letter printed on September 7, 1993, for repeatedly referring to "spending reductions" in the Clinton budget "when in fact the only proposed real decreases in spending are in the defense budget."

Losordo cited OMB figures to the effect that outlays (spending) will increase from $1.468 trillion [in 1993] to $1.781 trillion in 1998, while defense spending will drop from $277 billion to $239 billion over the same period. "How is this a spending cut?" Losordo asks, charging that the *Globe* is "simply repeating the distortions of fact presented by our politicians."

[In 1986] social scientists Robert Lichter, Stanley Rothman, and Linda Lichter published *The Media Elite*, a ground-breaking study of political leanings and perspectives among the nation's leading journalists and how those preferences affected their work. They concluded:

> The media elite are a homogeneous and cosmopolitan group, who were raised at some distance from the social and cultural traditions of small-town middle America. Drawn mainly from big cities in the Northeast and North Central states, their parents tended to be well-off, highly educated members of the middle class. Most have moved away from any religious heritage, and very few are regular churchgoers. In short, the typical leading journalist is the very model of the modern Eastern urbanite. The dominant perspective of this group is equally apparent. Today's leading journalists are politically liberal and alienated from traditional norms and institutions. Most place themselves to the left of center and regularly vote the Democratic ticket. Yet theirs is not the New Deal liberalism of the underprivileged, but the contemporary social liberalism of the urban sophisticate. They favor a strong welfare state within a capitalist framework. They differ most from the general public, however, on the divisive social issues that have emerged since the 1960s—abortion, gay rights, affirmative action, et cetera. Many are alienated from the "system" and quite critical of America's world role. They would like

to strip traditional powerbrokers of their influence and empower black leaders, consumer groups, intellectuals, and... the media.

These findings were complemented by an article in the summer 1986 edition of *Policy Review* magazine by Dinesh D'Souza, who analyzed television network conformism:

> No matter where he comes from... the aspiring TV journalist typically adopts a left-liberal worldview as he picks up the tools of his trade. There is nothing conspiratorial in this. To get their stories on the air, TV journalists have to embrace the culture of network news, either consciously or unconsciously.... And since the culture of television journalism is liberal, it is hardly surprising that reporters get their idea of what is news— ultimately the most ideological question in journalism—from a whole range of left-liberal assumptions, inclinations, and expectations.

THE EDITOR AS IDEOLOGICAL GATEKEEPER

In television as well as newspaper journalism, the reporter's role in the running of the newsroom and production of the final copy is subservient to that of the desk editor; it is certainly secondary or insignificant when measured against the power of managing editors and executive editors and of their television news counterparts. The reporter and the editor are both "journalists." It is the editor, however, in his function as gatekeeper, who determines which story will be covered, what news is "fit to print," and who gets hired and fired.

Take the *New York Times*, the nation's ranking and undisputedly liberal newspaper. Max Frankel, its executive editor, is not known for having hired any openly conservative reporter or editor during his seven-year tenure. Moreover, "one of the first things I did was stop the hiring of nonblacks and set up an unofficial little quota system," Frankel boasted in an interview with Ken Auletta.

Auletta, writing in the June 18, 1992, issue of the *New Yorker*, added: "The new publisher [Arthur Ochs Sulzberger, Jr.] applauded Frankel's hiring policies and also the newsroom's more extensive coverage of women and gays, despite grumbling by some members of the staff that the *Times* was becoming politically correct."

Grumbling over hiring practices and program content seems to be no longer an issue at the partly tax-supported National Public Radio (NPR), which is liberal to the core. (Think of Nina Totenberg, NPR's correspondent at the Supreme Court, and her stubborn effort to prevent Clarence Thomas from being confirmed as a justice of the Court.) A rare insight into the inner workings of NPR was offered in the Washington, D.C., weekly *City Paper* by Glenn Garvin, who conducted intensive research on the radio station:

It's not that the network's editorial brain trust meets each morning to plot the day's campaign to rid America of Republican taint. It's that the newsroom is composed almost entirely of like-minded people who share one another's major philosophical precepts.... Their thinking is apparent both in what they report and their approach to it. They believe that government is the fundamental agent of change, that government can and should solve most problems. They believe most of those solutions involve spending large sums of money. They believe that taxes are not only an appropriate way of raising money, but an impor-

tant social responsibility. They believe that, although individuals cannot always be trusted to make correct choices, bureaucrats usually can. In short, NPR reporters are the kind of people who voted for Michael Dukakis and Bill Clinton, not as the lesser evils, but enthusiastically, in the firm belief that what the world needs is better social engineering.

Like-minded people who share one another's major philosophical precepts and operate under unofficial but nonetheless binding rules of political correctness are not journalists. They are today's Media, less a profession than a culture and secular religion, attempting to reform society according to their left-radical agenda. The guiding motto of the *New York Times* —"All the news that's fit to print"—has been turned into a tool of self-censorship. Especially on feminism, the homosexual rights campaign, and pop culture, the *Times* "has in recent years become crassly partisan in an essentially frivolous way," writes critic Richard Neuhaus in the June/July edition of *First Things* magazine. "There is an absence of *gravitas*... it has become a generally vulgar and strident paper that is hostile to nuance and, it seems, editorially incapable of self-doubt or a modicum of intellectual curiosity."

The *Times* is still held to be the flagship of American journalism, but its traditional in-depth coverage of national and international events has been weakened by trendy treatment, obviously caused by imitating television coverage. Peter Steinfels, who writes the *Times*' Beliefs section, claims that journalists themselves know the problem: "The news media are sometimes less adept in telling truly new stories than in retelling old stories in new ways."

Steinfels, writing in the August 21, 1993, edition of the *Times*, offers a telling example of a tilt threatening to turn institutional: the coverage of Pope John Paul II's voyage to Colorado [summer 1993]. Steinfels observes:

> For the better part of a mid-August week some of the nation's most prized air time, from morning shows to evening newscasts, was devoted to Pope John Paul II's visit.... So were front-page stories in most newspapers.... No one can dispute that this reporting and commentary conveyed some powerful images of a charismatic religious leader and exuberant teenagers.... Nonetheless, fair questions can be raised about how much this impressive effort advanced the public's knowledge and understanding about the Pope, about the current state of Catholicism, about young people and about the moral issues that Pope John Paul II highlighted.

What was reported instead, in print and on the screen? "Journalists recounted," Steinfels wrote, "in some cases a bit breathlessly, the fact that many American Catholics disagree with their church's official teachings on birth control, ordaining women to the priesthood, and other questions about sex and roles for women." While the pope "repeatedly lamented the loss of belief in objective truth and in universally valid principles of morality," reporters wallowed in stereotypes: "Their estimates should have reflected the fact that the Pope's language might escape the ideological grid of American politics and the American news media."

The belief in objective truth and in universally valid principles, so central to Western culture, runs counter to the "anything goes" relativism of the counterculture, where truth is subject to debate and negotiation.

"Why do journalists tend to be liberals?" asks Michael Kinsley in a short, instructive essay tellingly titled "Bias and Baloney" in the December 14, 1992, edition of the *New Republic*. Conceding that the general liberal inclination of many journalists would be hard to deny, the much-in-demand liberal talk show host and columnist for the *Washington Post* and the *New Republic* states, only partly tongue-in-cheek:

> My own political views are more or less liberal. They were not genetically implanted, and I hold them under no form of compulsion except that of reason. It seems to me they are the sort of views a reasonable, intelligent person would hold. Since most journalists I meet are reasonable, intelligent people, the mystery to me is not why journalists tend to be liberals but why so many other reasonable, intelligent people are not.

Kinsley's smugness typifies the conviction of intellectual and moral superiority apparently shared by many contemporary liberal journalists. He rejects all conspiracy theories: "People freely choose their politics and freely choose their careers. No one is forcing journalists to hold liberal political views, and no one is preventing or even discouraging conservatives from becoming journalists. If it just happens to work out that way, so what?"

Kinsley also rejects the suspicion that a journalist's personal political worldview might taint his professional product through bias, claiming that "a political preference is not itself a 'bias.'"

THE DEATH OF PROFESSIONAL DETACHMENT AND OBJECTIVITY

Why, then, do political liberal preferences show so frequently, often blatantly, on network news programs, the average American's favored information watering holes? Why are the leading anchormen—Peter Jennings, Dan Rather, Tom Brokaw—known everywhere as liberal in their views and liberal in their presence on the screen? And why is there no conservative news anchor on network television? Is it because the medium of television, by its very nature, is hostile to balanced news presentation? That still would leave open the question of domination by liberals, a fact that had been documented and analyzed in John Corry's ground-breaking 1986 study *TV News and the Dominant Culture*.

Kinsley's flippant observation that "no one is preventing or even discouraging conservatives from becoming journalists" begs the larger question, which has nothing to do with personal political views or convictions: What happened to professional detachment, to objectivity?

Television news has long ceased to strive for objectivity, that forlorn ideal of yesteryear. Television news delivers "infotainment" instead, where whirl is king, tilt is trendy, and slant rules supreme. Likewise, objectivity has been driven from the pages of the nation's weekly newsmagazines. They also have surrendered to the lure of entertainment, allegedly expected or demanded by the viewing public, bored by print.

And commentary, the legitimate exercise of subjective opinion, once restricted to editorial and op-ed pages, is advancing glacierlike into the news pages of the *New York Times* and *Washington Post*, the nation's "prestige papers."

Driven by commercial television's soft assault, journalism attempts to adjust through imitation, thus betraying its mission and professional standards.

A new force is born: The Media. Or is it only show business with a mask?

NO

Martin A. Lee and Norman Solomon

POLITICIANS AND THE PRESS

More than 20 years after Vice President Spiro Agnew's famous attack on the American press, the myth of the "liberal media" endures.

Agnew decried "the trend toward the monopolization of the great public information vehicles and the concentration of more and more power over public opinion in fewer and fewer hands." True enough, but his oratory targeted only the *Washington Post* and other major media outlets lacking enthusiasm for the Nixon administration. "Agnew was hypocritical in his attack on press monopolies," a critic later remarked. "Giant chains like Newhouse and Hearst—among the good guys in Agnew's press lord pantheon—escaped his ire."

Likewise, conservative owners of magazines with huge circulations, like *Reader's Digest* and *Parade*, received no brickbats from the White House. An outspoken Federal Communications Commissioner, Nicholas Johnson, observed at the time that Agnew was simply going public with "what corporate and government officials have been doing for years in the privacy of their luncheon clubs and paneled offices. They cajoled and threatened publishers and broadcasters in an effort to manage news and mold images."

Agnew's rhetorical barrage in November 1969 was to reverberate into the century's last decade. However deceptive, it struck a populist chord of resentment against media conglomerates. Rather than challenge the "liberal media" myth, right-leaning owners have encouraged it—and media under their control have popularized it.

The Vice President conveniently neglected to mention that a year earlier the majority of endorsing newspaper editorials backed the Nixon-Agnew ticket. And three years later, running for reelection, the same Republican duo received a whopping 93 percent of the country's newspaper endorsements. (Since 1932 every Republican presidential nominee except Barry Goldwater has received the majority of endorsements from U.S. daily newspapers. Ronald Reagan got 77 percent in 1980, and 86 percent in 1984; George Bush got 70 percent in 1988.) Before resigning in disgrace from the vice presidency, Agnew never explained why the "liberal" media so consistently favored conservative presidential candidates.

From Martin A. Lee and Norman Solomon, *Unreliable Sources: A Guide to Detecting Bias in News Media* (Carol Publishing Group, 1992). Copyright © 1992 by Carol Publishing Group. Reprinted by permission.

Reporters' "liberalism" has been exaggerated quite a bit, as Duke University scholar Robert Entman found when he examined the study most commonly cited by purveyors of the cliché. Entman discovered that the study relied on "a non-random sample that vastly overrepresented perhaps the most liberal segment of journalism"—employees of public TV stations in Boston, New York and Washington. These journalists were much more heavily surveyed about their political attitudes than the personnel putting together the far more weighty *New York Times* and national CBS television news.

The much-ballyhooed conclusion that journalists are of a predominantly leftish bent failed to square with data compiled by researchers without a strongly conservative agenda. A Brookings Institution study, for instance, found that 58 percent of Washington journalists identified themselves as either "conservative or middle of the road."

A 1985 *Los Angeles Times* survey, comparing 3,000 journalists to 3,000 members of the general public, found that journalists were more conservative when asked if the government should act to reduce the gap between rich and poor. Fifty-five percent of the general public supported such measures, compared to only 50 percent of the "news staff" and 37 percent of the editors.

But all the heated number-crunching may be much ado about little. The private opinions of media workers are much less important than the end products. Mark Hertsgaard has astutely pinpointed "the deeper flaw in the liberal-press thesis" —"it completely ignored those whom journalists worked for. Reporters could be as liberal as they wished and it would not change what news they were allowed

to report or how they could report it. America's major news organizations were owned and controlled by some of the largest and richest corporations in the United States. These firms were in turn owned and managed by individuals whose politics were, in general, anything but liberal. Why would they employ journalists who consistently covered the news in ways they did not like?"

If there's a political tilt to news coverage, it derives principally from mass media owners and managers, not beat reporters. "Admittedly," said sociologist Herbert Gans, "some journalists have strong personal beliefs and also the position or power to express them in news stories, but they are most often editors; and editors, like producers in television, have been shown to be more conservative than their news staffs." To the extent that personal opinions influence news content, Gans added, "they are most often the beliefs of the President of the United States and other high federal, state and local officials, since they dominate the news."

However baseless, accusations by conservatives that the media lean left have made many journalists compensate by tilting in the other direction. In this sense, the liberal media canard has been effective as a pre-emptive club, brandished to encourage self-censorship on the part of reporters who "bend over backwards not to seem at all critical of Republicans," commented Mark Crispin Miller. "Eager to evince his 'objectivity,' the edgy liberal reporter ends up just as useful to the right as any ultra-rightist hack."

And there are plenty of those, dominating America's highest-profile forums for political commentary on television and newspaper editorial pages. "In terms of the syndicated columnists, if there is an ideological bias, it's more and more to the right," President Reagan's media point man David Gergen declared in a 1981 interview. As the decade wore on, the imbalance grew more extreme.

The syndicated likes of George Will, Patrick Buchanan, Robert Novak, William F. Buckley and John McLaughlin achieved monotonous visibility on national TV, thanks to producers casting nets wide for right-wing pundits. As a tedious ritual they were paired with bland centrists, so that supposed "debates" often amounted to center-right discussions —on PBS's *MacNeil/Lehrer NewsHour*, Gergen with the *Washington Post's* charmingly mild Mark Shields; on ABC's *This Week With David Brinkley*, Will with the network's stylized but politically tepid Sam Donaldson; on CNN's *Crossfire*, Buchanan or Novak with somnolent ex-CIA-exec Tom Braden. (In late 1989, Braden yielded his seat "on the left" to Michael Kinsley of the *New Republic* magazine, but this didn't make the show any less unbalanced. "Buchanan is much further to the right than I am to the left," Kinsley acknowledged. As Howard Rosenberg wrote in the *Los Angeles Times*, "*Crossfire* should at least get the labeling right: Pat Buchanan from the far right and Michael Kinsley from slightly left of center.")

In early 1989, columnist Jack Newfield counted eight popular political opinion talk shows on national television. "These shows all have certifiably right-wing hosts and moderators," wrote Newfield. "This is not balance. This is ideological imbalance that approaches a conservative monopoly… Buchanan, who calls AIDS a punishment from God for sin, and campaigns against the prosecution of Nazi war criminals hiding in America, is about as far right as you can get."

A fixture on CNN, and often made welcome on the biggest TV networks, Buchanan has flaunted his admiration for prominent fascists past and present, like the Spanish dictator Francisco Franco (who came to power allied with Hitler) and Chile's bloody ruler Augusto Pinochet. "A soldier-patriot like Franco, General Pinochet saved his country from an elected Marxist who was steering Chile into Castroism," Buchanan effused in a September 1989 column, going on to defend the apartheid regime in South Africa: "The Boer Republic is the only viable economy in Africa. Why are Americans collaborating in a U.N. conspiracy with sanctions?"

Sharing much of the remaining op-ed space are others from the hard right, including former U.N. ambassador Jeane Kirkpatrick; William Safire (like Buchanan, an ex-speechwriter for the Nixon-Agnew team); erstwhile segregationist James J. Kilpatrick; Charles Krauthammer; former NBC News correspondent and Moral Majority vice president Cal Thomas; neo-conservative prophet Norman Podhoretz, and Ray Price (yet another Nixon speechwriter). Aside from a handful of left-leaning liberals, most of the other op-ed mainstays are establishment-tied middle-roaders such as Flora Lewis, David Broder, Jeff Greenfield, Georgie Anne Geyer, and Meg Greenfield.

The more honest conservatives readily admit to an asymmetry in their favor. Blunt acknowledgement has come from Adam Meyerson, editor of *Policy Review* magazine at the Heritage Foundation, the Washington think tank that drew up much of the Reaganite agenda. "Journalism today is very different from what it was 10 to 20 years ago," he said in 1988. "Today, op-ed pages are dominated by conservatives." The media market's oversupply of right-wingers was not without a drawback: "If Bill Buckley were to come out of Yale today, nobody would pay much attention to him ... [His] ideas would not be exceptional at all, because there are probably hundreds of people with those ideas already there, and they have already got syndicated columns ..." As for becoming an editorial writer, Meyerson could not be encouraging. "There are still a few good jobs here and there, but there's a glut of opinions, especially conservative opinions."

Factor in the proliferation of televangelists and far-right religious broadcasters, and the complaints about the "liberal media" ring even more hollow. By 1987, religious broadcasting had become a $2 billion a year industry, with more than 200 full-time Christian TV stations and 1,000 full-time Christian radio stations. This means that evangelical Christians control about 14 percent of the television stations operating in the U.S. and 10 percent of the radio stations, which bombard the American public with a conservative theo-political message. TV ministries continue to thrive, despite the widely-publicized preacher sex and money scandals of the late 1980s.

Some journalists may reject the mythology about liberal prejudice, but when addressing what *is* going on they're prone to denial. Instead of identifying the thumbs on news-media scales, the preference is to call the whole contraption neutral. "Everybody talks about media biases to the right or the left," syndicated columnist Ellen Goodman pooh-poohed in 1989. "The real media bias is against complexity, which is usually terminated with the words: 'I'm sorry, we're out of time.'" Of course, electronic news media are surface-skimming operations. Views that seriously challenge the status quo, however, have few occasions to be interrupted, since they're so rarely heard at all.

As he celebrated Thanksgiving in 1989, Spiro Agnew had reason to be pleased on the twentieth anniversary of his bombast. Agnew's polemical legacy hadn't stopped refracting the light under which journalists in Washington furrowed their brows. Tagged as "liberal" despite the evidence, mass media continued to shy away from tough, independent reporting.

OFFICIAL SCANDALS: FROM WATERGATE TO CONTRAGATE

Although big media are an integral part of the American power structure, it doesn't mean that reporters never challenge a President or other members of the governing class. A number of Presidents have gotten into nasty spats with the press, which has been credited with exposing the Watergate scandal that drove Richard Nixon from the vestibules of authority.

While the orthodox view of Watergate depicts it as the ultimate triumph of a free and independent press, there is a contrary view held by award-winning investigative journalist Seymour Hersh. "Far from rooting Nixon out in Watergate, I would say the press made Watergate inevitable," Hersh told us.

Hersh's thesis is simple. During his first term, Nixon conducted several illegal and unconstitutional policies with hardly a whimper from the mainstream media: the secret bombing of Cambodia, subversive operations that toppled Chile's democratically-elected government, CIA domestic spying against antiwar dissenters, wholesale wiretapping of

American officials and other citizens. "If the press had been able to break any one of these stories in 1971," Hersh reflected, "we might have been able to save the President from himself. He might have been afraid to do some of the things he did in 1972, and this would have changed the course of history. But the press failed utterly to do anything during Nixon's first term, thereby making it easy for Nixon to walk into his own trap in Watergate."

Having gotten away with so much for so long, Nixon didn't think twice about launching a covert assault against leaders of the other established political party. When Nixon's private spies—the plumbers—were caught red-handed in the headquarters of the Democratic National Committee in June 1972, most media accepted White House claims that it was just a two-bit burglary. The pundits said there was no story there; *Washington Post* reporters Bob Woodward and Carl Bernstein were dismissed as a couple of precocious upstarts out to make trouble for the President.

Nearly all media were slow to delve into what proved to be a monumental political scandal. As Bernstein told an audience at Harvard University in 1989, "At the time of Watergate, there were some 2,000 full-time reporters in Washington, working for major news organizations. In the first six months after the break-in . . . 14 of those reporters were assigned by their news organizations to cover the Watergate story on a full-time basis, and of these 14, half-a-dozen on what you might call an investigative basis." Bernstein added: "The press has been engaged in a kind of orgy of self-congratulations about our performance in Watergate and about our performance in covering the

news since. And it seems to me no attitude could be more unjustified."

"We realize that we did a lousy job on Watergate," said United Press International's Helen Thomas of the White House press corps. "We just sat there and took what they said at face value." Television was even slower than print media. As author Donna Woolfolk Cross wrote, "TV news did not pursue the story until it was already a well-established matter of discussion in the press and among politicians. During the times when Americans might have profited most from a full exploration of the scandal—before a national election—TV news was still presenting the story as the administration billed it: a 'second-rate burglary.' "

When the Iran-contra scandal broke in November 1986, comparisons with Watergate quickly came into vogue. Once again there were tales of a crusading press corps—journalistic Davids slaying White House Goliaths. But the wrong analogy was being drawn. A more accurate appraisal of the two scandals would not have been very flattering to the U.S. media. For if members of the press corps snoozed through Nixon's first term, they also winked and nodded off during almost six years of the Reagan presidency. Small wonder there were those in the Reagan administration who felt they could get away with escapades even more outlandish than Watergate.

Nixon, of course, was eventually forced to resign from office. Reagan managed to elude such a fate, in part because his aides pursued a more sophisticated media strategy. Whereas Nixon's people were often overtly hostile to the press, waging both a public and private war against journalists, the Reagan White House eschewed brass-knuckle tactics in favor of a more amicable relationship. When the *Washington Post* persisted in publishing detrimental Watergate revelations, Nixon threatened to revoke the broadcasting license of the *Post's* parent company. The Reagan administration tried a more enticing approach, expanding the number of lucrative broadcast affiliates that media corporations could own.

Reagan also benefited from the fact that the media's ideological pendulum had swung rightward since Nixon's final days—largely in reaction to Watergate. Media executives felt that perhaps they had gone too far when Nixon resigned. Roger Wilkins, who wrote *Washington Post* editorials about Watergate, later remarked that the press sought to prove "in the wake of Watergate that they were not irresponsible, that they did have a real sense of the national interest, that they had wandered out of this corporate club... But that essentially they were members in good standing of the club and they wanted to demonstrate that."

Nixon's fall from grace in 1974 came during a period of intense conflict within America's governing circles about the Vietnam War, economic policy and other matters. Nixon loyalists believe, probably correctly, that Woodward and Bernstein were used by unnamed U.S. intelligence sources—including their main source, nicknamed "Deep Throat"—to derail the Nixon presidency. This is not to detract from their accomplishments, but Woodward and Bernstein clearly had help from powerful, well-placed sources.

Shadowboxing in Washington

When Reagan became President in 1981, there was a high degree of consensus within America's corporate and political elites about domestic and foreign policy.

Abdicating the role of a real opposition party, Democratic leaders in Congress were more eager to put on a show than put up a fight. Sometimes the media used the passivity of the Democrats to justify their own. Either way, as Walter Karp put it, "the private story behind every major non-story during the Reagan administration was the Democrats' tacit alliance with Reagan."

It was a convenient arrangement for each of the three principals. The Reagan administration got credit for superb political smarts, and—after its nadir, the unraveling of the Iran-contra scandal—admirable resiliency. ("Howard Baker restored order to the White House," etc.) The Democrats scored points for slugging it out with the Reaganites. And the media reported the shadowboxing as a brawl instead of a contest that kept being thrown before it ever got bloody.

"For eight years the Democratic opposition had shielded from the public a feckless, lawless President with an appalling appetite for private power," Karp wrote. "That was *the* story of the Reagan years, and Washington journalists evidently knew it. Yet they never turned the collusive politics of the Democratic party into news. Slavishly in thrall to the powerful, incapable of enlightening the ruled without the consent of the rulers, the working press, the 'star' reporters, the pundits, the sages, the columnists passed on to us, instead, the Democrats' mendacious drivel about the President's 'Teflon shield.' For eight years, we saw the effects of a bipartisan political class in action, but the press did not show us that political class acting, exercising its collective power, making things happen, contriving the appearances that were reported as news.

One of the chronically contrived appearances was President Reagan's great popularity—phenomenal only in that it was a distortion. In April 1989, the *New York Times* reminded readers that Reagan was "one of the most popular Presidents in American history." Authoritative, but false—as University of Massachusetts political science professor Thomas Ferguson promptly documented for the umpteenth time. "It is tiresome," he wrote in *The Nation* magazine, "always to be pointing out that this ever-popular and seemingly indestructible refrain monumentally distorts the truth. But it does." The past half-century of polling data from Gallup Report showed Reagan's average public approval rating while in office (52 percent) to be lower than Presidents Johnson (54 percent), Kennedy (70 percent), Eisenhower (66 percent), and Roosevelt (68 percent). What's more, Reagan barely bested his three immediate predecessors —Carter (47 percent), Ford (46 percent) and Nixon (48 percent). Of the last nine Presidents, Reagan's approval ranking was a mediocre fifth.

POSTSCRIPT

Does the News Media Have a Liberal Bias?

As the opposing arguments in this issue indicate, we can find critics on both the Left and the Right who agree that the media are biased. What divides such critics is the question of whether the bias is left-wing or right-wing. Defenders of the news media may seize upon this disagreement to bolster their own claim that "bias is in the eye of the beholder." But the case may be that the news media are unfair to both sides. If that were true, however, it would seem to take some of the force out of the argument that the news media have a distinct ideological tilt at all.

Edward Jay Epstein's *News from Nowhere* (Random House, 1973) remains one of the great studies of the factors that influence television news shows. In *Media Events: The Live Broadcasting of History* (Harvard University Press, 1992), Daniel Dayan and Elihu Katz argue that live television coverage of major events helps to create the events and serves an important integrative role for society by deepening most citizens' experience of a common history. A study by S. Robert Lichter et al., *The Media Elite* (Adler & Adler, 1986), tends to support Maitre's contention that the media slant leftward, as does William Rusher's *The Coming Battle for the Media* (William Morrow, 1988) and Allan Levite's "Bias Basics," *National Review* (October 28, 1996), whereas Ben Bagdikian's *The Media Monopoly* (Beacon Press, 1983) and Mark Hertsgaard's *On Bended Knee: The Press and the Reagan Presidency* (Schocken, 1989) lend support to Lee and Solomon's view. A more recent S. Robert Lichter book, coauthored with Linda Lichter and Stanley Rothman, is *Watching America* (Prentice Hall, 1991), which surveys the political and social messages contained in television "entertainment" programs. Lichter has also written a media textbook with Thomas Dye and Harmon Ziegler entitled *American Politics in the Media Age*, 4th ed. (Brooks-Cole, 1992). David Halberstam's *The Powers That Be* (Alfred A. Knopf, 1979), a historical study of CBS, the *Washington Post*, *Time* magazine, and the *Los Angeles Times*, describes some of the political and ideological struggles that have taken place within major media organizations.

Edward Jay Epstein's book, previously cited, uses as an epigraph the following statement by Richard Salant, president of CBS News in the 1970s: "Our reporters do not cover stories from *their* point of view. They are presenting them from *nobody's* point of view." Most probably, Salant had not intended to be facetious or ironic, but the statement so amused Epstein that he parodied it in the title of his book: *News from Nowhere*.

ISSUE 3

Is Third World Immigration a Threat to America's Way of Life?

YES: Peter Brimelow, from *Alien Nation: Common Sense About America's Immigration Disaster* (Random House, 1995)

NO: John Isbister, from *The Immigration Debate: Remaking America* (Kumarian Press, 1996)

ISSUE SUMMARY

YES: Peter Brimelow, a writer and senior editor of *Forbes* and *National Review*, asserts that the large influx of immigrants from non-European countries threatens to undermine the cultural foundations of American unity.

NO: John Isbister, a provost at the University of California, Santa Cruz, cites research showing that immigration does not have the many negative impacts that people like Brimelow fear. He argues that immigration has a negligible effect on earnings and public finances and that its cultural impacts "will make it more obvious that the United States is a plural and not a unicultural society."

In his 1996 State of the Union speech, President Bill Clinton promised a 50 percent increase in border patrols to try to dramatically reduce illegal immigration. Polls show that this stand is a popular one. There is also much support for cutting back on legal immigration.

Today the number of legal immigrants to America is close to 1 million per year, and illegal ("undocumented") immigrants probably number well over that figure. In terms of numbers, immigration is now comparable to the level it reached during the early years of the twentieth century, when millions of immigrants arrived from southern and eastern Europe. A majority of the new immigrants, however, do not come from Europe but from what has been called the "Third World"—the underdeveloped nations. The largest percentages come from Mexico, the Philippines, Korea, and the islands of the Caribbean, while European immigration has shrunk to about 10 percent. Much of the reason for this shift has to do with changes made in U.S. immigration laws during the 1960s. Decades earlier, in the 1920s, America had narrowed its gate to people from certain regions of the world by imposing quotas designed to preserve the balance of races in America. But in 1965 a series of amendments to the Immigration Act put all the world's people on an equal footing in terms of immigration. The result, wrote journalist Theodore

H. White, was "a stampede, almost an invasion" of Third World immigrants. Indeed, the 1965 amendments made it even easier for Third World immigrants to enter the country because the new law gave preference to those with a family member already living in the United States. Since most of the European immigrants who settled in the early part of the century had died off, and since few Europeans had immigrated in more recent years, a greater percentage of family-reuniting immigration came from the Third World.

Immigrants move to the United States for various reasons: to flee tyranny and terrorism, to escape war, or to join relatives who have already settled. Above all, they immigrate because in their eyes America is an island of affluence in a global sea of poverty; here they will earn many times what they could only hope to earn in their native countries. One hotly debated question is, What will these new immigrants do to the United States—or for it?

Part of the debate has to do with bread-and-butter issues: Will new immigrants take jobs away from American workers? Or will they fill jobs that American workers do not want anyway, which will help stimulate the economy? Behind these economic issues is a more profound cultural question: Will these new immigrants add healthy new strains to America's cultural inheritance, broadening and revitalizing it? Or will they cause the country to break up into separate cultural units, destroying America's unity? Of all the questions relating to immigration, this one seems to be the most sensitive.

In 1992 conservative columnist Patrick Buchanan set off a firestorm of controversy when he raised this question: "If we had to take a million immigrants next year, say Zulus or Englishmen, and put them in Virginia, which group would be easier to assimilate and cause less problems for the people of Virginia?" Although Buchanan later explained that his intention was not to denigrate Zulus or any other racial group but to simply talk about assimilation into Anglo-American culture, his remarks were widely characterized as racist and xenophobic (related to a fear of foreigners). Whether or not that characterization is justified, Buchanan's question goes to the heart of the cultural debate over immigration, which is the tension between unity and diversity.

In the selections that follow, Peter Brimelow contends that immigrants are harming America both economically and culturally. He argues that the sheer number of immigrants from other cultures threatens to overwhelm traditional safeguards against cultural disintegration. This foreign influx is changing America from a nation into a collection of separate nationalities. John Isbister challenges the economic harm thesis and argues that the cultural impacts of immigration "are positive, constructive changes, that most Americans will benefit from living in a more multicultural society and that the tension between the different ethnic groups can be alleviated."

YES

Peter Brimelow

ALIEN NATION: COMMON SENSE ABOUT AMERICA'S IMMIGRATION DISASTER

THE IMMIGRATION INUNDATION

In 1991, the year of Alexander's birth, the Immigration and Naturalization Service reported a total of over 1.8 million legal immigrants. That was easily a record. It exceeded by almost a third the previous peak of almost 1.3 million, reached eighty-four years earlier at the height of the First Great Wave of Immigration, which peaked just after the turn of the century.

The United States has been engulfed by what seems likely to be the greatest wave of immigration it has ever faced. The INS estimates that 12 to 13 million legal and illegal immigrants will enter the United States during the decade of the 1990s. The Washington, D.C.–based Federation for American Immigration Reform (FAIR), among the most prominent of the groups critical of immigration policy, thinks the total will range between 10 and 15 million. An independent expert, Daniel James, author of *Illegal Immigration—An Unfolding Crisis*, has argued that it could be as high as 18 million.

And the chaotic working of current U.S. immigration law has created a peculiar, but little-understood, reality. *The extraordinary truth is that, in almost all cases, Americans will have little more say over the arrival of these new claimants on their national community—and voters on their national future—than over the arrival of Alexander.*

This is because it's not just illegal immigration that is out of control. So is legal immigration. *U.S. law in effect treats immigration as a sort of imitation civil right, extended to an indefinite group of foreigners who have been selected arbitrarily and with no regard to American interests.*

Whether these foreigners deign to come and make their claim on America —and on the American taxpayer—is pretty much up to them.

AMERICA'S ONE-WAY IMMIGRATION DEBATE

Everyone knows that there are two sides to every question, except the typical American editor ordering up a story about immigration, for whom there is only one side: immigration good, concern about immigration bad.

This results in the anecdotal happy-talk good-news coverage of immigration that we all know and love:

XYZ was just Harvard's valedictorian —XYZ arrived in the U.S. speaking no English three months ago—XYZ PROVES THE AMERICAN DREAM IS STILL ALIVE!—despite those nasty nativists who want to keep all the XYZs out.

Now, the achievement of immigrants to the United States (more accurately, of some immigrants to the United States) is indeed one of the most inspiring, and instructive, tales in human history. Nevertheless, there are still two sides to the question. Thus we might, equally reasonably, expect to see balancing anecdotal coverage like this:

In January 1993, a Pakistani applicant for political asylum (and, simultaneously, for amnesty as an illegal immigrant) opens fire on employees entering CIA headquarters, killing two and wounding three! In February 1993, a gang of Middle Easterners (most illegally overstaying after entering on non-immigrant visas— one banned as a terrorist but admitted on a tourist visa in error) blow up New York's World Trade Center, killing six and injuring more than 1,000!! In December 1993, a Jamaican immigrant (admitted as a student but stayed, illegal status automatically regularized after marriage to a U.S. citizen) opens fire on commuters on New York's Long Island Rail Road, killing six and wounding 19!!! WHAT'S GOING ON??!!?

The case of Colin Ferguson, arrested in the Long Island Rail Road shootings, is particularly instructive. . . .

Ferguson's own writings showed him to be motivated by hatred of whites. And this racial antagonism is a much deeper problem. In any rational mind, it must raise the question: *Is is really wise to allow the immigration of people who find it so difficult and painful to assimilate into the American majority?*

Because the fact cannot be denied: if Ferguson and the others had not immigrated, those fourteen Americans would not have been killed.

Although we might reasonably expect to see such balancing media coverage of immigration, don't hold your breath. There are powerful taboos preventing it. . . . The result, however, is that the American immigration debate has been a one-way street. Criticism of immigration, and news that might support it, just tends not to get through.

This is no mere journalism-school game of balancing anecdotes. It involves the broadest social trends. For example, the United States is in the midst of a serious crime epidemic. Yet almost no Americans are aware that *aliens make up one quarter of the prisoners in federal penitentiaries*—almost three times their proportion in the population at large.

Indeed, many problems that currently preoccupy Americans have an unspoken *immigration dimension. . . .*

The education crisis. Americans are used to hearing that their schools don't seem to be providing the quality of education that foreigners get. Fewer of them know that the U.S. education system is also very expensive by international standards. Virtually none of them know anything about the impact of immigration on that education system.

Yet the impact of immigration is clearly serious. For example, in 1990 almost one child in every twenty enrolled in American public schools either could not speak English or spoke it so poorly as to need language-assistance programs.

This number is increasing with striking speed: only six years earlier, it had been one child in thirty-one. Current law is generally interpreted as requiring schools to educate such children in their native language. To do so, according to one California estimate, requires spending some 65 percent more per child than on an English-speaking child. . . .

[T]he immigration resulting from current public policy

1. is dramatically larger, less skilled and more divergent from the American majority than anything that was anticipated or desired
2. is probably not beneficial economically—and is certainly not necessary
3. is attended by a wide and increasing range of negative consequences, from the physical environment to the political
4. is bringing about an ethnic and racial transformation in America without precedent in the history of the world —an astonishing social experiment launched with no particular reason to expect success . . .

WHAT ABOUT MY GRANDFATHER?

Many Americans have difficulty thinking about immigration restriction because of a lurking fear: *This would have kept my grandfather out. . . .*

But it must also be stressed: *that was then; this is now.* There are important differences between the last Great Wave of Immigration and today's.

1. Then, there was an "Open Door" (essentially—and with the major exception of the restriction on Asians). Now, the 1965 reform has reopened the border in a perversely unequal way. Essentially, it has allowed immigrants from some countries to crowd out immigrants from others. . . .
2. Then, immigrants came overwhelmingly from Europe, no matter how different they seemed at the time; now, immigrants are overwhelmingly visible minorities from the Third World. Not withstanding which—
3. Then, there was an aggressive public and private "Americanization" campaign . . . ; now, there's "multiculturalism"—i.e., immigrants are officially not expected to assimilate.
4. Then, there was no welfare state and immigrants who failed often went home; now, there is a welfare state —and fewer immigrants leave.
5. Then, *immigration was stopped.* There was a pause for digestion—the Second Great Lull—that lasted some forty years. Now, there's no end in sight.

. . . [A]n implicit accusation of racism is the common reaction of a vocal minority of Americans to news of their country's shifting ethnic balance. . . .

I say a vocal minority because I think the vast majority of Americans regard as just a matter of common sense that the composition of a country's population cannot, in fact, be changed without risking dramatic consequences. . . .

[T]here are some extraordinary aspects of the impending ethnic revolution that, by any standard, deserve discussion in a democracy:

- *It is unprecedented in history.* No sovereign state has ever undergone such a radical and rapid transformation.
- *It is wholly and entirely the result of government policy.* Immigration is causing both the shifting American ethnic balance and also the projected massive increase in overall population.

Left to themselves, pre-1965 Americans would be stabilizing both their ethnic proportions and their overall numbers.

... [T]here's a plain fact to be considered: the evidence that multiracial societies work is—what shall we say?—*not very encouraging*.

There have, of course, been multiracial societies (strictly speaking, usually multiethnic) in the past. Famous examples are the Roman Empire, or the Arab Caliphate, which briefly ruled from Spain to Samarkand in the name of Muhammad. But these were old-fashioned despotisms, not modern democracies. And, even so, ethnic divisions still kept surfacing. The ancestors of the modern Iranians repeatedly rebelled against Arab rule, although they tended to justify their revolts in terms of a convenient Islamic heresy.

Heterogeneous empires that lasted, such as the Eastern Roman Empire of Byzantium, which survived until 1453, were generally based on a core ethnic group—distinctly like our old friend, the "racial hegemony of white Americans." In the case of Byzantium, for instance, this core group was Greek.

In modern times, there has been a lot of seductive murmuring about internationalism, united nations, new world orders, and so on. But, meanwhile, the role of ethnicity and race has proved to be elemental—absolute—fundamental. Look at the record, working back from the present:

- *Eritrea*, a former Italian colony ruled by Ethiopia since 1952, revolt begins in 1960s, finally splits off 1993.
- *Czechoslovakia*, founded 1918, splits into Czech and Slovak ethnic components, 1993.
- *Soviet Union*, founded 1922, splits into multiple underlying ethnic components, 1991. (Some of the underlying components are themselves promptly threatened with further ethnic fragmentation—Georgia, Moldova.)
- *Yugoslavia*, founded 1918, splits into multiple underlying ethnic components, 1991. (An earlier breakup averted by imposition of royal dictatorship, 1929.)
- *Lebanon*, founded 1920, progressive destabilization caused by its Muslim component's faster growth results in civil war, effective partition under Syrian domination, after 1975.
- *Cyprus*, independent 1960, repeated violence between Greeks and Turks results in military intervention by Turkey, effective partition with substantial ethnic cleansing, 1974.
- *Pakistan*, independent 1947, ethnically distinct eastern component rebels, splits off after Indian military intervention, 1971.
- *Malaysia*, independent 1963, political conflict between ethnic Malays and Chinese, Chinese-dominated Singapore expelled, 1965.

And these are just the cases where ethnic and racial differences have actually succeeded in breaking a country up. Many other cases are not yet resolved, because of often-bloody repression.

Here's a partial list: *India*—protracted separatist revolts by Sikhs, Kashmiris, northeastern hill tribes. *Sri Lanka*—protracted separatist revolt by Tamils. *Turkey, Iraq, Iran*—separatist revolts by Kurds. *Sudan, Chad*—endemic warfare between Arab north, black south. *Nigeria*—secession of Ibo-majority "Biafra" crushed in 1967–70 civil war. *Liberia*—English-speaking descendants of freed American slaves overthrown by tribal forces 1981, civil war renders more than half the population refugees. *Ulster*—protracted campaign by members of province's Catholic Irish minority to force the Ulster Protestant ("Scotch-Irish") majority to accept its transfer to the Irish Republic. Some of these conflicts have been very violent—over 1 million deaths each in Nigeria and Sudan.

And there's a whole further category of disputes that are being conducted, mostly, through political means. For example: *Belgium*—Flemish and Walloon; *Canada*—French and English; even *Brazil* —a movement in the predominantly white southern states Rio Grande do Sul, Santa Catarina and Paraná to separate from the mixed-race north.

What a record! You would think it would inspire at least some caution about the prospects for multiethnic, multiracial, multicultural harmony within the same political framework.

But you would be wrong. The recent record seems to have made very little impression on the American political elite. . . .

HOW MUCH ECONOMIC GROWTH ARE WE TALKING ABOUT ANYWAY?

Oddly, American economists have made very little effort to measure the overall economic benefits of immigration. But the answer seems to be clear: *immigration doesn't contribute that much to economic growth.* . . .

In 1992, the economic surplus generated by immigrants and accruing to native-born Americans was very small: about one to three tenths of 1 percent of total U.S. economic output, or between $6 billion and $18 billion.

That's 0.2 or 0.3 percent! In an economy whose long-run average annual growth is about 2 percent anyway!! Within the normal margin of error for economic projections—*so it may be, for practical purposes, infinitesimal!!!* . . .

Another point:

If immigration is indeed causing a net loss to taxpayers of $16 billion— as George Borjas estimates—that means its economic effects are neutral. It's a wash!!!

America is being transformed for— *nothing?*

Yep. That's what it looks like.

However, note that this Borjas back-of-the-envelope calculation has a subtle but ugly implication:

The overall economic surplus generated by immigrants and accruing to native-born Americans might be very small —but immigration might still be causing a significant redistribution of income within the native-born American community.

This happens because the small amount by which immigrants drive down the wages for all American workers, nationwide, adds up to a sizeable sum—which goes to American owners of capital. Borjas estimates it could be 2 percent of GNP, or as much as $120 billion. . . .

However, this is the ugly implication: the American elite's support for immigration may not be idealistic at all, but self-interested—as a way to prey on their fellow Americans. . . .

IS THE UNITED STATES STILL CAPABLE OF ABSORBING IMMIGRANTS?

Let's be clear about this: the American experience with immigration has been triumphant success. It has so far transcended anything seen in Europe as to make the application of European lessons an exercise to be performed with care.

But there are very clear reasons why the American nation has been able to absorb and assimilate immigrants. In considering further immigration, its enthusiasts must ask themselves honestly: *do these reasons still apply?*

One reason America could assimilate immigrants, as we have seen, is that there were regular pauses for digestion. Another reason is that the American political elite *wanted the immigrants to assimilate.* And it did not hesitate to ensure that they did.

Over two hundred years of U.S. history, a number of tried-and-true, but undeniably tough, assimilation techniques had been perfected. But today, they have been substantially abandoned.

The economic culture of the United States has changed significantly—from classical liberalism to government-regulated welfare statism. Earlier immigrants were basically free to succeed or fail. And many failed: as we have seen, as many as 40 percent of the 1880–1920 immigrants went back home. But now, public policy interposes itself, with the usual debatable results....

And it's not just the American economic culture that has changed. So has the political culture. Almost a century ago, the last Great Wave of immigrants were met with the unflinching demand that they "Americanize." Now they are told that they should retain and reinforce their diversity....

Is the United States still capable of absorbing immigrants? Is it still trying? Consider these policies:

1. *Massive, heterogeneous immigration.*
2. *"Bilingualism"*—i.e., foreign languageism—and
3. *"Multiculturalism"*—i.e., non-Americanism—in the education system.
4. *"Affirmative Action"*—i.e., government-mandated discrimination against white Americans.
5. *Systematic attack on the value of citizenship,* by making it easier for aliens to vote, receive government subsidies, etc.

Sounds much more like deconstructionism—the deconstruction of the American nation as it existed in 1965.

NO

John Isbister

THE IMMIGRATION DEBATE

THE DEBATE

Immigration has become one of the most contentious topics of debate in the United States. It is not surprising.

In 1965, Congress reformed the country's immigration law, removing the system of quotas based on national origins that had been in place since the 1920s. The architects of the 1965 act wanted to expunge what they saw as racial discrimination in the country's immigration legislation. They did not expect, however, that the new law would lead to much of a shift in either the number or the national origins of the country's immigrants. Yet, since 1965, an enormous change has occurred in both. The amount of immigration has reached levels seen only once before, at the turn of the present century. The United States now accepts more immigrants than all other countries combined. The principal sources of immigration have changed completely, from Europe with its white populations to the third world countries of Latin America and Asia. The pressure for immigration from foreign countries has grown faster than the legal gates have been opening, so the number of un-documented immigrants has increased too.

As immigration has grown, opposition to it has grown as well. The country is flooded with proposals to reduce the flow of immigrants, to change the pri-ority categories, to tighten controls at the border and to penalize immigrants, both legal and illegal. The Commission on Immigration Reform, headed by former Representative Barbara Jordan of Texas, recommended in 1995 that immigration be cut by one-third, and President Clinton endorsed the recom-mendation. The opposition is similar to the resistance that built up against the great influx of immigrants at the beginning of the century. Public opinion against that wave became so strong that Congress passed a series of acts in the 1920s severely restricting the number of new entrants. Today's critics of immigration would like to see the same sort of policy response.

Public opinion polls show strong resistance to immigration, even among some ethnic groups that include a large proportion of recent immigrants. A Roper poll showed that 55 percent of the population is in favor of a temporary freeze on immigration. A poll that divided its respondents by ethnicity showed that 70 to 80 percent of not only Anglos but also Mexican Americans, Puerto Ricans and Cuban Americans agreed with the statement, "There are too many immigrants coming to the U.S." A *Newsweek* poll found that 60 percent of Americans think that immigration is a "bad thing" for the country, and 62 percent think that immigrants take the jobs of American workers. In 1994, Californians voted by a 59–41 margin for Proposition 187, to cut undocumented immigrants and their children off from all public expenditures except emergency medical care. A Field poll showed that almost half of Californians favored a constitutional amendment to deny citizenship to the American-born children of undocumented immigrants. Any number of other polls show the same thing: the majority of Americans are at least skeptical about the value of immigration and, for the most part, are hostile to it.

Little about the debate is new; most of the arguments, both pro and con, have surfaced many times in the past. In the thirteen colonies of the eighteenth century, for example, the predominant opinion was that immigration was essential to prosperity and that any attempt to restrict it was illegitimate. Among the grievances listed in the Declaration of Independence was that the king had:

> endeavoured to prevent the population of these States; for that purpose obstructing the Laws for Naturalization of Foreigners; refusing to pass others to encourage their migration hither.

It had to be a certain *type* of immigrant, however; non-English newcomers were suspect. In the *Federalist Papers*, John Jay wrote,

> Providence has been pleased to give this one connected country to one united people—a people descended from the same ancestors, speaking the same language, professing the same religion, attached to the same principles of government, very similar in their manners and customs.

Benjamin Franklin, writing in 1775, was more explicitly racist:

> Why should the *Palatine Boors* be suffered to swarm into our settlements, and by herding together establish their language and manners to the exclusion of ours? Why should *Pennsylvania*, founded by the *English*, become a colony of *Aliens*, who will shortly be so numerous as to Germanize us instead of our Anglifying them, and will never adopt our language or customs, any more than they can acquire our complexion. . . .

The Economic Debate

Much of the debate has focused on the economic consequences of immigration, both short and long term. Some proponents of immigration argue that the newcomers contribute to the vitality of the American economy, helping to improve the standard of living of everyone, whether immigrant or native. Others do not go so far but argue that immigrants at least cause no economic harm to Americans. Those on the other side of the economic debate claim that immigrants impose significant material burdens on Americans and that they reduce the country's prospects for long-term prosperity. . . .

What the Empirical Studies Show

What do the cross-sectional studies tell us? Briefly, they show that immigration has little if any economic impact on the wages and employment opportunities of residents, even residents who are unskilled, low paid or racial minorities.

As an example, Robert LaLonde and Robert Topel used the 1970 and 1980 censuses to study the effects of immigration in 119 standard metropolitan statistical areas. They found that immigration had only a slight effect on earnings. According to their calculations, a 100 percent increase in immigration to a city would cause only a 3 percent decline in the earnings of the immigrants themselves and a 1 percent decline in the earnings of African American and Latino residents....

The rest of the cross-sectional empirical work leads to similar conclusions. The great majority of the studies find that immigration has little or no effect on the wages and employment of natives, even on the wages and employment of disadvantaged subgroups.

Can the Empirical Studies Be Reconciled with the Models?

We are left with a puzzle. Why is it that the theoretical models predict that immigration will harm the employment and wages of resident Americans, particularly disadvantaged Americans, yet most of the empirical research cannot identify such an effect? Normally in such a case, one would treat the models as hypotheses to be tested and conclude that the empirical tests have disproved the hypotheses. In this case, however, the models were not really tested directly, because time series studies were not possible.

It is easy to think of reasons why the cross-sectional empirical studies might be misleading. Perhaps immigration into a city tends to reduce the wages of low-skilled workers, as the models predict, but within a short time the flow of both labor and capital within the United States responds so as to negate the initial effect of immigration in those cities....

After dozens of sophisticated studies,... we are still uncertain about the short-run economic impact of immigration. Immigration may have negative economic effects that our statistical methods are incapable of detecting. The case is not proved, however. One can certainly come up with an argument to support the validity of the empirical studies. For example, if immigration attracts new capital into the country, it may have no overall effect on wages.

It is frustrating to learn that economists, with all their high-powered methodological tools, cannot give a clear answer to a simple, important question: how does immigration affect the earnings of American residents, in particular the most disadvantaged Americans? Nevertheless, that is the state of the professional literature.

Are Immigrants a Fiscal Burden?

... None of the research to date has been adequately designed to provide a fully persuasive answer to the question of whether immigration creates a fiscal burden on residents. The studies are in an accounting rather than an economic mode. They attempt to count the expenditures that are made on immigrants and the taxes paid by immigrants. Even this is exceptionally difficult to do, and every one of the studies can be criticized for being incomplete in one way or another. Few of them even attempt to measure the indirect market effects of immigration on the public finances. For example, if immigration leads to an increase in aggregate demand and the consequent creation of new jobs, some of which are held by previously unemployed natives, the taxes paid by these new employees and the reduction in unemployment insurance payments should be counted as a fiscal benefit of immigration....

It is hard to identify all the ways in which immigrants affect the revenues and expenditures of the different governments, let alone measure the effects. Taken together, however, most of the studies seem to indicate that immigrants have not been a net burden to U.S. governments—that government expenditures on the immigrants have not exceeded tax revenues paid by the immigrants. Immigrants may even have been a net asset....

... At the level of state governments, the situation may vary according to the state.

It appears... that in the country as a whole, immigrants probably impose no burden on resident taxpayers and may even contribute more than they use. At the state level, however, and even more so at the local level in communities where immigration has been heavy, there are a number of cases of immigrants imposing a fiscal burden. However, because every study to date has been seriously incomplete, we have only hints about the true fiscal impact of immigration, not proof....

MAKING A MULTICULTURAL SOCIETY WORK

The consequences of immigration into the United States are not limited to the economy. Just as important, perhaps more important, are the social and cultural impacts of immigration, particularly those resulting from changes in the ethnic composition of the population.... If immigration continues at its current rate, the time will come, a couple of generations hence, when Anglos will be a minority of the population and Latinos, not African Americans, will be the next largest group.

Many Americans oppose these changes, believing that their country is turning into something they do not like and did not agree to. Journalist Peter Brimelow writes, "The onus is on those who favor the major change in the ethnic balance entailed by current immigration levels to explain exactly what they have against the American nation as it had evolved by 1965 (90 per cent white, primarily from Italy, Germany, Ireland and Britain). While they're at it, they can explain just what makes them think that multi-racial societies work."

[The remainder of this selection] provides a response to Brimelow's challenge, arguing that the changes in the U.S. population caused by immigration are positive, constructive changes, that most Americans will benefit from living in a more multicultural society and that the tension between the different ethnic groups can be alleviated.

The Mosaic of American Life

American culture is based on a multitude of different nationalities and ethnicities. "It never happened that a group of people called Americans came together to form a political society called America," writes political philosopher Michael Walzer. "The people are Americans only by virtue of having come together." American culture does not derive from a single folk tradition; it is not based on a particular religion or a single race. It embodies many folkways, many religions, many races.

The principal metaphor for how the various traditions came together in America used to be the melting pot. The groups were thought to have mixed together so thoroughly that they created a new culture, one that was common to most Americans and that erased the immigrant past. The ideology of the melting pot is still alive, but at the end of the twentieth century it is weak. It is now apparent that the nineteenth-century immigrant groups did not assimilate as thoroughly as was once thought, that the melting pot never worked with African and Native Americans and that the latest waves of immigrants show few signs of disappearing into an undifferentiated brew. Replacing the melting pot is the pluralist, multicultural image of the mosaic, in which immigrants and their descendants are understood as retaining important parts of their ethnic identities, and together constituting a varied, diverse nation....

The metaphor of the melting pot misses... the essence of American culture. To be sure, the experience of being in America has changed people. African Americans are not Africans; neither, however, are they just Americans. They are African Americans, and their experience of the United States is strongly influenced by that fact. This is also true for the Jews, the Puerto Ricans, the Mexicans, the Chinese and many other groups that have come in large numbers to the United States. In their seminal 1963 study *Beyond the Melting Pot*, Nathan Glazer and Daniel Patrick Moynihan rejected the idea of a uniform American culture, at least in the neighborhoods of New York. Scholarly work since that time has expanded their ideas. In his 1993 book *A Different Mirror*, for example, Ronald Takaki interprets the full sweep of American history as being dominated by the interactions of immigrant and ethnic groups.

To the extent that the melting pot is a valid idea at all, its contents are white. The melting pot brought together English, Irish, Swedes, Italians, Hungarians, Russians and other European groups and made a country out of them. In the first part of the twentieth century, this seemed a remarkable achievement, because the history of immigration had been fraught with suspicion, disdain and discrimination. The English once thought of the Irish immigrants as scruffy and papist; at a later date, the English and Irish together thought that the Italians and Greeks were barbarian. Yet by the first half of the twentieth century, the distinctions between the European groups were blurring. They retained ethnic organizations, with the Jews being perhaps the strongest in maintaining their communities. They cooperated together in business and in politics, however; they sometimes moved into the same suburbs, and their children intermarried. The ethnic identities did not disappear, but they were on the road to becoming footnotes to an American identity.

If that sort of description rings true for some Irish and Poles, however, it does not for African and Native Americans. One can take the melting pot seriously as the central process of American civilization only if one thinks that non-white groups were not really part of that civilization. Many people have exactly that opinion. For example, Brimelow's popular book on immigration, *Alien Nation*, overflows with observations that the United States is properly a white nation and should stay that way. "The American nation has always had a specific ethnic core. And that core has been white," he writes. Later, he writes, "And—if only for my son Alexander's sake—I'd like it to stay that way." In spite of Brimelow's protestations that his views are not racist, the words speak for themselves.

Like it or not, non-whites have always been a fundamental component of American culture, since the first day a settler encountered a Native on the shore of the Atlantic, and since the first docking of a slave ship. Today, there are many more non-white groups. The majority of Latinos and Asians in the United States are the descendants of fairly recent immigrants, or immigrants themselves, so it is early to judge how those groups will assimilate into mainstream culture, or if mainstream culture will be there when they do. So far, however, they are not melting with other Americans nearly as completely as the different European groups did. They face racial discrimination that is different from and deeper than anything the Europeans faced. Their ethnic organizations and ethnic identities seem to be stronger.

If immigration continues at its current pace, therefore, and if third world countries of origin still predominate, so that non-Anglo ethnic groups continue to grow as proportions of the population, each passing decade will make it more obvious that the United States is a plural and not a unicultural society. . . .

Immigration as a Threat to the Dominant Culture

The majority of white Americans think of themselves as Americans, not any particular kind of Americans. They often think of themselves as people without any particular culture, just "people." The truth, however, is that they have merged not into a common American culture but into the dominant American culture, so dominant that they can be blinded into thinking of it as the only culture. Thus Bette Hammond . . . complains that today's immigrants want to be in America but they do not want to be American. She means, presumably, that they do not want to be part of the predominantly white, Anglo, middle-class culture that the melting pot has produced. The non-white groups tend to see it differently. They cannot be part of that dominant culture, they believe, because they are excluded from it and oppressed by it.

Anglos who fear the new immigration understand this on some level. They know, and fear, that the forces of the melting pot are not strong enough to assimilate the latest wave of newcomers completely . . . Today's immigrants look different, they speak differently, they have different values, different family structures, different commitments, different heritages. Mainstream-culture Americans often fear that this new multiculturalism is altering the life to which they are accustomed. . . .

Immigration Seen through Multicultural Lenses

Those who see the country as pluralist, myself included, do not share the fears of the uniculturalists. The essence of American life is that it is composed of different groups, different cultures, races, religions, attitudes, folkways and ideologies, differences that give the country its distinctiveness. Current immigration is sure to change the mixture, but change is not new; the cultural mixture of America has been changing continuously.

Brimelow's question was: what was wrong with the American nation as it was in 1965, 90 percent white? The answer is that there were serious problems, as the civil rights movement and the explosions in the central cities revealed. America has always been multicultural, but it has been a peculiar kind of multiculturalism: not equally powerful cultures enriching one another on a reciprocal basis, but a dominant culture set against subservient cultures fighting to secure places for themselves. Today's immigration creates the possibility that the United States may become a country without a dominant race and without a dominant culture. If Anglos become a minority by the second half of the twenty-first century, and if the different ethnic groups achieve political representation, they will have the power to protect their interests and their cultures. As the sizes of the different racial and ethnic groups become more comparable, the likelihood of one group dominating the others will become correspondingly less.

The alternative to an egalitarian, reciprocal, multicultural society is not the single culture imagined by the uniculturalists. The implication of Brimelow's description ("90 per cent white, primarily from Italy, Germany, Ireland and Britain") is that the United States really could be a country with a single culture, much like some imagine France or Japan to be. It never has been, however, and it cannot be. The most important theme in American cultural history, since the seventeenth century, has been racial conflict. The conflicts have been marked by slavery, unequal power, widely disparate economic statuses, personal prejudice and institutional discrimination. Although the terms of the confrontation have shifted, whites and non-whites are still unequal in status. The alternatives before the country, therefore, are not a single culture versus many cultures, but multiculturalism marked by dominance, subordination and conflict versus multiculturalism marked by equality of status and reciprocity.

How can the first kind of country be transformed into the second? There is no single answer. I am enough of an optimist, however, to think that I have been living in the United States during a generation of change—through the civil rights movement, through political action, through education, through the assertion of legal rights, through cooperation by people of good will and through immigration. The shift in immigration legislation from a racist to a nondiscriminatory basis in 1965 has allowed and will continue to allow the relative numbers of the different ethnic groups to change in such a way that they confront one another on a more equal basis.

Numbers matter. In order for the different groups to relate to one another on an equal basis, without the members of one group feeling that they have to suppress their values and their interests, all the groups need to be not equal in size but well represented. As Anglos move toward minority status, and as Latinos and Asian Americans grow proportionately and African Americans retain their current relative representation, the interactions among the different groups may become more direct, clearer, more reciprocal, more equal. The United States will not become multicultural because it always has been, but its multiculturalism will become healthier, its citizens less constrained by structures of discrimination. . . .

What will be distinctive about the United States is that the mix of cultures will be so rich. Even today, the representation of different groups in the United States is broader than in any other country; as immigration proceeds, the combination of ethnic groups will approach that of the world as a whole. Anglos will probably continue to be overrepresented and Asians underrepresented, in comparison to their proportions in the world's population, but the former will be less than half and the latter will constitute a substantial number.

One of the reasons that it is important for America to become a country in which different cultural groups encounter one another on the basis of equality and respect is that America could become a model to the world. The world needs models of cultural respect.

POSTSCRIPT

Is Third World Immigration a Threat to America's Way of Life?

Former representative Silvio Conte (R-Massachusetts) said at a citizenship ceremony, "You can go to France, but you will never be a Frenchman. You can go to Germany but you will never be a German. Today you are all Americans, and that is why this is the greatest country on the face of the earth." At one time America's open doors to immigrants was one of the prides of America. For some people, like Isbister, it still is. He thinks that an integrated, multicultural society is a culturally rich society and that immigration is making America stronger. Many people disagree because they fear the consequences of today's immigration. Brimelow worries that, although the new immigrants may want to assimilate, they have reached such a critical mass that the United States has lost the ability to absorb everyone into its own, slowly dissipating culture. The result is that immigrants are encouraged to maintain and promote the cultures that they arrive with, which further dilutes the original culture of America. Isbister counters that Brimelow's fears are that the white America that he identifies with will lose some of its dominance. That is, the America that Brimelow wants to protect is a racist, white America. Isbister argues that America has always been multicultural and that it will gain from being multicultural.

For a fascinating study of the roots of American traditional culture, see David Hackett Fischer, *Albion's Seed: Four British Folkways in America* (Oxford University Press, 1989). Stanley Lieberson and Mary C. Waters, in *From Many Strands* (Russell Sage Foundation, 1988), argue that ethnic groups with European origins are assimilating, marrying outside their groups, and losing their ethnic identities. Richard D. Alba's study "Assimilation's Quiet Tide," *The Public Interest* (Spring 1995) confirms these findings.

Several major works debate whether or not immigrants, on average, economically benefit America and can assimilate. Sources that argue that immigrants largely benefit America include Julian L. Simon, *The Economic Consequences of Immigration* (Basil Blackwell, 1989) and *Immigration: The Demographic and Economic Facts* (Cato Institute, 1995); Sanford J. Unger, *Fresh Blood: The New American Immigrants* (Simon & Schuster, 1995); Joel Millman, *The Other Americans: How Immigrants Renew Our Country, Our Economy, Our Values* (Viking, 1997); John C. Harles, *Politics in the Lifeboat: Immigrants and the American Democratic Order* (Westview Press, 1993); and Thomas Muller, *Immigrants and the American City* (New York University Press, 1993). See also Ben Wattenberg and Karl Zinmeister, "The Case for More Immigration," *Commentary* (April 1990); Glenn Garvin, "No Fruits, No Shirts, No Service," *Reason*

(April 1995) and "Bringing the Border War Home," *Reason* (October 1995); and Nathan Glazer, "Immigration and the American Future," *The Public Interest* (Winter 1995).

Those who argue that immigrants have more negative than positive impacts include George Borjas, in *Friends or Strangers* (Basic Books, 1990) and "Know the Flow," *National Review* (April 17, 1995); Roy Beck, *The Case Against Immigration* (W. W. Norton, 1996); Lawrence Auster, *The Path to National Suicide: An Essay on Immigration and Multiculturalism* (AICF, 1990); and Richard D. Lamm, "Enough," *Across the Board* (March 1995). Vernon M. Biggs, Jr., and Stephen Moore debate each other on the economic impacts of immigration in *Still an Open Door? U.S. Immigration Policy and the American Economy* (American University Press, 1994), and a variety of issues are debated in *Immigration: Debating the Issues* edited by Nicholas Capaldi (Prometheus Books, 1997). Lawrence E. Harrison, in "America and Its Immigrants," *National Interest* (Summer 1992), argues in favor of selective immigration, which would allow only those people with the "correct" skills and values to immigrate to the United States. Given the great need for a haven for those who must flee persecution and desperation, there are many humanitarian aspects to the immigration issue that must be brought into the discussion. See Gil Loescher, *Beyond Charity: International Cooperation and the Global Refugee Crisis* (Oxford University Press, 1993).

On the Internet . . .

American Men's Studies Association

The American Men's Studies Association is a not-for-profit professional organization of scholars, therapists, and others interested in the exploration of masculinity in modern society. *http://www.cybersales.net/amsa/*

American Studies Web

This eclectic site provides links to a wealth of resources on the Internet related to gender studies. *http://www.georgetown.edu/crossroads/asw/*

Feminism and Women's Resources

This site for feminism and women's resources includes information on and links to women's organizations, women's resources, and other organizations and links of interest. *http://zeno.ibd.nrc.ca/~mansfield/feminism/*

Feminist Internet Gateway

The Feminist Internet Gateway provides affirmative action links, resources from the feminist majority foundation, information for empowering women in business, sexual harassment information, and much more. *http://www.feminist.org/gateway/sd_exec2.html*

GLAAD: Gay and Lesbian Alliance Against Defamation

GLAAD, formed in New York in 1985, seeks to improve the public's attitudes toward homosexuality and to put an end to discrimination against lesbians and gay men. *http://www.glaad.org/*

The Men's Issues Page

This site for men's issues has links to such topics as battered men, false rape/abuse/molestation reporting, men's physical and mental health, and men's organizations. *http://www.vix.com/men/index.html*

SocioSite

This site provides insights into a number of issues that affect family relationships. It covers wide-ranging issues regarding women and men, family and children, and much more. *http://www.pscw.uva.nl/sociosite/TOPICS/Women.html*

PART 2

Sex Roles, Gender, and the Family

The modern feminist movement has advanced the causes of women to the point where there are now more women in the workforce in the United States than ever before. Professions and trades that were traditionally regarded as the provinces of men have opened up to women, and women now have easier access to the education and training necessary to excel in these new areas. But what is happening to sex roles, and what are the effects of changing sex roles? How have related problems such as male-female communication difficulties and the deterioration of the traditional family structure affected men, women, and children? Is feminism as a universal philosophy harmful in any way? The issues in this part address these sorts of questions.

■ Is Feminism a Harmful Ideology?

■ Are Communication Problems Between Men and Women Largely Due to Radically Different Conversation Styles?

■ Should Society Be More Accepting of Homosexuality?

■ Is the Decline of the Traditional Family a National Crisis?

ISSUE 4

Is Feminism a Harmful Ideology?

YES: Robert Sheaffer, from "Feminism, the Noble Lie," *Free Inquiry* (Spring 1995)

NO: William H. Chafe, from *The Paradox of Change: American Women in the Twentieth Century* (Oxford University Press, 1991)

ISSUE SUMMARY

YES: Robert Sheaffer, a consulting editor for *Skeptical Inquirer,* faults feminism for supporting its political agenda with fraudulent research and for trying to impose an inappropriate equality on men and women that conflicts with basic biological differences between the genders.

NO: William H. Chafe, a professor at Duke University, demonstrates the value of feminism by reviewing the history of feminism since the early 1960s and pointing to the injustices that the feminist movement largely helped to correct. He maintains that the obvious need to end continuing discrimination demonstrates the value of feminism.

The publication of Betty Friedan's *The Feminine Mystique* (W. W. Norton, 1963) is generally thought of as the beginning of the modern women's movement, and since that time significant changes have occurred in American society. Occupations and professions, schools, clubs, associations, and governmental positions that were by tradition or law previously reserved for men only are now open to women. Women are found in increasing numbers among lawyers, judges, physicians, and elected officials. In 1981 President Ronald Reagan appointed the first woman, Sandra Day O'Connor, to the Supreme Court. In 1983 the first American woman astronaut, Sally Ride, was included in the crew of a space shuttle, and women have been on more recent space shuttle missions as well. The service academies have accepted women since 1976, and women in the military participated in the U.S. invasion of Panama in December 1989 and the Persian Gulf War in 1990–1991. There are ongoing debates in Congress and among the armed services about whether or not to lift restrictions on women serving in combat. And Elizabeth Watson became the first woman to head a big-city police department when the mayor of Houston appointed her chief of police in January 1990.

These sorts of changes—quantifiable and highly publicized—may signal a change in women's roles, at least to this extent: women now engage in occupations that were previously exclusive to men, and women can pursue the necessary training and education required to do so. But three decades after Friedan's book, to what extent do females and males have equal standing? Are femininity and femaleness prized or valued the same as maleness and masculinity? What is happening to society's concepts of both? Even as changes are occurring in the public world, what is happening on a personal level to the roles of men and women? How do we value the domestic sphere? What is happening to child care? to our concept of the family?

Feminism—an ideology that, in its most basic form, directly opposes sexism by supporting gender equality and portraying women and men as essentially equals—has been a driving force in shaping the modern women's movement. The final legal victory of the women's movement was supposed to be the passage of the Equal Rights Amendment to the Constitution (ERA), which would have made a person's sex an irrelevant distinction under the law. The ERA passed both houses of Congress by overwhelming margins in 1972, but it failed to win ratification from the required three-fourths of the state legislatures. The amendment was not ratified in part due to the efforts of a coalition of groups, composed overwhelmingly of women, who went to battle against it. Thus, the women's movement did not represent the views of all women; many continued to believe in traditional gender roles.

The picture has since become more complicated. In addition to feminists and antifeminists, now there are the uninvolved. The feminists of the 1960s and 1970s fought passionately for gender equality. Today they find their daughters largely disinterested in such issues. The reason for this is that women today *expect* to be treated equally, have plenty of opportunity, and achieve more parity in family roles. In other words, the women's movement has succeeded to the point that the younger generation of women is without a cause. Paula Span, in "It's a Girl's World," *The Washington Post Magazine* (June 22, 1997), quotes her daughter as saying, "Most of my girlfriends and I feel like we could do anything. . . . Being female isn't a restriction." Has the success of feminism and the women's movement made feminism irrelevant? Span believes that it is widely perceived as passé. "I'm not too dismayed by the work that still remains to achieve equality, having learned way back to take the long view, but I'm worried about whether young women have any interest in undertaking the task," she says.

In the readings that follow, Robert Sheaffer argues that feminists falsely reconstruct gender realities to deny that biological differences contribute significantly to gender inequalities. Sheaffer asserts that feminists assume that current inequalities are due to socialization and are thus malleable, or are due to discrimination and are thus best redressed by regulations. But he concludes that their program of action will have largely adverse impacts. A favorable view of feminism is presented by William H. Chafe, who defines feminism by what feminists have tried to change. He discusses three variants of feminism, all of which he says have brought about important reforms in society.

YES

Robert Sheaffer

FEMINISM, THE NOBLE LIE

In the *Republic*, Plato argues that, in order to build a proper Utopia, it would be necessary to depict the gods as virtuous. Hence censorship and deception were seen as requisite for instilling virtue: "The lie in words is in certain cases useful and not hateful."[1] This has come to be known as Plato's "Noble Lie." In the present age, another would-be builder of utopias has, almost unnoticed, adopted the Noble Lie in pursuit of its goals, while somehow yet retaining an aura of moral rectitude: the politically correct feminist movement, which reigns virtually unchallenged in academe and in government.

The world as depicted by contemporary feminism is a peculiar one. It teaches a history that is at variance with that taught in history departments, a view of science incorporating only selectively that taught in science departments, and a paradoxical, illiberal approach to morality in which the correctness of an action depends to a large extent on who is performing it. The world-view created by contemporary feminism has much in common with that of the illusionist, who can conjure an impressive scenario, but only when viewed from a certain angle, and only when all attempts at critical scrutiny are muted. Indeed, it is difficult to quell the suspicion that the reason feminists have always insisted on a separate department for Women's Studies is because they require exemption from the peer review and critical scrutiny that their material would otherwise receive were it taught as history, philosophy, or science.

Feminists have largely gotten away with these deceptions because the widespread and highly successful inculcation of male guilt allows them to claim that any critical scrutiny of their claims amounts to "blaming the victim." Additionally, chivalrous feelings make most men feel it is somehow unfair to attack women, even if those same women are spouting bizarre nonsense in the process of vigorously attacking men. The result has been that a great deal of selective truth, half-truth, and even untruth has been unquestioningly accepted by a large portion of the educated public. In Plato's Utopian state, the rulers would have a monopoly on the right to tell lies; through the enforcement of "hostile speech" codes on campus (and in some instances questioning feminist doctrine has been construed as hostile speech), modern-day academic feminists seek the same privilege.

* * *

... The harsh reality is that the entire history of the human race, from the present to the earliest written texts, is an unbroken record of so-called patriarchy, presumably extending back at least as far as our early primate ancestors (since chimp society displays extreme male dominance). In every human society, without exception, leadership is associated with the male and the nurturing of children with the female.

Those who argue that socialization must somehow explain sex roles find themselves unable to explain *why* socialization always proceeds in a uniform direction, when according to their assumptions it ought to proceed randomly, resulting in a patchwork of matriarchies, interspersed with patriarchies. Why does every society, without exception, socialize men for leadership and women for domestic tasks? Why not the reverse?

Thus, the strict environmentalist explanation falls into an infinite regress, and finds itself postulating an uncaused cause: the male dominance we observe in every society is said to be caused by socialization, yet the socialization has no cause, and somehow always was.

Steven Goldberg argues persuasively that the popular claim of socialization to explain sex roles gets the causality backward. He writes that feminist theorists "make the mistake of treating the social environment as an independent variable, thereby failing to explain *why* the social environment always conforms to limits set by, and takes a direction concordant with, the physiological (i.e., never

does environment act as sufficient counterpoise to enable a society to avoid male dominance of hierarchies)."[2] Societies observe the patterns of behavior that biology seems to render inevitable, then attempt to socialize women and men into roles that it expects they will be able to fulfill. Hence, according to Goldberg, socialization is the *dependent* variable, not the independent one, as is commonly supposed.

If sex roles really are arbitrary constructs of society, created to keep women "in their place," why is it necessary to give transsexuals—individuals who already display many characteristics of the opposite sex—hormones of that opposite sex, prior to and separate from any surgery, to enable them to genuinely fit into their new role? Invariably these male or female hormones are reported as having profound mood-altering characteristics. For example, in the documentary film *Max* by the lesbian director Monika Treut, a pre-surgical female-to-male transsexual comments on the profound effects experienced upon being administered male hormones in the course of treatment. She reported that her energy level suddenly increased dramatically, as did her sex drive. Her moods were greatly affected, and she found herself unable to cry as much and as easily as she did before. Feminists, however, attribute such behavior in men to "socialization."

Now if the feminist "society-is-responsible" hypothesis were true, sex hormones would have no effect on behavior, and transsexuals could presumably be trained into their new roles just by reading a book. The reason that the feminist theorist attempts to force us to ignore the powerful role of male and female hormones as determinants of behavior is that we would then have to acknowledge that sex roles are not only arbitrary, but are in fact permanent and ineradicable (short of radical medical intervention).

Contemporary politically correct feminists, like Marxists, feel obligated to postulate a purely environmental explanation for all sex-related differences in behavior, because, as soon as biological differences are admitted as relevant factors, the presumption that women's career choices are forced by discrimination cannot be supported. Should any male/female differences in behavior and career choices be admitted as innate and real, then the null hypothesis—the assumption that in the absence of discrimination, no differences in the two groups would be observed—is no longer tenable. The feminist would then be placed in the position of needing to separate the effects of so-called discrimination from those of biology, a clearly impossible task. Hence, male/female differences in biology must be declared *ipso facto* to have no possible observable consequences. Biologist Garrett Hardin notes that the epithet "biological determinism," carrying "implications of absolute rigidity," is "a straw man set up for the convenience of polemicists; we would do well to ignore it." He adds,

> to suppose that human behavior is uninfluenced by heredity is to say that man is not a part of nature. The Darwinian assumption is that he is; Darwinians insist that the burden of proof falls on those who assert the contrary.

Philosopher Michael Levin wryly describes feminist theory as a form of Creationism, which he defines as

> any refusal to apply evolutionary theory to man. It is irrelevant whether this refusal is sustained by a literal reading of scripture or commitment to a secular ideology.

He chides scientists like Richard Lewontin and Stephen Jay Gould, who take a wholly naturalistic stance toward all living creatures apart from man.[3]

The fact that men have much greater physical strength than women cannot possibly be admitted as a factor causing men to predominate in strenuous jobs; the dearth of women in such jobs is instead attributed to a hostile working environment created by sexist men. If it is admitted that few women actually *want* to do such work, this must be explained away as a consequence of them having been brainwashed into accepting negative patriarchal stereotypes. That men predominate in higher-paying positions is itself seen as evidence of a vast conspiracy to keep women out of better jobs, in spite of the fact that, when we correct for factors such as the number of hours worked, the number of years of education and in the position, etc., the differences all but vanish.[4] If it were really true that women were being paid fifty-nine cents (or whatever number you choose to believe) for every dollar that men make, for doing the same work at the same level of skill, then no business could possibly be competitive if it employed any men.

That differences in career choices might arise from mutual preferences and independent choices made by two groups having significant innate psychological differences is not a permissible hypothesis, even though it has seemed obvious to every other society except our own. No explanation will be satisfactory to contemporary feminists unless it depicts men as exploiters and women as victims (a depiction that itself belies the feminists' claim to believe in strict equality).

In order to defend the employment conspiracy hypothesis, feminists must argue either that there are no genuine, innate differences in the skills, attitudes, and abilities of women and men, or else that such differences may exist but have absolutely no observable effect. As soon as such differences are admitted as a meaningful factor influencing career choices and performance, the case for the supposed omnipresent discrimination vanishes.

Most feminists will reluctantly admit that, at least in sports, the difference in performance between women and men is a result of innate factors and not social conditioning. No amount of political indoctrination will transform a female athlete into a respectable linebacker for the National Football League. This then places the feminist in the curious position of arguing that innate factors account for the profound difference in male/female performance in sports, but in absolutely nothing else. This violates parsimony. Michael Levin argues that it is absurd to claim that there is *no* paid job outside athletics where the kind of skill, stamina, and speed manifested in athletics conveys advantage.[5] Truly, it is ideology, not logic, that prompts the hypothesis of absolute male/female interchangeability (most feminists will disavow the claim of interchangeability, yet vigorously defend everything that follows from it!).

Contemporary politically correct feminism with its emphasis on group rights and group offenses is fundamentally illiberal, a dramatic break from the long humanistic tradition that emphasizes individual rights, rewards, and punishments. It attacks free speech wherever freedom is used in ways it does not approve; many feminists have recently joined forces with the religious right to attack so-called pornography. (Another coalition of feminists with the religious right, crusading against alleged satanic cults, threatens to become a witch-hunt in a literal sense! And the zealous use of highly dubious "repressed memories" to uncover supposed "forgotten incest" is largely a feminist-led campaign.)

This ideology seeks to replace the liberal ideal of "equality under the law" with the sinister "some are more equal than others," awarding women special rights and special protections unavailable to men. One of the most glaring examples concerns the status of single-sex schools. The small number of remaining all-male colleges, mostly of military orientation, such as Virginia Military Institute and The Citadel, are under unrelenting political and legal pressure from feminists to end their single-sex policy, which is held to be discriminatory. Yet, when a few years back the directors of all-female Mills College decided to begin admitting men students, this same relentless feminist juggernaut came down upon them to *preserve* same-sex education, forcing them to reverse their decision.

The justification offered was that men tend to dominate classroom environments owing to their greater aggressiveness. Feminists who argue this way, however, are in the delicate position of maintaining that, while male dominance of classrooms is caused by the male's greater aggressiveness, male dominance of the business world is entirely the result of a conspiracy against women.

* * *

It is invariably objected that the kinds of positions and doctrines described above are those of extremists and that reasonable feminists and feminist organizations do not hold them. The question I next ask is: just *where are* all these reasonable feminists? The answer invariably is that they are sitting next to me, or in the office down the hall; yet somehow these supposed voices of moderation manage to play absolutely no role whatsoever in the formulation of public policy. We are asked to believe that the largest feminist organization in America, and the largest-circulation feminist magazine, each of which endlessly promotes the image of women as victims while vigorously lobbying for special preferences and quotas (and each is or recently was headed up by a lesbian), are somehow unrepresentative of what the supposedly typical feminist does and believes. Again, this is just a cheap rhetorical trick: by definition, the largest organizations and publications in any movement are representative of that movement. Were they unrepresentative, some other spokeswomen would step forth, and gather a following larger still.

No reasonable person could deny that women and men ought to have the same legal rights in matters of a career, property ownership, etc. Likewise, no reasonable person could expect that equality of opportunity would automatically turn into equality of result when two groups are as different as women and men. It also seems to me that no reasonable person could deny the moral equality of women and men: that neither sex has any credible claim to greater goodness or cooperative behavior than the other. Yet, this is precisely what contemporary feminism attempts to deny, with its incessant depiction of men as cruel exploiters and women as their innocent victims.

The rhetoric of the feminist movement portrays history as a dismal scenario of the unending oppression and subjugation of women for the selfish benefit of men. (That men might themselves be a "victim" class, given that men have made up almost 100 percent of the cannon fodder of every battle in history, is not worthy of consideration.) But the depiction of woman as perpetual victim does not survive critical scrutiny. Whatever rights women may not have had at various points in history, such as the right to vote, had typically only been won by men a short time earlier. Throughout most of history, *nobody* had any rights, outside the ruling elite! And the very real *informal* power women hold in families and other situations is simply ignored when painting the weepy scenario.

As for contemporary American society: women live an average of seven years longer than men; female-headed households have a net worth that averages 41 percent higher than those of male-headed ones (and this in spite of the fact that the average woman works far fewer hours per year than the average man). Women, supposedly discriminated against in education, make up 55 percent of current college graduates. They claim to be discriminated against in politics, yet cast seven million more votes than men in electing presidents. They win almost automatically in child custody disputes. Victims of violent crime are overwhelmingly male, and wives assault husbands *more frequently* than the reverse. Women can murder a sleeping husband or lover in cold blood, then claim the "battered woman" defense and very likely receive only the lightest sentence or perhaps even no sentence at all, even in the absence of any proof that they were actually battered. (There is no "battered man" defense.)

If convicted of a felony, a man serves out a sentence averaging more than 50 percent longer than a woman convicted of the same crime, and a man in prison is more than ten times as likely to die there than is a woman. Men's suicide rate is four times that of women. Twenty-four out of the twenty-five jobs ranked worst in terms of pay and working conditions by the Jobs Related Almanac have one thing in common: they are all 95 percent to 100 percent male. Of those killed in work-related accidents, 94 percent are men, as were 96 percent of those killed in the Gulf War. If men have supposedly arranged everything to be so wonderful for themselves, then why are they dying, being mutilated, murdered, or killing themselves at rates vastly higher than those of women, who end up having more money in spite of having worked less?[6] It makes much more sense to call contemporary American women "privileged" than "oppressed!"

The world-view erected by contemporary politically correct feminism, the only kind that plays any role in shaping public policy, is a house of cards. It requires its adherents to jump from one unsteady limb to another, never quite sure whether sex differences in behavior are illusory or very real but insignificant; uncertain whether women behave exactly the same as men, or are emotionally and morally superior, oriented toward life (unlike men, who love death); switching from "absolute *égalité*" to "special provisions," depending on which confers greater advantage. Women are simultaneously strong and independent, fully prepared to prevail in the hell of combat, yet at the same time so weak as to need special rules under which they receive compensatory advantages to assist them in competition with men; they also need special protection against unwanted sexual advances and dirty jokes. This is much like a magician's silk that appears to have a different color each time it is revealed. It is predictable that this article will be answered far more with *ad hominem* insults and expressions of moral outrage than with reasoned argument; such are the defenses employed by illusionists who are infuriated when their deceptions are revealed.

But there can be great harm in falsehood unopposed, especially when it results in suspicion, hostility, and envy between the sexes, where love frequently used to exist as recently as a generation before. In no other countries has politically correct feminism gained such power as in the United States and Canada (which is itself interesting: why have European women largely declined to fight in the war against men?). As a consequence, we have here what is almost certainly the highest divorce rate in the world, a crumbling educational system, and a seemingly unstoppable spiral of rising crime and related social pathology. Recent studies demonstrated a powerful correlation between this social pathology and the children of fatherless families.[7] It remains to be seen whether any society can remain intact largely without viable families in which to raise psychologically healthy children. One can argue that the U.S. family died of natural causes at precisely the same time feminists began shooting at it; after examining the depth and ferocity of the feminist attack against women's roles as wives and mothers, one can be convinced.

Nietzsche warned against systems of morality grounded in what he called *ressentiment*, pretending to represent compassion while actually embodying the covert destructiveness of those who impotently desire revenge against those they envy. He cited Christian morality as the primary example of such a system.[8] While feigning an attitude of passivity and love, the early Christian actually worked to bring down any person or institution esteemed for worldly success. We must not fail to note that contemporary politically correct feminism and Marxism are both manifestations of *ressentiment*.[9]

In spite of its success in masquerading as a harmless, even noble, movement dedicated to simple fairness, the contemporary feminist movement is in fact a Noble Lie. No matter how many people may have been sincerely persuaded to believe its pronouncements, the empress has no clothes. And a Noble Lie is nonetheless a lie.

NOTES

1. *The Republic,* Book II (382c).

2. Steven Goldberg, *When Wish Replaces Thought* (Buffalo, N.Y.: Prometheus Books, 1991) p. 173.

3. Garrett Hardin, *Naked Emperors: Essays of a Taboo Stalker* (Los Altos, Calif.: William Kaufmann, Inc., 1982), Chapter 8. Michael Levin, *Feminism and Freedom* (New Brunswick, N.J.: Transaction Books, 1987), Chapter 3.

4. See, for example, George Gilder's *Wealth and Poverty* (New York: Bantam Books, 1982) Chapter 12.

5. Michael Levin, *Feminism and Freedom* (New Brunswick, N.J.: Transaction Books, 1987) Chapter 10.

6. These statistics come from Warrent Farrell *The Myth of Male Power* (New York: Simon & Schuster, 1993).

7. See "Dan Quayle Was Right," *Atlantic Monthly,* April 1993.

8. Nietzsche, *The Genealogy of Morals,* Book 1. See also Robert Sheaffer, *The Making of the Messiah* (Prometheus Books, 1991) Chapter 2.

9. Simone de Beauvoir is generally acknowledged as the Founding Mother of contemporary feminism. In her tome *The Second Sex,* she plainly grounds her theory of the "exploitation" of women in "historical materialism" (i.e., Marxism), and in particular in the now-discredited historical speculations of Engels. Today, the feminist establishment and socialists, are on the same side of every significant political issue.

NO

William H. Chafe

THE POSTWAR REVIVAL OF FEMINISM

THE REVIVAL OF FEMINISM

HELMAN: Before all else, you are a wife and mother.
NORA: That I no longer believe. I believe that before all else, I am a human being, just as much as you are—or at least that I should try to become one.

—Henrik Ibsen, *A Doll's House* (1879)

In the fall of 1962, the editors of *Harper's* observed a curious phenomenon. An extraordinary number of women seemed "ardently determined to extend their vocation beyond the bedroom, kitchen and nursery," but very few showed any interest in feminism. Both observations were essentially correct. In the years during and after World War II, millions of women had joined the labor force, many of them leaving the home to take jobs; but the expansion of their "sphere" occurred without fanfare and was not accompanied either by progress toward equality or an organized effort to protest traditional definitions of "woman's place." If many women were dissatisfied with what one housewife called the endless routine of "dishwashing, picking up, ironing and folding diapers," they had no collective forum to express their grievances. Women examined their futures privately and with an unmilitant air. There seemed to be no sanctioned alternative.

Eight years later, feminism competed with the war in Vietnam, student revolts, and inflation for headlines in the daily press. Women activists picketed the Miss America pageant, demonstrated at meetings of professional associations to demand equal employment opportunities, and insisted on equal access to previously all-male bars and restaurants in New York. They called a national strike to commemorate the 50th anniversary of woman suffrage, wrote about the oppression of "sexual politics," and sat in at the editorial offices of *Newsweek* and the *Ladies' Home Journal*. In an era punctuated by protest, feminism had once again come into its own. If not all women enlisted in the new struggle for equality, few could claim to be unaffected by it.

The evolution of any protest movement, of course, is a complicated process. In general, however, a series of preconditions are necessary: political currency and sanction for the ideas around which a movement grows; a catalyst to initiate protest; support from an energetic minority, at least, of the aggrieved group; and a social atmosphere that is conducive to reform. To an extent unmatched since the last days of the suffrage fight, all these elements were present during the 1960s. The accumulated grievances of individual women found expression in a growing number of feminist voices whose writings gave focus to the movement; the civil-rights struggle helped to trigger a renewal of women's rights activism; a substantial number of women, young and old, were ready to respond; and the society at large was more sensitive than at any time in the twentieth century to the quest for social justice. No one development could have fostered the resurgence of feminism, but the several acting together created a context in which, for the first time in five decades, feminism became again a force to be reckoned with.

* * *

The most widely noted indictment of America's system of sex inequality came from the pen of Betty Friedan. Although other books and articles exerted just as much influence on key groups of women activists, Friedan's acerbic look at *The Feminine Mystique* (1963) generated the kind of attention that made feminism a popular topic of conversation once again. According to Friedan, American women had been held captive by a set of ideas that defined female happiness as total involvement in the roles of wife and mother. Advertisers manipulated women into believing that they could achieve fulfillment by using the latest model vacuum cleaner or bleaching their clothes a purer white. Women's magazines romanticized domesticity and presented an image of women as "gaily content in a world of bedroom, kitchen, sex, babies and home." And psychiatrists popularized the notion that any woman unhappy with a full-time occupation as housewife must be neurotic. As a result, Friedan charged, a woman's horizons were circumscribed from childhood on by the assumption that her highest calling in life was to be a servant to her husband and children. In effect, the home had become a "comfortable concentration camp" that infantilized its female inhabitants and forced them to "give up their adult frame of reference." Just as Victorian culture had repressed women's sexual instincts, modern American culture had destroyed their minds and emotions.

Other observers came to the same conclusions. Adopting a more academic perspective, Ellen and Kenneth Keniston pointed out that young women had no positive models of independent women to emulate and that with no culturally approved alternative to homemaking, many women accepted a "voluntary servitude" in the home rather than risk losing their femininity. The sociologist Alice Rossi made the same point. "There are few Noras in contemporary society," she observed, "because women have deluded themselves that a doll's house is large enough to find complete fulfillment within it." As a result, however, children were treated like "hothouse plants," women overidentified with their offspring, and a vicious cycle of repression and frustration ensured. The family became a breeding ground for discontent and unhappiness, with suburban bliss exploding into skyrocketing divorce rates, addiction to pills and alcohol, and an epidemic of mental illness.

At the heart of this diagnosis was the assertion that women had been deprived of the chance to develop an identity of their own. Assigned to a "place" solely on the basis of their sex, women were kept from seeing themselves as unique human beings. All women participated equally in the undifferentiated roles of housewife and mother, but many lacked a more precise image of themselves as individuals. As one young mother wrote to Friedan:

> I've tried everything women are supposed to do—hobbies, gardening, pickling, canning, and being very social with my neighbors.... I can do it all, and I like it, but it doesn't leave you anything to think about—any feeling of who you are.... I love the kids and Bob and my home.... But I'm desperate. I begin to feel that I have no personality. I'm a server of food and putter-on of pants and a bedmaker, somebody who can be called on when you want something. But who am I?

To Friedan and others like her, the question struck at the core of the alienation of modern women and could be answered only if wives and mothers rejected cultural stereotypes and developed lives of their own. If women pursued their own careers, Alice Rossi noted, they would demand less of their husbands, provide a "living model" of independence and responsibility to their children, and regain a sense of their own worth as persons. With an independent existence outside the home, they would cease to be parasites living off the activities of those around them and, instead, became full and equal partners in the family community.

There were a number of problems with this analysis. First, it reflected an extraordinary middle- and upper-class bias, ignoring both the circumstances and aspirations of those women who were not white and not affluent. Second, it failed to do justice to those women who were content with their lives—three out of five according to a 1962 Gallup poll. And third, it presumed that the ideas of "the feminine mystique" were a post–world War II phenomenon, when in fact they went even further back than the "cult of true womanhood" in the nineteenth century. Nor could it fairly be said that women in the 1950s were more "victimized" than they had been at other times in history.

Nevertheless, the fact that a feminist analysis had gained political currency proved to be enormously important. For years, talk about women's discontent had been rife, but now there was an assessment of that discontent that compelled attention. With eloquence and passion, Friedan had dramatized through case studies the boredom and alienation of those afflicted by "the problem that has no name." In addition, she was able to take her readers behind the scenes to editorial offices and advertising firms where they could see firsthand the way in which the image of the feminine mystique was formed. It was hard not to be outraged after reading how advertising men—who themselves viewed housework as menial—tried to sell cleaning products as an answer to drudgery and as a means of expressing creativity. If, as Friedan claimed, the women frustrated by such manipulation were legion, her book helped to crystallize a sense of grievance and to provide an ideological explanation with which the discontented could identify. *The Feminine Mystique* sold more than a million copies, and if not all its readers agreed with the conclusions, they could not help but reexamine their own lives in light of the questions it raised.

... [T]he time was right in the mid-1960s for feminism to make a profound impact, with substantial support from both younger and older women. Fortuitously, the woman's movement of the 1960s and 1970s was operating in tandem with rather than in opposition to long-term social developments. During the 1910s and 1920s, suffragist calls for greater economic and social independence for women ran counter to patterns of behavior that found most married and middle-class women still conforming to traditional norms. Now, feminist calls for the same kind of independence coincided with women leaving the home in ever greater numbers and learning firsthand how pervasive sex discrimination was. Fertility rates, attitudes toward sexuality and the double standard, changes in long-term employment curves—all these seemed to be working *for*, not against, the demands of women activists....

* * *

Although outside observers were impressed by the apparent fervor with which large numbers of activists supported abortion reform, ERA [Equal Rights Amendment], and child care, there existed beneath the surface of the women's movement an ongoing set of conflicts over the tactics, goals, and values of the new feminism. From the nineteenth century onward, women's rights activists had struggled with a series of troubling dilemmas. Were women different from men or similar to them? *Should* women accept or seek differential treatment from society? Was the best method

of securing equality to assimilate into the society, adopting integration as a means as well as an end, or did separatism make more sense as a strategy and tactic? Should women join in coalition with others in behalf of shared goals, or should women act only on their own behalf and pursue their own agenda regardless of potential alliances? Was reform or revolution the goal, and if revolution, who was the enemy to be overthrown? Obviously, such questions were not easy to answer, nor did they pose the kind of choices that could readily be solved by compromise....

At least three different kinds of feminism competed during the early 1970s for the allegiance of women activists. Broadly defined, these can be labeled as liberal feminism, radical feminism, and socialist feminism. Each in its own way developed a different analysis and set of answers to the key questions of the sources of women's oppression, the possibilities of coalition to end that oppression, and the goal of reform or revolution. Radical feminism and socialist feminism shared in common a collectivist approach to women's dilemma and an antipathy to the individualist priorities of liberal feminism. Yet both radicals and socialists at different times shared a commitment to some of the programmatic goals of liberal feminism and might join the ranks of such liberal organizations as NOW [National Organization for Women] and WEAL [Women's Equity Action League]. The conflicts were stark, but it was not at all unlikely that the same person could—at different stages of ideological perception—be identified with all three kinds of feminism.

To casual observers, liberal feminism was clearly the dominant force in women's rights activity in the years after

1968. Associated primarily with personalities like Betty Friedan and organizations like NOW, liberal feminism sought to work politically within the existing social and economic framework to secure reforms for women and progress toward full equality of opportunity between the sexes....

[T]he goal of liberal feminism was complete integration of women into American society. Assimilation, not separatism, was the desired end, with victory being defined as the total acceptance of women—as individuals—in all jobs, political organizations, and voluntary associations *without regard to their sex*. Implicitly, then, NOW and other liberal feminist groups embraced a natural-rights philosophy that all individuals should be treated the same, that sex and gender should be discounted, and that eradication of a "separate-sphere" ideology was a *sine qua non* [essential] for progress toward equality.

Within this framework, liberal feminists concentrated on a series of pragmatic reforms. Recognizing that equal access for women into the "opportunity structure" necessitated at least acknowledging past barriers, NOW and other similar groups endorsed affirmative-action programs to promote women in compensation for prior neglect and the creation of social institutions such as federally funded child-care centers to ease conflicts between family and work. Liberal feminists emphasized compliance with equal-opportunity legislation, enactment of the ERA to guarantee that women would be treated exactly like men under the law, and advancement of women into careers that previously had been dominated by men. Typical of NOW's initiatives in the late 1960s were campaigns to eliminate sex identifica- tion from employment advertisements in newspapers ("Male Only Jobs," "Female Only Jobs"), a blistering indictment of one airline that offered "Men only" executive flights from Chicago to New York at the end of the business day, and insistence on open admission to clubs and bars previously off-limits to women. Clearly, the message was that women wanted to join, as individuals with equal rights, all the institutions of the society and that separate classification of spheres by sex was no longer acceptable.

Although for many Americans at the time these positions seemed extreme, liberal feminists themselves were —within the overall women's movement —perceived to be pragmatic and even conservative. They were "liberals," after all, who believed in incremental change and the possibility of persuading individuals through reason of the need for reform. They neither wished to topple the power structure nor to create their own. Rather, they wanted to join the existing social and economic system. As a consequence, they were more likely to eschew radical rhetoric and shy away from controversy, lest they alienate some of those *within* the structure of power whom they needed as allies. Thus, in the early years at least, NOW preferred to avoid the issue of sexual preference, lest lesbian-baiting be used to defeat their other goals. When NOW did take a strong stand in favor of abortion reform and reproductive freedom, some of its members were distressed enough to form the Women's Equity Action League (WEAL) in 1969, a group that would concentrate exclusively on economic and political issues in an effort to avoid losing the backing of those who adamantly opposed abortion and gay rights.

Within the overall spectrum of women's activism, then, the position of liberal feminists was fairly clear. They were political, and they were activist—but their activism focused on reform of mainstream institutions, often through the existing electoral system, with the goal of integration by women as individuals within the prevailing social and economic order. Groups like the National Women's Political Caucus might be formed to promote women's issues and women politicians, but any such "separatist" tactics were premised on acceptance of the fundamental health of American institutions and on a belief that reform would eventually eliminate the need for such separate organizations. Although NOW and other liberal feminist groups espoused programs that would benefit poor and minority women as well as the middle class, it was clear that their primary constituency consisted of well-educated, upwardly mobile and independent women who wished to take their place next to men in America's dominant social and economic institutions.

Radical feminists, by contrast, saw men as the enemy, patriarchy as a system that must be overthrown, and separatism as an important strategy and tactic—for achieving the revolution. The adjective "radical" naturally evokes an association with the New Left or the student movements of the late 1960s but in reality it speaks more to the position of activists on a woman-defined scale, not one dictated by male political affiliations —that is, feminists were radical vis à vis their diagnosis of women's oppression as a function of male supremacy rather than vis à vis their position on the war in Vietnam or capitalism.

At the same time, it would be a mistake not to recognize the extent to which New Left machismo played a role in shaping radical feminism. In the early stages of the women's liberation movement, for example, women participants in the civil-rights struggle and the anti-war movement sought repeatedly to bring their concerns before male-dominated New Left organizations. Yet when they did so, they were treated with disdain, contempt, and outrageous sexism. *Ramparts* magazine, one journalistic voice of the New Left, dismissed women petitioners at a Students for a Democratic Society (SDS) conference as a "mini-skirted caucus." When Jo Freeman and Shulamith Firestone brought resolutions on women's rights to the National Conference on New Politics in December 1967, they were told that their concerns were irrelevant. "Calm down, little girl," the man presiding at the convention said. And when a representative of women's groups sought to present two statements on women's issues to the anti-Vietnam War mobilization rally in November 1968, she was greeted with raucous heckling. "Take it off," men around the platform yelled. . . . Eventually, the speaker was forced to leave the stage, a male anti-war leader saying it was "for her own good." "If radical men can be so easily provoked into acting like red-necks," one woman observer noted, "what can we expect from others? What have we gotten ourselves into?"

Such experiences simply reinforced the inclination of many women to organize separate groups, free of interruption and domination by men. "We need not only separate groups, but a separate movement, free of preconceptions," Ellen Willis wrote. "It is also clear that a genuine alliance with male radicals will not be possible until sexism sickens them as much as racism. This will not be accomplished through persuasion, conciliation or love, but through independence and solidarity." ...

By virtue of their analysis and prescription for change, radical feminists were identified with a series of issues and processes that while shared with other groups as well were perhaps more characteristic of radical feminist groups than others. Consciousness-raising, for example, provided an organizational tactic for most women's liberation groups, but the process was especially associated with radical feminists. When groups of ten to fifteen women gathered to share their common concerns about the second-class treatment women were accorded in American society, one of the bonds that united them was the stories they told each other about growing up female, being pressured into subservient roles, responding to sexual pressures from men, having to "perform" for an audience with a preordained script on how women should act. As the stories became more intimate and the sense of solidarity more profound, consciousness-raising became the symbol for women standing together against men and society. They found within their group identity and process the model for separatist institution-building and the empowerment to pursue change. If becoming woman-identified was the philosophical core of radical feminism, what better way to initiate and perpetuate the process than by reinforcing every week the experiences and bonds that tied women to each other.

Similarly, while gay rights represented an issue with which every feminist group eventually identified, radical feminists were more likely than others to see the question of sexual preference as pivotal. Not only did lesbianism embody the politics of being a "woman-identified woman"; it also clearly celebrated the empowerment of being self-sufficient and free of men in *every* aspect of life, including the sexual. Women who lived together, worked together, and slept together made separatism the pragmatic as well as philosophical *raison d'être* of their lives. In an age of reproductive technology that promised to bypass heterosexuality as a precondition for pregnancy, it was possible to envision an entire life free of men. And if women could thereby establish their freedom from patriarchy, they could create a world where class oppression based on sex no longer existed.

Toward that end, radical feminists also focused their energies on developing women-run institutions. To break the shackles of the male-dominated health professions, especially gynecology, women built their own health clinics, taught self-examination, and with books like *Our Bodies, Our Selves* created a mass-market resource that would liberate countless others from medical views of women that reflected a man's point of view. Feminist publishing houses commissioned, edited, and printed their own literature, from children's books that were nonsexist to literary and political journals. Abortion clinics, child-care centers, separate caucuses in professional associations, and food cooperatives all represented ways in which women could structure their own lives and institutions so that men were not in control. Although usually associated with groups like New York Radical Women (1968) and New York Radical Feminists (1970), the radical feminist perspective was widespread throughout the country and helped substantially to shape the ideological direction of the entire movement. While not political in electoral or legislative terms, radical feminism gave support to causes, institutions, and alliances that reflected the power of separatist thinking and the importance of women's distinctive cultural voice in reshaping gender relations in society at large.

The third major expression of feminist thought was also radical, but more in the mainstream sense than in a "woman-identified" sense. Comprised of people often referred to as "politicos," these women were Marxist, called themselves socialist-feminists, and emphasized the inextricable links between race, class, and gender oppression. Rather than advocating separatism, with men as the enemy, socialist-feminists championed solidarity by oppressed peoples everywhere, male or female, with capitalism as the enemy. Like radical feminists, the socialists were contemptuous of the existing social order and sought revolution, but theirs was a revolution where men were potential allies and where the goal was a complete abolition of race, gender, and class hierarchies, not a separate, woman-defined world. . . .

Socialist-feminists saved their harshest criticism, however, for the reformism of liberal feminist groups like NOW. Marlene Dixon, a Marxist, regretted the extent to which "the political consciousness of women [was frozen] at a very primitive level: the struggle against the attitudinal expression of institutionalized white male supremacy . . . particularly as it impinged upon sexual relationships. The early actions of the movement—bra burnings, Miss America protests, Playboy Club demonstrations—reflected a political consciousness which had been stunted in the long debate confined within personal relationships."

. . . [S]ocialist-feminists adopted perhaps the most visionary scheme of all. Not only should women organize to liberate themselves from oppression, but they should constitute a vanguard revolutionary force who—together with blacks, Hispanics, Indians, the poor, and other "victims" of capitalism—could transform the entire social and economic order. Women could be free only if the reign of capitalism ended, but women's captivity was neither separate nor different from the captivity of other groups. Hence, alliance with these groups, whatever the limitations of *their* sexual politics, was a prerequisite for change. Of all the activist visions that inspired women in the late 1960s and early 1970s, the socialist-feminists' was perhaps the most programmatic and political, and certainly the most collectivist, the most severely critical of traditional liberal individualism. . . .

To outside observers, . . . the unity, vigor, and enthusiasm of feminism seemed far more impressive (or threatening) than any internal divisions. Although comedians might scorn women's liberation and ridicule women who insisted on being admitted to "men's" bars or who protested the Miss America pageant as a "meat market," the measure of derision was, in fact, a testimony to how effectively feminists were entering the public consciousness with their positions. By the early 1970s, countless Americans were debating what could only be described as "feminist" issues, whether the focus was on the Equal Rights Amendment, child care, abortion, "open marriage," greater sharing of household responsibilities, or the sexual revolution. In every kitchen, living room, and bedroom, feminists contended, women—and men—were facing, for the first time in their lifetimes, the centrality of women's liberation to *all aspects* of daily life.

Indeed, what remained most impressive was the growing support that feminist positions seemed to be gathering in the body politic. In 1962, George Gallup asked a cross-section of American women whether they felt themselves to be victims of discrimination. Two-thirds of the women responding said no. Eight years later—three years after the women's movement began—the same question was asked again. This time, 50 percent of the respondents said that they were victims of discrimination. In 1974, the question was asked a third time. Now, with more than seven years of experience with the women's movement, two out of three respondents said that they were victims of discrimination, and even more supported such feminist policies as the Equal Rights Amendment and the right of a woman to have an abortion.

... By the early 1970s, the pollster Daniel Yankelovich commented on the "wide and deep" acceptance of women's liberation positions among the young. In two years, the number of students who viewed women as an oppressed group had doubled, and nearly 70 percent of college women declared agreement with the statement that "the idea that a woman's place is in the home is nonsense." The expression of such feminist viewpoints coincided with the greatest period of success in securing support for public policies promoting sex equality that had occurred in more than half a century....

THE BEST OF TIMES, THE WORST OF TIMES

In many respects, the 1970s and 1980s provided an ideal barometer for measuring the impact on women's status of the changes that had occurred during the postwar era. The 1940s and 1950s had been a time of paradox, with significant behavioral changes in women's economic activities occurring simultaneously with a resurgence of traditional patriarchal attitudes that defined women's "place"—rigidly and anachronistically—as being strictly in the home. With the revitalization of a dynamic feminist movement in the 1960s, however, an opportunity arose for reconciling attitudes and behavior and, potentially at least, for creating an ideological mandate for moving toward substantive equality between the sexes.

As the 1970s and 1980s unfolded, however, it became clear that the relationship between attitudes and practice would remain complicated. The feminist movement careened through its own roller-coaster journey, achieving enormous successes, only to have these followed by disastrous defeats. Extraordinary changes continued to occur in the family and workplace, resulting in giant strides forward for a number of women who, two decades earlier, would have been unable even to conceive of some of the choices they now faced; yet other women, caught in the same vortex of change, saw their opportunities diminish and the degree of their oppression deepen, not diminish. In the end, the story of these two decades was reminiscent of what Charles Dickens wrote in *The Tale of Two Cities*: "it was the best of times, it was the worst of times; it was a spring of hope, a winter of discontent." The fact that both characterizations were true said worlds about the divided mind of American society when it came to women's role in life and about the continuing power of race and class to interact with gender and shape women's possibilities and circumstances.

As a result, it was possible to predict that by the beginning of a new century, some white women of decent education and economic security would have more equality with men than women had ever experienced in America before and that many poor women—especially of minority background—would be caught in a cycle of poverty and hopelessness not exceeded at any time before in the twentieth century. . . .

* * *

One explanation for why the 1970s and 1980s were "the best of times, the worst of times" centers on the extent to which America was becoming much more a two-tiered society. The 1960s had spawned passionate crusades for social justice. With a degree of energy, collective mobilization, and ideological fervor not seen for more than a century, Americans from a variety of backgrounds had come together to struggle against racism, sexism, poverty, and war. Many of these movements had gone through similar stages of evolution. Beginning as moderate reform efforts, premised on the ability of social institutions to respond readily to proof of injustice, they had become rapidly radicalized as the depth of resistance to change became more obvious. By the end of each movement's history, some participants had become revolutionaries, some had dropped out, and some had joined in accepting whatever reforms had been achieved, choosing to work within the established order rather than try to overthrow it. . . .

When looking carefully at the experience of women during these decades, it seems clear that important reforms did take place, resulting in substantial elimination of barriers in law and custom that had denied women the freedom to pursue their own destinies. Just as the civil-rights movements led to the passage of public-accommodations laws, desegregation of many educational institutions, and destruction of Jim Crow, the women's rights movement brought a toppling of ancient barriers to women in the professions and support for a whole series of freedoms in personal behavior that had not been permitted before. Whether the issue was reproductive freedom, access to a career in corporate America, or greater flexibility of choice in one's mating or childbearing patterns, enormous changes had taken place. It would not be going too far to say that within the framework of the legal system at least, barriers to individual freedom based on race and gender had largely been eliminated.

What this meant, in reality, was that individual women and individual members of minority groups now had the opportunity to join the mainstream (a) as long as they had the economic base and educational qualifications for doing so; and (b) as long as they accepted the rules that governed mainstream institutions and agreed to operate within the prevailing norms of the status quo. Thus, large numbers of black Americans, including women, succeeded in getting college degrees in desegregated institutions and in joining the middle class through securing access to well-paid positions in corporate America. Similarly, large numbers of women, including some minorities, were able to enter business and professional schools, move into elite law firms and corporations, and create a life that combined professional achievement and personal fulfillment in a way that had never been available to their mothers and grandmothers.

In all of this, those in positions of power responded, albeit reluctantly, as long as basic structures remained intact. It was all right to admit blacks, Hispanics, or women into the corporate boardroom; it was not all right to abolish the boardroom or place blacks, Hispanics, or women in control. Reform was permissible; structural change was not.

In this context, the demands of liberal feminism were far more tolerable than those of radical feminism or of socialist-feminism. Liberal feminists wanted access for women to decent jobs, prestigious clubs, high-powered meetings; they wanted to abolish "male only" or "female only" job classifications; they sought the kind of self-determination for women as individuals that men had always had as individuals. And frequently, they asked for more radical changes as well. But it was impossible for those with power to respond to the first set of demands because these were familiar requests, with compelling morality and logic behind them, and *they could be accepted without changing the rules of the game*, except in terms of defining who could play.

Radical feminists and socialist-feminists, by contrast, sought to redesign both the ballpark and the rules. Both insisted in placing collective priorities ahead of individual freedom of choice. In one case, it was all women *qua* women seeking to be treated as a class, with their own separatist institutions and values dedicated to ending patriarchy; in the other case, it was all oppressed people as a class seeking to destroy capitalism. But in both cases, the goal was radical transformation, not moderate accommodation.

In contradiction to the reform aspirations of the liberal feminists, the revolutionary demands of radical feminists and socialist-feminists were not absorbable. Basic structures would be challenged and changed. Power would be redistributed. The rules would be altered. And countless Americans—women and men—who were devoted to a different view of gender roles mobilized to resist these demands. Those in the opposition also organized to defeat the more frightening ideas of liberal feminists, or at least their version of these ideas. Hence, the ERA went down to defeat because antifeminists said that it threatened to abolish all distinctions between the sexes, subvert the family, and sanction sexual deviancy. Still, people might resist the ERA and also be pleased that their own daughters could go to law school or become a bank manager....

Ultimately, the paradox of these years being both the best and the worst of times is no paradox at all. It is rather the key to how American society has functioned in this era and a vantage point from which to better understand the persistent power of race and class—together with sex—to determine women's experience.

POSTSCRIPT

Is Feminism a Harmful Ideology?

Sheaffer states that his most convincing arguments are made against extremist positions, which "reasonable feminists" might not hold. But since he cannot find the voice of reasonable feminists in the current public debate, he feels justified in representing all feminists by their extreme positions. But do feminists deny the significance of hormones and other biological differences between women and men? Does their demand for truly equal opportunity and affirmative action only require the premise that the similarities between men and women are greater than the differences? On the other hand, have feminists cultivated an antipathy to men as their oppressors? Has the feminist program adversely affected the family and gender relations? Do feminists deny that nondiscriminatory bases exist for many inequalities between men and women?

Over the past 30 years, there has been a deluge of books, articles, and periodicals devoted to expounding feminist positions. Among the earliest feminist publications was Betty Friedan's book *The Feminine Mystique* (W. W. Norton, 1963). Friedan later wrote *The Second Stage* (Summit Books, 1981), which was less antagonistic to men and more accepting of motherhood and traditional women's roles. Important statements by feminist leaders are Gloria Steinem, *Outrageous Acts and Everyday Rebellions,* 2d ed. (Henry Holt, 1995) and "Revving Up for the Next 25 Years," *Ms.* (September/October 1997), and Patricia Ireland, *What Women Want* (Penguin, 1996). For an attack on the attackers and misrepresentors of the women's movement, see Susan Faludi's *Backlash: The Undeclared War on American Women* (Crown Publishers, 1991). A superb analysis of the full range of gender issues is found in *Paradoxes of Gender* by Judith Lorber (Yale University Press, 1994). Christine Hoff Sommers advocates equity (liberal) feminism while criticizing feminist extremists and sloppy research in *Who Stole Feminism? How Women Have Betrayed Women* (Simon & Schuster, 1994). For radical feminist views, see Catharine A. MacKinnon's *Feminism Unmodified* (Harvard University Press, 1987); Marilyn French's *Beyond Power* (Summit Books, 1985); and Margaret Randall's *Gathering Rage: The Failure of Twentieth-Century Revolutions to Develop a Feminist Agenda* (Monthly Review Press, 1992). For a radical feminist analysis of the oppression of women, see Marilyn French, *The War Against Women* (Summit Books, 1992). An analytical and historical discussion of women's movements over the past century and a half is provided by Steven M. Buechler in *Women's Movements in the United States: Suffrage, Equal Rights, and Beyond* (Rutgers University Press, 1990). For an insightful analysis of how ideology has been used by men to mute the rebellion of women against exploitative and subordinate relations, see Mary R. Jackman, *The Velvet Glove: Paternalism and Conflict in Gender, Class, and Race Relations* (University of California Press, 1994). A rich analysis of gender inequality and its social and psychological roots is provided by Sandra Lipsitz Bem in *The Lenses of Gender: Transforming the Debate on Sexual Inequality* (Yale University Press, 1994). For recent views on feminism, see Elizabeth Fox-Genovese, *Feminism Is Not the Story of My Life: How Today's Feminist Elite Has Lost Touch With the Real Concerns of Women* (Doubleday, 1996); Ellen R. Klein, *Feminism Under Fire* (Prometheus, 1996); and Sheila Tobias, *Faces of Feminism* (Westview Press, 1997). Other important feminist voices are Suzanne Gordon, *Prisoners of Men's Dreams: Striking Out for a New Feminine Future* (Little, Brown, 1991); Paula Kamen, *Feminist Fatale: Voices from the "Twentysomething" Generation Explore the Future of the "Women's Movement"* (Donald I. Fine, 1991); Barbara Findlen, ed., *Listen Up: Voices from the Next Feminist Generation* (Seal Press, 1995); and Naomi Wolf, *Fire With Fire: The New Female Power and How It Will Change the Twenty-First Century* (Random House, 1993).

Antifeminist works are rarer. One antifeminist, Nicholas Davidson, charges that it is "extremely difficult to find a publisher for a work critical of feminism." See Davidson's *The Failure of Feminism* (Prometheus Books, 1988). Other antifeminist arguments may be found in Elizabeth Powers, "A Farewell to Feminism," *Commentary* (January 1997); Maggie Gallagher's *Enemies of Eros* (Bonus Books, 1993); Michael Levin's *Feminism and Freedom* (Transaction Books, 1987); Midge Decter's *The New Chastity and Other Arguments Against Women's Liberation* (Putnam, 1974); George Gilder's *Sexual Suicide* (Times Books, 1973); and Phyllis Schlafly's *The Power of Positive Woman* (Arlington House, 1977). For a defense of men against the accusations of feminists see Warren Farrell, *The Myth of Male Power* (Simon & Schuster, 1993) and David Thomas, *Not Guilty: The Case in Defense of Men* (William Morrow, 1993).

ISSUE 5

Are Communication Problems Between Men and Women Largely Due to Radically Different Conversation Styles?

YES: Deborah Tannen, from *You Just Don't Understand: Women and Men in Conversation* (Ballantine Books, 1991)

NO: Mary Crawford, from *Talking Difference: On Gender and Language* (Sage Publications, 1995)

ISSUE SUMMARY

YES: Deborah Tannen, a professor of sociolinguistics, argues that men and women have strikingly different communication styles, in that men's concerns about maintaining or enhancing their status greatly affects what they hear and say, while women's concern about connections and closeness greatly affects their communication.

NO: Professor of psychology Mary Crawford argues that the thesis that men and women have radically different communication styles is greatly exaggerated in the media and is based on simplistic stereotypes.

In 1992 John Gray published his best-selling book *Men Are from Mars, Women Are from Venus* (HarperCollins), which promises greatly improved relationships between men and women if they understand that men and women are different and if they accept rather than resent their differences. Here are some selections from the book:

> One of the biggest differences between men and women is how they cope with stress. Men become increasingly focused and withdrawn while women become increasingly overwhelmed and emotionally involved. At these times, a man's needs for feeling good are different from a woman's. He feels better by solving problems while she feels better by talking about problems. Not understanding and accepting these differences creates unnecessary friction in our relationships (p. 29).

> When a Martian gets upset he never talks about what is bothering him. He would never burden another Martian with his problem unless his friend's assistance was necessary to solve the problem. Instead he becomes very quiet and goes to his private cave to think about his problem, mulling it over to find a solution. When he has found a solution, he feels much better and comes out of his cave (p. 30).

When a Venusian becomes upset or is stressed by her day, to find relief, she seeks out someone she trusts and then talks in great detail about the problems of her day. When Venusians share feelings of being overwhelmed, they suddenly feel better. This is the Venusian way.

On Venus sharing your problems with another actually is considered a sign of love and trust and not a burden. Venusians are not ashamed of having problems. Their egos are dependent not on looking "competent" but rather on being in loving relationships....

A Venusian feels good about herself when she has loving friends with whom to share her feelings and problems. A Martian feels good when he can solve his problems on his own in his cave (p. 31).

Some people claim to be greatly helped by Gray's message; it helps them to understand the strange ways of the opposite sex. Others find it demeaning to characterize women as irrational, passive, and overly dependent on others. Critics also feel that it counsels women to accept boorish and uncaring behavior in men, while telling men that they only have to listen to women more to make them happy. Others put Gray's book down as too stereotyped to be helpful, and some even find it harmful. Gray depicts men and women as so different that they are best symbolized as coming from different planets. Some people feel that ideology is blatantly false. After all, boys and girls and men and women spend a lot of time talking to each others, so their worlds cannot be too far apart. In any case, Gray's message gets a strong reaction because it addresses a very important issue: how can men and women better understand each other?

This issue fascinates sociologists because it plunges them into questions about the construction of reality, perceptions of reality, differential socialization, and power in male-female relationships. Gray himself is constructing reality as he sees it in his book, and according to his reality many difficulties between men and women are not anyone's fault but are just misunderstandings. His reality leaves power out, but a sociologist will always take it into account. In fact, sociologists would note that men and women differ not only in their socialization but also in their relative power in their relationships. Relative power has a large effect on people's communication patterns. The person with greater income, education, and job status will feel freer to determine when, where, how, and about what the pair talks.

The differences in male-female communication styles that Deborah Tannen identifies in the following selection are similar to Gray's, but she lodges them in a deeper analysis of the differential needs of men and women. She says that men are more concerned about hierarchy and that women are more concerned about relationships, but it is a matter of degree. She, like Gray, works for better understanding between men and women. In the second selection, Mary Crawford reacts strongly to the proponents of gender differences in communication because she feels that their construction of gendered reality is superficial and puts women down.

YES
Deborah Tannen

YOU JUST DON'T UNDERSTAND

Recognizing gender differences frees individuals from the burden of individual pathology. Many women and men feel dissatisfied with their close relationships and become even more frustrated when they try to talk things out. Taking a *sociolinguistic* approach to relationships makes it possible to explain these dissatisfactions without accusing anyone of being crazy or wrong, and without blaming—or discarding—the relationship. If we recognize and understand the differences between us, we can take them into account, adjust to, and learn from each other's styles.

The sociolinguistic approach I take... shows that many frictions arise because boys and girls grow up in what are essentially different cultures, so talk between women and men is cross-cultural communication. A cross-cultural approach to gender differences in conversational style differs from the work on gender and language which claims that conversations between men and women break down because men seek to dominate women. No one could deny that men as a class are dominant in our society, and that many individual men seek to dominate women in their lives. And yet male dominance is not the whole story. It is not sufficient to account for everything that happens to women and men in conversations—especially conversations in which both are genuinely trying to relate to each other with attention and respect. The effect of dominance is not always the result of an intention to dominate....

* * *

Many years ago I was married to a man who shouted at me, "I do not give you the right to raise your voice to me, because you are a woman and I am a man." This was frustrating, because I knew it was unfair. But I also knew just what was going on. I ascribed his unfairness to his having grown up in a country where few people thought women and men might have equal rights.

Now I am married to a man who is a partner and friend. We come from similar backgrounds and share values and interests. It is a continual source of pleasure to talk to him. It is wonderful to have someone I can tell everything to, someone who understands. But he doesn't always see things as I do, doesn't

Excerpted from Deborah Tannen, *You Just Don't Understand: Women and Men in Conversation* (Ballantine Books, 1991), pp. 17–29, 42–48. Copyright © 1990 by Deborah Tannen. Reprinted by permission of William Morrow & Company, Inc.

always react to things as I expect him to. And I often don't understand why he says what he does.

At the time I began working on this book, we had jobs in different cities. People frequently expressed sympathy by making comments like "That must be rough," and "How do you stand it?" I was inclined to accept their sympathy and say things like "We fly a lot." Sometimes I would reinforce their concern: "The worst part is having to pack and unpack all the time." But my husband reacted differently, often with irritation. He might respond by de-emphasizing the inconvenience: As academics, we had four-day weekends together, as well as long vacations throughout the year and four months in the summer. We even benefited from the intervening days of uninterrupted time for work. I once overheard him telling a dubious man that we were lucky, since studies have shown that married couples who live together spend less than half an hour a week talking to each other; he was implying that our situation had advantages.

I didn't object to the way my husband responded—everything he said was true—but I was surprised by it. I didn't understand why he reacted as he did. He explained that he sensed condescension in some expressions of concern, as if the questioner were implying, "Yours is not a real marriage; your ill-chosen profession has resulted in an unfortunate arrangement. I pity you, and look down at you from the height of complacence, since my wife and I have avoided your misfortune." It had not occurred to me that there might be an element of one-upmanship in these expressions of concern, though I could recognize it when it was pointed out. Even after I saw the point, though, I was inclined to regard my husband's response as slightly odd, a personal quirk. He frequently seemed to see others as adversaries when I didn't.

... I now see that my husband was simply engaging the world in a way that many men do: as an individual in a hierarchical social order in which he was either one-up or one-down. In this world, conversations are negotiations in which people try to achieve and maintain the upper hand if they can, and protect themselves from others' attempts to put them down and push them around. Life, then, is a contest, a struggle to preserve independence and avoid failure.

I, on the other hand, was approaching the world as many women do: as an individual in a network of connections. In this world, conversations are negotiations for closeness in which people try to seek and give confirmation and support, and to reach consensus. They try to protect themselves from others' attempts, to push them away. Life, then, is a community, a struggle to preserve intimacy and avoid isolation. Though there are hierarchies in this world too, they are hierarchies more of friendship than of power and accomplishment.

Women are also concerned with achieving status and avoiding failure, but these are not the goals that are *focused* on all the time, and they tend to pursue them in the guise of connection. And men are also concerned with achieving involvement and avoiding isolation, but they are not *focused* on these goals, and they tend to pursue them in the guise of opposition.

Discussing our differences from this point of view, my husband pointed out to me a distinction I had missed: He reacted the way I just described only if expressions of concern came from men in whom he sensed an awareness of hierarchy. And there were times when I too disliked people's expressing sympathy about our commuting marriage. I recall being offended by one man who seemed to have a leering look in his eye when he asked, "How do you manage this long-distance romance?" Another time I was annoyed when a women who knew me only by reputation approached us during the intermission of a play, discovered our situation by asking my husband where he worked, and kept the conversation going by asking us all about it. In these cases, I didn't feel put down; I felt intruded upon. If my husband was offended by what he perceived as claims to superior status, I felt these sympathizers were claiming inappropriate intimacy.

INTIMACY AND INDEPENDENCE

Intimacy is key in a world of connection where individuals negotiate complex networks of friendship, minimize differences, try to reach consensus, and avoid the appearance of superiority, which would highlight differences. In a world of status, *independence* is key, because a primary means of establishing status is to tell others what to do, and taking orders is a marker of low status. Though all humans need both intimacy and independence, women tend to focus on the first and men on the second. It is as if their lifeblood ran in different directions.

These differences can give women and men differing views of the same situation, as they did in the case of a couple I will call Linda and Josh. When Josh's old high-school chum called him at work and announced he'd be in town on business the following month, Josh invited him to stay for the weekend. That evening he informed Linda that they were going to have a houseguest, and that he and his chum would go out together the first

night to shoot the breeze like old times. Linda was upset. She was going to be away on business the week before, and the Friday night when Josh would be out with his chum would be her first night home. But what upset her the most was that Josh had made these plans on his own and informed her of them, rather than discussing them with her before extending the invitation.

Linda would never make plans, for a weekend or an evening, without first checking with Josh. She can't understand why he doesn't show her the same courtesy and consideration that she shows him. But when she protests, Josh says, "I can't say to my friend, 'I have to ask my wife for permission'!"

To Josh, checking with his wife means seeking permission, which implies that he is not independent, not free to act on his own. It would make him feel like a child or an underling. To Linda, checking with her husband has nothing to do with permission. She assumes that spouses discuss their plans with each other because their lives are intertwined, so the actions of one have consequences for the other. Not only does Linda not mind telling someone, "I have to check with Josh"; quite the contrary—she likes it. It makes her feel good to know and show that she is involved with someone, that her life is bound up with someone else's.

Linda and Josh both felt more upset by this incident, and others like it, than seemed warranted, but it cut to the core of their primary concerns. Linda was hurt because she sensed a failure of closeness in their relationship: He didn't care about her as much as she cared about him. And he was hurt because he felt she was trying to control him and limit his freedom.

A similar conflict exists between Louise and Howie, another couple, about spending money. Louise would never buy anything costing more than a hundred dollars without discussing it with Howie, but he goes out and buys whatever he wants and feels they can afford, like a table saw or a new power mower. Louise is disturbed, not because she disapproves of the purchases, but because she feels he is acting as if she were not in the picture.

Many women feel it is natural to consult with their partners, at every turn, while many men automatically make more decisions without consulting their partners. This may reflect a broad difference in conceptions of decision making. Women expect decisions to be discussed first and made by consensus. They appreciate the discussion itself as evidence of involvement and communication. But many men feel oppressed by lengthy discussions about what they see as minor decisions, and they feel hemmed in if they can't just act without talking first. When women try to initiate a freewheeling discussion by asking, "What do you think?" men often think they are being asked to decide....

ASYMMETRIES

If intimacy says, "We're close and the same," and independence says, "We're separate and different," it is easy to see that intimacy and independence dovetail with connection and status. The essential element of connection is symmetry: People are the same, feeling equally close to each other. The essential element of status is asymmetry: People are not the same; they are differently placed in a hierarchy....

The symmetry of connection is what creates community: If two people are struggling for closeness, they are both struggling for the same thing. And the asymmetry of status is what creates contest: Two people can't both have the upper hand, so negotiation for status is inherently adversarial. In my earlier work, I explored in detail the dynamics of intimacy (which I referred to as involvement) and independence, but I tended to ignore the force of status and its adversarial nature. Once I identified these dynamics, however, I saw them all around me. The puzzling behavior of friends and co-workers finally became comprehensible.

Differences in how my husband and I approached the same situation, which previously would have been mystifying, suddenly made sense. For example, in a jazz club the waitress recommended the crab cakes to me, and they turned out to be terrible. I was uncertain about whether or not to send them back. When the waitress came by and asked how the food was, I said that I didn't really like the crab cakes. She asked, "What's wrong with them?" While staring at the table, my husband answered, "They don't taste fresh." The waitress snapped, "They're frozen! What do you expect?" I looked directly up at her and said, "We just don't like them." She said, "Well, if you don't like them, I could take them back and bring you something else."

After she left with the crab cakes, my husband and I laughed because we realized we had just automatically played out the scripts I had been writing about. He had heard her question "What's wrong with them?" as a challenge that he had to match. He doesn't like to fight, so he looked away, to soften what he felt was an obligatory counterchallenge: He felt instinctively that he had to come up with something wrong with the crab cakes to justify my complaint. (He was fighting for me.) I had taken the question "What's wrong with them?" as a request for information. I instinctively sought a way to be right without making her wrong. Perhaps it was because she was a women that she responded more favorably to my approach. . . .

MALE-FEMALE CONVERSATION IS CROSS-CULTURAL COMMUNICATION

If women speak and hear a language of connection and intimacy, while men speak and hear a language of status and independence, then communication between men and women can be like cross-cultural communication, prey to a clash of conversational styles. Instead of different dialects, it has been said they speak different genderlects.

The claim that men and women grow up in different worlds may at first seem patently absurd. Brothers and sisters grow up in the same families, children to parents of both genders. Where, then, do women and men learn different ways of speaking and hearing?

IT BEGINS AT THE BEGINNING

Even if they grow up in the same neighborhood, on the same block, or in the same house, girls and boys grow up in different worlds of words. Others talk to them differently and expect and accept different ways of talking from them. Most important, children learn how to talk, how to have conversations, not only from their parents but from their peers. After all, if their parents have a foreign or regional accent, children do not emulate it; they learn to speak with the pronunciation of the region where they grow up. Anthropologists Daniel Maltz and Ruth Borker summarize research showing that boys and girls have very different ways of talking to their friends. Although they often play together, boys and girls spend most of their time playing in same-sex groups. And, although some of the activities they play at are similar, their favorite games are different, and their ways of using language in their games are separated by a world of difference.

Boys tend to play outside, in large groups that are hierarchically structured. Their groups have a leader who tells others what to do and how to do it, and resists doing what other boys propose. It is by giving orders and making them stick that high status is negotiated. Another way boys achieve status is to take center stage by telling stories and jokes, and by sidetracking or challenging the stories and jokes of others. Boys' games have winners and losers and elaborate systems of rules that are frequently the subjects of arguments. Finally, boys are frequently heard to boast of their skill and argue about who is best at what.

Girls, on the other hand, play in small groups or in pairs; the center of a girl's social life is a best friend. Within the group, intimacy is key: Differentiation is measured by relative closeness. In their most frequent games, such as jump rope and hopscotch, everyone gets a turn. Many of their activities (such as playing house) do not have winners or losers. Though some girls are certainly more skilled than others, girls are expected not to boast about it, or show that they think they are better than the others. Girls don't give orders; they express their preferences as suggestions, and suggestions are likely to be accepted. Whereas boys say, "Gimme that!" and

"Get outta here!" girls say, "Let's do this," and "How about doing that?" Anything else is put down as "bossy." They don't grab center stage—they don't want it —so they don't challenge each other directly. And much of the time, they simply sit together and talk. Girls are not accustomed to jockeying for status in an obvious way; they are more concerned that they be liked. . . .

[One] study suggests that boys and girls both want to get their way, but they tend to do so differently. Though social norms encourage boys to be openly competitive and girls to be openly cooperative, different situations and activities can result in different ways of behaving. Marjorie Harness Goodwin compared boys and girls engaged in two task-oriented activities: The boys were making slingshots in preparation for a fight, and the girls were making rings. She found that the boys' group was hierarchical: The leader told the others what to do and how to do it. The girls' group was egalitarian: Everyone made suggestions and tended to accept the suggestions of others. But observing the girls in a different activity —playing house—Goodwin found that they too adopted hierarchical structures: The girls who played mothers issued orders to the girls playing children, who in turn sought permission from their play-mothers. Moreover, a girl who was a play-mother was also a kind of manager of the game. This study shows that girls know how to issue orders and operate in a hierarchical structure, but they don't find that mode of behavior appropriate when they engage in task activities with their peers. They do find it appropriate in parent-child relationships, which they enjoy practicing in the form of play.

These worlds of play shed light on the world views of women and men in relationships. The boys' play illuminates why men would be on the lookout for signs they are being put down or told what to do. The chief commodity that is bartered in the boys' hierarchical world is status, and the way to achieve and maintain status is to give orders and get others to follow them. A boy in a low-status position finds himself being pushed around. So boys monitor their relations for subtle shifts in status by keeping track of who's giving orders and who's taking them.

These dynamics are not the ones that drive girls' play. The chief commodity that is bartered in the girls' community is intimacy. Girls monitor their friendships for subtle shifts in alliance, and they seek to be friends with popular girls. Popularity is a kind of status, but it is founded on connection. It also places popular girls in a bind. By doing field work in a junior high school, Donna Eder found that popular girls were paradoxically—and inevitably—disliked. Many girls want to befriend popular girls, but girls' friendships must necessarily be limited, since they entail intimacy rather than large group activities. So a popular girl must reject the overtures of most of the girls who seek her out—with the result that she is branded "stuck up."

THE KEY IS UNDERSTANDING

If adults learn their ways of speaking as children growing up in separate social worlds of peers, then conversation between women and men is cross-cultural communication. Although each style is valid on its own terms, misunderstandings arise because the styles are different. Taking a cross-cultural approach to male-female conversations makes it possible to explain why dissatisfactions are justified without accusing anyone of being wrong or crazy.

Learning about style differences won't make them go away, but it can banish mutual mystification and blame. Being able to understand why our partners, friends, and even strangers behave the way they do is a comfort, even if we still don't see things the same way. It makes the world into more familiar territory.

NO

Mary Crawford

TALKING DIFFERENCE: ON GENDER AND LANGUAGE

TALKING ACROSS THE GENDER GAP

People believe in sex differences. As one best-selling book puts it, when it comes to communication, *Men are from Mars, Women are from Venus* (Gray, 1992). Social scientists have helped to create and confirm that belief by conducting innumerable studies of every conceivable linguistic and stylistic variation between the sexes and by developing theories that stress differences rather than similarities and overlap (West and Zimmerman, 1985). In *Language and Woman's Place* (1975) the linguist Robin Lakoff proposed that women use a speech style that is ineffectual because it is overly polite, hesitant, and deferent. The assertiveness training movement of the 1970s and 1980s—a therapeutic fad led by psychologists whose clients were largely women—engaged perhaps hundreds of thousands of people in attempts to change their way of communicating. A rationale for the movement was that some people (especially women) suffer from poor communication skills and irrational beliefs that prevent them from expressing themselves clearly and directly. More recently, linguists and communication experts have created another conceptual bandwagon by applying theories of cross-cultural communication to women and men. According to this view, 'men from Mars' and 'women from Venus' are fated to misunderstand each other unless they recognize their deeply socialized differences.

The view of gender and language encoded in these writings and therapies is that fundamental differences between women and men shape the way they talk. The differences are conceived as located within individuals and prior to the talk—as differences in personality traits, skills, beliefs, attitudes, or goals. For the millions of people who have become acquainted with issues of gender and language through reading best-selling books telling women how to be more assertive or how to understand the 'opposite' sex, or through watching television talk shows featuring communication experts who claim that talk between women and men is cross-cultural communication, a powerful narrative frame is provided and validated: that gender is difference, and difference is static, bipolar, and categorical. Absorbing such messages, it would be very difficult *not* to believe that women and men are indeed opposite sexes when it comes to talk. . . .

TWO SEXES, TWO CULTURES

Cross-Cultural Talk . . .

Talking Across the Gender Divide
. . . When we think of distinct female and male subcultures we tend to think of societies in which women and men spend virtually their entire lives spatially and interactionally segregated; for example, those which practice purdah. In Western societies, however, girls and boys are brought up together. They share the use of common space in their homes; eat, work, and play with their siblings of both sexes; generally attend co-educational schools in which they are aggregated in many classes and activities. Both sexes are supervised, cared for, and taught largely by women in infancy and early childhood, with male teachers and other authority figures becoming more visible as children grow older. Moreover, they see these social patterns mirrored and even exaggerated in the mass media. How can the talk of Western women and men be seen as talk across cultures?

The two-cultures model was first applied to the speech of North American women and men by Daniel Maltz and Ruth Borker, who proposed that difficulties in cross-sex and cross-ethnic communication are 'two examples of the same larger phenomenon: cultural difference and miscommunication' (1982: 196). Maltz and Borker acknowledge the argument that American women and men interact with each other far too much

to be characterized as living in different subcultures. However, they maintain that the social rules for friendly conversation are learned between the ages of approximately 5 and 15, precisely the time when children's play groups are maximally segregated by sex. Not only do children voluntarily choose to play in same-sex groups, they consciously exaggerate differences as they differentiate themselves from the other sex. Because of the very different social contexts in which they learn the meanings and goals of conversational interaction, boys and girls learn to use language in different ways.

Citing research on children's play, Maltz and Borker (1982) argue that girls learn to do three things with words:

1. to create and maintain relationships of closeness and equality;
2. to criticize others in acceptable (indirect) ways;
3. to interpret accurately and sensitively the speech of other girls.

In contrast, boys learn to do three very different things with words:

1. to assert one's position of dominance;
2. to attract and maintain an audience;
3. to assert oneself when another person has the floor.

The Two-Cultures Approach as Bandwagon
. . . The new twist in the two-cultures model of communication is to conceive relationship difficulties not as women's deficiencies but as an inevitable result of deeply ingrained male–female differences. The self-help books that encode a two-cultures model make the paradoxical claim that difference between the sexes is deeply socialized and/or fundamental to masculine and feminine natures, and at the same time subject to change

and manipulation if the reader only follows prescribed ways of talking. Instead of catchy slogans and metaphors that stigmatize women (*Women who Love too Much*, Doris Doormat v. Agatha Aggressive) the equally catchy new metaphors glorify difference.

... Deborah Tannen's *You just don't Understand: Women and Men in Conversation* (1990)... has become a phenomenal success in the US. Acclaimed in the popular press as the 'Rosetta Stone that at last deciphers the miscommunication between the sexes' and as 'a Berlitz guidebook to the language and customs of the opposite gender [sic]'... Tannen claims that childhood play has shaped world views so that, when adult women and men are in relationships 'women speak and hear a language of connection and intimacy, while men speak and hear a language of status and independence' (1990:42). The contrasting conversational goals of intimacy and independence lead to contrasting conversational styles. Women tell each other of their troubles, freely ask for information and help, and show appreciation of others' helping efforts. Men prefer to solve problems rather than talk about them, are reluctant to ask for help or advice, and are more comfortable in the roles of expert, lecturer, and teacher than learner or listener. Men are more talkative in public, women in private. These different styles are labelled 'report talk' (men's) and 'rapport talk' (women's).

Given the stylistic dichotomy between the sexes, miscommunication is almost inevitable; however, no one is to blame. Rather, another banner proclaims, 'The Key is Understanding:' 'Although each style is valid on its own terms, misunderstandings arise because the styles are different. Taking a cross-cultural approach

to male–female conversations makes it possible to explain why dissatisfactions are justified without accusing anyone of being wrong or crazy' (1990:47).

You just don't Understand makes its case for the two-cultures model skillfully and well using techniques that have become standard in popular writing about behavior: characterizations of 'most' women and men, entertaining anecdotes, and the presentation of research findings as fact.... Instead of advocating conversational formulae or regimented training programs for one sex, it recommends simply that people try to understand and accept sex differences and to be as flexible in style as possible....

The Two-Cultures Approach: an Evaluation

Beyond Deficiencies and Blame

Proponents of the two-cultures model maintain that it is an advance over approaches that blame particular groups for miscommunication....

Unlike earlier approaches, the two-cultures model does not characterize women's talk as deficient in comparison to a male norm. In contrast to the notion of an ineffectual 'female register' or the prescriptive masculine ideals of the assertiveness training movement, the two-cultures model problematizes the behavior of men as well as women. To John Gray, neither Mars nor Venus is a superior home. To Deborah Tannen, 'report talk' and 'rapport talk' are equally limiting for their users in cross-sex communication. The speech style attributed to men is no longer 'standard' speech or 'the language,' but merely one way of negotiating the social landscape.

A model of talk that transcends woman-blaming is less likely to lead to woman-as-problem research programs or to widespread attempts to change women through therapy and skills training. Moreover, ways of talking thought to characterize women can be positively revalued within this framework. In a chapter on gossip, Tannen notes that the negative connotation of the word reflects men's interpretation of women's ways of talking. But gossip can be thought of as 'talking about' rather than 'talking against.' It can serve crucial functions of establishing intimacy and rapport....

Doing Gender, Doing Power

The two-cultures approach fails to theorize how power relations at the structural level are recreated and maintained at the interactional level. The *consequences* of 'miscommunication' are not the same for powerful and powerless groups. As Deborah Cameron (1985: 150) points out, 'The right to represent and stereotype is not mutual.' Stereotypes of less powerful groups (immigrants, people of color) as inadequate speakers serve to ensure that no one need take seriously what these people say. People of color may have their own set of negative stereotypes of white people, but 'these are the ideas of people without power. They do not serve as a base for administrative procedures and decisions, nor do they get expressed routinely in mass media.' Recent research on the relationship between power and stereotyping suggests that people in power stereotype others partly as a cognitive 'shortcut' that minimizes the need to attend to them as individuals. People without power, of course, must attend carefully to their 'superiors' in order to avoid negative judgment or actual harm and cannot afford to use schematic shortcuts (Fiske, 1993).

'Negotiating status' is an evaluatively neutral term for interpersonal behaviors that consolidate power and maintain dominance. Ignoring the enactment of power and how it connects to structural power in gender relations does a disservice to sociolinguistics, distorting its knowledge base and undermining other more legitimate research approaches (Freed, 1992). Moreover, it badly misrepresents communication phenomena. Nancy Henley and Cheris Kramarae (1991) provide a detailed analysis of six 'cultural differences' in female–male speech styles taken from Maltz and Borker (1982), showing that they may be more plausibly interpreted as manifestations and exercises of power. For example, men's tendency to interpret questions as requests for information, and problem-sharing as an opportunity to give expert advice, can be viewed as prerogatives of power. In choosing these speech strategies, men take to themselves the voice of authority.

This failure to recognize structural power and connect it with international power has provoked the strongest criticisms of the two-cultures approach. In a review of *You just don't Understand*, Senta Troemel-Ploetz (1991) pointed out that if the majority of relationships between women and men in our society were not fundamentally asymmetrical to the advantage of men,

we would not need a women's liberation movement, women's commissions, houses for battered women, legislation for equal opportunity, antidiscrimination laws, family therapy, couple therapy, divorce... If you leave out power, you do not understand any talk, be it the discussion after your speech, the conversation at your own dinner-table, in a doctor's office, in the back yards of West

Philadelphia, in an Italian village, on a street in Turkey, in a court room or in a day-care center, in a women's group or at a UN conference. It is like saying Black English and Oxford English are just two different varieties of English, each valid on its own; it just so happens that the speakers of one variety find themselves in high-paying positions with a lot of prestige and power of decision-making, and the others are found more in low-paying jobs, or on the streets and in prisons. They don't always understand each other, but they both have the best intentions; if they could only learn a bit from each other and understand their differences as a matter of style, all would be well. (Troemel-Ploetz, 1991: 497–8)

No one involved in debating the two-cultures approach denies that men have more social and political power than women. Maltz and Borker (1982: 199) acknowledge that power differentials 'may make some contribution' to communication patterns. However, they do not theorize the workings of power in interaction or advocate structural changes to reduce inequity.

The Bandwagon Revisited
There is no inherent limitation to the two-cultures approach that would prevent its development as a theory of difference *and* dominance, a theory that could encompass the construction of gendered subjectivities, the reproduction of inequality in interaction, and the role of interaction in sustaining gendered social structures. It is therefore the more disappointing that in the popularized versions that have influenced perhaps millions of people, it is flattened into an account of sex dichotomies. And this is why the model has been so harshly evaluated by feminist scholars. Perhaps unfortunately,

the more egregious versions have been largely ignored and the more scholarly one attacked. Deborah Tannen's critics have charged that, despite the absence of overt women-blaming and the positive evaluation of 'feminine' modes of talk, the interpretations she offers often disguise or gloss over inequity, and privilege men's interpretations (Freed, 1992; Troemel-Ploetz, 1991). They have accused her of being an apologist for men, excusing their insensitivity, rudeness, and dominance as mere stylistic quirks, and encouraging women to make the adjustments when needs conflict (Freed, 1992). Indeed, the interpretations Tannen offers for the many anecdotes that enliven her book often read as though the past two decades of women's studies scholarship had never occurred, and there were no feminist analyses available with which to contextualize gendered behavior (Troemel-Ploetz, 1991).

You just don't Understand is apolitical —a choice which is in itself a political act, and a significant one at that, given that the book has sold well over a million copies. Like the popular psychology of the assertiveness training movement, it does not threaten the status quo (Troemel-Ploetz, 1991). Like its pop-psychology companions on the bookstore shelves, it offers something to both the powerful and those over whom they have power: to men, a compelling rationale of blame-free difference and to women a comforting promise of mutual accommodation.

Let us consider [two] examples, from [two] types of conversational setting, to illustrate how the accounts of interaction in *You just don't Understand* might be reinterpreted in light of research on women and gender. The first is an anecdote about Josh and Linda. When an old friend calls Josh at work with plans for a visit nearby on business, Josh invites him to spend the weekend and makes plans to go out with him Friday night. These plans are made without consulting with Linda, who protests that Josh should have checked with her, especially since she will be returning from a business trip herself that day. Tannen's explanation of the misunderstanding is in terms of an autonomy/intimacy dichotomy. Linda likes to have her life entwined with Josh's, to consult and be consulted about plans. Josh feels that checking with her implies a loss of independence. 'Linda was hurt because she sensed a failure of closeness in their relationship ... he was hurt because he felt she was trying to control him and limit his freedom' (1990: 27).

No resolution of the conflict is provided in the anecdote; the implication is that Josh's plans prevail. Interpreting this story in terms of women's needs for intimacy and men's for autonomy glosses the fact that Josh has committed mutual resources (living space, food, the time and work required to entertain a houseguest) on behalf of himself and his partner without acknowledgement that the partner should have a voice in that decision. His behavior seems to reflect the belief that the time and energy of others (women) are to be accommodated to men. As a test of the fairness of his behavior, imagine that Josh were living with a male housemate. To invite a mutual weekend guest without consulting the housemate would be considered overtly rude. The housemate (but not the woman in a heterosexual couple) would be warranted in refusing to cooperate, because he is seen as entitled to make his own plans and control his own resources. A sense of entitlement to act entirely on one's own and

make decisions unilaterally is 'part of the social empowerment that men enjoy. It has precious little to do with communicative style or language' (Freed, 1992: 4). ...

In a section titled 'First Me, Then Me,' Tannen describes her own experience of discourse in a professional setting. Seated at a faculty dinner next to a woman, she enjoyed a mutually informative and pleasant discussion in which each talked about her research and explored connections and overlaps. Turning to a male guest, she initiated a conversation in a similar way. However, the conversation proceeded very differently:

> During the next half hour, I learned a lot about his job, his research, and his background. Shortly before the dinner ended there was a lull, and he asked me what I did. When I said I was a linguist, he became excited and told me about a research project he had conducted that was related to neurolinguistics. He was still telling me about his research when we all got up to leave the table. (1990: 126)

Lecturing, says Tannen, is part of a male style. And women let them get away with it. Because women's style includes listening attentively and not interrupting, they do not jump in, challenge, or attempt to deflect the lecturer. Men assume that if their partner had anything important to say, she would say it. The two styles interact to produce silent women, who nod and smile although they are bored, and talkative men, who lecture at length though they themselves may be bored and frustrated by the lack of dialogue. Thus, apparent conversational dominance is not something men deliberately do to women. Neither is it something women culpably permit. The imbalance is created by 'habitual styles.'

The stylistic interpretation discounts the possibility that the male academic in this example did not want to hear about his female dinner companion's research because he did not care about it. That women and what they do are valued less than men and what they do is one of the fundamental insights of feminism. The history of women in the professions provides ample evidence of exclusion, discrimination, and marginalization. Methods vary: plagiarizing women's work (Spender, 1989), denigrating them as unfeminine while stealing their ideas (Sayre, 1975), denying them employment (Crawford, 1981; Scarborough and Furumoto, 1987) and recognition (Nochlin, 1971). When women compete successfully in male domains, they are undermined by sexual harassment (Gutek, 1985) and by being represented as sex objects (a long-running 1980s ad campaign featured female physicians and attorneys making medical rounds and appearing in court in their underwear) (Lott, 1985). In short, there is not yet much reason to believe that women in the professions are routinely taken as seriously as their male peers. And the academy is no exception. What Tannen explains as mere stylistic differences have the effect of keeping women and their work invisible, and have had documented consequences on women's hiring, promotion, and tenure (Caplan, 1993)....

A Rhetoric of Reassurance

The rhetoric of difference makes everyone—and no one—responsible for interpersonal problems. Men are not to blame for communication difficulties; neither is a social system in which gender governs access to resources. Instead, difference is reified: 'The culprit, then is not an individual man or even men's styles alone, but the difference between women and men's styles' (Tannen, 1990: 95).

One of the most striking effects achieved in these books is to reassure women that their lot in heterosexual relationships is normal. Again and again, it is stressed that no one is to blame, that miscommunication is inevitable, that unsatisfactory results may stem from the best of intentions. As these explanations dominate the public realm of discourse about gender, they provide 'one more pseudo-explanation' and 'one more ingenious strategy for not tackling the root causes of women's subordinate status' (Cameron, in press).

Its very ubiquity has made inequality of status and power in heterosexual relationships seem unremarkable, and one of the most important contributions of feminist research has been to make it visible (Wilkinson and Kitzinger, 1993). In the discourse of miscommunication the language feminists have developed to theorize status and power is neutralized. Concepts such as sexism, sex discrimination, patriarchy, and gender inequity are barely mentioned, and conversational strategies that have the effect of silencing women are euphemized as stylistic 'asymmetries.' For example, Tannen explains that when men do most of the talking in a group, it is not because they intend to prevent women from speaking or believe that women have nothing important to say. Rather, they see the women as *equals*, and expect them to compete in the same style they themselves use. Thus, an inequity that feminists have conceptualized in terms of power differentials is acknowledged, but explained as an accidental imbalance created by style and having little to do with a gendered social order.

Power dynamics in heterosexual relationships are obscured by the kinds of intentions imputed to speakers. Both books presume an innocence of communicative intent. In the separate and simplistic worlds of Martians and Venusians, women just want to be cherished and men just want to be needed and admired. In the separate worlds of 'report talk' and 'rapport talk', the goal may be sex-specific but the desire is the same: to be understood and responded to in kind. In *You just don't Understand*, each anecdote is followed by an analysis of the intentions of *both* speakers, a practice that Tannen (1992) feels reflects her fairness to both sexes. But this symmetry is false, because the one kind of intention that is never imputed to any speaker is the intent to dominate. Yet people are aware of such intentions in their talk, and, when asked, can readily describe the verbal tactics they use to 'get their own way' in heterosexual interactions (Falbo, 1982; Falbo and Peplau, 1980; Kelley et al., 1978). Tannen acknowledges the role of power in conversational dynamics (cf. p. 283, 'We enact and create our gender, and our inequality, with every move we make'). But the rhetorical force of the anecdotes is about difference. When an anecdote seems obviously explainable in terms of dominance strategies, the possibility of such an account is often acknowledged but discounted. The characteristics that the two-cultures model posit for females' speech are ones appropriate to friendly conversation, while the characteristics posited for men's speech are not neutral, but indicate uncooperative, dominating and disruptive interaction (Henley and Kramarae, 1991). Whose needs are being served when intent to dominate is ruled out *a priori* in accounting for cross-sex conversation?

Many of the most compelling anecdotes describe situations in which a woman is hurt, frustrated or angered by a man's apparently selfish or dominating behavior, only to find that her feelings were unwarranted because the man's intentions were good. This is psychologically naive. There is no reason to believe that *post hoc* stated intentions are a complete and sufficient description of conversational motives.…

The emphasis on interpreting a partner's intentions is problematic in others ways as well. As Nancy Henley and Cheris Kramarae (1991: 42) point out, '[F]emales are required to develop special sensitivity to interpret males' silence, lack of emotional expressiveness, or brutality, and to help men express themselves, while men often seem to be trained deliberately to misinterpret much of women's meaning.' Young girls are told that hitting, teasing, and insults are to be read as signs of boys' 'liking.' Adolescent girls are taught to take responsibility for boys' inexpressiveness by drawing them out in conversation, steering talk to topics that will make them feel comfortable, and being a good listener.…

Analyzing conversation in terms of intentions has a very important implication: it deflects attention from *effects*, including the ways that everyday action and talk serve to recreate and maintain current gender arrangements.

POSTSCRIPT

Are Communication Problems Between Men and Women Largely Due to Radically Different Conversation Styles?

One of Crawford's concerns is the demeaning picture of women that the literature on gender differences in communication styles often suggests. Men are problem solvers and stand on their own two feet, while women are people pleasers and dependent. Men, however, could also feel put down. According to the theory, men are predominantly interested in defending and advancing their status, even to the point of stepping on toes and jeopardizing closeness. This makes men out to be rather immoral. Self-promotion and the need to dominate others is not sanctioned by most religions or appreciated much by most people. Women come closer to religious and popular ideals than men do. To their credit, they bond, love, and share more through communication than men do, and women do so without necessarily sacrificing their competence in the process.

Many issues regarding gender differences in communication styles remain murky. Everyone, including Crawford, acknowledges that there are talking differences between genders, but how big are these differences? This relates to the large question of how different men and women are on other significant dimensions. What causes these differences? To what extent are they biological and hormonal, and to what extent are they due to differential socialization and different positions in society? How changeable are these differences? Should they be changed?

The past two decades have produced considerable research on gender differences in communication styles, which is reflected in several readers and academic works. Tannen and Crawford are prominent in this literature. In addition to the books from which the selections were drawn, see Tannen's *Gender and Discourse* (Oxford University Press, 1994) and her edited book *Gender and Conversational Interaction* (Oxford University Press, 1993). See also Deborah Cameron, ed., *The Feminist Critique of Language: A Reader*, 2d ed. (Routledge, 1998); Jennifer Coates, ed., *Language and Gender: A Reader* (Blackwell, 1998); Ruth Wodak, ed., *Gender and Discourse* (Sage Publications, 1997); Louise Goueffic, ed., *Breaking the Patriarchal Code: The Linguistic Basis of Sexual Bias* (Knowledge, Ideas & Trends, 1996); Mary Ritchie Key, *Male/Female Language* (Scarecrow Press, 1996); Victoria L. Bergwall, Janet M. Bing, and Alice F. Freed, eds., *Rethinking Language and Gender Research: Theory and Practice* (Longman, 1996); and Kira Hall and Mary Bucholtz, eds. *Gender Articulated: Language and the Socially Constructed Self* (Routledge, 1995).

ISSUE 6

Should Society Be More Accepting of Homosexuality?

YES: Richard D. Mohr, from *A More Perfect Union: Why Straight America Must Stand Up for Gay Rights* (Beacon Press, 1994)

NO: Carl F. Horowitz, from "Homosexuality's Legal Revolution," *The Freeman* (May 1991)

ISSUE SUMMARY

YES: Philosophy professor Richard D. Mohr argues that homosexuals suffer from unjust discrimination and that homosexuality is neither immoral nor unnatural.

NO: Carl F. Horowitz, a policy analyst at the Heritage Foundation, argues that legal acceptance of homosexuality has gone too far. He maintains that open displays of homosexual affection, the creation of gay neighborhoods, and gay mannerisms are deeply offensive to heterosexuals.

In 1979 in Sioux Falls, South Dakota, Randy Rohl and Grady Quinn became the first acknowledged homosexual couple in America to receive permission from their high school principal to attend the senior prom together. The National Gay Task Force hailed the event as a milestone in the progress of human rights. It is unclear what the voters of Sioux Falls thought about it, since it was not put up to a vote, but if their views were similar to those of voters in Dade County, Florida; Houston, Texas; Wichita, Kansas; and various localities in the state of Oregon, they probably were not as enthusiastic as the National Gay Task Force. In referenda held in these and other areas, voters have reversed decisions by legislators and local boards to ban discrimination by sexual preference. Even in New York City, which is well known for its liberal attitudes, parents in some school districts have fought battles against school administrators over curricula that promote tolerance of gay lifestyles.

Yet the attitude of Americans toward gay rights is not easy to pin down. On one hand, voting majorities in many localities have defeated or overturned resolutions designating sexual orientation as a protected right. In 1993 alone, 19 localities passed measures that are considered antihomosexual by gay rights leaders. However, voters have also defeated resolutions like the one in California in 1978 that would have banned the hiring of gay schoolteachers, or the one on the Oregon ballot in 1992 identifying homosexuality as "abnormal, wrong, unnatural and perverse." In some states, notably Colorado, voters have approved initiatives widely perceived as antigay, but, almost invariably, these resolutions have been carefully worded so as to appear to oppose "special" rights for gays. In general, polls show that a large majority of Americans believe that homosexuals should have equal rights with heterosexuals with regard to job opportunities. On the other hand, many persist in viewing homosexuality as morally wrong.

President Bill Clinton experienced both of these views in 1992 and 1993. When he ran for president, Clinton caused no particular stir when he openly supported gay rights and promised that if elected he would issue an executive order lifting the ban on homosexuals in the military services. Once in office, however, and faced with demands from gay rights groups to deliver on his pledge, Clinton encountered bitter opposition. The locus of the opposition was the armed services and their supporters in Congress, but these vocal opponents also enjoyed considerable support from the public at large. Clinton ended up accepting a modified version of what he had promised—a "don't ask, don't tell, don't pursue" policy that fell far short of fully accepting homosexuality in the armed services.

Homosexuality was once commonly viewed as "deviant." The adjective may still be acceptable by both sides of the controversy if it simply means behavior considered different by the majority. But in popular usage, "deviant" means considerably more than this. It carries the connotation of "sick" and "immoral," which is why homosexuals are working hard to redefine homosexuality as normal, natural, and an acceptable lifestyle in a pluralist society. A more accepting attitude seems to be growing, especially among younger, college-educated Americans, but the recent referendum results suggest that widespread opposition to gay rights measures still exists.

In the selections that follow, Richard D. Mohr argues that the refusal to accept homosexuality is simply another form of bigotry, in the same category as racial or sexual discrimination, and that the time is long past due for granting full civil rights to homosexuals. Carl F. Horowitz argues that society's legal acceptance of homosexuality is already excessive because the rights of homosexuals are impinging on those of heterosexuals.

YES

Richard D. Mohr

PREJUDICE AND HOMOSEXUALITY

Who are gays anyway? Though the number of gays in America is hotly disputed, studies agree that gays are distributed through every stripe and stratum of Americans. Who are homosexuals? They are your friends, your minister, your teacher, your bankteller, your doctor, your mailcarrier, your officemate, your roommate, your congressional representative, your sibling, parent, and spouse. They are we. We are everywhere, virtually all ordinary, virtually all unknown.

Ignorance about gays, however, has not stopped people's minds from being filled with stereotypes about gays. Society holds two oddly contradictory groups of anti-gay stereotypes. One revolves around an individual's allegedly confused gender identity: lesbians are females who want to be, or at least look and act like, men—bulldykes, diesel dykes; while gay men are males who want to be, or at least look and act like, women—queens, fairies, nances, limp-wrists, nellies, sissies, aunties. These stereotypes of mismatches between biological sex and socially defined gender provide the materials through which lesbians and gay men become the butts of ethniclike jokes. These stereotypes and jokes, though derisive, basically view lesbians and gay men as ridiculous. For example: "How many fags does it take to change a light bulb?" Answer: "Eight—one to replace it and seven to scream 'Faaaaaabulous!'"

The other set of stereotypes revolves around gays as a pervasive sinister conspiratorial threat. The core stereotype here is that of the gay person—especially gay man—as child molester, and more generally as sex-crazed maniac. Homosexuality here is viewed as a vampirelike corruptive contagion. These stereotypes carry with them fears of the very destruction of family and civilization itself. Now, that which is essentially ridiculous can hardly have such a staggering effect. Something must be afoot.

Clarifying the nature of stereotypes can help make sense of this incoherent amalgam. Stereotypes are not simply false generalizations from a skewed sample of cases examined. Admittedly, false generalizing plays some part in the stereotypes society holds about gays and other groups. If, for instance, one takes as one's sample gay men who are in psychiatric hospitals or prisons, as was done in nearly all early investigations, not surprisingly one will

From Richard D. Mohr, *A More Perfect Union: Why Straight America Must Stand Up for Gay Rights* (Beacon Press, 1994). Copyright © 1994 by Richard D. Mohr. Reprinted by permission of Beacon Press.

probably find them to be of a crazed or criminal cast. Such false generalizations, though, simply confirm beliefs already held on independent grounds, ones that likely led the investigator to the prison and psychiatric ward to begin with. Evelyn Hooker, who in the late 1950s carried out the first rigorous studies of nonclinical gay men, found that psychiatrists, when presented with case files including all the standard diagnostic psychological profiles—but omitting indications of sexual orientation—were unable to distinguish gay files from non-gay ones, even though they believed gay men to be crazy. These studies proved a profound embarrassment to the psychiatric establishment, which has profited throughout the century by attempting to "cure" allegedly insane gays. The studies led eventually to the decision by the American Psychiatric Association in 1973 to drop homosexuality from its registry of mental illnesses. Nevertheless, the stereotype of gays as "sick" continues to thrive in the mind of America....

* * *

Partly because lots of people suppose they don't know any gay people and partly through the maintaining of stereotypes, society at large is unaware of the many ways in which gays are subject to discrimination in consequence of widespread fear and hatred. Contributing to this social ignorance of discrimination is the difficulty for gay people, as an invisible minority, even to complain of discrimination. If one is gay, the act of registering a complaint suddenly targets oneself as a stigmatized person, and so, especially in the absence of any protection against discrimination, simply invites additional discrimination. So, discrimination against gays, like rape, goes seriously underreported. Even so, known discrimination is massive.

Annual studies by the National Gay and Lesbian Task Force have consistently found that over 90 percent of gay men and lesbians have been victims of violence or harassment in some form on the basis of their sexual orientation. Greater than one in five gay men and nearly one in ten lesbians have been punched, hit, or kicked; a quarter of all gays have had objects thrown at them; a third have been chased; a third have been sexually harassed, and 14 percent have been spit on, all just for being perceived to be gay.

The most extreme form of anti-gay violence is queerbashing—where groups of young men target a person who they suppose is a gay man and beat and kick him unconscious and sometimes to death amid a torrent of taunts and slurs. Few such cases with gay victims reach the courts. Those that do are marked by inequitable procedures and results. Frequently judges will describe queerbashers as "just all-American boys." A District of Columbia judge handed suspended sentences to queerbashers whose victim had been stalked, beaten, stripped at knife point, slashed, kicked, threatened with castration, and pissed on, because the judge thought the bashers were good boys at heart—they went to a religious prep school. In 1989, a judge in Dallas handed a sentence he acknowledged as light to the eighteen-year-old murderer of two gay men because the murderer had killed them in a gay cruising zone, where the judge said they might have been molesting children. The judge thereby justified a form of vigilantism that bears a striking resemblance to the lynching of black men on the grounds that they might molest white women. Indeed, queerbashing has the same function that past lynchings of blacks had—to keep a whole stigmatized group in line. As with lynchings, society has routinely averted its eyes, giving its permission or even tacit approval to violence and harassment.

Police and juries often will simply discount testimony from gays; they frequently construe assaults on and murders of gays as "justified" self-defense. The killer simply claims his act was an understandably panicked response to a sexual overture. Alternatively, when guilt seems patent, juries will accept highly implausible "diminished capacity" defenses, as in the case of Dan White's 1978 assassination of openly gay San Francisco city councilman Harvey Milk. Hostess Twinkies made him do it, or so the successful defense went. These inequitable procedures collectively show that the life and liberty of gays, like those of blacks, simply count for less than the life and liberty of members of the dominant culture.

Gays are also subject to widespread discrimination in employment. Governments are leading offenders here. They do a lot of discriminating themselves, require that others do it, and set precedents favoring discrimination in the private sector. First and foremost, the armed forces discriminate against lesbians and gay men. The federal government has also denied gay men and lesbians employment in the CIA, FBI, and the National Security Agency—and continues to defend such discrimination in the courts. The government refuses to give security clearances to gays and so forces the country's considerable private sector military and aerospace contractors to fire employees known to be gay and to avoid hiring those perceived to be gay. State and local governments regularly fire gay teachers, policemen, firemen, social workers, and

anyone who has contact with the public. Further, state licensing laws (though frequently honored only in the breach) officially bar gays from a vast array of occupations and professions—everything from doctors, lawyers, accountants, and nurses to hairdressers, morticians, even used-car dealers.

Gays are subject to discrimination in a wide variety of other ways, including private-sector employment, public accommodations, housing, insurance of all types, custody, adoption, and zoning regulations that bar "singles" or "nonrelated" couples from living together. A 1988 study by the Congressional Office of Technology Assessment found that a third of America's insurance companies openly admit that they discriminate against lesbians and gay men. In nearly half the states, same-sex sexual behavior is illegal.

Legal sanctions, discrimination, and the absorption by gays of society's hatred all interact to impede and, for some, block altogether the ability of gay men and lesbians to create and maintain significant personal relations with loved ones. Every facet of life is affected by discrimination. Only the most compelling reasons could possibly justify it.

* * *

Many people suppose society's treatment of gays is justified because they think gays are extremely immoral. To evaluate this claim, different senses of "moral" must be distinguished. Sometimes "morality" means the values generally held by members of a society—its mores, norms, and customs. On this understanding, gays certainly are not moral: lots of people hate them, and social customs are designed to register widespread disapproval of gays. The problem here is that this sense of morality is merely a descriptive one. Every society has this kind of morality—even Nazi society, which had racism and mob rule as central features of its "morality" understood in this sense. Before one can use the notion of morality to praise or condemn behavior, what is needed is a sense of morality that is prescriptive or normative.

As the Nazi example makes clear, the fact that a belief or claim is descriptively moral does not entail that it is normatively moral. A lot of people in a society saying that something is good, even over aeons, does not make it so. The rejection of the long history of the socially approved and state-enforced institution of slavery is another good example of this principle at work. Slavery would be wrong even if nearly everyone liked it. So consistency and fairness require that one abandon the belief that gays are immoral simply because most people dislike or disapprove of gays.

Furthermore, recent historical and anthropological research has shown that opinion about gays has been by no means universally negative. It has varied widely even within the larger part of the Christian era and even within the Church itself. There are even current societies—most notably in Papua New Guinea—where compulsory homosexual behavior is integral to the rites of male maturity. Within the last thirty years, American society has undergone a grand turnabout from deeply ingrained, nearly total condemnation to nearly total acceptance on two emotionally charged "moral" or "family" issues—contraception and divorce. Society holds its current descriptive morality of gays not because it has to, but because it chooses to.

Clearly popular opinion and custom are not enough to ground moral condem-

nation of homosexuality. Religious arguments are also frequently used to condemn homosexuality. Such arguments usually proceed along two lines. One claims that the condemnation is a direct revelation of God, usually through the Bible. The other sees condemnation in God's plan as manifested in nature; homosexuality (it is claimed) is "contrary to nature."

One of the more remarkable discoveries of recent gay research is that the Bible may not be as univocal in its condemnation of homosexuality as many have believed. Christ never mentions homosexuality. Recent interpreters of the Old Testament have pointed out that the story of Lot at Sodom is probably intended to condemn inhospitality rather than homosexuality. Further, some of the Old Testament condemnations of homosexuality seem simply to be ways of tarring those of the Israelites' opponents who happen to accept homosexual practices when the Israelites themselves did not. If so, the condemnation is merely a quirk of history and rhetoric rather than a moral precept.

What does seem clear is that those who regularly cite the Bible to condemn an activity like homosexual sex do so by reading it selectively. Do clergy who cite what they take to be condemnations of homosexuality in Leviticus maintain in their lives all the hygienic, dietary, and marital laws of Leviticus? If they cite the story of Lot at Sodom to condemn homosexuality, do they also cite the story of Lot in the Cave to condone incestuous rape? It seems then not that the Bible is being used to ground condemnations of homosexuality as much as society's dislike of homosexuality is being used to interpret the Bible.

Even if a consistent portrait of condemnation could be gleaned from the

Bible, what social significance should it be given? One of the guiding principles of society, enshrined in the Constitution as a check against the government, is that decisions affecting social policy are not made on religious grounds. The Religious Right has been successful in thwarting sodomy law reform, in defunding gay safe-sex literature and gay art, and in blocking the introduction of gay materials into school curriculums. If the real ground of the alleged immorality invoked by governments to discriminate against gays is religious (as it seems to be in these cases), then one of the major commitments of our nation is violated. Religious belief is a fine guide around which a person might organize his own life, but an awful instrument around which to organize someone else's life.

In the second kind of religious argument, people try to justify society's treatment of gays by saying they are unnatural. Though the accusation of unnaturalness looks whimsical, it is usually hurled against homosexuality with venom of forethought. It carries a high emotional charge, usually expressing disgust and evincing queasiness. Probably it is nothing but an emotional charge. For people get equally disgusted and queasy at all sorts of things which are perfectly natural and which could hardly be fit subjects for moral condemnation. Two typical examples in current American culture are some people's responses to mothers breastfeeding in public and to women who do not shave body hair. Similarly people fling the term "unnatural" at gays in the same breath and with the same force as when they call gays "sick" and "gross." When people have strong emotional reactions, as they do in these cases, without being able to give good reasons for them, they can hardly be thought of as operating morally, but more likely as obsessed and manic.

When "nature" is taken in technical rather than ordinary usages, it also cannot ground a charge of homosexual immorality. When unnatural means "by artifice" or "made by humans," it can be pointed out that virtually everything that is good about life is unnatural in this sense. The chief feature that distinguishes people from other animals is people's very ability to make over the world to meet their needs and desires. Indeed people's well-being depends upon these departures from nature. On this understanding of human nature and the natural, homosexuality is perfectly unobjectionable; it is simply a means by which some people adapt nature to fulfill their desires and needs. . . .

But (it might also be asked) aren't gays willfully the way they are? It is widely conceded that if sexual orientation is something over which an individual—for whatever reason—has virtually no control, then discrimination against gays is presumptively wrong, as it is against racial and ethnic classes.

Attempts to answer the question whether or not sexual orientation is something that is reasonably thought to be within one's own control usually appeal simply to various claims of the biological or "mental" sciences. But the ensuing debate over genes, hormones, hypothalamuses, twins, early childhood development, and the like is as unnecessary as it is currently inconclusive. All that is needed to answer the question is to look at the actual experience of lesbians and gay men in current society, and it becomes fairly clear that sexual orientation is not likely a matter of choice.

. . . [I]f people were persecuted, threatened with jail terms, shattered careers, loss of family and housing, and the like for eating, say, Rocky Road ice cream, no one would ever eat it. Everyone would pick another easily available flavor. That gay people abide in being gay even in the face of persecution suggests that being gay is not a matter of easy choice.

... Typically, gays-to-be simply find themselves having homosexual encounters and yet, at least initially, resisting quite strongly the identification of being homosexual. Such a person even very likely resists having such encounters, but ends up having them anyway. Only with time, luck, and great personal effort, but sometimes never, does the person gradually come to accept her or his orientation, to view it as a given material condition of life, coming as all materials do with certain capacities and limitations. The person begins to act in accordance with his or her orientation and its capacities, seeing its actualization as a requisite for an integrated personality and as a central component of personal well-being. As a result, the experience of coming out to oneself has for gays the basic structure of a discovery, not the structure of a choice. And far from signaling immorality, coming out to others affords one of the few remaining opportunities in ever more bureaucratic, technological, and socialistic societies to manifest courage.

How would society at large be changed if gays were socially accepted? Suggestions to change social policy with regard to gays are invariably met with claims that to do so would invite the destruction of civilization itself: after all isn't that what did Rome in? Actually, Rome's decay paralleled not the flourishing of homosexuality but its repression under the later Christianized emperors. Predictions of American civilization's imminent demise have been as premature as they have been frequent. Civilization has shown itself to be rather resilient here, in large part because of the country's traditional commitments to respect for privacy, to individual liberties, and especially to people minding their own business. These all give society an open texture and the flexibility to try out things to see what works. And because of this, one now need not speculate about what changes reforms in gay social policy might bring to society at large. For many reforms have already been tried.

Half the states have decriminalized lesbian and gay male sex acts. Can you guess which of the following states still have sodomy laws: Wisconsin, Minnesota; New Mexico, Arizona; Vermont, New Hampshire; Nebraska, Kansas? One from each pair does and one does not have sodomy laws. And yet one would be hard pressed to point out any substantial social differences between the members of each pair. (If you're interested: the second of each pair still has them.) Empirical studies have shown that there is no increase in other crimes in states that have decriminalized homosexual sex acts.

Neither has the passage of legislation barring discrimination against gays ushered in the end of civilization. Nearly a hundred counties and municipalities, including some of the country's largest cities (like Chicago and New York City), have passed such statutes, as have eight states: Wisconsin, Connecticut, Massachusetts, Hawaii, New Jersey, Vermont, California, and Minnesota. Again, no more brimstone has fallen on these places than elsewhere. Staunchly anti-gay cities, like Miami and Houston, have not been spared the AIDS crisis.

Berkeley, California, followed by a couple dozen other cities including New York, has even passed "domestic partner" legislation giving gay couples at least some of the same rights to city benefits as are held by heterosexually married couples, and yet Berkeley has not become more weird than it already was. A number of major universities (including Harvard, Stanford, and the University of Chicago) and respected corporations (including Levi Strauss and Company, the Montefiore Medical Center of New York, and Apple Computer, Inc.) have also been following Berkeley's lead. Lesbian and gay marriages are legal in Denmark (as of 1989) and in Norway (1993). In May of 1993, Hawaii's Supreme Court ruled that the state's law requiring spouses to be of different genders is a violation of the state's Equal Rights Amendment and can be upheld in further litigation only if the law's discrimination against same-sex couples (implausibly) can be shown to be necessary to a compelling state interest.

Seemingly hysterical predictions that the American family would collapse if such reforms passed have proven false, just as the same dire predictions that the availability of divorce would lessen the ideal and desirability of marriage proved unfounded. Indeed if current discrimination, which drives gays into hiding and into anonymous relations, ended, far from seeing gays destroying American families, one would see gays forming them.

If discrimination ceased, gay men and lesbians would enter the mainstream of the human community openly and with self-respect. The energies that the typical gay person wastes in the anxiety of leading a day-to-day existence of systematic disguise would be released for use in personal flourishing. From this release would be generated the many benefits that accrue to a society when its individual members thrive.

Society would be richer for acknowledging another aspect of human diversity. Families with gay members would develop relations based on truth and trust rather than lies and fear. And the heterosexual majority would be better off for knowing that they are no longer trampling their gay friends and neighbors.

Finally and perhaps paradoxically, in extending to gays the rights and benefits it has reserved for its dominant culture, America would confirm its deeply held vision of itself as a morally progressing nation, a nation itself advancing and serving as a beacon for others—especially with regard to human rights. The words with which our national pledge ends—"with liberty and justice for all"—are not a description of the present, but a call for the future. America is a nation given to a prophetic political rhetoric which acknowledges that morality is not arbitrary and that justice is not merely the expression of the current collective will. It is this vision that led the black civil rights movement to its successes. Those senators and representatives who opposed that movement and its centerpiece, the 1964 Civil Rights Act, on obscurantist grounds, but who lived long enough and were noble enough, came in time to express their heartfelt regret and shame at what they had done. It is to be hoped and someday to be expected that those who now grasp at anything to oppose the extension of that which is best about America to gays will one day feel the same.

NO

Carl F. Horowitz

HOMOSEXUALITY'S LEGAL REVOLUTION

Last April, a brief series of events occurred in a Madison, Wisconsin, restaurant that spoke volumes about the current character of the homosexual rights movement. An employee of the Espresso Royal Cafe asked two women—presumably lesbians—to refrain from passionately kissing as they sat at a window table. Madison's gay community was not amused. The very next day, about 125 homosexual demonstrators showed up on the premises, and conducted a "kiss-in" for several minutes. A spokeswoman for the protesters, Malvene Collins, demanded, "You say gays and lesbians cannot show affection here? Why not here but in every other restaurant in Madison?" The establishment's chastised owner, Donald Hanigan, assured the crowd, "I regret that this incident ever happened. I want all of you to come in here every day."

In October, several dozen homosexual males, many of them dressed in women's clothing, openly hugged and kissed in a terminal of Seattle-Tacoma Airport, and handed out condoms and leaflets to travelers. Matt Nagel, spokesman for the Seattle chapter of . . . [the] homosexual organization, Queer Nation, seemed to sum up the feeling among militants in the local homosexual community. "We're going to homophobic bars, we're going to pack them, we're going to be openly affectionate, we're going to dance together and make it uncomfortable for all the straight people there."

At the same time in Chicago, six homosexual couples staged a "kiss-in" at the cosmetics counter of a Bloomingdale's department store until they were escorted out by security guards. Far from being deterred, the couples shortly went down to the cafeteria of a nearby office building, where they resumed their public display of affection.

A BID FOR LEGITIMACY

After some two decades of confrontation, the homosexual rights movement is consolidating its bid for legitimacy. The phrase, "Out of the closet, and into the streets," sounds quaint. That battle has already been won. Openly

From Carl F. Horowitz, "Homosexuality's Legal Revolution," *The Freeman* (May 1991). Copyright © 1991 by *The Freeman*. Reprinted by permission of *The Freeman*, Foundation for Economic Education, Irvington-on-Hudson, NY. Notes omitted.

homosexual adults are certainly in the streets—and in stores, airports, and "homophobic" bars. Openly gay television characters, each with handsome, well-scrubbed looks, populate daytime and evening drama. Gay-oriented news programming is available on radio and television. Homosexual activists have all but completed their campaign to persuade the nation's educational establishment that homosexuality is normal "alternative" behavior, and thus any adverse reaction to it is akin to a phobia, such as fear of heights, or an ethnic prejudice, such as anti-Semitism.

The movement now stands on the verge of fully realizing its use of law to create a separate homosexual society paralleling that of the larger society in every way, and to intimidate heterosexuals uncomfortable about coming into contact with it. Through aggressive lobbying by such gay organizations as the Human Rights Campaign Fund, the Lambda Legal Defense and Education Fund, and the National Gay and Lesbian Task Force, the first part of that mission has enjoyed enormous success. About 90 counties and municipalities now have ordinances banning discrimination on the basis of gender orientation. There are roughly 50 openly gay public officials, up from less than a half-dozen in 1980.

Gay couples are increasingly receiving the full benefits of marriage, if not through state recognition of homosexual marriage ceremonies, then through enactment of domestic partnership laws. The State of California recently took a big step toward legalization of such marriages: this December [1990] it announced that "non-traditional" families, including homosexual couples, could formally register their unions as "unincorporated non-profit associations." Divorced gay

parents are receiving with increasing frequency the right to custody of natural children. Gay adults without children are increasingly receiving the right to adopt them. Aspiring homosexual clergy are demanding—and receiving—the right to be ordained. Openly gay teachers are teaching in public schools. Homosexual soldiers, aware that their sexual orientation is grounds for expulsion from the military, openly declare their proclivities.

A Federal gay rights bill is the ultimate prize, and homosexual activists are blunt and resolute in pursuing such legislation. For example, Jeff Levi, spokesman for the National Gay and Lesbian Task Force, remarked at a press conference coinciding with the national gay march on Washington in October 1987:

... we are no longer seeking just a right to privacy and a protection from wrong. We also have a right—as heterosexual Americans already have—to see government and society affirm our lives.... until our relationships are recognized in the law —through domestic partner legislation or the definition of beneficiaries, for example—until we are provided with the same financial incentives in tax law and government programs to affirm our family relationships, then we will not have achieved equality in American society.

Yet, homosexual activists know that this legal revolution will never succeed without the unpleasant task of coercing heterosexuals into masking their displeasure with homosexuality. It is thus not enough merely to break down all existing barriers to homosexual affection being expressed through marriage, child-rearing, or employment. The law must additionally be rewritten to make it as difficult as possible for heterosexuals to avoid contact with such displays, or to show discomfort toward them.

This two-edged approach would create a world in which stringent laws at all levels, aggressively enforced and strictly interpreted, force business owners to refuse to discriminate against the openly homosexual in patronage, leasing, and hiring. Removing overtly homosexual patrons from a bar, an airport, or any other public space would result in heavy fines and even jail sentences against property owners or their employees (or in lieu of these sanctions, mandatory purgation). Derogatory remarks directed at homosexuals, even with sexuality only incidental, would likewise result in criminal penalties.

1990: A PIVOTAL YEAR

The year 1990 was pivotal for the homosexual legal revolution. The states of Massachusetts and Wisconsin in the late 1980s had enacted laws forbidding discrimination against homosexuals. The victories would come quickly now, especially at the local level. In March, the City of Pittsburgh voted to include sexual orientation as a right protected under the City Code. In October, Stanford University allowed homosexual couples to qualify for university student housing. In November, voters in San Francisco, buoyed by a heavy turnout of that city's large gay population, produced a "lavender sweep," not only passing Proposition K, a city initiative to allow homosexuals to register as domestic partners at City Hall (a similar measure was defeated in 1989), but electing two openly lesbian candidates to the City Board of Supervisors, and an openly homosexual male candidate to the Board of Education.

Voters in Seattle refused to repeal an existing gender orientation ordinance. Congress did its part early in the year by overwhelmingly passing the Hate Crimes Statistics Act (or Hate Crimes Act), which requires the Justice Department to publish hate crime statistics according to classifications that include sexual orientation....

"GAY CIVIL RIGHTS"

The homosexual lobby speaks of itself as struggling for "civil rights." "The gay community's goal is integration—just as it was with Martin Luther King," argues homosexual activist and San Francisco Board of Supervisors President Harry Britt.[10] Yet, underneath the surface, gay civil rights seems analogous to black "civil rights" *after* Reverend King's death. Far from seeking integration with the heterosexual world, it vehemently avoids it. More important, the movement seeks to win sinecures through the state, and over any objections by "homophobic" opposition. With a cloud of a heavy fine or even a jail sentence hanging over a mortgage lender, a rental agent, or a job interviewer who might be discomforted by them, homosexuals under these laws can win employment, credit, housing, and other economic entitlements. Heterosexuals would have no right to discriminate against homosexuals, but apparently, not vice versa. Libertarians as well as traditionalists ought to be troubled by this.

Consider a recent controversy in Madison, Wisconsin, as noted earlier a national bastion of "enlightened" attitudes. Three single women had recently moved into the same apartment, and one announced that she was a lesbian. The other two, not unreasonably, asked her to move. The lesbian filed a grievance with the local Human Rights Board, and, predictably, won. The shock came in the punishment. The two heterosexual women had to pay

$1,500 in "damages" to the lesbian, send her a public letter of apology, attend a two-hour "briefing" on homosexuality (conducted, needless to say, by homosexuals), and submit to having their living arrangements monitored for two years.

With such laws in effect, this outcome would not be so much played out as simply avoided. Let one hypothetical example suffice, one that no doubt *has* been played out regularly, and that goes a long way in explaining why in any metropolitan area gays tend to cluster in a few neighborhoods.

A man enters an apartment rental office, inquiring about a vacancy. He openly indicates he is a homosexual, or at least implies as much through certain mannerisms. For good measure, he brings along his lover. The rental manager fudges, clears his throat, and says, "Well, er, several people are looking at the apartment. Call me later." An hour later, a second man, alone, walks in. He does not announce his sexuality. Who gets the apartment?

In the absence of gay protectionism, and assuming equal incomes, the manager (sighing with relief) would probably award the apartment to the second applicant. Gay militants would cry, "Discrimination!"—and miss the point. Discrimination based on sexual orientation is fundamentally different from that based on race. Homosexuality constitutes a behavioral, not a genetic trait. It is within the moral right of a landlord, job interviewer, banker, or anyone else performing a "gatekeeper" function to discourage economically risky behavior, sexual or otherwise. Libertarian columnist Doug Bandow articulates this:

> The point is, homosexuals have no right to force others to accept or support their

lifestyle. Certainly government has no business discriminating against them: Anti-sodomy laws, for instance, are a vicious intrusion in the most intimate form of human conduct. And gays who pay taxes have as much right to government services and employment as anyone else.

But someone who decides to live openly as a homosexual should accept the disapproval of those around him. For many Americans still believe that there is a fundamental, unchangeable moral code by which men are to live....

Using government to bludgeon homophobics into submission is even more intolerant than the original discrimination.

Under normal circumstances, the rental manager would not want to lease to gays who, once moved in, might tell their friends that the neighborhood could have possibilities as a "gay" one. Word-of-mouth travels fast within their world. Beyond a certain "tipping-point," many heterosexual residents near and within the complex, rather than risk feeling stigmatized, would choose to move. Their places largely would be taken by overt homosexuals.

In fact this is exactly how neighborhoods such as Castro (San Francisco), West Hollywood (formerly part of Los Angeles, now separately incorporated largely due to gay pressure), the West Village (New York City), and Dupont Circle (Washington, D.C.) all rapidly developed reputations as "gay neighborhoods," and how large sections of Martha's Vineyard, Fire Island, and Rehoboth Beach became "gay resorts." The tipping-point principle also applies to public facilities such as restaurants. At the Grapevine Cafe in Columbus, Ohio, for example, heterosexual customers stopped coming when the clientele became heavily gay.

What would happen with a sexual orientation law in place? The rental manager knows that if he turns down an openly homosexual applicant, he risks prosecution. Any rejection can serve as proof of discriminatory intent, even with factors such as length of employment, income, and previous tenant record taken into account. In response to such a fear, the manager, though reluctantly, is likely to award the apartment to the homosexual.

For gay activists, therein lies the pay-off. By codifying into law "protection" of homosexual mannerisms, they can intimidate gatekeepers into providing job security and housing for the openly homosexual. Thus, without necessarily mentioning anything about quotas or, for that matter, homosexuality, law in the U.S. is increasingly mandating *homosexual affirmative action.* . . .

THE GROWING THREAT OF VIOLENCE

There is something about encountering homosexuality in its militant and pugnacious form that touches a deep, almost reflexive anger, even among most heterosexual liberals. That is why attempts at "mainstreaming" gay culture, even when holding an olive branch, are bound to fail. One of the saddest books to appear in recent years is *After the Ball: How America Will Conquer Its Fear and Hatred of Gays in the 90s.*[29] The authors, Marshall Kirk and Hunter Madsen, both homosexual, advocate a national campaign to cheerfully "sell" gay culture. They suggest, for example, that gay organizations buy up advertising space in "straight" newspapers with pictures of historical figures such as

Alexander the Great, asking: "Did you know he was gay?"

Kirk and Madsen, like their surlier compatriots, fail to grasp that public homosexuality strikes at both a heterosexual's fear of loss of sexual identity and sense of belonging to a family. For even in this age of artificial insemination, families are not sustainable without heterosexuality. No matter how much the homosexual activist naively protests, "Gays are people, too," such a plea will receive in return grudging respect, and little else.

In a summary piece for *Newsweek's* March 12, 1990, cover story, "The Future of Gay America," Jonathan Alter revealed a rare understanding of this dynamic. He notes, "'Acting gay' often involves more than sexual behavior itself. Much of the dislike for homosexuals centers not on who they are or what they do in private, but on so-called affectations —'swishiness' in men, the 'butch' look for women—not directly related to the more private sex act." Quite rightly so—one doubts if more than a tiny fraction of heterosexuals have even *inadvertently* witnessed a homosexual act. Alter then gets to the core of the issue. "Heterosexuals," he writes, "tend to argue that gays can downplay these characteristics and 'pass' more easily in the straight world than blacks can in a white world. . . . This may be true, but it's also irrelevant. For most gays those traits aren't affectations but part of their identities; attacking their swishiness is the same as attacking *them.*"

Yet if gays, through their carefully practiced "gay" mannerisms, know fully well they are antagonizing many heterosexuals, then why do they display them? Is it not in part to make heterosexuals sweat? By aggressively politicizing these traits, and demanding that those objecting must grin and bear it, they are in a sense restricting heterosexual freedom of speech. Male and even female opposition to persons with these traits is slowly taking a nasty turn, moving from violence of language to violence of fists. And yet, given the emerging legal climate, one discovers within oneself a disquieting empathy with the inchoate rage behind such acts.

Most heterosexuals are reasonably libertarian; an October 1989 Gallup Poll indicated that by a 47-to-36 margin (with the remainder undecided), Americans prefer legalization of homosexual relations between consenting adults. This is all to the good. Anti-sodomy laws serve no purpose but to intimidate people out of private, consensual acts. On the other hand, the brazen, *open* display of homosexuality—as if to taunt, to tease, to maliciously sow confusion into sexual identities—is something most heterosexuals do not handle gracefully. With an unofficial government mandate for preferential treatment, it is not difficult to imagine a backlash....

The principal motive of the gay movement is coming into focus with each passing month: to bait heterosexuals' less morally sturdy side, goading them into verbal or (better) physical assaults against the openly homosexual. That way, cries of homosexual victimhood would carry even more self-fulfilling prophecy, so much the better to vilify heterosexuals.

Gay militants aren't hesitant about admitting to such motives. Some want nothing less than war in the streets. Homosexual playwright and ACT-UP founder, Larry Kramer, recently called upon a gay audience to take gun practice for use in eventual combat against police and gay-bashers. "They hate us anyway," he rationalized. A cover of a recent issue of *Outweek* displayed a lesbian pointing a gun at the reader, with the headline, "Taking Aim at Bashers," while another cover announced, "We Hate Straights." ...

The crowning legacy of the new gay legalism may yet be widespread violence, a violence brought on by state inhibition of rational dialogue at the behest of gay radicals, and in the name of "sensitivity." That alone is enough reason to oppose it.

POSTSCRIPT

Should Society Be More Accepting of Homosexuality?

The issue of gay rights raises many issues of social control. Most people would agree that all members of a just society should have equal rights and should not have to endure the harassment and discrimination that Mohr reports gays and lesbians often experience. But how many Americans will fully defend with actions the rights of people with dramatically different lifestyles? This is where people's commitment to democracy and justice meets a real test. Tolerance for alternative lifestyles is increasing in America, but will tolerant citizens take actions against the harassment of homosexuals? On the other hand, the few gays and lesbians who practice a flagrant gay lifestyle can be criticized for offending the values of the community. Shouldn't gays respect community norms? But does full subordination to community norms deny gays the right to maintain a lifestyle that does not harm others? (Harmful lifestyles, whether homosexual or heterosexual, are rightfully condemned.) Finally, the normalization of gay lifestyles requires that it be openly practiced. So the issue is partly a matter of rights and partly a matter of courteous respect for others, whether homosexuals or heterosexuals.

There is a considerable literature on homosexuality. A basic source is Wayne Dynes, ed., *The Encyclopedia of Homosexuality* (Garland Publishing, 1990). Other general works include Michelangelo Signorile, *Queer in America: Sex, the Media, and the Closets of Power* (Random House, 1993) and Didi Herman, *Rights of Passage: Struggles for Lesbian and Gay Equality* (University of Toronto Press, 1994). Randy Shilts, in *Conduct Unbecoming: Gays and Lesbians in the U.S. Military* (St. Martin's Press, 1993), investigates the situation of lesbians and gays in the military over the last three decades. See also Lois Shawver, *And the Flag Was Still There: Straight People, Gay People, and Sexuality in the U.S. Military* (Haworth Press, 1995). Eugene T. Gomulka, in "Why No Gays?" *Proceedings* (December 1992), makes the case for maintaining the ban on gays in the military. Joseph Nicolosi argues that homosexuality can be cured and sexual orientation changed in "Let's Be Straight: A Cure Is Possible," while Carlton Cornett answers him in "Gay Ain't Broke; No Need to Fix It," *Insight on the News* (December 6, 1993). Cornett's view is supported by Andrew Sullivan in *Virtually Normal* (Alfred A. Knopf, 1995). Sullivan also has a reader on the same-sex marriage issue, *Same-Sex Marriage, Pro and Con: A Reader* (Random House, 1997). The best work on human sexual practices is Edward O. Laumann, John H. Gagnon, Robert T. Michael, and Stuart Michaels, *The Social Organization of Sexuality: Sexual Practices in the United States* (University of Chicago Press, 1994).

ISSUE 7

Is the Decline of the Traditional Family a National Crisis?

YES: David Popenoe, from "The American Family Crisis," *National Forum: The Phi Kappa Phi Journal* (Summer 1995)

NO: Stephanie Coontz, from *The Way We Really Are: Coming to Terms With America's Changing Families* (Basic Books, 1997)

ISSUE SUMMARY

YES: Sociologist David Popenoe contends that families play important roles in society but how the traditional family functions in these roles has declined dramatically in the last several decades, with very adverse effects on children.

NO: Family historian Stephanie Coontz argues that current discussion of family decline includes a false idealization of the traditional family of the past and misleading interpretations of current data on families. She finds that the trends are both positive and negative.

The state of the American family deeply concerns many Americans. About 40 percent of marriages end in divorce, and only 27 percent of children born in 1990 are expected to be living with both parents by the time they reach age 17. Most Americans, therefore, are affected personally or are close to people who are affected by structural changes in the family. Few people can avoid being exposed to the issue: violence in the family and celebrity divorces are standard fare for news programs, and magazine articles decrying the breakdown of the family appear frequently. Politicians today try to address the problems of the family. Academics have affirmed that the family crisis has numerous significant negative effects on children, spouses, and the rest of society.

Sociologists pay attention to the role that the family plays in the functioning of society. For a society to survive, its population must reproduce (or take in many immigrants), and its young must be trained to perform adult roles and to have the values and attitudes that will motivate them to contribute to society. Procreation and socialization are two vital roles that families traditionally have performed. In addition, the family provides economic and emotional support for its members, which is vital to their effective functioning in society.

Today the performance of the family is disappointing in all of these areas. Procreation outside of marriage has become common, and it has been found to lead to less than ideal conditions for raising children. The scorecard on American family socialization is hard to assess, but there is concern about such issues as parents' declining time with and influence on their children and latchkey children whose parents work and who must therefore spend part of the day unsupervised. There is a prevalence of poverty among single-parent families as well as a potential for financial difficulties within families that have only one income earner. These indicators suggest that the modern family will fail economically unless each family contains two spouses that both work.

Although most experts agree that the American family is in crisis, there is little agreement about what, if anything, should be done about it. After all, most of these problems result from the choices that people make to try to increase their happiness. People end unhappy marriages. Married women work for fulfillment or financial gain. Unwed mothers decide to keep their children. The number of couples who choose to remain childless is growing rapidly. The high divorce rate and the frequency of child and spouse abuse indicate that the modern family fails to provide adequate social and emotional support.

Individual choices are not the only factors that have contributed to the weakening of the family (economic and legal changes have also played an important role). This trend cannot be changed unless people start choosing differently. As yet there is no sign of this happening. Does this mean that the weakening of the family is desirable? Few would advocate such an idea, but is it a reasonable position if free choice is a leading value? Sociologists recognize that the free choices of individuals do not always produce good results at the aggregate or societal level. For example, people choose to smoke, drink, and take drugs for their pleasure, but the costs in lost production, medical services, and socially harmful behaviors are immense. Is the traditional family undergoing this type of problem?

In the selections that follow, David Popenoe argues that the family is the key institution in society. Since it plays many important roles, its functional decline, which is largely due to cultural trends, has many adverse social impacts, including greatly harming children. He concludes by suggesting what needs to be done to strengthen families and family life. Stephanie Coontz provides a much different assessment of the present state of the family as compared with earlier times. She maintains that the family crisis thesis ignores the many strengths of American families today, overemphasizes certain negative trends, and misinterprets several of them. She tries to set the record straight and to counter much of the misinformation that the media produces.

YES

David Popenoe

THE AMERICAN FAMILY CRISIS

Throughout our nation's history, we have depended heavily on the family to provide both social order and economic success. Families have provided for the survival and development of children, for the emotional and physical health of adults, for the special care of the sick, injured, handicapped, and elderly, and for the reinforcement of society's values. Today, America's families face growing problems in each of these areas, and by many measures are functioning less well than ever before—less well, in fact, than in other advanced, industrialized nations.

The most serious negative effects of the functional decline of families have been on children. Evidence suggests that today's generation of children is the first in our nation's history to be less well-off psychologically and socially than their parents were at the same age. Alarming increases have occurred in such pathologies as juvenile delinquency, violence, suicide, substance abuse, eating disorders, nonmarital births, psychological stress, anxiety, and unipolar depression.

Such increases are especially troubling because many conditions for child well-being have improved. Fewer children are in each family today; therefore, more adults are theoretically available to care for them. Children are in some respects healthier and materially better off; they have completed more years in school, as have their parents. Greater national concern for children's rights, for child abuse, and for psychologically sound childrearing practices is also evident.

FAMILY ORIGINS AND HISTORY

As the first social institution in human history, the family probably arose because of the need for adults to devote a great amount of time to childrearing. Coming into the world totally dependent, human infants must, for a larger portion of their lives than for any other species, be cared for and taught by adults. To a unique degree, humans nurture, protect, and educate their offspring. It is hard to conceive of a successful society, therefore, that does not have families that are able to raise children to become adults who have the capacity to love and to work, who are committed to such positive social values as honesty, respect, and responsibility, and who pass these values on to the next generation.

Infants and children need, at minimum, one adult to care for them. Yet, given the complexities of the task, child-rearing in all societies until recent years has been shared by many adults. The institutional bond of marriage between biological parents, with the essential function of tying the father to the mother and child, is found in virtually every society. Marriage is the most universal social institution known; in no society has non-marital childbirth, or the single parent, been the cultural norm. In all societies the biological father is identified where possible, and in almost all societies he plays an important role in his children's upbringing, even though his primary task is often that of protector and breadwinner.

In the preindustrial era, however, adult family members did not necessarily consider childrearing to be their primary task. As a unit of rural economic production, the family's main focus typically was economic survival. According to some scholars, rather than the family being for the sake of the children, the children, as needed workers, were for the sake of the family. One of the most important family transitions in history was the rise in industrial societies of what we now refer to as the "traditional nuclear family": husband away at work during the day and wife taking care of the home and children full time. This transition took place in the United States beginning in the early 1800s. The primary focus of this historically new family form was indeed the care and nurturing of children, and parents dedicated themselves to this effort.

Over the past thirty years, the United States (along with other modern societies) has witnessed another major family transformation—the beginning of the end of the traditional nuclear family. Three important changes have occurred:

- The divorce rate increased sharply (to a level currently exceeding 50 percent), and parents increasingly decided to forgo marriage, with the consequence that a sizable number of children are being raised in single-parent households, apart from other relatives.
- Married women in large numbers left the role of full-time mother and housewife to go into the labor market, and the activities of their former role have not been fully replaced.
- The focus of many families shifted away from childrearing to the psychological well-being and self-development of their adult members. One indication of this latter focus is that, even when they have young children to raise, parents increasingly break up if their psychological and self-fulfillment needs are unmet in the marriage relationship.

We can never return to the era of the traditional nuclear family, even if we wanted to, and many women and men emphatically do not. The conditions of life that generated that family form have changed. Yet the one thing that has not changed through all the years and all the family transformations is the need for children to be raised by mothers and fathers. Indeed, in modern, complex societies in which children need an enormous amount of education and psychological security to succeed, active and nurturing relationships with adults may be more critical for children than ever.

Unfortunately, the amount of time children spend with adults, especially their parents, has been dropping dramatically. Absent fathers, working mothers, distant grandparents, anonymous schools, and transient communities have become hallmarks of our era. Associated with this trend in many families, and in society as a whole, is a weakening of the fundamental assumption that children are to be loved and valued at the highest level of priority.

THE INDIVIDUALISM TREND

To understand fully what has happened to the family, we must look at the broader cultural changes that have taken place, especially changes in the values and norms that condition everyday choices. Over recent centuries in industrialized and industrializing societies, a gradual shift has occurred from a "collectivist" culture (I am using this term with a cultural and not a political meaning) toward an individualistic culture. In the former, group goals take precedence over individual ones. "Doing one's duty," for example, is more important than "self-fulfillment," and "social bonds" are more important than "personal choice." In individualistic cultures, the welfare of the group is secondary to the importance of such personal goals as self-expression, independence, and competitiveness.

Not surprisingly, individualistic societies rank higher than collectivist societies in political democracy and individual development. But the shift from collectivism to individualism involves social costs as well as personal gains —especially when it proceeds too far. Along with political democracy and individual development, individualistic societies tend to have high rates of individual deviance, juvenile delinquency, crime, loneliness, depression, suicide, and social alienation. In short, these societies have more free and independent citizens but less social order and probably a lower level of psychological well-being.

"Communitarian" Individualism

The United States has long been known as the world's most individualistic society. Certainly, we place a high value on this aspect of our society, and it is a major reason why so many people from other countries want to come here. Yet for most of our history, this individualism has been balanced, or tempered, by a strong belief in the sanctity of accepted social organizations and institutions, such as the family, religion, voluntary associations, local communities, and even the nation as a whole. While individualistic in spirit, people's identities were rooted in these social units, and their lives were directed toward the social goals that they represented. Thus, the United States has been marked for much of its history, not by a pure form of individualism, but by what could be termed a "communitarian" or balanced individualism.

"Expressive" Individualism

As the individualism trend has advanced, however, a more radical or "expressive" individualism has emerged, one that is largely devoted to "self-indulgence" or "self-fulfillment" at the expense of the group. Today, we see a large number of people who are narcissistic or self-oriented, and who show concern for social institutions only when these directly affect their own well-being. Unfortunately, these people have a tendency to distance themselves from the social and community groupings that have long been the basis for personal security and social order. Since the 1950s, the number of people being married, visiting informally with others, and belonging to voluntary associations has decreased, and the number of people living alone has increased.

In turn, the traditional community groupings have been weakened. More people are viewing our once accepted social institutions with considerable skepticism. As measured by public opinion polls, confidence in such public institutions as medicine, higher education, the law, the press, and organized religion has declined dramatically. As measured by people voting with their feet, trust in the institution of marriage also had declined dramatically. And, as we see almost every night on the news, our sense of cultural solidarity seems to be diminishing.

The highly disturbing actions of inner-city residents that we have witnessed in the urban riots of recent years could be considered less a departure from everyday American cultural reality than a gross intensification of it. Few social and cultural trends found in the inner city are not also present in the rest of the nation. Indeed, with respect to the family, the characteristics of the African American family pronounced by President Lyndon Johnson in 1965 to be in a state of "breakdown" are very similar to the family characteristics of America as a whole in 1994!

In summary, for the good of both the individual and society, the individualism trend in the United States has advanced too far. The family holds the key. People need strong families to provide them with the identity, belonging, discipline, and values that are essential for full individual development. The social institutions of the surrounding community depend on strong families to teach those "civic" values—honesty, trust, self-sacrifice, personal responsibility, respect for others—that enable them to thrive. But let us not forget that strong families depend heavily on cultural and social supports. Family life in an unsupportive community is always precarious and the social stresses can be overwhelming.

NOT TO FORGET THE GAINS

While I have presented a fairly grim picture in describing these cultural changes, it is important to add that not every aspect of our society has deteriorated. In several key areas, this nation has seen significant social progress. For instance, we are a much more inclusive society today—segregation and racism have diminished, and we now accept more African Americans, Hispanics, and other minority groups into the mainstream. The legal, sexual, and financial emancipation of women has become a reality as never before in history. With advances in medicine, we have greater longevity and, on the whole, better physical health. And our average material standard of living, especially in the possession of consumer durables, has increased significantly.

THE NUCLEAR FAMILY AND MARRIAGE

Given our nation's past ability to accept positive social change, we can have some confidence in our capacity to solve the problem of family decline. In seeking solutions, we should first consider what family structure is best able to raise children who are autonomous and socially responsible, and also able to meet adult needs for intimacy and personal attachment. Considering the available evidence, as well as the lessons of recent human experience, unquestionably the family structure that works best is the nuclear family. I am not referring to the traditional nuclear family, but rather to the nuclear family that consists of a male and a female who marry and live together and share responsibility for their children and for each other.

Let us look, for a moment, at other family forms. No advanced, Western society exists where the three-generation extended family is very important and where it is not also on the wane. Some scholars suggest that a new extended family has emerged with the trend toward "step" and "blended" families. "Isn't it nice," they say, "that we now have so many new relatives!" The final verdict is not yet in on stepfamilies, but preliminary evidence from the few empirical studies that have been done sends quite the opposite message, and it is a chilling one. For example, a recent British study of 17,000 children born in 1958 concluded that "the chances of stepchildren suffering social deprivation before reaching twenty-one are even greater than those left living after divorce with a lone parent." Similar findings are turning up in the United States.

How are the single-parent families doing? Accumulating evidence on the personal and social consequences of this family type paints an equally grim picture. A 1988 survey by the National Center for Health Statistics found, for example, that children from single-parent families are two to three times more likely to have emotional and behavioral problems than children from intact families, and reduced family income is by no means the only factor involved. In their new book *Growing Up With a Single Parent*, Sara McLanahan and Gary Sandefur, after examining six nationally representative data sets containing over 25,000 children from a variety of racial and social class backgrounds, conclude that "children who grow up with only one of their biological parents are disadvantaged across a broad array of outcomes... they are twice as likely to drop out of high school, 2.5 times as likely to become teen mothers, and 1.4 times as likely to be idle—out of school and out of work—as children who grow up with both parents." The loss of economic resources, they report, accounts for only about 50 percent of the disadvantages associated with single parenthood.

TOWARD SOLUTIONS

Of course, many people have no other choice than to live in step- and single-parent families. These families can be successful, and their members deserve our continuing support. Nevertheless, the benefits that strong nuclear families bring to a high-achieving, individualistic, and democratic society are absolutely clear. For example, a committed marriage, which is the basis of the strong nuclear family, brings enormous benefits to adults. It is ironic in this age of self-fulfillment, when people are being pulled away from marriage, that a happy marriage seems to provide the best source of self-fulfillment. By virtually every measure, married individuals are better off than single individuals.

Another reason for supporting strong nuclear families is that society gains enormously when a high percentage of men are married. While unmarried women take relatively good care of themselves, unmarried men often have difficulty in this regard. In general, every society must be wary of the unattached male, for he is universally the cause of numerous social ills. Healthy societies are heavily dependent on men being attached to a strong moral order, which is centered in families, both to discipline sexual behavior and to reduce competitive aggression. Men need the moral and emotional instruction of women more than vice versa. Family life, especially having children, is for men a civilizing force of no mean proportions.

We should be seriously concerned, therefore, that men currently spend more time living apart from families than at probably any other time in American history. About a quarter of all men aged twenty-five to thirty-four live in nonfamily households, either alone or with an unrelated individual. In 1960, average Americans spent 62 percent of their adult lives with spouse and children, which was the highest in our history; by 1980, they spent 43 percent, the lowest in our history. This trend alone may help to account for the high and rising crime rates over the past three decades. During this period, the number of reported violent crimes per capita, largely committed by unattached males, increased by 355 percent.

Today, a growing portion of American men are highly involved in child care, providing more help with the children than their own fathers did. Yet, because they did not stay with or marry the mothers of their children, or because of divorce, a large number of men have abandoned their children entirely.

Between 1960 and 1990 the percentage of children living apart from their biological fathers more than doubled, from 17 percent to 36 percent. In general, child-rearing women have become increasingly isolated from men. This is one of the main reasons why nothing would benefit the nation more than a national drive to promote strong marriages.

THE NEW FAMILISM: A HOPEFUL TREND

One bright spot in this picture is what some of us have called "the new familism," a growing realization in America that, "yes, the family really is in trouble and needs help." Public opinion polls indicate that nearly two-thirds of Americans believe "family values have gotten weaker in the United States." Both major political parties and our President now seem to be in agreement.

Two primary groups are involved in this cultural mini-shift: the maturing baby boomers, now at the family stage of their life cycle, and the "babyboom echo" children of the divorce revolution. The middle-aged baby boomers, spurred by growing evidence that children have been hurt by recent family changes, have been instrumental in shifting the media in a profamily direction. And many of the echo children of the 1970s, with their troubled childhoods, are coming into adulthood with a resolve not to repeat their parents' mistakes. They tend to put a high premium on marital permanence, perhaps because they have been unable to take the family for granted as many of their parents—the children of the familistic 1950s—did. But one concern is this: will they have the psychological stability to sustain an intimate relationship, or will their insecure childhoods make it impossible for them to fulfill their commitment to a lasting marriage?

Unfortunately, studies of the long-term effects of divorce on children and adolescents provide no optimism in this regard.

A couple of other factors seem to be working in a profamily direction. One is AIDS, which has now noticeably slowed the sexual revolution. As one entertainment figure recently said (with obvious dismay), "dating in Hollywood just isn't what it used to be." Neither, I must add, is dating what it used to be on the college campus, but the changes so far have not been very remarkable. Another factor is that cultural change is often reflected in cycles, and some cycles of change are patterned in generational terms. We know that not all cultural values can be maximized simultaneously. What one generation comes to value because they have less of it, their parents' generation rejected. This factor leads us to believe that the nation as a whole may be primed in the 1990s to run away from the values of radical individualism and more fully embrace the ideals of family and other social bonds.

CONCLUSION

In thinking about how to solve America's family crisis, we should keep the following considerations uppermost in mind:

- As a society, we cannot return to the era of the traditional nuclear family. But, we must do everything possible to strengthen the husband-wife nuclear family that stays together and takes responsibility for its children. Every child both wants—and needs—a mother and a father.
- Fundamental to strengthening the nuclear family is a renewed emphasis on the importance of marriage, which is the social institution designed primarily to hold men to the mother-child unit. It is extremely important for our children, and for our society, that men are attached to childrearing families.
- With even the strongest of marriages, parents have great difficulty raising children in an unsupportive and hostile environment. We must seek to renew the sinews of community life that can support families, maintain social order, and promote the common good. We should give as much attention to recreating a "family culture" as we are now giving to strengthening a "work culture."
- As an overall approach to promoting family life, nothing is more important than trying to diminish and even turn back the trend toward radical individualism. Social bonds, rather than personal choice, and community needs, rather than individual autonomy, must be accorded a higher priority in our culture—and in our lives.

NO

Stephanie Coontz

THE WAY WE REALLY ARE

INTRODUCTION

Five years ago I wrote a book called *The Way We Never Were: American Families and the Nostalgia Trap*. As a family historian bothered by widespread misconceptions in the popular press about "traditional" families, I hoped to get people to look more realistically at the strengths, weaknesses, and surprising variability of family life in the past.

My book went to press just as Dan Quayle issued his famous condemnation of Murphy Brown, the fictional television character who decided to bear her child out of wedlock. The ensuing polemics over whether Murphy Brown was setting a bad example for our nation's youth were followed by an all-out war over family values as the 1992 election approached. Since much of the discussion focused on the contrast between today's families and "the way things used to be," I began to get calls from congressional committees, reporters, and television producers asking me for a historical perspective on these issues. Soon I found myself in the thick of a national debate over what was happening to the American family....

In my last book, I demonstrated the tremendous variety of family types that have worked—and not worked—in American history. When families succeeded, it was often for reasons quite different than stereotypes about the past suggest—because they were flexible in their living arrangements, for example, or could call on people and institutions beyond the family for assistance or support. And when families failed, the results were often devastating. There never was a golden age of family life, a time when all families were capable of meeting the needs of their members and protecting them from poverty, violence, or sexual exploitation.

The "traditional" sexual double standard, for example, may have led more middle-class girls to delay sex at the end of the nineteenth century than today, but it also created higher proportions of young female prostitutes. Respect for elders may have received more lip service in the past, but elders were until very recently the segment of the population most likely to be destitute.

Yet knowing there was no golden age in history does not satisfy most people. Okay, they say, so the past wasn't great, and people have been lamenting the "breakdown of the family" or the "crisis of modern youth" since colonial days. It may be entertaining to know that John Watson, the most famous child psychiatrist of the early twentieth century, predicted in 1928 that marriage would be dead by 1977, and that in 1977, noted sociologist Amitai Etzioni announced that "by mid-1990 not one American family will be left." But even a stopped clock is right twice a day. What if these fears are finally coming true? Am I claiming that the more things change, the more they remain the same? Do I think people are crazy to feel anxious about recent trends in family life?

"Perhaps it's good to have our illusions about the past shattered," people often say, "but once we reject the lies and the myths, what do we put in their place?" Are the only lessons from history negative? Isn't there anything positive families can learn from history and sociology? . . .

Boosting Our Social Intelligence: Putting Family and Personal Trends in Context

Understanding the history of families and the structural constraints under which they operate can prevent our emotional and social IQs from being stunted by what sometimes seems like a national campaign to "dumb us down." Politicians have become experts in squeezing the complexity out of issues to produce compressed, thirteen-second sound bites. Think-tank publicists bombard us with the out-of-context snippets of information sometimes called "factoids." . . .

Care must be taken in interpreting headlines about the explosion of unwed motherhood. Unwed motherhood has increased dramatically since 1970, but it's easy to overstate *how* dramatically, because much illegitimacy was covered up in the past and reporting methods have recently become much more sophisticated. In the past, notes Sam Roberts, many unwed mothers would tell census workers that they were separated, "resulting in the anomaly of many more 'separated' women than men." At least 80 percent of the increase in unwed motherhood reported between 1981 and 1983, explains Steve Rawlings of the Census Bureau, came from "refinements in survey procedures that were introduced early in the 1980s. This represents 10 to 15 percent of the total increase between 1970 and 1993 (or 20 to 25 percent of the increase since 1980)." And though newspapers routinely use unwed motherhood and single parenthood interchangeably, many unwed mothers are part of cohabitating couples. Five states, including California, further distort the statistics by assuming a woman is unmarried if she has a different last name than the father listed on the birth certificate!

It's also important to distinguish between the ratio of unmarried to married births and the rate of births to unmarried women. Between 1960 and 1990, the nonmarital birth ratio increased by more than 500 percent, from 5.3 percent of all births to 28 percent. But birth rates to unmarried women only increased by a factor of 1.73, not quite twofold. What explains the larger figure is that births to unmarried women rose while births to married women fell, increasing the *relative* proportion of unmarried births much more than their *absolute* numbers. In some cases, a fall in marital fertility may be so large that unwed births become a larger proportion of all births even when rates of unwed childbearing are flat or falling. The probability that an unmarried African-American woman would have a child actually fell from 9.8 to 9.0 percent between 1960 and 1990, for example; but because married-couple childbearing decreased among African Americans even more sharply, the proportion of black children born to unwed mothers rose.

I'm not saying that the media intend to mislead. But in many cases, lack of historical perspective makes intelligent, dedicated reporters vulnerable to manipulation by people who wish to magnify one particular set of the factoids that continuously streak across our information horizon. . . .

The result is that many pronouncements about the family, often by the same commentators, have a peculiarly manic-depressive quality. On the one hand, there are the doomsday predictions. New consensus spokesman David Popenoe warns that the decay of family life is "unique and unprecedented" and that the final collapse of "the last vestige of the traditional family unit" is imminent. "Marriage is dying," says Robert Rector of the Heritage Foundation; the next ten years will "decide whether or not marriage and family survive in this nation." Our failure to halt the decay of marriage, says the Council on Families in America, is "nothing less than an act of cultural suicide."

On the other hand, these catastrophic assertions are periodically interspersed with cheerful assurances that things may be turning around. Popenoe sees hopeful signs of a "new familism" in "the nation as a whole." Charles Murray of the American Enterprise Institute thinks we may be moving toward "the restoration of a culture in which family, parenthood, . . . morality, and the virtues are all perceived and valued in ways that our grandparents would find familiar."

Such wild fluctuations in assessments result from a lack of historical context. By contrast, once people understand the complicated *mix* of long-term changes in family trends, social institutions, and cultural mores, they are less likely to think that any one-size-fits-all quick fix can turn everything around, for better or for worse. They're more likely to be realistic about what can and can't be changed, what we need to adjust to and what we may be able to resist.

For example, take the question of whether marriage is a dying institution. In 1867 there were 9.6 marriages per 1,000 people. A hundred years later, in 1967, there were 9.7. The rate reached a low of 7.9 in 1932 and an all-time high of 16.4 in 1946, a peak quickly followed by a brief but huge surge in divorce. Marriage rates fell again from the early 1950s to 1958, rose slowly until the end of the 1960s, and then began to decline again. But the proportion of women who remain single all their lives is *lower* today than at the turn of the century, and fewer women now feel they have to forgo marriage entirely in order to do anything else in their lives. Periodic predictions to the contrary, it is unlikely that we will someday record the demise of the last married couple in America.

Nevertheless, marriage is certainly a *transformed* institution, and it plays a smaller role than ever before in organizing social and personal life. One reason is that marriage comes much later, for most people, than in the past. Men's average age at first marriage today is not unprecedented, though it has now regained the previous record high of

1890. But the average age of marriage for contemporary women is two years higher than its historical peak in 1890 and almost four years higher than in the 1950s. This figure approaches the highest age ever recorded for Western Europe, a region where marriage has always taken place later than almost anywhere else in the world. And although fewer women stay single all their lives than in 1900, a higher proportion of women than ever before experience a period of independent living and employment before marriage. Women's expectations of both marriage and work are unlikely to ever be the same as in the past.

The second reason for marriage's more limited role in people's lives is that it is no longer expected to last "until death do us part." Divorce rates in America rose steadily until World War II, fell briefly during the 1950s, and took off again during the late 1960s. The divorce rate crested near the end of the 1970s, leveled off in the 1980s, and very slightly receded from 1988 to 1993. This last trend was heralded by many commentators as a "real turnaround," a sign that Americans "are turning conservative, pro-family." But while demographers now say that only 40 percent, rather than 50 percent, of marriages will end in divorce, these remain among the highest divorce rates ever recorded. Furthermore, the cumulative effects of past divorces continue to mount. In 1960 there were 35 divorced men and women for every 1,000 married ones. By 1990 there were 140 divorced individuals for every 1,000 married ones.

People often misunderstand what statisticians mean when they estimate that one in every two or three marriages will end in divorce. The calculations refer to the chances of a marriage ending in divorce within 40 years. While rising divorce rates have increased the number of marriages at risk for dissolution, the gradual extension of life spans ensures that a marriage today has the potential to last three times longer than one of 200 years ago. Thus while the number of people who divorce is certainly unprecedented, so is the number of couples who celebrate their fortieth wedding anniversaries. In fact, the chances of doing so have never been better.

On the other hand, the average marriage that ends in divorce lasts only 6.3 years. We may be seeing more marriages that last longer and are more fulfilling than at any time in our history. But we are also seeing more marriages that are *less* committed and of shorter duration than in the past. Sociologist Valerie Oppenheimer suggests we are experiencing growing polarization between increasing numbers of very "high-quality," long-lasting marriages *and* increasing numbers of short-lived, medium- to "low-quality" ones where the partners are not committed enough to stay and work things through. Understanding this polarization helps explain some of the ambivalence Americans have about modern families. Very few people in a modern high-quality marriage would trade it for an older model where limited communication and a high degree of sexual dissatisfaction were taken for granted. And few adults in a very low-quality marriage, or their children, want to be trapped there for life. But the commitments and consequences of "medium-quality" marriages are more ambiguous, especially for kids, and this worries many Americans.

Often their worry takes the form of a debate over whether we should return to the family forms and values of the 1950s. That decade is still close enough that many people derive their political position on the issue from personal experience. At forums I've conducted across the country, some people raised in 1950s families tell of tormented childhoods in alcoholic, abusive, or conflict-ridden families. They cannot understand, they say vehemently, why anyone would regret the passing of the 1950s for a single moment. My research validates their experience. These individuals were not alone.

But other people remember 1950s families that shielded them from adult problems and disputes. Many had unmistakably happy parents. Others had secure childhoods but learned later that one or both of their parents were miserable. Some of these individuals are now sorry that their parents stayed together, but many more say they are glad not to have known about their parents' problems and grateful for whatever kept their families together. They are also thankful that the media did not expose them to many adult realities that today's children see or read about every day. My research validates their experience too.

The only way to get past the polarized personal testimonies for and against 1950s families is to put their strengths and weaknesses into historical perspective. This permits a more balanced assessment of what we have gained and lost since then. It also helps us distinguish historical precedents we may be able to draw on from new issues requiring new responses....

WHY WORKING MOTHERS ARE HERE TO STAY

The 1950s was clearly out of balance in one direction, with almost half the adult population restricted in their access to economic and political roles beyond the family. But the last few decades have been out of balance in the opposite direction. Many of us now feel that our expanding roles beyond the family have restricted our access to family life.

At first glance, it appears that the new imbalance results from women, especially mothers, entering the workforce. Certainly, that trend has produced a dramatic change in relation to the decade that most people use as their measure of "traditional" family life. In 1950, only a quarter of all wives were in the paid labor force, and just 16 percent of all children had mothers who worked outside the home. By 1991, more than 58 percent of all married women, and nearly two-thirds of all married women with children, were in the labor force. Of the total number of children in the country, 59 percent, including a majority of preschoolers, had mothers who worked outside the home.

But to analyze today's family imbalance as a conflict between work and mothering is to misread family history and to misdirect future family policy. Historically, productive work by mothers as well as fathers (and by young people) has not only been compatible with family life but has also strengthened family relationships. What's really out of balance is the relationship between market activities and nonmarket ones (including community as well as family ties). Our jobs don't make room for family obligations. The purchase of goods and services often substitutes for family or neighborhood activities. Phone calls, beepers, faxes and e-mail constantly intrude into family time. To correct this imbalance, we need to reorganize work to make it more compatible with family life. We need to reorganize family life to make sure that all members share in the work needed to sustain it. We need to redirect technology so that it serves rather than dominates our social and interpersonal relationships.

Instead, however, the family consensus brokers encourage us to cobble together personal marital arrangements that combine what they consider to be the best family features from both the 1950s and the 1990s. They reason that if we could convince women to take time off from work while their children are young, bolster male wages enough that more families could afford to make this choice, increase the incentives for marriage, and combat the excesses of individualism that lead to divorce or unwed motherhood, then surely we could solve the conflicts that parents now experience in balancing work and family. While recommending that men should help out more at home and expressing abstract support for equal pay and promotion opportunities for women on the job, the family values think tanks nevertheless propose that parents revive "relatively traditional marital gender roles" for the period "when children are young," cutting back on mothers' paid work.

In the absence of wider social change in work policies and family support systems, this is the individual solution that many men and women try to work out. And it may be a reasonable stopgap measure for parents who can afford it. But when such personal accommodations are put forward as an overarching political program for family life, they cease to sound quite so reasonable. . . .

Women, the argument goes, are happy to care for children, but men's biological drives point them in a different direction. Men have to be coaxed and guided into responsible fatherhood, and societies have historically achieved this by granting husbands special status as moral educators, family authority figures, and breadwinners. When society stops viewing breadwinning "as a father's special task," we lose our most powerful way "to motivate fathers to provide for their children."

The family values crusaders believe that all men and women, at least during their parenting years, should organize their families with the man as primary provider and protector and the wife as primary nurturer. Before and after child rearing, a woman is welcome to work; but unless she has no other option, she should engage in "sequencing"— alternating work and child raising rather than trying to combine them. Popenoe proposes the wife take "at least a year" off work, then work part-time until her children are in their early to mid-teens. Even when both husband and wife are employed, the woman should remain primarily responsible for nurturing, with the man as "junior partner" at home. Husbands should help out more than in the past, but anything that smacks of "androgyny" is to be avoided like the plague. Society, he argues, must "disavow the popular notion of radical feminists that 'daddies can make good mommies.'"

Hostility to women's economic independence is a consistent subtext in "new consensus" writing. "Policies that encourage mothers to work instead of marry" are a large part of America's social problem, says Wade Horn of the National Fatherhood Initiative. Without providing any evidence, Dan Quayle claims studies show "that children whose parents work are *less likely* to have Mommy's undivided attention than children whose mothers stay home." Isn't it odd how quickly a discussion of working *parents* becomes an indictment of *Mommy*? According to this agenda, a male breadwinner—female homemaker division of labor is not an individual family choice but the correct model for every family. Women are told that there are compensations for giving up their aspirations to economic equality: "Even though the man is the head of the family, the woman is the neck, and she turns the head any way she wants." But if women are not willing to "give back" family leadership, groups such as the Promise Keepers advise men to "take it back. . . . Be sensitive. Treat the lady gently and lovingly. But lead!"

While we can debate the *merits* of these proposals for America's families, I am more interested in examining their *practicality*. How likely is it that a majority of mothers will once more withdraw from paid employment during the early years of child rearing? What can historical and sociological analysis teach us about how realistic it is to propose that we revive the breadwinner identity as the basis for men's commitment to marriage and child raising?

The Late Birth and Short Life of the Male Breadwinner Family

One of the most common misconceptions about modern marriage is the notion that coprovider families are a new invention in human history. In fact, today's dual-earner family represents a return to older norms, after a very short interlude that people mistakenly identify as "traditional."

Throughout most of humanity's history women as well as men were family breadwinners. Contrary to cartoons of cavemen dragging home food to a wife waiting at the campfire, in the distant past of early gathering and hunting societies

women contributed as much or more to family subsistence as men. Mothers left the hearth to forage for food, hunt small animals, trade with other groups, or tend crops.

On this continent, neither Native American, African-American, nor white women were originally seen as economic dependents. Among European colonists, men dominated women, but their authority was based on legal, political, and religious coercion, not on men's greater economic importance. The most common words for wives in seventeenth- and eighteenth-century colonial America were "yoke-mates" or "meet-helps," labels that indicated women's economic partnership with men. Until the early nineteenth century, men and women worked together on farms or in small household businesses, alongside other family members. Responsibility for family life and responsibility for breadwinning were not two different, specialized jobs.

But in the early 1800s, as capitalist production for the market replaced home-based production for local exchange and a wage-labor system supplanted widespread self-employment and farming, more and more work was conducted in centralized workplaces removed from the farm or home. A new division of labor then grew up within many families. Men (and older children) began to specialize in work outside the home, withdrawing from their traditional child-raising responsibilities. Household work and child care were delegated to wives, who gave up their older roles in production and barter. While slaves and free blacks continued to have high labor force participation by women, wives in most other ethnic and racial groups were increasingly likely to quit paid work outside the home after marriage.

But it's important to remember that this new division of work between husbands and wives came out of a *temporary* stage in the history of wage labor and industrialization. It corresponded to a transitional period when households could no longer get by primarily on things they made, grew, or bartered, but could not yet rely on purchased consumer goods. For example, families no longer produced their own homespun cotton, but ready-made clothing was not yet available at prices most families could afford. Women still had to sew clothes from cloth that men purchased with their pay. Most families still had to grow part of their food and bake their own bread. Food preparation and laundering required hours of work each day. Water often had to be hauled and heated.

Somebody had to go out to earn money in order to buy the things the family needed; but somebody else had to stay home and turn the things they bought into things they could actually use. Given the preexisting legal, political, and religious tradition of patriarchal dominance, husbands (and youths of both sexes) were assigned to work outside the home. Wives assumed exclusive responsibility for domestic matters that they had formerly shared with husbands or delegated to older children and apprentices. Many women supplemented their household labor with income-generating work that could be done at or around home—taking in boarders, doing extra sewing or laundering, keeping a few animals, or selling garden products. But this often arduous work was increasingly seen as secondary to wives' primary role of keeping house, raising the children, and getting dinner on the table.

The resulting identification of masculinity with economic activities and femininity with nurturing care, now often seen as the "natural" way of organizing the nuclear family, was in fact a historical product of this nineteenth-century transition from an agricultural household economy to an industrial wage economy. So even as an ideal, the male breadwinner family was a comparatively late arrival onto the historical scene. As a reality—a family form in which most people actually lived—it came about even later....

The Revival of Women's Role as Family Coprovider

... For approximately 50 years, from the 1920s through the 1960s, the growth in married women's work outside the home was smaller than the decline in child labor, so that the male breadwinner family became increasingly dominant. But even at its high point in the 1950s, less than 60 percent of American children spent their youth in an Ozzie and Harriet-type family where dad went to work and mom stayed home. And by the 1970s the fifty-year reign of this family form was definitely over....

After 1973, real wages for young men began falling, creating a larger proportion of families where the mother worked just to keep the family afloat. Housing inflation meant that families with young children were especially likely to need the wife to work, in order to afford the new home that their growing family motivated them to buy. By 1989, almost 80 percent of all home buyers came from two-income households. Another incentive was the rising cost of higher education, which increased nearly three times faster than household income between 1980 and 1994.

Today most families can no longer think of the earnings that wives and mothers bring home as a bonus that can be put aside when family needs call. Nor, increasingly, do the jobs women hold allow them the luxury of choosing to cut back or quit when family priorities change, any more than their husbands' jobs would. By 1993, married women working full-time contributed 41 percent of their families' incomes. Indeed, in 23 percent of two-earner couples, the wives earned *more* than their husbands.

The sequencing of mothering and paid employment that characterized many women's activities over the past 100 years is becoming a thing of the past. Through most of this century, even though labor participation rates for women rose steadily, they dropped significantly when women were in their twenties and thirties. By 1990, however, labor-force participation rates no longer dipped for women in their child-raising years. Today, fewer and fewer women leave their jobs while their children are very young.

Proponents of the modified male breadwinner family believe that if we could drastically reduce the number of single-mother households, raise wages for men, and convince families to get by on a little less, we might be able to get wives to quit work during their child-raising years. Polls consistently show that many women would like to cut back on work hours, though not quit entirely (and it's interesting that an almost equal number of men would also like to cut back their hours). But a return to the norm of male breadwinner families is simply not feasible for most Americans.

Why Wives and Mothers Will Continue to Work Outside the Home

It's not just a dollars-and-cents issue. Most women would not give up the satisfactions of their jobs even if they could afford to quit. They consistently tell interviewers they like the social respect, self-esteem, and friendship networks they gain from the job, despite the stress they may face finding acceptable child care and negotiating household chores with their husbands. In a 1995 survey by Louis Harris & Associates, for example, less than a third of working women said they would prefer to stay home even if money were no object.

Another reason women do not want to quit work is that they are not willing to surrender the increased leverage it gives them in the family. The simple truth is that women who do not earn income have much less decision-making power in marital relations than women who do. And no amount of goodwill on the part of husbands seems to lessen this imbalance. In one in-depth study of American families, researchers found that the primary determinant of power in all couples was who brings in the money. The only exception was among lesbians. Lesbian couples might be persuaded to have one partner stay home with the kids and the other earn the money, but I doubt that the Institute for American Values would consider this a positive step in the direction of "marital role complementarity."

Aside from women's own motivations to remain at work, the issue of whether a family can afford to have the wife stay home is quite debatable. One of the most longstanding American traditions, much older than the ideal of the male breadwinner, is the search for socioeconomic mobility. That's why many families came to America in the first place. It's what people were seeking when they crossed the plains in covered wagons, why farmers switched from diversified family crops to specialized market production, what parents have expected education to provide for their children.

From the mid-nineteenth to the mid-twentieth century, there were three main routes to family economic advancement. One was child labor, allowing parents to accumulate enough to buy a house and possibly send a later generation to school. Another was the move from farm to city, to take advantage of higher wage rates in urban areas. The third was investment in increased training and education for male members of the family.

But child labor was abolished in the early twentieth century, and even before 1950 most men had already obtained nonfarm jobs. By the mid-1960s there were diminishing returns to the gains families could expect from further education or training for men.

As these older strategies ceased to guarantee continued mobility, women's employment became so central to family economic advancement that it could less and less often be postponed or interrupted for full-time child raising.

In other words, even for families where the uninterrupted work of wives isn't essential for minimum family subsistence, it is now the main route to even a modest amount of upward mobility. Those who tell women who "don't need to work" that they should go back to full-time child rearing are contradicting many of the other ideals most Americans hold dear. We're talking about abandoning the American dream here. The only way to get a significant number of families to make this choice would be to foster a thoroughly untraditional —some might even say un-American— acceptance of a stationary standard of living, a no-growth family economy. Some families may harbor such subversive ideals; yet the chances are slim that this will become a mass movement any time soon.

POSTSCRIPT

Is the Decline of the Traditional Family a National Crisis?

Popenoe admits that there are many positive aspects to the recent changes that have affected families, but he sees the negative consequences, especially for children, as necessitating actions to counter them. He recommends a return to family values and speaks out against the individualistic ethos. Coontz contends that the traditional family form that people like Popenoe are nostalgic for was atypical in American history and cannot be re-created. Furthermore, a closer look at the data indicates that the institution of the family is not in crisis. While admitting that many marriages fail, Coontz asserts that many families are strong.

Support for Coontz's point of view can be found in E. L. Kain, *The Myth of Family Decline* (D. C. Heath, 1990); J. F. Gubrium and J. A. Holstein, *What Is a Family?* (Mayfield, 1990); and Rosalind C. Barnett and Caryl Rivers, *She Works/He Works: How Two-Income Families Are Happier, Healthier, and Better Off* (HarperCollins, 1997). Recent works describing the weakening of the family and marriage include Richard T. Gill, *Posterity Lost: Progress, Ideology, and the Decline of the American Family* (Rowman & Littlefield, 1997); Dana Mack, *The Assault on Parenthood: How Our Culture Undermines the Family* (Simon & Schuster, 1997); Maggie Gallagher, *The Abolition of Marriage: How We Destroy Lasting Love* (Regnery, 1996); and Barbara Dafoe Whitehead, *The Divorce Culture: How Divorce Became an Entitlement and How It Is Blighting the Lives of Our Children* (Alfred A. Knopf, 1997). David Popenoe and Jean Bethke Elshtain's book *Promises to Keep: Decline and Renewal of Marriage in America* (Rowman & Littlefield, 1996) discusses the decline but also signs of renewal of marriage. Arlene Skolnick argues that not only is the family changing but it is also in a crisis in *Embattled Paradise: The American Family in an Age of Uncertainty* (Basic Books, 1991). In contrast to the family crisis view, Andrew M. Greeley presents a positive portrait of the family in *Faithful Attraction* (Tor Books, 1991). Change is emphasized in Andrew Cherlin's two books *Marriage, Divorce, Remarriage,* rev. ed. (Harvard University Press, 1992) and *The Changing American Family and Public Policy* (Urban Institute Press, 1988). For major works on aspects of familial changes see David Blankenhorn, *Fatherless America: Confronting Our Most Urgent Social Problem* (Basic Books, 1995); Martha Albertson Fineman, *The Neutered Mother, the Sexual Family and Other Twentieth Century Tragedies* (Routledge, 1995); Ailsa Burns and Cath Scott, *Mother-Headed Families and Why They Have Increased* (Lawrence Erlbaum, 1994); and Sara McLanahan and Gary Sandefur, *Growing Up With a Single Parent: What Hurts and What Helps* (Harvard University Press, 1994).

On the Internet . . .

http://www.dushkin.com

Poverty in America Research Index

This page offers definitions and tables related to poverty and poverty areas in the United States. The site provides facts about poverty and discussions of poverty myths versus realities. Welfare reform is also addressed.
http://www.mindspring.com/~nexweb21/povindex.htm

The Urban Institute

This organization offers lengthy discussions of issues related to welfare and its reform. This page starts with the assertion, "No one likes the current welfare system."
http://www.urban.org/welfare/overview.htm

Yahoo! Full Coverage: Affirmative Action

This links you to the Yahoo! search engine for the topic of affirmative action.
http://gnn.yahoo.com/society_and_culture/affirmative_action/

PART 3

Stratification and Inequality

Although the ideal of equal opportunity for all is strong in the United States, many charge that the American political and economic system is unfair. Various affirmative action programs have been implemented to remedy unequal opportunities, but some argue that this is discrimination in reverse. Others argue that minorities should depend on themselves, not the government, to overcome differences in equality. Does poverty continue to exist in the United States despite public assistance programs because it has become a deeply ingrained way of life for individuals? Or is poverty a result of the failure of policymakers to live up to U.S. egalitarian principles? Social scientists debate these questions in this part.

■ Is Increasing Economic Inequality a Serious Problem?

■ Are the Poor Largely Responsible for Their Poverty?

■ Has Affirmative Action Outlived Its Usefulness?

ISSUE 8

Is Increasing Economic Inequality a Serious Problem?

YES: Paul Krugman, from "The Spiral of Inequality," *Mother Jones* (November/December 1996)

NO: Christopher C. DeMuth, from "The New Wealth of Nations," *Commentary* (October 1997)

ISSUE SUMMARY

YES: Economist Paul Krugman demonstrates the dramatic increase in income inequality by comparing data on income shares for 1970 and 1994. He assesses some of the potential nightmarish impacts of increasing inequality, including societal disintegration.

NO: Christopher C. DeMuth, president of the American Enterprise Institute for Public Policy Research, argues that the "recent increase in income inequality... is a very small tick in the massive and unprecedented leveling of material circumstances that has been proceeding now for almost three centuries and in this century has accelerated dramatically."

The cover of the January 29, 1996, issue of *Time* magazine bears a picture of 1996 Republican presidential candidate Steve Forbes and large letters reading: "DOES A FLAT TAX MAKE SENSE?" During his campaign Forbes expressed his willingness to spend $25 million of his own wealth in pursuit of the presidency, with the major focus of his presidential campaign being a flat tax, which would reduce taxes substantially for the rich. It seems reasonable to say that if the rich pay less in taxes, others would have to pay more. Is it acceptable for the tax burden to be shifted away from the rich in America? Forbes believed that the flat tax would benefit the poor as well as the rich. He theorized that the economy would surge ahead because investors would shift their money from relatively nonproductive, but tax-exempt, investments to productive investments. This is an example of the trickle-down theory, which claims that helping the rich stimulates the economy, which helps the poor. In fact, the trickle-down theory is the major rationalization for the view that great economic inequality benefits all of society.

Inequality is not a simple subject. For example, America is commonly viewed as having more social equality than the more hierarchical societies of Europe and Japan, but America has more income inequality than almost all other industrial societies. This apparent contradiction is explained when one recognizes that American equality is not in income but in the opportunity to obtain higher incomes. The issue of economic inequality is further complicated by other categories of equality/inequality, which include political power, social status, and legal rights.

Americans believe that everyone should have an equal opportunity to compete for jobs and awards. This belief is backed up by free public school education, which provides poor children with a ladder to success, and by laws that forbid discrimination. Americans, however, do not agree on many specific issues regarding opportunities or rights. For example, should society compensate for handicaps such as disadvantaged family backgrounds or the legacy of past discrimination? This issue has divided the country. Americans do not agree on programs such as income-based scholarships, quotas, affirmative action, or the Head Start compensatory education program for poor preschoolers. In the abstract, everyone supports equality of legal rights, but it is often violated in practice.

America's commitment to political equality is strong in principle, though less strong in practice. Everyone over 18 years old gets one vote, and all votes are counted equally. However, the political system tilts in the direction of special interest groups; those who do not belong to such groups are seldom heard. Furthermore, as in the case of Forbes, money plays an increasingly important role in political campaigns.

The final dimension of equality/inequality is status. Inequality of status involves differences in prestige, and it cannot be eliminated by legislation. Ideally, the people who contribute the most to society are the most highly esteemed. To what extent does this principle hold true in the United States?

The Declaration of Independence proclaims that "all men are created equal," and the Founding Fathers who wrote the Declaration of Independence went on to base the laws of the land on the principle of equality. The equality they were referring to was equality of opportunity and legal and political rights for white, property-owning males. They did not mean equality of income or status, though they recognized that too much inequality of income would jeopardize democratic institutions. In the two centuries following the signing of the Declaration, nonwhites and women struggled for and won considerable equality of opportunity and rights. Meanwhile, income gaps in the United States have been widening (except from 1929 to 1945, when the stock market crash harmed the wealthy and wartime full employment favored the poor).

In the readings that follow, Paul Krugman argues that inequality in America has increased so much since 1970 that most people no longer "live more or less the same kind of life." He maintains that politics and power explain much of the income polarization that threatens the unity of American society. Christopher C. DeMuth admits that incomes have become more unequally distributed, but he argues that consumption, a better indicator of living conditions, has become much more equally distributed.

YES

Paul Krugman

THE SPIRAL OF INEQUALITY

Ever since the election of Ronald Reagan, right-wing radicals have insisted that they started a revolution in America. They are half right. If by a revolution we mean a change in politics, economics, and society that is so large as to transform the character of the nation, then there is indeed a revolution in progress. The radical right did not make this revolution, although it has done its best to help it along. If anything, we might say that the revolution created the new right. But whatever the cause, it has become urgent that we appreciate the depth and significance of this new American revolution—and try to stop it before it becomes irreversible.

The consequences of the revolution are obvious in cities across the nation. Since I know the area well, let me take you on a walk down University Avenue in Palo Alto, California.

Palo Alto is the de facto village green of Silicon Valley, a tree-lined refuge from the valley's freeways and shopping malls. People want to live here despite the cost—rumor has it that a modest three-bedroom house sold recently for $1.6 million—and walking along University you can see why. Attractive, casually dressed people stroll past trendy boutiques and restaurants; you can see a cooking class in progress at the fancy new kitchenware store. It's a cheerful scene, even if you have to detour around the people sleeping in doorways and have to avoid eye contact with the beggars. (The town council plans to crack down on street people, so they probably won't be here next year, anyway.)

If you tire of the shopping district and want to wander further afield, you might continue down University Avenue, past the houses with their well-tended lawns and flower beds—usually there are a couple of pickup trucks full of Hispanic gardeners in sight. But don't wander too far. When University crosses Highway 101, it enters the grim environs of East Palo Alto. Though it has progressed in the past few years, as recently as 1992 East Palo Alto was the murder capital of the nation and had an unemployment rate hovering around 40 percent. Luckily, near the boundary, where there is a cluster of liquor stores and check-cashing outlets, you can find two or three police

From Paul Krugman, "The Spiral of Inequality," *Mother Jones* (November/December 1996). Copyright © 1996 by The Foundation for National Progress. Reprinted by permission of *Mother Jones*. Notes omitted.

cruisers keeping an eye on the scene— and, not incidentally, serving as a thin blue line protecting the nice neighborhood behind them. . . .

What few people realize is that this vast gap between the affluent few and the bulk of ordinary Americans is a relatively new fixture on our social landscape. People believe these scenes are nothing new, even that it is utopian to imagine it could be otherwise.

But it has not always been thus—at least not to the same extent. I didn't see Palo Alto in 1970, but longtime residents report that it was a mixed town in which not only executives and speculators but schoolteachers, mailmen, and sheet-metal workers could afford to live. At the time, I lived on Long Island, not far from the old *Great Gatsby* area on the North Shore. Few of the great mansions were still private homes then (who could afford the servants?); they had been converted into junior colleges and nursing homes, or deeded to the state as historic monuments. Like Palo Alto, the towns contained a mix of occupations and education levels—no surprise, given that skilled blue-collar workers often made as much as, or more than, white-collar middle managers.

Now, of course, Gatsby is back. New mansions, grander than the old, are rising by the score; keeping servants, it seems, is no longer a problem. A couple of years ago I had dinner with a group of New York investment bankers. After the business was concluded, the talk turned to their weekend homes in the Hamptons. Naively, I asked whether that wasn't a long drive; after a moment of confused silence, the answer came back: "But the helicopter only takes half an hour."

You can confirm what your eyes see, in Palo Alto or in any American community, with dozens of statistics. The most straightforward are those on income shares supplied by the Bureau of the Census, whose statistics are among the most rigorously apolitical. In 1970, according to the bureau, the bottom 20 percent of U.S. families received only 5.4 percent of the income, while the top 5 percent received 15.6 percent. By 1994, the bottom fifth had only 4.2 percent, while the top 5 percent had increased its share to 20.1 percent. That means that in 1994, the average income among the top 5 percent of families was more than 19 times that of the bottom 20 percent of families. In 1970, it had been only about 11.5 times as much. (Incidentally, while the change in distribution is most visible at the top and bottom, families in the middle have also lost: The income share of the middle 20 percent of families has fallen from 17.6 to 15.7 percent.) These are not abstract numbers. They are the statistical signature of a seismic shift in the character of our society.

The American notion of what constitutes the middle class has always been a bit strange, because both people who are quite poor and those who are objectively way up the scale tend to think of themselves as being in the middle. But if calling America a middle-class nation means anything, it means that we are a society in which most people live more or less the same kind of life.

In 1970 we were that kind of society. Today we are not, and we become less like one with each passing year. As politicians compete over who really stands for middle-class values, what the public should be asking them is, *What* middle class? How can we have common "middle-class" values if whole segments of society live in vastly different economic universes?

If this election was really about what the candidates claim, it would be devoted to two questions: Why has America ceased to be a middle-class nation? And, more important, what can be done to make it a middle-class nation again?

THE SOURCES OF INEQUALITY

Most economists who study wages and income in the United States agree about the radical increase in inequality—only the hired guns of the right still try to claim it is a statistical illusion. But not all agree about why it has happened.

Imports from low-wage countries—a popular villain—are part of the story, but only a fraction of it. The numbers just aren't big enough. We invest billions in low-wage countries—but we invest trillions at home. What we spend on manufactured goods from the Third World represents just 2 percent of our income. Even if we shut out imports from low-wage countries (cutting off the only source of hope for the people who work in those factories), most estimates suggest it would raise the wages of low-skill workers here by only 1 or 2 percent.

Information technology is a more plausible villain. Technological advance doesn't always favor elite workers, but since 1970 there has been clear evidence of a general "skill bias" toward technological change. Companies began to replace low-skill workers with smaller numbers of high-skills ones, and they continue to do so even though low-skill workers have gotten cheaper and high-skill workers more expensive.

These forces, while easily measurable, don't fully explain the disparity between the haves and the have-nots. Globalization and technology may explain why a college degree makes more differ-

ence now than it did 20 years ago. But schoolteachers and corporate CEOs typically have about the same amount of formal education. Why, then, have teachers' salaries remained flat while those of CEOs have increased fivefold? The impact of technology and of foreign trade do not answer why it is harder today for most people to make a living but easier for a few to make a killing. Something else is going on.

VALUES, POWER, AND WAGES

In 1970 the CEO of a typical Fortune 500 corporation earned about 35 times as much as the average manufacturing employee. It would have been unthinkable to pay him 150 times the average, as is now common, and downright outrageous to do so while announcing mass layoffs and cutting the real earnings of many of the company's workers, especially those who were paid the least to start with. So how did the unthinkable become first thinkable, then doable, and finally—if we believe the CEOs—unavoidable?

The answer is that values changed—not the middle-class values politicians keep talking about, but the kind of values that helped to sustain the middle-class society we have lost.

Twenty-five years ago, prosperous companies could have paid their janitors minimum wage and still could have found people to do the work. They didn't, because it would have been bad for company morale. Then, as now, CEOs were in a position to arrange for very high salaries for themselves, whatever their performance, but corporate boards restrained such excesses, knowing that too great a disparity between the top man and the ordinary worker would cause problems. In short, though America was a society with large disparities between economic classes, it had an egalitarian ethic that limited those disparities. That ethic is gone.

One reason for the change is a sort of herd behavior: When most companies hesitated to pay huge salaries at the top and minimum wage at the bottom, any company that did so would have stood out as an example of greed; when everyone does it, the stigma disappears.

There is also the matter of power. In 1970 a company that appeared too greedy risked real trouble with other powerful forces in society. It would have had problems with its union if it had one, or faced the threat of union organizers if it didn't. And its actions would have created difficulties with the government in a way that is now unthinkable. (Can anyone imagine a current president confronting a major industry over price increases, the way John F. Kennedy did the steel industry?)

Those restraining forces have largely disappeared. The union movement is a shadow of its former self, lucky to hold its ground in a defensive battle now and then. The idea that a company would be punished by the government for paying its CEO too much and its workers too little is laughable today: since the election of Ronald Reagan the CEO would more likely be invited to a White House dinner.

In brief, much of the polarization of American society can be explained in terms of power and politics. But why has the tide run so strongly in favor of the rich that it continues regardless of who is in the White House and who controls the Congress?

THE DECLINE OF LABOR

The decline of the labor movement in the United States is both a major cause of growing inequality and an illustration of the larger process under way in our society. Unions now represent less than 12 percent of the private workforce, and their power has declined dramatically. In 1970 some 2.5 million workers participated in some form of labor stoppage; in 1993, fewer than 200,000 did. Because unions are rarely able or willing to strike, being a union member no longer carries much of a payoff in higher wages.

There are a number of reasons for the decline of organized labor: the shift from manufacturing to services and from blue-collar to white-collar work, growing international competition, and deregulation. But these factors can't explain the extent or the suddenness of labor's decline.

The best explanation seems to be that the union movement fell below critical mass. Unions are good for unions: In a nation with a powerful labor movement, workers have a sense of solidarity, one union can support another during a strike, and politicians take union interests seriously. America's union movement just got too small, and it imploded.

We should not idealize the unions. When they played a powerful role in America, they often did so to bad effect. Occasionally they were corrupt, often they extracted higher wages at the consumer's expense, sometimes they opposed new technologies and enforced inefficient practices. But unions helped keep us a middle-class society—not only because they forced greater equality within companies, but because they provided a counterweight to the power of wealthy individuals and corporations. The loss of that counterweight is clearly bad for society.

The point is that a major force that kept America a more or less unified society went into a tailspin. Our whole society is now well into a similar downward spiral, in which growing inequality creates the political and economic conditions that lead to even more inequality.

THE POLARIZING SPIRAL

Textbook political science predicts that in a two-party democracy like the United States, the parties will compete to serve the interests of the median voter—the voter in the middle, richer than half the voters but poorer than the other half. And since ordinary workers are more likely to lose their jobs than strike it rich, the interests of the median voter should include protecting the poor. You might expect, then, the public to demand that government work against the growing divide by taxing the rich more heavily and by increasing benefits for lower-paid workers and the unemployed.

In fact, we have done just the opposite. Tax rates on the wealthy—even with Clinton's modest increase of 1993—are far lower now than in the 1960s. We have allowed public schools and other services that are crucial for middle-income families to deteriorate. Despite the recent increase, the minimum wage has fallen steadily compared with both average wages and the cost of living. And programs for the poor have been savaged: Even before the recent bipartisan gutting of welfare, AFDC payments for a typical family had fallen by a third in real terms since the 1960s.

The reason why government policy has reinforced rather than opposed this growing inequality is obvious: Well-off people have disproportionate political weight. They are more likely to vote—the median voter has a much higher income than the median family—and far more likely to provide the campaign contributions that are so essential in a TV age.

The political center of gravity in this country is therefore not at the median family, with its annual income of $40,000, but way up the scale. With decreasing voter participation and with the decline both of unions and of traditional political machines, the focus of political attention is further up the income ladder than it has been for generations. So never mind what politicians say; political parties are competing to serve the interests of families near the 90th percentile or higher, families that mostly earn $100,000 or more per year.

Because the poles of our society have become so much more unequal, the interests of this political elite diverge increasingly from those of the typical family. A family at the 95th percentile pays a lot more in taxes than a family at the 50th, but it does not receive a correspondingly higher benefit from public services, such as education. The greater the income gap, the greater the disparity in interests. This translates, because of the clout of the elite, into a constant pressure for lower taxes and reduced public services. . . .

If public schools and other services are left to deteriorate, so will the skills and prospects of those who depend on them, reinforcing the growing inequality of incomes and creating an even greater disparity between the interests of the elite and those of the majority.

Does this sound like America in the '90s? Of course it does. And it doesn't take much imagination to envision what our

society will be like if this process continues for another 15 or 20 years. We know
all about it from TV, movies, and best-
selling novels. While politicians speak
of recapturing the virtues of small-town
America (which never really existed), the
public—extrapolating from the trends it
already sees—imagines a *Blade Runner*-
style dystopia, in which a few people live
in luxury while the majority grovel in
Third World living standards.

STRATEGIES FOR THE FUTURE

There is no purely economic reason
why we cannot reduce inequality in
America. If we were willing to spend
even a few percent of national income
on an enlarged version of the Earned
Income Tax Credit, which supplements
the earnings of low-wage workers, we
could make a dramatic impact on both
incomes and job opportunities for the
poor and near-poor—bringing a greater
number of Americans into the middle
class. Nor is the money for such policies
lacking: America is by far the least
heavily taxed of Western nations and
could easily find the resources to pay for
a major expansion of programs aimed at
limiting inequality.

But of course neither party advanced
such proposals during the electoral campaign. The Democrats sounded like Republicans, knowing that in a society
with few counterweights to the power
of money, any program that even hints at
redistribution is political poison. It's no
surprise that Bill Clinton's repudiation of
his own tax increase took place in front
of an audience of wealthy campaign contributors. In this political environment,
what politician would talk of taxing the
well-off to help the low-wage worker?

And so, while the agenda of the GOP
would surely accelerate the polarizing
trend, even Democratic programs now
amount only to a delaying action. To
get back to the kind of society we had,
we need to rebuild the institutions and
values that made a middle-class nation
possible. . . .

In particular, we also need to apply
strategic thinking to the union movement. Union leaders and liberal intellectuals often don't like each other very
much, and union victories are often of
dubious value to the economy. Nonetheless, if you are worried about the cycle of polarization in this country, you
should support policies that make unions
stronger, and vociferously oppose those
that weaken them. There are some stir-
rings of life in the union movement—a
new, younger leadership with its roots
in the service sector has replaced the
manufacturing-based old guard, and has
won a few political victories. They must
be supported, almost regardless of the
merits of their particular case. Unions are
one of the few *political* counterweights to
the power of wealth.

Of course, even to talk about such
things causes the right to accuse us of
fomenting "class warfare." They want
us to believe we are all members of
a broad, more or less homogeneous,
middle class. But the notion of a middle-
class nation was always a stretch. Unless
we are prepared to fight the trend toward
inequality, it will become a grim joke.

NO

Christopher C. DeMuth

THE NEW WEALTH OF NATIONS

The Nations of North America, Western Europe, Australia, and Japan are wealthier today than they have ever been, wealthier than any others on the planet, wealthier by far than any societies in human history. Yet their governments appear to be impoverished—saddled with large accumulated debts and facing annual deficits that will grow explosively over the coming decades. As a result, government spending programs, especially the big social-insurance programs like Social Security and Medicare in the United States, are facing drastic cuts in order to avert looming insolvency (and, in France and some other European nations, in order to meet the Maastricht treaty's criteria of fiscal rectitude). American politics has been dominated for several years now by contentious negotiations over deficit reduction between the Clinton administration and the Republican Congress. This past June, first at the European Community summit in Amsterdam and then at the Group of Eight meeting in Denver, most of the talk was of hardship and constraint and the need for governmental austerity ("Economic Unease Looms Over Talks at Denver Summit," read the *New York Times* headline).

These bloodless problems of governmental accounting are said, moreover, to reflect real social ills: growing economic inequality in the United States; high unemployment in Europe; an aging, burdensome, and medically needy population everywhere; and the globalization of commerce, which is destroying jobs and national autonomy and forcing bitter measures to keep up with the bruising demands of international competitiveness.

How can it be that societies so surpassingly wealthy have governments whose core domestic-welfare programs are on the verge of bankruptcy? The answer is as paradoxical as the question. We have become not only the richest but also the freest and most egalitarian societies that have ever existed, and it is our very wealth, freedom, and equality that are causing the welfare state to unravel.

* * *

That we have become very rich is clear enough in the aggregate. That we have become very equal in the enjoyment of our riches is an idea strongly resisted by many. Certainly there has been a profusion of reports in the media and political speeches about increasing income inequality: the rich, it is said, are getting richer, the poor are getting poorer, and the middle and working classes are under the relentless pressure of disappearing jobs in manufacturing and middle management.

Although these claims have been greatly exaggerated, and some have been disproved by events, it is true that, by some measures, there has been a recent increase in income inequality in the United States. But it is a very small tick in the massive and unprecedented leveling of material circumstances that has been proceeding now for almost three centuries and in this century has accelerated dramatically. In fact, the much-noticed increase in measured-income inequality is in part a result of the increase in real social equality. Here are a few pieces of this important but neglected story.

• First, progress in agriculture, construction, manufacturing, and other key sectors of economic production has made the material necessities of life—food, shelter, and clothing—available to essentially everyone. To be sure, many people, including the seriously handicapped and the mentally incompetent, remain dependent on the public purse for their necessities. And many people continue to live in terrible squalor. But the problem of poverty, defined as material scarcity, has been solved. If poverty today remains a serious problem, it is a problem of individual behavior, social organization, and public policy. This was not so 50 years ago, or ever before.

• Second, progress in public health, in nutrition, and in the biological sciences and medical arts has produced dra-matic improvements in longevity, health, and physical well-being. Many of these improvements—resulting, for example, from better public sanitation and water supplies, the conquest of dread diseases, and the abundance of nutritious food—have affected entire populations, producing an equalization of real personal welfare more powerful than any government redistribution of income.

The Nobel prize-winning economist Robert Fogel has focused on our improved mastery of the biological environment—leading over the past 300 years to a doubling of the average human life span and to large gains in physical stature, strength, and energy—as the key to what he calls "the egalitarian revolution of the 20th century." He considers this so profound an advance as to constitute a distinct new level of human evolution. Gains in stature, health, and longevity are continuing today and even accelerating. Their outward effects may be observed, in evolutionary fast-forward, in the booming nations of Asia (where, for example, the physical difference between older and younger South Koreans is strikingly evident on the streets of Seoul).

• Third, the critical *source* of social wealth has shifted over the last few hundred years from land (at the end of the 18th century) to physical capital (at the end of the 19th) to, today, human capital—education and cognitive ability. This development is not an unmixed gain from the standpoint of economic equality. The ability to acquire and deploy human capital is a function of intelligence, and intelligence is not only unequally distributed but also, to a significant degree, heritable. As Charles Murray and the late Richard J. Herrnstein argue in *The Bell Curve,* an economy that rewards sheer brainpower replaces one old source of inequality, socioeconomic advantage, with a new one, cognitive advantage.

* * *

But an economy that rewards human capital also tears down far more artificial barriers than it erects. For most people who inhabit the vast middle range of the bell curve, intelligence is much more equally distributed than land or physical capital ever was. Most people, that is, possess ample intelligence to pursue all but a handful of specialized callings. If in the past many were held back by lack of education and closed social institutions, the opportunities to use one's human capital have blossomed with the advent of universal education and the erosion of social barriers.

Furthermore, the material benefits of the knowledge-based economy are by no means limited to those whom Murray and Herrnstein call the cognitive elite. Many of the newest industries, from fast food to finance to communications, have succeeded in part by opening up employment opportunities for those of modest ability and training—occupations much less arduous and physically much less risky than those they have replaced. And these new industries have created enormous, widely shared economic benefits in consumption; I will return to this subject below.

• Fourth, recent decades have seen a dramatic reduction in one of the greatest historical sources of inequality: the social and economic inequality of the sexes. Today, younger cohorts of working men and women with comparable education and job tenure earn essentially the same incomes. The popular view would have it that the entry of women into the workforce has been driven by falling male earnings and the need "to make ends meet" in middle-class families. But the popular view is largely mistaken. Among married women (as the economist Chin-hui Juhn has demonstrated), it is wives of men with high incomes who have been responsible for most of the recent growth in employment.

• Fifth, in the wealthy Western democracies, material needs and desires have been so thoroughly fulfilled for so many people that, for the first time in history, we are seeing large-scale voluntary reductions in the amount of time spent at paid employment. This development manifests itself in different forms: longer periods of education and training for the young; earlier retirement despite longer life spans; and, in between, many more hours devoted to leisure, recreation, entertainment, family, community and religious activities, charitable and other non-remunerative pursuits, and so forth. The dramatic growth of the sports, entertainment, and travel industries captures only a small slice of what has happened. In Fogel's estimation, the time devoted to nonwork activities by the average male head of household has grown from 10.5 hours per week in 1880 to 40 hours today, while time per week at work has fallen from 61.6 hours to 33.6 hours. Among women, the reduction in work (including not only outside employment but also household work, food preparation, childbearing and attendant health problems, and child rearing) and the growth in nonwork have been still greater.

There is a tendency to overlook these momentous developments because of the often frenetic pace of modern life. But our busy-ness actually demonstrates the point: time, and not material things, has become the scarce and valued commodity in modern society.

* * *

One implication of these trends is that in very wealthy societies, income has become a less useful gauge of economic welfare and hence of economic equality. When income becomes to some degree discretionary, and when many peoples' incomes change from year to year for reasons unrelated to their life circumstances, *consumption* becomes a better measure of material welfare. And by this measure, welfare appears much more evenly distributed: people of higher income spend progressively smaller shares on consumption, while in the bottom ranges, annual consumption often exceeds income. (In fact, government statistics suggest that in the bottom 20 percent of the income scale, average annual consumption is about twice annual income—probably a reflection of a substantial underreporting of earnings in this group.) According to the economist Daniel Slesnick, the distribution of consumption, unlike the distribution of reported income, has become measurably *more* equal in recent decades.

If we include leisure-time pursuits as a form of consumption, the distribution of material welfare appears flatter still. Many such activities, being informal by definition, are difficult to track, but Dora Costa of MIT has recently studied one measurable aspect—expenditures on recreation—and found that these have become strikingly more equal as people of lower income have increased the amount of time and money they devote to entertainment, reading, sports, and related enjoyments.

Television, videocassettes, CD's, and home computers have brought musical, theatrical, and other entertainments (both high and low) to everyone, and have enormously narrowed the differences in cultural opportunities between wealthy urban centers and everywhere else. Formerly upper-crust sports like golf, tennis, skiing, and boating have become mass pursuits (boosted by increased public spending on parks and other recreational facilities as well as on environmental quality), and health clubs and full-line book stores have become as plentiful as gas stations. As some of the best things in life become free or nearly so, the price of pursuing them becomes, to that extent, the "opportunity cost" of time itself.

The substitution of leisure activities for income-producing work even appears to have become significant enough to be contributing to the recently much-lamented increase in inequality in measured income. In a new AEI study, Robert Haveman finds that most of the increase in earnings inequality among U.S. males since the mid-1970's can be attributed not to changing labor-market opportunities but to voluntary choice—to the free pursuit of nonwork activities at the expense of income-producing work.

Most of us can see this trend in our own families and communities. A major factor in income inequality in a wealthy knowledge economy is age—many people whose earnings put them at the top of the income curve in their late fifties were well down the curve in their twenties, when they were just getting out of school and beginning their working careers. Fogel again: today the average household in the top 10 percent might consist of a professor or accountant married to a nurse or secretary, both in their peak years of earning. As for the stratospheric top 1 percent, it includes not only very rich people like Bill Cosby but also people like Cosby's fictional Huxtable family: an obstetrician married to a corporate lawyer. All these individuals would have appeared well down the income distribution as young singles, and that is where their young counterparts appear today.

That more young people are spending more time in college or graduate school, taking time off for travel and "finding themselves," and pursuing interesting but low- or non-paying jobs or apprenticeships before knuckling down to lifelong careers is a significant factor in "income inequality" measured in the aggregate. But this form of economic inequality is in fact the social equality of the modern age. It is progress, not regress, to be cherished and celebrated, not feared and fretted over.

POSTSCRIPT

Is Increasing Economic Inequality a Serious Problem?

This debate can be posed in terms of two contradictory statements by the two authors: "If calling America a middle-class nation means anything, it means that we are a society in which most people live more or less the same kind of life. In 1970 we were that kind of society. Today we are not, and we become less like one with each passing year" (Krugman); "We have become very equal in the enjoyment of our riches" (DeMuth). Both authors support their statements with indicators that measure trends, but they select different indicators. The reader has to decide which set of indicators better describes his or her idea of inequality.

Inequality, stratification, and social mobility are central concerns of sociology, and they are addressed by a large literature. Two important discussions of income inequality are *The Inequality Paradox: Growth of Income Disparity* edited by James A. Auerbach and Richard S. Belous (National Policy Association, 1998) and *When Earnings Diverge: Causes, Consequences, and Cures for the New Inequality in the U.S.* by Richard B. Freeman (National Policy Association, 1997). Two classic publications on stratification theory based on research on census statistics are Peter M. Blau and Otis Dudley Duncan's *The American Occupational Structure* (John Wiley & Sons, 1967) and Robert M. Hauser and David L. Featherman's *The Process of Social Stratification* (Academic Press, 1972). Blau's other major works on stratification include *Structural Contexts of Opportunities* (University of Chicago Press, 1994). Richard J. Herrnstein and Charles Murray's *The Bell Curve: Intelligence and Class Structure in American Life* (Free Press, 1994) is a controversial work that concludes that the major cause of income inequality is differences in intelligence. This book is vigorously attacked by Claude S. Fischer et al. in *Inequality by Design: Cracking the Bell Curve Myth* (Princeton University Press, 1996). For a structural explanation of inequality see Sheldon Danziger and Peter Gottschalk, *America Unequal* (Harvard University Press, 1995). For an examination of the full range of explanations of poverty, see William A. Kelso, *Poverty and the Underclass: Changing Perceptions of the Poor in America* (New York University Press, 1994). A number of important works look at the poor and their disadvantages, including Elliot Liebow, *Tell Them Who I Am: The Lives of Homeless Women* (Free Press, 1993); Lawrence M. Mead, *The New Politics of Poverty* (Basic Books, 1992); Richard H. Ropers, *Persistent Poverty* (Plenum, 1992); Mickey Kaus, *The End of Inequality* (Basic Books, 1992); and Thomas Lyson and William W. Falk, *Forgotten Places: Uneven Development in Rural America* (University of Kansas Press, 1993).

ISSUE 9

Are the Poor Largely Responsible for Their Poverty?

YES: Nicholas Eberstadt, from "Prosperous Paupers and Affluent Savages," *Society* (January/February 1996)

NO: David M. Gordon, from "Values That Work," *The Nation* (June 17, 1996)

ISSUE SUMMARY

YES: Nicholas Eberstadt, a researcher with the American Enterprise Institute and the Harvard University Center for Population and Development Studies, contends that poverty and numerous problems "devolve from predictably injurious patterns of individual and parental behavior."

NO: The late professor of economics David M. Gordon attacks the values explanation for poverty and other problems because they ignore the structure and behavior of the economic system. He maintains that the decline of decent paying and steady jobs for workers without college educations is the real explanation for these problems.

The Declaration of Independence proclaims the right of every human being to "life, liberty, and the pursuit of happiness." It never defines happiness, but Americans tend to agree that it includes doing well financially, getting ahead in life, and maintaining a comfortable standard of living.

The fact is that millions of Americans do not do well and do not get ahead. They are mired in poverty and seem unable to get out of it. On the face of it, this fact poses no contradiction to America's commitment to the pursuit of happiness. To pursue is not necessarily to catch. It only means the unhindered opportunity to catch through hard work and risk taking. It certainly does not mean that everyone should feel entitled to a life of material prosperity. The prototypical American slogan is "equality of opportunity," which is vastly different from the socialist dream of "equality of condition." This is probably one reason why socialism has so few adherents in America.

The real difficulty in reconciling the American ideal with American reality is not the problem of income differentials but the *persistence* of poverty from generation to generation. Often, parent, child, and grandchild seem to be locked into a hopeless cycle of destitution and dependence. There are two basic explanations for this problem: one largely blames the poor, and the other largely blames their circumstances and, thus, society.

The explanation that blames the poor is most strongly identified with the culture-of-poverty thesis, according to which a large segment of the poor does not really try to get out of poverty. In its more extreme form this view portrays the poor as lazy, stupid, or base. Their poverty is not to be blamed on defects of American society but on their own defects. After all, many successful Americans have worked their way up from humble beginnings, and many immigrant groups have made progress in one generation. Therefore, the United States provides opportunities for those who work hard.

According to this view, available opportunities are ignored by the portion of the poor that embraces the culture of poverty. This *culture* breeds poverty because it is antithetical to the self-discipline and hard work that enable others to overcome poverty. In other words, the poor have a culture all their own that is at variance with middle-class culture and that hinders their success. Although it may keep people locked into what seems to be an intolerable life, this culture nevertheless has its own compensations and pleasures: it is full of "action," and it does not demand that people postpone pleasure, save money, or work hard.

The culture of poverty does not play a major role in today's version of the poor-are-to-blame theory. According to recent versions of this theory, having children out of wedlock, teenage pregnancy, divorce, latchkey children, absent fathers, crime, welfare dependency, and child abuse are what contribute to poverty. Culture contributes to these practices by being permissive or even condoning. This culture, however, is not antithetical to but is shared in part by much of the middle class.

According to the second explanation of poverty, the poor have few opportunities and many obstacles to overcome to climb out of poverty. Most of the poor will become self-supporting if they are given a chance. Their most important need is for decent jobs that have potential for advancement. But poor people often cannot find jobs, and when they do, the jobs are dead-end or degrading.

The culture-of-poverty thesis shields the economic system from blame for poverty and honors Americans who are better off. But most of the poor are as committed to taking care of themselves and their families through hard work as is the middle class, and a sense of dignity is common to all classes. Critics judge the culture-of-poverty thesis to be a self-righteous justification by spokesmen for the middle and upper classes for an economic system that rewards them while subjecting the poor to an intolerable existence. How different is the culture of the poor from the culture of the middle class? If their material conditions were altered, would the culture of the poor change?

In the following selections, Nicholas Eberstadt acknowledges that mental afflictions and other disabilities are responsible for some poverty, but he blames most poverty on the behavior of the poor or their parents. David M. Gordon argues that the key to understanding poverty today is the fact that the opportunities for those without a college education have greatly diminished over the past couple of decades.

YES
Nicholas Eberstadt

PROSPEROUS PAUPERS AND AFFLUENT SAVAGES

My assignment is to discuss the problems of poverty and poverty alleviation in the modern United States. To appreciate the nature and context of a contemporary problem, it is sometimes helpful to frame it in historical perspective. To understand the dilemmas we confront today, we would do well to consider how the struggle against deprivation and material poverty has changed in our country over the past sixty years.

Imagine with me that we find a time machine. . . .

Let us use our time machine to bring [a] New Deal [reformer] to the present for a moment and list six things our visitor from the past will quickly learn about the current condition of U.S. society:

First of all, we would surely have to mention the failure, for a full generation, to achieve any appreciable reduction in the official index of poverty in America. In 1993, in fact, the officially measured poverty rate for the population as a whole was slightly higher than it had been in 1966, twenty-seven years earlier. More ominously, the officially measured poverty rate for U.S. families has registered a steady rise for over two decades. Most troubling of all, the official poverty rate for children in the early 1990s was reported to be nearly one-and-a-half times as high as in the late 1960s, and distinctly higher than it had been in the mid-1960s, when the "War on Poverty" commenced.

Second, we would have to mention the progressive rise in the proportion of U.S. children living in fatherless homes. In 1993, only 74 percent of America's families with children had both a mother and a father in the home—a lower proportion than in 1946, despite the disruption imposed, and the casualties inflicted, by World War II. By 1993, nearly a quarter of the nation's children under eighteen years of age would be living in a female-headed household. Over 40 percent of the country's children would be in families that did not include their biological father.

Third, our visitor could hardly help but notice that hundreds of thousands of persons—persons often desperate and deranged—are now wandering homeless through the streets in U.S. cities.

From Nicholas Eberstadt, "Prosperous Paupers and Affluent Savages," *Society* (January/February 1996). Copyright © 1996 by Transaction Publishers. Reprinted by permission. References omitted.

Fourth, our New Deal reformer might be interested to learn that over a million persons, at any given time, were incarcerated in correctional facilities in the United States in the early 1990s—a figure that speaks to a huge increase in criminality since the Great Depression. In 1992, 1.3 million prisoners were being held at any given moment in local jails and state or federal prisons. Over four times as many persons were serving time in prison in 1992 as in the early 1960s. In 1992, nearly 12 million arrests were processed for criminal offenses— three times as many as thirty years before. In 1990—the most recent year for which such figures are available from the Bureau of Justice Statistics— roughly one adult American in forty was under "correctional supervision": in jail, in prison, on probation, or on parole. For men over eighteen years of age, that ratio was one in twenty-four; for African-American adults, one in thirteen; for black males over eighteen, roughly one in seven.

Fifth, despite the overall improvement in health in the modern United States, our visitor would learn that health trends for vulnerable groups were much less favorable. The proportion of babies born with dangerously low birth weights, for example, was higher in 1993 (the most recent figure available) than in 1980; the incidence of low birth weight over those years rose for both black and white infants. In contrast to the Depression decade of the 1930s, during which life expectancy at birth for nonwhites increased by fully five years, life expectancy for African Americans stagnated between 1982 and 1991. Over those years, life expectancy at birth for black males actually registered a slight decline.

Sixth, and by no means least, our visitor from the past would learn that a higher fraction of Americans were on "relief"—or what we now call "means-tested public assistance"—in the early 1990s than had been in the depths of the Great Depression. The U.S. Census Bureau publishes an annual report on poverty in the United States; its estimates are instructive. For the nation as a whole in 1992, 24 percent of the population, almost a quarter, lived in households that received some form of means-tested assistance. Among African Americans, the proportion of the population in households receiving some form of means-tested assistance was nearly 53 percent; over 28 percent were obtaining means tested *cash* assistance. By contrast, in January 1935, according to the National Resources Planning Board, an estimated 26 percent of the country's African Americans were on relief. Lest one presume that the pattern is particular to African Americans, we can look at the trends for the white population. That same Depression-era report estimated that 16 percent of U.S. whites were on relief in January 1935; by 1992, according to the Census Bureau, nearly 20 percent of the country's whites were seeking and obtaining some kind of means-tested assistance. In 1992, over 30 percent of the white children under six years of age resided in a household receiving at least one type of means-tested assistance; every seventh white child under the age of six lived in a household obtaining publicly provided, means-tested cash.

Now, what would our New Deal reformer make of these facts? . . .

It is true, to be sure, that some rays of sunshine would greet our time traveler upon stepping out of the capsule and into the modern United States. He or she would learn, for example, about the near elimination of financial poverty among the elderly: Between 1959 and 1991 the official poverty rate for persons sixty-five and over dropped by two-thirds—or by as much as five-sixths, if one of the Census Bureau's alternative official measures is to be trusted.

He or she would learn about dramatic increases in per capita income, after appropriate adjustments for inflation, for the country's African-American population: Between 1967 and 1993 alone, per capita income for black Americans increased by over 75 percent.

And he or she would also learn about the equalization of incomes between black and white two-parent families: By 1990, to go by median earnings, African-American married couples in their late thirties or early forties were making 92 cents for every dollar earned by their white counterparts. (Appropriate adjustments for differences in educational attainment, one may note, would narrow that earnings differential still further.)

But quite clearly, from the perspective of a New Deal reformer, there would be something very, very wrong with the picture of modern America. Despite tremendous material advances, revolutionary improvements in knowledge and technology, and a vast augmentation of national wealth, the country's domestic social problems have by no means been eliminated. Paradoxically, in the early 1990s such problems as crime, dependency, and family breakdown were far more acute than they had been during the Great Depression, when general income levels, and general levels of schooling, were so much lower. For a reformer or an idealist from an earlier time, the social problems with which we must currently cope, I submit, would be especially

troubling because they would be so completely unexpected. Contemplating our social problems today, I suspect, a visitor from the past would be stricken with a severe bout of cognitive dissonance. It is precisely that dissonance that I wish to discuss.

How is the dissonance to be explained? There are a number of serious issues possibly bearing on the nature of our domestic problems today that I will not touch upon at all. The workings of the U.S. labor market (especially with respect to low-pay employees), recent trends in economic inequality within our society, and the apparent slowdown in improvements in productivity in our economy since the early 1970s are all matters of legitimate concern. Despite the categorical pronouncements we occasionally hear about these three problems, they seem to me extremely complex—not yet adequately understood by objective, impartial researchers, despite the considerable attention they rightly receive.

My objective is more modest. I simply wish to suggest that part of the dissonance to which I have alluded can be explained by the fact that ours is now a nation whose social and economic problems are no longer familiar, nor in any real sense traditional. The modern United States is a country inhabited by large numbers of prosperous paupers and affluent savages. As mass phenomena, these are quite new. The patterns of mass behavior attendant upon these syndromes constitute major problems for our society today. It is precisely these patterns, I submit, that account for much of what would surprise or dismay earlier eyes on surveying our contemporary landscape. . . .

We are well aware that troubling things are occurring in our society—things with very real and distinctly adverse implications for the material well-being of our nation and our children.

Let me mention just one of these, and its ramifications. Marxist utopians of the nineteenth and twentieth centuries have talked at great length about the withering away of the state. That withering away has not occurred in any of the societies for which this possibility was under discussion. But we *have* witnessed an amazing, perhaps even revolutionary, "withering away" of a central social institution in the modern United States: This is the withering away of the family. (That is to say, of the family as traditionally understood: a mother-father union with children. If one is sufficiently sophisticated or inventive, any household configuration including human beings can be defined as a "family," and a "crisis of the family" becomes a definitional impossibility.)

The trends of the past thirty-five years have been both striking and consequential. Around 1959, only about 10 percent of the children in the United States were living outside of two-parent families. By 1990, that proportion was over 27 percent—a near tripling in only thirty years. Trends have been most extreme for African-American families, where something like a sea-change has been registered. In barely a generation, the two-parent family went from being the norm to the exception for our African-American population. By 1990, over half of all black children in the United States were living in mother-headed families. Less than 38 percent were living in two-parent families. By 1990, moreover, fewer than a quarter of the country's African-American children were living under the same roof as their biological mother and their biological father.

But trends for America's white population were only different in degree—not in direction. By 1990, according to one Census Bureau study, fewer than two-thirds of America's white children were living with both their biological father and their biological mother. Ten years earlier, the corresponding fraction had been over three-fourths—that is to say, over ten points higher.

Despite the tremendous improvements in the odds of survival for the partners in a marriage between the Great Depression and the 1990s, the survival prospects for marriages themselves [have] been falling over time. With increasing frequency, marriages that have produced children are disrupted, not by death, but by divorce, separation, and desertion.

Another recent Census Bureau study puts our proclivities toward family breakup in quantitative perspective. The results are arresting. Between 1985 and 1987, 7.4 percent of the white two-parent families with children under eighteen in the survey suffered "discontinuation"; for their African-American counterparts, the corresponding "discontinuation" rate was 12.2 percent. Projecting this two-year breakup rate forward, one produces figures suggesting that only half of the white babies—and less than one-third of the black babies—born to married parents can expect to reach adulthood in intact homes. For technical reasons, those unadjusted, aggregate projections overstate somewhat the actual odds of breakup for particular marital unions. But given the trends in family breakup that we have witnessed over the past forty years, it is by no means impossible that these rough numbers will finally *understate* the prevalence of broken homes around children born to married parents in the mid-1980s. It is strange: The richer and the more educated our country has become, the weaker our family units seem to become.

It is tempting, indeed, to speak of the *anomalization* of the marital union. African Americans are in the vanguard of this movement. In 1975, nearly 77 percent of black women in their late twenties had been married at some time in their lives. By 1990, the corresponding figure was 45 percent—a drop of over thirty points in fifteen years! For black women in their early thirties, the fall-off is almost as steep: a drop from 87 percent in 1975 to 61 percent in 1990, or over twenty-five points. If this pace of change continues for the rest of our decade, by the year 2000 less than a quarter of America's black women in their late twenties, and fewer than 45 percent of those in their early thirties, will ever have been married.

High rates of non-marriage, of course, can no longer be interpreted as signifying high rates of childlessness. Paralleling the breakup of two-parent families is the rise of families never fully formed. Over the past four decades, our country has experienced a veritable explosion of out-of-wedlock births. In 1960, about 5 percent of the births in the United States were reportedly to unmarried mothers. By 1992, the proportion exceeded 30 percent. When the figures are in for 1995, we can expect the proportion to be higher still. And as these large fractions should indicate, out-of-wedlock birth is not only, or even predominantly, a black phenomenon.

To be sure, the situation is more extreme for our African-American population. By 1992, more than two out of three black babies were born out-of-wedlock. But black babies no longer comprise the majority of the infants born outside marriage in the United States. In 1992, 37 percent of the country's illegitimate births

were black; 63 percent were *not*. The stereotype of the unwed mother as a black teenager, furthermore, is by now completely outdated: In 1992, that group accounted for fewer than *one-eighth* of the illegitimate births in the United States.

Illegitimacy has become a "white thing" over the past generation. In 1960, 2.3 percent of the country's babies were reportedly born out-of-wedlock. By 1992, 22.6 percent were born out of wedlock —a tenfold increase in thirty-two years. In recent decades, in fact, the fastest increase in out-of-wedlock births has been for white mothers, and not for white teenagers but, rather, for mothers over the age of twenty-five. Between 1973 and 1992, the absolute number of illegitimate births to white teenagers rose by about 70 percent; for white women in their thirties, the total jumped by a factor of ten. (By contrast, the total number of illegitimate births to black teenagers increased by "only" 16 percent between 1973 and 1992.)

By the 1960s, the plight of the African-American family had become a topic of national policy discussion. All too seldom recognized today is the fact that illegitimacy ratios for the country's white population are generally higher than were the country's black ratios at the time of the now-famous Moynihan report. Consider: In 1960, roughly 42 percent of the babies born to nonwhite girls between the ages of fifteen and nineteen were reportedly illegitimate. In 1992, over 60 percent of the babies born to white girls those same ages were reportedly out-of-wedlock. In 1970, the illegitimacy ratio for black babies born to mothers in their early twenties was 31 percent; in 1992, the corresponding white illegitimacy ratio was 32 percent. At the moment, it would seem as if illegitimacy ratios for white America are roughly one generation behind the trends established by black America.

What are the consequences of the now pervasive tendencies of family breakup, and failure of families to form, for the United States? Three come immediately to mind. The first, of course, is financial and economic hardship. Many studies have been done on the financial consequences of divorce for children and for mothers; none of them have shown economic improvement in the situation of the typical fatherless household. All of them have shown serious drops in income, although the estimates vary from one study to the next. A Census Bureau report on the problem may be the most comprehensive to date: By its estimates, in families with children where the father moves out and where the mother does not reconcile or remarry, household income falls by an average of 40 percent in the first year, and per capita income drops by an average of 25 percent. The financial situation is even worse for the families of unwed mothers. The Census Bureau does not make a practice of disaggregating the income levels of various types of single-mother families, but my colleague Douglas Besharov has taken that extra step in some of his research. For 1990, he found a fateful difference between the incomes of never-married mothers with children and divorced mothers with children. For blacks and whites alike, the median incomes of these never-married single-mother households were lower by 40 percent or more.

Breakup of families, or failure of families to form, has also resulted in a great rise in dependence upon government assistance programs. In 1992, according to the Census Bureau, over 70 percent of those living in female-headed families with children were seeking and getting means-tested benefits; 44 percent of this population was using means-tested public cash. Among black female-headed families with children, reliance upon means-tested public benefits is now the norm: 86 percent of such households obtained at least one form of means-tested assistance in 1992, and 56 percent were getting means-tested public cash. But participation in government aid programs is fast becoming the norm for white single mothers, too; in fact, by 1992 over two-thirds of this group was drawing upon at least one form of means-tested aid, and nearly 43 percent were spending means-tested government money. Long-term dependence upon public assistance programs is a very real prospect for the single-mother family. Recent research suggests that 14 percent of the country's divorced mothers with children had spent over ten years on the Aid to Families with Dependent Children (AFDC) program; among never-married mothers, roughly 40 percent had been on AFDC for a decade or more. Those rates, of course, were calculated on the basis of past patterns. We have every reason to expect that the likelihood of long-term dependence would be higher for a single mother starting out today.

Finally, family breakup and illegitimacy are associated with the rise in crime in our nation. In the modern United States, the relationship between family breakdown and crime is not just strong; it is *very* strong. I could quote any number of studies to this effect, but here is Barbara Defoe Whitehead, from her widely read *Atlantic Monthly* article of April 1993:

> The relationship [between single parent families and crime] is so strong that controlling for family configuration erases

the relationship between race and crime and between low income and crime. This conclusion shows up time and again in the literature. The nation's mayors, as well as police officers, social workers, probation officers, and court officials, consistently point to family breakup as the most important source of rising rates of crime.

... To sum up: Today's antipoverty efforts confront problems that were not faced by the New Dealers—and may not even have been imagined by them. (These problems, on the other hand, *were* imagined by the Puritans—although it is doubtful that many Puritans would have predicted such problems would ever be so rampant in their City on a Hill.) The problems to which I refer devolve from predictably injurious patterns of individual and parental behavior. These injurious patterns do not explain all of the social problems that we confront in our nation today. But they may account for a great fraction of the domestic problems we confront.

A revolution in personal behavior and personal attitudes has taken place in the United States since the New Deal. That revolution has coincided with a great surge in policy experimentation, as we have attempted to apply the techniques of problem-solving governance to an increasingly ambitious agenda of social concerns. For better or worse, we have been living through interesting years.

We have learned, to our sorrow, that the state is a limited and highly imperfect father for the family. Given the comprehensive proposals currently pending for the restructuring of our health care system, I fear that we may learn that the state is also a limited and highly imperfect mother for the family. No matter how expertly devised the policy, no matter how dedicated the civil servants, no matter how generously funded the initiatives, antipoverty and social policy programs will be judged a failure in any confrontation against the perverse patterns of behavior that characterize so much of what troubles us about modern U.S. life.

The reassertion of individual and familial responsibilities, I believe, is central to the revitalization of our society. It is also central, I believe, to dealing with the dysfunctions that sadden and dismay us most about our national condition. But how such a resurgence is to be accomplished generally and effectively—much less how our governmental institutions are to abet in such a resurgence—is far from clear to me.

NO

David M. Gordon

VALUES THAT WORK

Conservative pundits and politicians love to find symbolic scapegoats to blame for social problems. Their targets shift constantly: teen pregnancy. Lazy workers. Ungrateful immigrants. Violent movies and ugly rap lyrics. Welfare chiselers. Gangsta teens. Racial quotas. Behind all social problems, they insist, are corroding values.

I would argue instead that the wage squeeze and the confrontational strategy underlying it account for many of the most notorious economic and social problems in the United States. Name the problem—"family breakdown," "welfare dependency," "teen pregnancy"—and we can find falling real wages or job insecurity lurking in the background. The U.S. corporate production system and the kinds of jobs it provides—or fails to provide—holds the key to much of what we currently debate in the policy arena. Conservatives have shifted the discussion toward cultural factors, blaming people and their values for many of their own problems. We need to redress the balance and bring the quality of people's jobs back into the discussion. Values matter, of course. But jobs matter at least as much, if not more.

For example, conservatives cast welfare as an issue of family values. Welfare ruins families, Republicans and their Democratic allies lament. Families will be stronger—and our economy more productive—if we can push parasites off the dole. The villain here is the culture of poverty. Moms with kids on welfare "choose" welfare instead of employment because they are too weak to appreciate the independence that employment provides.

Yet most welfare mothers participate in the labor market at least intermittently, moving in and out of welfare, in and out of jobs. For example, a study by scholars at the Institute for Women's Policy Research found that a substantial majority of A.F.D.C. recipients participated in the labor force over a two-year period: 43 percent of mothers on welfare had worked at least 300

From David M. Gordon, "Values That Work," *The Nation* (June 17, 1996). Copyright © 1996 by David M. Gordon. Reprinted by permission of *The Nation*.

hours of paid work, while another 30 percent spent a significant portion of time looking for work. Over the two-year period, the mothers in the sample spent 77 percent of their time on welfare and 23 percent off the rolls. During the period they were on the rolls, they spent more than 30 percent of their total time working or looking for work.

* * *

Only one-quarter of A.F.D.C. recipients is totally dependent on A.F.D.C. income, the study shows; the remaining three-quarters package A.F.D.C. together with some combination of income from paid work, earnings and benefits of other family members, and other resources. But if they're so interested in working, the conservative critics will ask, why don't welfare mothers depend entirely on income from paid employment? The answer seems fairly clear: Many women with children either earn such low wages or work at such bad jobs (or both) that even if they worked full time they could not come close to supporting their families at or above the poverty level, even as it is measured by the meager official standard.

Consider the economics. Laura Lein and Kathryn Edin have interviewed poor single mothers in the Boston, Chicago, San Antonio and Charleston, South Carolina, metropolitan areas and have begun to put together a detailed portrait of their income and expenditures. A typical welfare mother with two children in Chicago in the early nineties had an income from A.F.D.C. and food stamps alone of only $7,356 in 1993 dollars, considerably below the poverty line. However, Lein and Edin found that the typical A.F.D.C. mother was able to lift her family a bit above the poverty level

through paid work (with the earnings mostly unreported to welfare), some support from the absent father and additional support from relatives and friends.

Would she be better off if she worked full time, year-round at the minimum wage of $4.25? Assuming that the minimum-wage job does not provide health coverage, her fate depends entirely on the availability of child care: If she is able to find free care for her kids, perhaps from a grandmother, then she can improve her standard of living by 20 percent. But, under the more likely eventuality that she cannot find free child care and has to pay the going rate, her standard of living (remember that under this scenario she's off the welfare rolls) would decline by 20 percent.

Working full time, year-round at $6 an hour doesn't change the picture at all: Hourly earnings increase, but food stamp benefits and the earned-income tax credit decline. Worse still, with the somewhat higher earnings from paid work, she loses eligibility for Medicaid benefits. So the basic economics remain almost exactly the same: If free child care is available, a roughly 20 percent improvement in standard of living by leaving the rolls; no free child care, roughly 20 percent decline.

These numbers would be less devastating, obviously, if we had different systems of providing health insurance and child care. But health care reform has fallen flat on its face and a substantial expansion of publicly subsidized child care isn't even on the drawing board. With our current job market, in which welfare mothers' primary jobs when they worked paid an average of $4.88 an hour (in 1994 dollars), "self-sufficiency" won't allow a woman with a couple of children to escape from poverty. In 1993, 29 percent of working women earned less than $6 an hour. At wages like that, supporting children as a single mother is just about impossible.

* * *

Another issue exposes us to the classic debate about the relative importance of the "culture of poverty" and the world of work. It is said that we have a new "underclass" in the United States—a generation outside the mainstream, mostly male, mostly black, many of them teens, mostly in core inner-city neighborhoods. Their tough lives have developed even tougher attitudes: callous, violent, impervious to conventional social standards. If they survive their teens, they will be destitute or living on a different dole, in prison cells.

But these public presuppositions have tended to overlook the role of deteriorating job opportunities. For many young African-American men in the United States, job prospects are slim. Wages, when they work, are spare, and job security elusive. Since the seventies, hourly earnings have declined more sharply for African-American men than for white men. And relative rates of joblessness have deteriorated among black men as well.

Why has the plight of younger African-American men grown more acute? Many assume that these different aspects of the "underclass" phenomenon can be attributed to the characteristics of the "underclass" themselves. They have become relatively less skilled, less intelligent or less committed. If they behaved differently, or acquired more advantageous characteristics, they could lift themselves out of the "underclass." (Of course, if disadvantages for African-Americans are substantially due to lower intelligence, as it is newly fashionable for conservatives to claim, and relatively lower average intelligence is genetically determined, then the victims can be blamed but can't be helped.)

But we find relatively little evidence to confirm this explanation. There has not been any increase in the numbers of men who have dropped out of school before high school completion and, in particular, dropout rates among African-Americans have declined fairly substantially since the sixties. Nor does it appear, despite all the publicity about falling S.A.T. scores and virtual illiteracy among inner-city youth, that there has been a general decline in cognitive skills among those coming out of school. The S.A.T. evidence is somewhat misleading because only students who want to go to college take the test. A much more comprehensive standard is the National Assessment of Educational Progress, administered since 1970 to all high school students. By this evidence, average cognitive skills have been improving or holding steady. And, especially striking given the popular stereotypes, average cognitive achievement among African-American high school students has increased fairly steadily since the seventies.

* * *

In addition, educational attainment has grown more equal by race over the past twenty years. Perhaps more important, standard measures of reading and writing skills have also grown relatively more equal by race over the past twenty years. In one systematic analysis, John Bound and Richard B. Freeman conclude that interracial differences in educational attainment explain little or none of the deterioration of African-American men's labor market position since 1973. Nor do they find evidence that a widening of the gap in skills not picked up at school can help explain that deterioration.

Then what does explain it? As a number of analysts have made clear, the stark and sharp decline in job opportunities, especially in the bottom half of the earnings distribution, has had especially strong impact. In the Midwest, for example, Bound and Freeman find that a major role is played by the "huge drop in the proportion of young black workers in manufacturing"—jobs that in the Midwest had been relatively high paying and had contributed to the gradual improvement in the economic fortunes of African-American men in the sixties and early seventies. Northwestern University sociologist Christopher Jencks thinks that the decline in decent jobs may help explain some of the very particular patterns that have helped shape popular impressions of the "underclass"—intermittent work habits among many younger African-American men, with many older African-American men eventually dropping out of the labor force altogether. He hypothesizes:

- "Good" jobs (that is, steady jobs that paid enough to support a family) became scarcer after 1970.
- Firms increasingly reserved these jobs for the college-educated and for men with good work histories.
- Young men without higher education therefore found it harder to get good jobs. They responded by postponing marriage and by taking poorly paid, short-term jobs.
- The substitution of short-term jobs for steady jobs drove up the percentage of young men who were idle in a typical week but had little effect on

the percentage who were idle for long periods.

- As young men get older, they become increasingly reluctant to take poorly paid short-term jobs. Some find steady jobs. Others drop out of the labor market entirely.

But even with this scenario, which places such paramount importance on declining job opportunities, many might nonetheless fault African-American men for giving up too quickly. Two factors seem especially important in responding to this concern. First, when job opportunities for which younger African-American men can reasonably qualify improve, their employment rates, work records and earnings all tend to improve dramatically. Complementary studies by Richard Freeman and by M.I.T. economist Paul Osterman found, for example, that young black male economic fortunes improved dramatically in the mid- to late eighties where acute labor shortages developed in central-city areas and where low-end earnings were bid up as a result.

Osterman conducted some special labor-market surveys in Boston in the eighties, where the "Massachusetts miracle" was helping drive employment and spread prosperity even into the inner city. And welfare benefits remained among the nation's most generous during this period (before the current Republican Governor, William Weld, began his scorched-earth program). "If the neoconservatives are right" about the intractability of the "underclass," as Osterman frames the problem, "generosity should have inhibited the response of poor people to the economic opportunities afforded by long-term growth. If the liberals are right, the combination of full employment and active social policy should have paid off in a reduction of poverty rates." As far as the data would allow reasonably firm conclusions, Osterman reports that the "liberals" win this face-off. "Full employment does in fact deliver many of the benefits its advocates have promised. Poverty rates fell substantially in Boston, and it is very clear that the poor did respond to economic opportunity when it was offered."

* * *

Second, it is not even all that obvious that young African-Americans "behave" all that differently from whites. Their opportunities differ, clearly, but it's not clear that they respond to these opportunities differently than whites do or would.

To consider this possibility, we need to distinguish carefully between "joblessness" and, among other conditions, "shiftlessness." The jobless are either unemployed or out of the labor force. The "shiftless"—try to pin a precise definition on that loaded term—are those who evidently don't want to work, because, as University of Chicago sociologists Marta Tienda and Haya Stier write, "they are lazy and prefer other forms of support, even if the support is grossly inadequate to maintain a decent life-style." Are a large proportion of the "jobless" in inner-city neighborhoods truly "shiftless"?

According to some special surveys undertaken of the Chicago inner city, Tienda and Stier think not. In general, most inner-city adults work, and most of those who do not work nonetheless appear committed to working if they can find suitable opportunities. Something like 5 or 6 percent of inner-city adults might reasonably conform to their definition of "shiftlessness"—being not only jobless but also showing virtually no inter-

est in working even though they are capable of it. The percentages are higher among African-American men who are not parents than for others, but this is a relatively small group. "Most of the evidence," Tienda and Stier conclude, "showed that willingness to work was the norm in Chicago's inner city."

One key to assessing behavior in this context involves what economists call the "reservation wage"—the wage in available work below which potential workers may decide that it's simply not worth the effort. The conservatives sometimes seem to maintain that workers ought to be willing to work at any wage, that the dignity of employment should be enough by itself. But both standard economic theory and survey results suggest that *everyone* will have some "reservation wage," a self-defined minimum below which they won't accept a job.

If the underclass were truly incorrigible, we ought to find that their reservation wages were relatively or "unrealistically" high, that they were unwilling to work at wage levels that more "reasonable" or ambitious workers would be willing to accept. There is much that we don't know on this issue. And we need to be careful in reaching conclusions in any case, since what people may say is their "reservation wage" may not be very reliable. But it does not appear, in general, that African-American men are holding themselves out of the labor market simply or primarily because their wage standards are too high. In the Chicago inner-city survey, for example, Tienda and Stier found that "black men appeared most willing and white men least willing to accept low-paying jobs"—the average wage rate expected by those who had worked and wanted a job was $5.50 an hour for black men, $6.20 for Mexican and Puerto Rican men, and $10.20 for white men. It is a measure of how low our wage standards have sunk in the more than two decades of the wage squeeze that $5.50 an hour may strike some readers as an "unreasonably" high standard. But if there are other ways of surviving at a roughly comparable living standard, should everyone always prefer working at a chump's job for chump change? How many meals can the "dignity" of paid employment actually provide?

POSTSCRIPT

Are the Poor Largely Responsible for Their Poverty?

In *Reducing Poverty in America* edited by Michael R. Darby (Sage Publications, 1996), James Q. Wilson summarizes the debate on the causes of poverty as the clash between two views: "The first is incentives or objective factors: jobs, incomes, opportunities. The second is culture: single-parent families, out-of-wedlock births, and a decaying work ethic." Sociologists expect the structural versus individual explanations of poverty to be debated for a long time because both are partially true. The cultural explanation derives from the anthropological studies of Oscar Lewis and was proposed as a major cause of urban poverty in America by Edward Banfield in *The Unheavenly City* (Little, Brown, 1970). The most vigorous proponent of the culture-of-poverty thesis today is Lawrence E. Harrison, who wrote *Who Prospers? How Cultural Values Shape Economic and Political Success* (Basic Books, 1992). In *The Dream and the Nightmare: The Sixties' Legacy to the Underclass* (William Morrow, 1993), Myron Magnet blames the culture of the underclass for their poverty, but he also blames the upper classes for contributing greatly to the underclass's culture. Charles Murray, in *Losing Ground* (Basic Books, 1984), attempts to provide empirical support for the idea that welfare is a cause of poverty and not its solution, and he concludes that welfare should be abolished.

The counter to the cultural explanation of poverty is the structural explanation. Its most current version focuses on the loss of unskilled jobs. This is the thrust of William Julius Wilson's analysis of the macroeconomic forces that impact so heavily on the urban poor in *The Truly Disadvantaged* (University of Chicago Press, 1987) and in *When Work Disappears: The World of the New Urban Poor* (Alfred A. Knopf, 1996). If Jeremy Rifkin's analysis in *The End of Work: The Decline of the Global Labor Force and the Dawn of the Post-Market Era* (Putnam, 1995) is right, this situation will get worse, not better, because new technologies will lengthen unemployment lines unless the economy or the working world is radically restructured. For a similar view, see Stanley Aronowitz and William DiFazio, *The Jobless Future: Sci-Tech and the Dogma of Work* (University of Minnesota Press, 1994)

There are countless works that describe the adverse conditions of the poor. The nineteenth-century English novelist Charles Dickens was a crusader for the poor, and many of his novels, still in print and certainly considered classics, graphically depict the wretchedness of poverty. Michael Harrington described poverty in America in his influential nonfiction book *The Other America* (Macmillan, 1963) at a time when most of the country was increasingly affluent.

ISSUE 10

Has Affirmative Action Outlived Its Usefulness?

YES: Walter E. Williams, from "Affirmative Action Can't Be Mended," *Cato Journal* (Spring/Summer 1997)

NO: Clarence Page, from *Showing My Color* (HarperCollins, 1996)

ISSUE SUMMARY

YES: Professor of economics Walter E. Williams asserts that "the civil rights struggle for blacks is over and won," so affirmative action policies are unjust and adversely affect society.

NO: Journalist Clarence Page argues that affirmative action has largely opened doors for blacks that they should have gone through many years earlier and that, with prejudice and discrimination still virulent, some affirmative action is still needed to equalize opportunities.

In America, equality is a principle as basic as liberty. "All men are created equal" is perhaps the most well known phrase in the Declaration of Independence. More than half a century after the signing of the Declaration, the French social philosopher Alexis de Tocqueville examined democracy in America and concluded that its most essential ingredient was the equality of condition. Today we know that the "equality of condition" that Tocqueville perceived did not exist for women, blacks, Native Americans, and other racial minorities, nor for other disadvantaged social classes. Nevertheless, the ideal persisted.

When slavery was abolished after the Civil War, the Constitution's newly ratified Fourteenth Amendment proclaimed, "No State shall ... deny to any person within its jurisdiction the equal protection of the laws." Equality has been a long time coming. For nearly a century after the abolition of slavery, American blacks were denied equal protection by law in some states and by social practice nearly everywhere. One-third of the states either permitted or forced schools to become racially segregated, and segregation was achieved elsewhere through housing policy and social behavior. In 1954 the Supreme Court reversed a 58-year-old standard that had found "separate but equal" schools compatible with equal protection of the law. A unanimous decision in *Brown v. Board of Education* held that separate is *not* equal for the members of the discriminated-against group when the segregation "generates a feeling of inferiority as to their status in the community that may affect their hearts and minds in a way unlikely ever to be undone." The 1954 ruling on public elementary education has been extended to other areas of both governmental and private conduct, including housing and employment.

Even if judicial decisions and congressional statutes could end all segregation and racial discrimination, would this achieve equality—or simply perpetuate the status quo? Consider that the unemployment rate for blacks today is more than twice that of whites. Disproportionately higher numbers of blacks experience poverty, brutality, broken homes, physical and mental illness, and early deaths, while disproportionately lower numbers of them reach positions of affluence and prestige. It seems possible that much of this inequality has resulted from 300 years of slavery and segregation. Is termination of this ill treatment enough to end the injustices? No, say the proponents of affirmative action.

Affirmative action—the effort to improve the educational and employment opportunities for minorities—has had an uneven history in U.S. federal courts. In *Regents of the University of California v. Allan Bakke* (1978), which marked the first time the Supreme Court dealt directly with the merits of affirmative action, a 5–4 majority ruled that a white applicant to a medical school had been wrongly excluded in favor of a less qualified black applicant due to the school's affirmative action policy. Yet the majority also agreed that "race-conscious" policies may be used in admitting candidates—as long as they do not amount to fixed quotas. The ambivalence of *Bakke* has run through the Court's treatment of the issue since 1978. More recent decisions suggest that the Court is beginning to take a dim view of affirmative action. In 1989, for example, the Court ruled that a city council could *not* set aside a fixed percentage of public construction projects for minority contractors.

Affirmative action is hotly debated outside the courts, and white males have recently been vocal on talk shows and in print about being treated unjustly because of affirmative action policies. In the following selections, Walter E. Williams and Clarence Page debate the merits of affirmative action. In Williams's view, affirmative action has outlived its usefulness, and the government should follow a policy of strict race neutrality. Page, on the other hand, considers affirmative action an essential means for undoing some of the effects of white racism.

YES

Walter E. Williams

AFFIRMATIVE ACTION
CAN'T BE MENDED

For the last several decades, affirmative action has been the basic component of the civil rights agenda. But affirmative action, in the form of racial preferences, has worn out its political welcome. In Gallup Polls, between 1987 and 1990, people were asked if they agreed with the statement: "We should make every effort to improve the position of blacks and other minorities even if it means giving them preferential treatment." More than 70 percent of the respondents opposed preferential treatment while only 24 percent supported it. Among blacks, 66 percent opposed preferential treatment and 32 percent supported it (Lipset 1992: 66–69).

The rejection of racial preferences by the broad public and increasingly by the Supreme Court has been partially recognized by even supporters of affirmative action. While they have not forsaken their goals, they have begun to distance themselves from some of the language of affirmative action. Thus, many business, government, and university affirmative action offices have been renamed "equity offices." Racial preferences are increasingly referred to as "diversity multiculturalism." What is it about affirmative action that gives rise to its contentiousness?

For the most part, post-World War II America has supported civil rights for blacks. Indeed, if we stick to the uncorrupted concept of civil rights, we can safely say that the civil rights struggle for blacks is over and won. Civil rights properly refer to rights, held simultaneously among individuals, to be treated equally in the eyes of the law, make contracts, sue and be sued, give evidence, associate and travel freely, and vote. There was a time when blacks did not fully enjoy those rights. With the yeoman-like work of civil rights organizations and decent Americans, both black and white, who fought lengthy court, legislative, and street battles, civil rights have been successfully secured for blacks. No small part of that success was due to a morally compelling appeal to America's civil libertarian tradition of private property, rule of law, and limited government.

Today's corrupted vision of civil rights attacks that civil libertarian tradition. Principles of private property rights, rule of law, freedom of association, and limited government are greeted with contempt. As such, the agenda of today's civil rights organizations conceptually differs little from yesteryear's restrictions that were the targets of the earlier civil rights struggle. Yesteryear civil rights organizations fought *against* the use of race in hiring, access to public schools, and university admissions. Today, civil rights organizations fight *for* the use of race in hiring, access to public schools, and university admissions. Yesteryear, civil rights organizations fought *against* restricted association in the forms of racially segregated schools, libraries, and private organizations. Today, they fight *for* restricted associations. They use state power, not unlike the racists they fought, to enforce racial associations they deem desirable. They protest that blacks should be a certain percentage of a company's workforce or clientele, a certain percentage of a student body, and even a certain percentage of an advertiser's models.

Civil rights organizations, in their successful struggle against state-sanctioned segregation, have lost sight of what it means to be truly committed to liberty, especially the freedom of association. The true test of that commitment does not come when we allow people to be free to associate in ways we deem appropriate. The true test is when we allow people to form those voluntary associations we deem offensive. It is the same principle we apply to our commitment to free speech. What tests our commitment to free speech is our willingness to permit people the freedom to say things we find offensive.

ZERO-SUM GAMES

The tragedy of America's civil rights movement is that it has substituted today's government-backed racial favoritism in the allocation of resources for yesteryear's legal and extra-legal racial favoritism. In doing so, civil rights leaders fail to realize that government allocation of resources produces the kind of conflict that does not arise with market allocation of resources. Part of the reason is that any government allocation of resources, including racial preferential treatment, is a zero-sum game.

A zero-sum game is defined as any transaction where one person's gain necessarily results in another person's loss. The simplest example of a zero-sum game is poker. A winner's gain is matched precisely by the losses of one or more persons. In this respect, the only essential difference between affirmative action and poker is that in poker participation is voluntary. Another difference is the loser is readily identifiable, a point to which I will return later.

The University of California, Berkeley's affirmative action program for blacks captures the essence of a zero-sum game. Blacks are admitted with considerably lower average SAT scores (952) than the typical white (1232) and Asian student (1254) (Sowell 1993: 144). Between UCLA and UC Berkeley, more than 2,000 white and Asian straight A students are turned away in order to provide spaces for black and Hispanic students (Lynch 1989: 163). The admissions gains by blacks are exactly matched by admissions losses by white and Asian students. Thus, any preferential treatment program results in a zero-sum game almost by definition.

More generally, government allocation of resources is a zero-sum game primarily because government has no resources of its very own. When government gives some citizens food stamps, crop subsidies, or disaster relief payments, the recipients of the largesse gain. Losers are identified by asking: where does government acquire the resources to confer the largesse? In order for government to give to some citizens, it must through intimidation, threats, and coercion take from other citizens. Those who lose the rights to their earnings, to finance government largesse, are the losers.

Government-mandated racial preferential treatment programs produce a similar result. When government creates a special advantage for one ethnic group, it necessarily comes at the expense of other ethnic groups for whom government simultaneously creates a special disadvantage in the form of reduced alternatives. If a college or employer has X amount of positions, and R of them have been set aside for blacks or some other group, that necessarily means there are $(X - R)$ fewer positions for which other ethnic groups might compete. At a time when there were restrictions against blacks, that operated in favor of whites, those restrictions translated into a reduced opportunity set for blacks. It is a zero-sum game independent of the race or ethnicity of the winners and losers.

Our courts have a blind-sided vision of the zero-sum game. They have upheld discriminatory racial preferences in hiring but have resisted discriminatory racial preferences in job layoffs. An example is the U.S. Supreme Court's ruling in *Wygant v. Jackson Board of Education* (1986), where a teacher union's collective-bargaining agreement protected black teachers from job layoffs in order to maintain racial balance. Subsequently, as a result of that agreement, the Jackson County School Board laid off white teachers having greater seniority while black teachers with less seniority were retained.

A lower court upheld the constitutionality of the collective bargaining agreement by finding that racial preferences in layoffs were a permissible means to remedy societal discrimination (*Wygant* 1982: 1195, 1201). White teachers petitioned the U.S. Supreme Court, claiming their constitutional rights under the Equal Protection clause were violated. The Court found in their favor. Justice Lewis F. Powell delivered the opinion saying, "While hiring goals impose a diffuse burden, only closing one of several opportunities, layoffs impose the entire burden of achieving racial equity on particular individuals, often resulting in serious disruption of their lives. The burden is too intrusive" (*Wygant* 1986: 283). . . .

There is no conceptual distinction in the outcome of the zero-sum game whether it is played on the layoff or the hiring side of the labor market. . . . The diffuseness to which Justice Powell refers is not diffuseness at all. It is simply that the victims of hiring preferences are less visible than victims of layoff preferences as in the case of *Wygant*. The petitioners in *Wygant* were identifiable people who could not be covered up as "society." That differs from the cases of hiring and college admissions racial preferences where those who face a reduced opportunity set tend to be unidentifiable to the courts, other people, and even to themselves. Since they are invisible victims, the Supreme Court and others can blithely say racial hiring goals (and admission goals) impose a diffuse burden.

TENTATIVE VICTIM IDENTIFICATION

In California, voters passed the California Civil Rights Initiative of 1996 (CCRI) that says: "The state shall not discriminate against, or grant preferential treatment to, any individual or group on the basis of race, sex, color, ethnicity, or national origin in the operation of public employment, public education, or public contracting." Therefore, California public universities can no longer have preferential admission policies that include race as a factor in deciding whom to admit. As a result, the UCLA School of Law reported accepting only 21 black applicants for its fall 1997 class—a drop of 80 percent from the previous year, in which 108 black applicants were accepted. At the UC Berkeley Boalt Hall School of Law, only 14 of the 792 students accepted for the fall 1997 class are black, down from 76 the previous year. At the UCLA School of Law, white enrollment increased by 14 percent for the fall 1997 term and Asian enrollment rose by 7 percent. At UC Berkeley, enrollment of white law students increased by 12 percent and Asian law students increased by 18 percent (Weiss 1997)....

In the case of UC Berkeley's preferential admissions for blacks, those whites and Asians who have significantly higher SAT scores and grades than the admitted blacks are victims of reverse discrimination. However, in the eyes of the courts, others, and possibly themselves, they are invisible victims. In other words, no one can tell for sure who among those turned away would have gained entry to UC Berkeley were it not for the preferential treatment given to blacks....

AFFIRMATIVE ACTION AND SUPPLY

An important focus of affirmative action is statistical underrepresentation of different racial and ethnic groups on college and university campuses. If the percentages of blacks and Mexican-Americans, for example, are not at a level deemed appropriate by a court, administrative agency, or university administrator, racial preference programs are instituted. The inference made from the underrepresentation argument is that, in the absence of racial discrimination, groups would be represented on college campuses in proportion to their numbers in the relevant population. In making that argument, little attention is paid to the supply issue— that is, to the pool of students available that meet the standards or qualifications of the university in question.

In 1985, fewer than 1,032 blacks scored 600 and above on the verbal portion of the SAT and 1,907 scored 600 and above on the quantitative portion of the examination. There are roughly 58 elite colleges and universities with student body average composite SAT scores of 1200 and above (Sowell 1993: 142). If blacks scoring 600 or higher on the quantitative portion of the SAT (assuming their performance on the verbal portion of the examination gave them a composite SAT score of 1200 or higher) were recruited to elite colleges and universities, there would be less than 33 black students available per university. At none of those universities would blacks be represented according to their numbers in the population.

There is no evidence that suggests that university admissions offices practice racial discrimination by turning away blacks with SAT scores of 1200 or higher. In reality, there are not enough blacks to be admitted to leading colleges and universities on the same terms as other students, such that their numbers in the campus population bear any resemblance to their numbers in the general population.

Attempts by affirmative action programs to increase the percent of blacks admitted to top schools, regardless of whether blacks match the academic characteristics of the general student body, often produce disastrous results. In order to meet affirmative action guidelines, leading colleges and universities recruit and admit black students whose academic qualifications are well below the norm for other students. For example, of the 317 black students admitted to UC Berkeley in 1985, all were admitted under affirmative action criteria rather than academic qualifications. Those students had an average SAT score of 952 compared to the national average of 900 among all students. However, their SAT scores were well below UC Berkeley's average of nearly 1200. More than 70 percent of the black students failed to graduate from UC Berkeley (Sowell 1993: 144).

Not far from UC Berkeley is San Jose State University, not one of the top-tier colleges, but nonetheless respectable. More than 70 percent of its black students fail to graduate. The black students who might have been successful at San Jose State University have been recruited to UC Berkeley and elsewhere where they have been made artificial failures. This pattern is one of the consequences of trying to use racial preferences to make a student body reflect the relative importance of different ethnic groups in the general population. There is a mismatch between black student qualifications and those of other students when the wrong students are recruited to the wrong universities.

There is no question that preferential admissions is unjust to both white and Asian students who may be qualified but are turned away to make room for less-qualified students in the "right" ethnic group. However, viewed from a solely black self-interest point of view, the question should be asked whether such affirmative action programs serve the best interests of blacks. Is there such an abundance of black students who score above the national average on the SAT, such as those admitted to UC Berkeley, that blacks as a group can afford to have those students turned into artificial failures in the name of diversity, multiculturalism, or racial justice? The affirmative action debate needs to go beyond simply an issue of whether blacks are benefited at the expense of whites. Whites and Asians who are turned away to accommodate blacks are still better off than the blacks who were admitted. After all, graduating from the university of one's second choice is preferable to flunking out of the university of one's first choice.

To the extent racial preferences in admission produce an academic mismatch of students, the critics of California's Proposition 209 may be unnecessarily alarmed, assuming their concern is with black students actually graduating from college. If black students, who score 952 on the SAT, are not admitted to UC Berkeley, that does not mean that they cannot gain admittance to one of America's 3,000 other colleges. It means that they will gain admittance to some other college where their academic characteristics will be more similar to those of their peers. There will not be as much of an academic mismatch. To the extent this is true, we may see an *increase* in black graduation rates. Moreover, if black students find themselves more similar to their white peers in terms of college grades and graduation honors, they are less likely to feel academically isolated and harbor feelings of low self-esteem.

AFFIRMATIVE ACTION AND JUSTICE

Aside from any other question, we might ask what case can be made for the morality or justice of turning away more highly credentialed white and Asian students so as to be able to admit more blacks? Clearly, blacks as a group have suffered past injustices, including discrimination in college and university admissions. However, that fact does not spontaneously yield sensible policy proposals for today. The fact is that a special privilege cannot be created for one person without creating a special disadvantage for another. In the case of preferential admissions at UCLA and UC Berkeley, a special privilege for black students translates into a special disadvantage for white and Asian students. Thus, we must ask what have those individual white and Asian students done to deserve punishment? Were they at all responsible for the injustices, either in the past or present, suffered by blacks? If, as so often is the case, the justification for preferential treatment is to redress past grievances, how just is it to have a policy where a black of today is helped by punishing a white of today for what a white of yesterday did to a black of yesterday? Such an idea becomes even more questionable in light of the fact that so many whites and Asians cannot trace the American part of their ancestry back as much as two or three generations.

AFFIRMATIVE ACTION AND RACIAL RESENTMENT

In addition to the injustices that are a result of preferential treatment, such treatment has given rise to racial resentment where it otherwise might not exist. While few people support racial resentment and its manifestations, if one sees some of affirmative action's flagrant attacks on fairness and equality before the law, one can readily understand why resentment is on the rise.

In the summer of 1995, the Federal Aviation Administration (FAA) published a "diversity handbook" that said, "The merit promotion process is but one means of filling vacancies, which need not be utilized if it will not promote your diversity goals." In that spirit, one FAA job announcement said, "Applicants who meet the qualification requirements ... cannot be considered for this position.... Only those applicants who do not meet the Office of Personnel Management requirements ... will be eligible to compete" (Roberts and Stratton 1995: 141).

According to a General Accounting Office report that evaluated complaints of discrimination by Asian-Americans, prestigious universities such as UCLA, UC Berkeley, MIT, and the University of Wisconsin have engaged in systematic discrimination in the failure to admit highly qualified Asian students in order to admit relatively unqualified black and Hispanic students (U.S. GAO 1995).

In Memphis, Tennessee, a white police officer ranked 59th out of 209 applicants for 75 available positions as police sergeant, but he did not get promoted. Black officers, with lower overall test scores than he, were moved ahead of him and promoted to sergeant. Over a two-year period, 43 candidates with lower scores were moved ahead of him and made sergeant (Eastland 1996: 1–2).

There is little need to recite the litany of racial preference instances that are clear violations of commonly agreed upon standards of justice and fair play. But the dangers of racial preferences go beyond matters of justice and fair play. They lead to increased group polarization ranging from political backlash to mob violence and civil war as seen in other countries. The difference between the United States and those countries is that racial preferences have not produced the same level of violence (Sowell 1990). However, they have produced polarization and resentment.

Affirmative action proponents cling to the notion that racial discrimination satisfactorily explains black/white socioeconomic differences. While every vestige of racial discrimination has not been eliminated in our society, current social discrimination cannot begin to explain all that affirmative action proponents purport it explains. Rather than focusing our attention on discrimination, a higher pay-off can be realized by focusing on real factors such as fraudulent education, family disintegration, and hostile economic climates in black neighborhoods. Even if affirmative action was not a violation of justice and fair play, was not a zero-sum game, was not racially polarizing, it is a poor cover-up for the real work that needs to be done.

REFERENCES

Eastland, T. (1996) *Ending Affirmative Action: The Case for Colorblind Justice.* New York: Basic Books.

Lipset, S. M. (1992) "Equal Chances Versus Equal Results." In H. Orlans and J. O'Neill (eds.) *Affirmative Action Revisited; Annals of the American Academy of Political and Social Science* 523 (September): 63–74.

Lynch, F. R. (1989) *Invisible Victims: White Males and the Crisis of Affirmative Action.* New York: Greenwood Press.

Roberts, P. C., and Stratton, L. M. (1995) *The Color Line: How Quotas and Privilege Destroy Democracy.* Washington, D.C.: Regnery.

Sowell, T. (1990) *Preferential Policies: An International Perspective.* New York: William Morrow.

Sowell, T. (1993) *Inside American Education: The Decline, The Deception, The Dogmas.* New York: The Free Press.

United States General Accounting Office (1995) *Efforts by the Office for Civil Rights to Resolve Asian-American Complaints.* Washington, D.C.: Government Printing Office. (December).

Weiss, K. R. (1997) "UC Law Schools' New Rules Cost Minorities Spots." *Los Angeles Times,* 15 May.

Wygant v. Jackson Board of Education (1982) 546 F. Supp. 1195.

Wygant v. Jackson Board of Education (1986) 476 U.S. 267.

NO

Clarence Page

SUPPLY-SIDE AFFIRMATIVE ACTION

Occasionally I have been asked whether I ever benefited from affirmative action in my career. Yes, I respond. You might say that my first jobs in newspapers came as a result of an affirmative action program called "urban riots."

Most newspapers and broadcast news operations in America were not much interested in hiring black reporters or photographers when I graduated from high school in 1965. Nevertheless, I asked the editor of the local daily if he had any summer jobs in his newsroom. I knew I was good. I was an honors graduate and feature editor at the local high school's student newspaper. I had a regional award already glistening on my short resume. Still, I was not picky. I would be delighted to mop floors just to get a job in a real newsroom.

And it was not as if I did not have connections. The editor had known me since I had been one of his newspaper's carriers at age twelve. Still, it was not to be. He told me the budget would not allow any summer jobs for any young folks that year. Then the very next day I found out through a friend that the newspaper did have an opening after all. The editors had hired a white girl a year younger than I, who also happened to be a reporter under my supervision at the student newspaper, to fill it.

Don't get mad, my dad advised me, just get smart. Get your education, he said. "Then someday you can get even!"

My saintly, interminably patient schoolteacher grandmother, dear old Mother Page, also helped ease my tension. "Son," she said, "just prepare yourself, for someday the doors of opportunity will open up. When they do, you must be ready to step inside."

Little did she know that that very summer, riots would erupt in the Watts section of Los Angeles. More than four hundred riots would explode across the nation over the next three years. Suddenly editors and news directors across the country were actively looking to hire at least a few reporters and photographers who could be sent into the "ghetto" without looking too conspicuous.

Many of the black journalists hired in that talent raid, much of it waged on the staffs of black publications and radio stations, would bring Pulitzers and other honors to their new bosses, dispelling the notion that they were mere "tokens" and confirming the depth of talent that had been passed over for so long. Women soon followed. So did Hispanics, some of whom had worked for years with Anglo pseudonyms to get past anti-Latino prejudices; Asians; and Native Americans.

Times have changed. Twenty-two years after it became the first newspaper to turn me down for a job, my hometown daily became the first to purchase my newly syndicated column. The advice of my elders ("Just prepare yourself") had come to fruition.

You might say that it took me only twenty years to become an "overnight success."

Yet it is significant that I and other "first blacks" hired in the nation's newsrooms felt pretty lonely through several years of "tokenism" before affirmative hiring—or, if you prefer, "diversity hiring"—policies began to take hold at the dawn of the 1970s. The message to us journalists of color was clear: White managers did not mind hiring a few of us now and then, but they didn't want to make a habit of it, not until policies came down from the top stating in military fashion that "you *will* hire more women and minorities."

So, of all the arguments I have heard various people make against affirmative action, I find the least persuasive to be the charge that it makes its recipients feel bad. Stanford law professor Barbara Babcock had the proper response to that notion when President Jimmy Carter appointed her to head the civil rights division of the Justice Department. When she was asked in a press conference how it felt to think that she had gotten the job because she was a woman, she replied that it felt a lot better than thinking that she had *not* gotten the job because she was a woman.

True enough. Most white males have not felt particularly bad about the special preferences they have received because of their race and gender for thousands of years. Why should we? Believe me, compared to the alternative, preferential treatment feels better.

Nor have I heard many express a nagging doubt about their ability to "hack it" in fair competition with others. Quite the opposite, privileged groups tend to look upon their privilege as an entitlement. Whatever guilt or misgivings they may have are assuaged by the cottage industry that has grown up around bolstering the self-esteem of white people. Books like Charles Murray and Richard J. Herrnstein's *Bell Curve* are intended, at bottom, to answer this deep yearning. Much is made in the book about how whites perform fifteen percentage points higher on average than blacks do on standardized tests and that this may easily explain why whites earn more money than blacks. Little is made of how Asian Americans perform fifteen percentage points higher than whites, yet they have hardly taken over management or ownership of American corporations.

Or, as one of my black professional friends put it, "Since we all know that hardly any of us is really all-black, I want to know how come we only got all the dumb white folks' genes?"

The notion that Babcock should feel bad about her appointment is based on the pernicious presumption that, simply and solely because she is a woman, she must be less qualified than the man who normally would be preferred simply because he was a man.

Charles Sykes, in *A Nation of Victims: The Decay of the American Character* (1993), says that those who insist on affirmative action really are arguing that "minorities" (he speaks little of women) cannot meet existing standards, and that ultimately affirmative action forces all minorities to "deal with the nagging doubt that its policies stigmatize all successful minority individuals."

Another critic of affirmative action, Dinesh D'Souza, resident scholar at the American Enterprise Institute, goes so far as to say in his inflammatory *The End of Racism: Principles for a Multiracial Society* (1995) that most of us middle-class blacks should be stigmatized because we owe our prosperity, such as it is, to affirmative action. He then speculates that middle-class blacks must suffer "intense feelings of guilt" because "they have abandoned their poor brothers and sisters, and realize that their present circumstances became possible solely because of the heart-wrenching sufferings of the underclass."

Yet nothing in affirmative action law calls for the unqualified to be hired regardless of merit. Even "special admissions" minority students are selected from among those who already have met the standards required to do the college's work.

Affirmative action calls only for "merit" standards to be more inclusive. Affirmative action, properly implemented, *widens the pool* of qualified candidates who will be considered. This often benefits qualified white males, too, who would otherwise have been bypassed because of nepotism, favoritism, and other unnecessarily narrow criteria. My favorite example is the University of Indiana Law School's decision in 1969 to broaden its acceptance criteria to open doors to bright, promising applicants who showed high potential but, for the present, had not scored as well as other applicants in a highly competitive field. The goal of the program was to offer a second chance to disadvantaged students like those who could be found in abundance in Gary and other urban centers, but the program was not limited to them. Several white students got in, too. One was a well-heeled De Pauw University graduate named J. Danforth Quayle. He later became vice president of the United States. He apparently had not scored well enough to qualify for the law school under existing criteria, but, like him or not, he did have potential. Some people are late bloomers....

Arguments against affirmative action fall under the following general categories:

"We don't need it anymore." The work of early feminists and the civil rights movement did their job, but now it is time to move on. The nation has outgrown employment and educational discrimination. Nonwhite skin may actually be an advantage in many businesses and schools. The market is ultimately color-blind and would be fair, if only those infernal lawyers and government regulators would get out of the way.

Comment: Americans hate intrusions into their marketplace, unless the intrusions benefit them. I would argue that bias is as natural as xenophobia and as common as apple pie. Until opportunities are equalized enough to encourage women and minorities to have more trust in the free marketplace, there will be a glaring demand for extraordinary measures to target what is actually only a quite modest amount of jobs, scholarships, and contracts to minorities.

"Racism has reversed." This is David Duke's claim. Whites, particularly white males, now suffer a distinct disadvantage in the workplace and in college applications. Affirmative action sets racial "quotas" that only reinforce prejudices. Besides, two wrongs do not make a right.

Comment: Not anymore. Conservative court decisions in the 1990s actually have shifted the burden of proof in hiring, promotions, publicly funded scholarships, and contract set-aside cases from whites and males to minorities and women. If women and minorities ever had a time of supremacy under the law, it is gone. Conservative court opinions have worked hastily to restore white male primacy.

"It cheats those who need help most." The biggest beneficiaries of affirmative action have been, first, middle-class women and, second, advantaged minorities. It misses the less qualified "underclass."

Comment: It is easy to criticize a program that fails to reach goals it never was intended to achieve. The argument that affirmative action benefits those who need help the least falsely presumes affirmative action to be (1) an antipoverty program and (2) a program that forces employers and colleges to accept the unqualified. It is neither. It is an equal opportunity process that, by that definition, helps most those who are best equipped to take advantage of opportunities once they are opened. I find it ironic that many of the same critics who argue that affirmative action is anticompetitive and bad for business can so quickly spin on a dime to complain that it also is uncharitable.

For example, the biggest black beneficiaries of affirmative action have been working-class blacks who had skills but were shut out of slots for which they were fully qualified in higher-paying blue-collar semiskilled, service, craft, police, and firefighter jobs because of restrictive unions and other discriminatory policies. Before President Nixon signed an executive order in 1972 calling for vigorous affirmative action among federal contractors, few black carpenters, plumbers, and other skilled building tradesmen were allowed to receive union cards. Only when construction boomed high enough to hire all available whites were skilled black tradesmen given union cards, and then only temporary cards, on a last-hired, first-fired basis. Significantly, within months of signing the executive order, Nixon was campaigning for reelection against racial "quotas." His executive order had come not so much out of his best intentions for blacks as out of a keen desire to drive a political wedge between minorities and labor-union whites.

Other examples can be found in the southern textile industry, which, under government pressure in the middle and late 1960s, finally hired blacks into their predominantly female workforce as laborers, operatives, and service and craft workers. "As a result, these black women—many of whom had spent their working lives cleaning other people's homes for a few dollars a day—tripled their wages, an enormous improvement in the quality of their lives," Gertrude Ezorsky, a Brooklyn College philosophy professor, wrote in *Racism & Justice: The Case for Affirmative Action* (1991). "I conclude that affirmative action has not merely helped a 'few fortunate' blacks."

"Be like the model minorities." Behave more like Asians and, for that matter, hardworking immigrant African and West Indian blacks who appear to get along just fine despite racism and without affirmative action. In one notable screed, backlash journalist Jared Taylor's *Paved with Good Intentions: The Failure of Race Relations in America,* asks the question: Why do blacks continue in spite of civil rights reforms and outright preferential treatment to bring so much trouble on themselves and others with family failures, violent crimes, and drug abuse? Black leaders are no help, says Taylor, for they have become "shakedown artists" who encourage excuses, handouts, and self-pity that generate a "denial of individual responsibility." Why, oh why, asks Taylor, don't blacks simply behave more like Asian immigrants in "taking possession of their own lives"?

Comment: Opponents of affirmative action invented the "model minority" myth to stereotype Asian-American success in misleading ways that don't benefit Asians or anyone else. According to the myth, Asians succeed better academically and earn higher household income than whites despite racial discrimination and without the benefit of affirmative action. Quite the contrary, goes the myth, affirmative action sets quota ceilings on Asian participation, much like those that once limited enrollment of Jews in the Ivy League. So, therefore, affirmative action actually is harmful, both to minority initiative and to Asian success.

It's an attractive myth, but reality is a bit more complicated. There is a significant difference, for example, between *household* income and *individual* income. Asian household income, like the household income of immigrant blacks from the West Indies, exceeds white household income because more individuals in the house are likely to be working. Asian individual income still lags behind whites at every income level, from the bottom,

where low-income Hmongs and many Filipinos, in particular, suffer poverty not unlike that of poor blacks and Hispanics, to the upper levels of corporate management, where a new set of myths continue to stereotype Asians as "not quite American" or "good at rational skills, but not 'people skills.'" Asian-American friends whose families have been here for several generations speak of being asked routinely, "You speak such good English; how long have you been in this country?" More ominous to many Asians are the horror stories like that of Vincent Chin, a Chinese-American who was beaten to death one night in the early 1980s by two disgruntled Detroit auto workers who were angry at competition by Japanese automakers....

"Give meritocracy a chance."   Free market zealots like University of Chicago law professor Richard Epstein, who believes all "irrational discrimination" would disappear in an unfettered marketplace, have called for the elimination of anti-discrimination laws, saying the market will punish those who turn aside talented workers or customers with money in their pockets just because of race or ethnicity. D'Souza agrees with Epstein's bold assertion that anti-discrimination laws actually get in the way of women and minorities who would prefer to hire family members. He calls for an end to all anti-discrimination laws except those that apply solely to government.

Comment: "Merit" by whose standard? Market forces do count, but so do culture and personal prejudices. Segregation cost white businesses valuable consumer business, yet, even in the North, where it was required only by local custom, not by government, many refused to serve blacks anyway.

Any intrusions into the marketplace trouble free-market conservatives like Epstein and D'Souza, but the larger question we Americans must ask ourselves is this: What kind of country do we want? There is no neutral "color-blind" approach to the law that has for centuries been tilted against women and minorities. It either defends the status quo, which is imbalanced by race and gender, it shifts some benefits to certain groups, or it shifts benefits away from those groups. Do we want rampant irrational completely unfair discrimination reminiscent of the Jim Crow days that dehumanizes large numbers of Americans while we wait for the vagaries of the marketplace to catch up? Or do we want to shape law and social practice to encourage people to mix, get to know each other better, and ultimately reduce tensions?

"It encourages balkanization." Affirmative action opens social wedges that threatens to replace the basic American melting pot creed with a new "balkanization."

Comment: Anyone who thinks American society was *less* balkanized in the 1950s and 1960s was not only color-blind but also quite deaf to the complaints of people of color. If there were less racial or gender friction in major newsrooms, campuses, and other workplaces, it is only because there was no race or gender in them except white men.

Racism and sexism have not disappeared, it is widely agreed, they have only become more subtle—"gone underground"—making them less easy to detect, harder to root out. Most of us tend to ignore our own prejudices un-

less someone points them out. If individuals wish to discriminate in their private social world, that's their business. But discrimination in hiring and promotional practices is everyone's business. With the courts already jammed and the complaint mechanisms of the Equal Employment Opportunity Commission suffering backlogs of two years or worse, especially after Americans with Disabilities Act cases were layered onto its already overtaxed, underfunded enforcement mechanisms, promises of enforcement of individual complaints were simply not enough to make up for cruel realities. Even when the courts do reach guilty verdicts, they often impose racial or gender quotas onto the plaintiffs as part of the penalty and remedies. Such court-ordered mandates are, by the way, the only real "quotas" that are allowed under civil rights law and only as a last resort to remedy particularly egregious cases of historic discrimination, such as the police and fire department hiring and promotion practices in cities like Chicago, Memphis, and Birmingham. Yet even these quotas have been quite modest, used sparingly, and, beginning in the 1980s, steadily rolled back by the courts, even while the numbers showed modest progress in the face of the enormous problem.

What most people call rigid "quotas" are actually quite flexible goals and timetables, a distinction that has diminished in the public mind in recent years as conservative politicians have, with remarkable success, attacked flexible goals and timetables with as much vigor as they once reserved for attacking rigid quotas.

"Focus on class not race." In attempts to salvage some rudiments of affirmative action in the face of a conservative onslaught, some centrists have argued for programs that reach out to the most needy, regardless of race or gender. If such programs are conducted equitably, a preponderance of minorities will be brought in anyway, without the dubious air of unfairness.

The ghetto "underclass" has not benefited from affirmative action, University of Chicago sociology professor William Julius Wilson writes in *The Truly Disadvantaged* (1987) because this group is "outside the mainstream of the American occupational system." For this group, Wilson advocates macroeconomic policies aimed at promoting economic growth to replace inner-city manufacturing jobs lost since the 1950s and on-the-job training programs.

Each of these arguments has some merit and much myth. Left to our own devices, most of us unfortunately will discriminate, often in ways too subtle for us to notice even when we do it. Either way, such irrational discrimination occurs and is not healthy for a diverse society....

America will not have racial equality until opportunities are equalized, beginning at the preschool level, to build up the supply of qualified applicants for the new jobs emerging in information-age America. The American ideal of equal opportunity still produces rewards, when it is given a real try. It needs to be tried more often. Affirmative action is not a perfect remedy, but it beats the alternative, if the only alternative is to do nothing.

POSTSCRIPT

Has Affirmative Action Outlived Its Usefulness?

Despite their basic disagreement, both Williams and Page desire a colorblind society. The authors' main disagreement is on the need for affirmative action today to achieve this goal. Page suggests that in order to *bring about* color blindness, it may be necessary to become temporarily color conscious. But for how long? And is there a danger that this temporary color consciousness may become a permanent policy, as Williams fears? Williams observes that Americans support "soft affirmative action" but are opposed to more aggressive affirmative action. Could less aggressive affirmative action be the way to greater national unity on the race issue?

The writings on this subject are diverse and numerous. For a personal reading of black and white attitudes, see Studs Terkel, *Race: How Blacks and Whites Think and Feel About the American Obsession* (New Press, 1992). For a more academic reading of white racial attitudes, see Paul M. Sniderman and Thomas Piazza, *The Scar of Race* (Harvard University Press, 1993). One way to learn about racism is to read Gregory Howard Williams's story about living as a black after years as a white in *Life on the Color Line: The True Story of a White Boy Who Discovered He Was Black* (E. P. Dutton, 1995). Two works that portray the experiences of racism by the black middle class are Ellis Close, *The Rage of a Privileged Class* (HarperCollins, 1993) and Joe R. Feagin and Melvin P. Sikes, *Living With Racism: The Black Middle-Class Experience* (Beacon, 1994). Two personal accounts of this experience are Brent Staples, *Parallel Time: Growing Up in Black and White* (Pantheon, 1994) and Henry Louis Gates, *Colored People* (Free Press, 1994). Steven L. Carter's *Reflections of an Affirmative Action Baby* (Basic Books, 1991) is based on the author's own experiences under affirmative action. Andrew Hacker argues that affirmative action has relatively minor adverse consequences for whites in *Two Nations: Black and White, Separate, Hostile, Unequal* (Charles Scribner's Sons, 1992). Lee Sigleman and Susan Welch, in *Black Americans' Views of Racial Inequality: The Dream Deferred* (Cambridge University Press, 1991), argue that blacks and whites have basically different perspectives of the racial situation. Dinesh D'Souza, in *The End of Racism* (Free Press, 1995), argues that white racism has pretty much disappeared in the United States. The opposite is argued by Joe Feagin and Hernan Vera in *White Racism: The Basics* (Routledge, 1995) and by Stephen Steinberg in *Turning Back* (Beacon Press, 1995). Further support for the thesis of continuing racism is supplied by Douglas S. Massey and Nancy A. Denton in *American Apartheid: Segregation and the Making of the Underclass* (Harvard University Press, 1993).

On the Internet . . .

Economic Report of the President
This report includes current and anticipated trends in the United States and annual numerical goals concerning topics such as employment, production, real income, and federal budget outlays. The database notes employment objectives for significant groups of the labor force, annual numeric goals, and a plan for carrying out program objectives.
http://www.library.nwu.edu/gpo/help/econr.html

HandsNet on the Web
This site from HandsNet is meant to serve as a clearing-house for information about current welfare reform efforts at the national, state, and local levels.
http://www.igc.apc.org/handsnet2/welfare.reform/index.html

National Center for Policy Analysis
Through this site you can read discussions that are of major interest in the study of American politics and government from a sociological perspective.
http://www.public-policy.org/~ncpa/pd/pdindex.html

Policy.com
Visit this site of the "policy community" to examine major issues related to social welfare, welfare reform, social work, and many other topics. The site includes substantial resources for researching issues online.
http://www.policy.com/

PART 4

Political Economy and Institutions

Are political power and economic power merged within a "power elite" that dominates the U.S. political system? The first issue in this part explores that debate. The second issue concerns the proper role of government in the economy. Some believe that the government must correct for the many failures of the market, while others think that the government usually complicates the workings of the free market. The next debate concerns public policy: How should we assess the impact and efficacy of welfare programs? The fourth issue examines the role of the government in public education. Finally, the last issue in this part looks at doctor-assisted suicide for terminally ill patients.

■ Is Government Dominated by Big Business?

■ Should Government Intervene in a Capitalist Economy?

■ Will Welfare Reform Benefit the Poor?

■ Are Vouchers the Solution to the Ills of Public Education?

■ Should Doctor-Assisted Suicide Be Legalized for the Terminally Ill?

ISSUE 11

Is Government Dominated by Big Business?

YES: G. William Domhoff, from *Who Rules America? Power and Politics in the Year 2000,* 3rd ed. (Mayfield Publishing, 1998)

NO: Jeffrey M. Berry, from "Citizen Groups and the Changing Nature of Interest Group Politics in America," *The Annals of the American Academy of Political and Social Science* (July 1993)

ISSUE SUMMARY

YES: Political sociologist G. William Domhoff argues that the "owners and top-level managers in large income-producing properties are far and away the dominant power figures in the United States" and that they have inordinate influence in the federal government.

NO: Jeffrey M. Berry, a professor of political science, contends that public interest pressure groups that have entered the political arena since the end of the 1960s have effectively challenged the political power of big business.

Since the framing of the U.S. Constitution in 1787, there have been periodic charges that America is unduly influenced by wealthy financial interests. Richard Henry Lee, a signer of the Declaration of Independence, spoke for many Anti-Federalists (those who opposed ratification of the Constitution) when he warned that the proposed charter shifted power away from the people and into the hands of the "aristocrats" and "moneyites."

Before the Civil War, Jacksonian Democrats denounced the eastern merchants and bankers who, they charged, were usurping the power of the people. After the Civil War, a number of radical parties and movements revived this theme of antielitism. The ferment—which was brought about by the rise of industrial monopolies, government corruption, and economic hardship for western farmers—culminated in the founding of the People's Party at the beginning of the 1890s. The Populists, as they were more commonly called, wanted economic and political reforms aimed at transferring power away from the rich and back to "the plain people."

By the early 1900s the People's Party had disintegrated, but many writers and activists have continued to echo the Populists' central thesis: that the U.S. democratic political system is in fact dominated by business elites. Yet the thesis has not gone unchallenged. During the 1950s and the early 1960s, many social scientists subscribed to the *pluralist* view of America.

Pluralists argue that because there are many influential elites in America, each group is limited to some extent by the others. There are some groups, like the business elites, that are more powerful than their opponents, but even the more powerful groups are denied their objectives at times. Labor groups are often opposed to business groups; conservative interests challenge liberal interests, and vice versa; and organized civil libertarians sometimes fight with groups that seek government-imposed bans on pornography or groups that demand tougher criminal laws. No single group, the pluralists argue, can dominate the political system.

Pluralists readily acknowledge that American government is not democratic in the full sense of the word; it is not driven by the majority. But neither, they insist, is it run by a conspiratorial "power elite." In the pluralist view, the closest description of the American form of government would be neither majority rule nor minority rule but *minorities* rule. (Note that in this context, "minorities" does not necessarily refer to race or ethnicity but to any organized group of people with something in common—including race, religion, or economic interests—not constituting a majority of the population.) Each organized minority enjoys some degree of power in the making of public policy. In extreme cases, when a minority feels threatened, its power may take a negative form: the power to derail policy. When the majority—or, more accurately, a coalition of other minorities—attempts to pass a measure that threatens the vital interests of an organized minority, that group may use its power to obstruct their efforts. (Often cited in this connection is the use of the Senate filibuster, which is the practice of using tactics during the legislative process that cause extreme delays or prevent action, thus enabling a group to "talk to death" a bill that threatens its vital interests.) But in the pluralist view negative power is not the only driving force: when minorities work together and reach consensus on certain issues, they can institute new laws and policy initiatives that enjoy broad public support. Pluralism, though capable of producing temporary gridlock, ultimately leads to compromise, consensus, and moderation.

Critics of pluralism argue that pluralism is an idealized depiction of a political system that is in the grip of powerful elite groups. Critics fault pluralist theory for failing to recognize the extent to which big business dominates the policy-making process. In the selections that follow, G. William Domhoff supports this view, identifies the groups that compose the power elite, and details the way they control or support social, political, and knowledge-producing associations and organizations that advance their interests. Jeffrey M. Berry, in opposition, argues that, thanks to new consumer, environmental, and other citizen groups, big business no longer enjoys the cozy relationship it once had with Washington policymakers.

YES

G. William Domhoff

WHO RULES AMERICA?

POWER AND CLASS IN THE UNITED STATES

...[T]he owners and top-level managers in large income-producing properties are far and away the dominant power figures in the United States. Their corporations, banks, and agribusinesses come together as a *corporate community* that dominates the federal government in Washington. Their real estate, construction, and land development companies form *growth coalitions* that dominate most local governments. Granted, there is competition within both the corporate community and the local growth coalitions for profits and investment opportunities, and there are sometimes tensions between national corporations and local growth coalitions, but both are cohesive on policy issues affecting their general welfare, and in the face of demands by organized workers, liberals, environmentalists, and neighborhoods.

As a result of their ability to organize and defend their interests, the owners and managers of large income-producing properties have a very great share of all income and wealth in the United States, greater than in any other industrial democracy. Making up at best 1 percent of the total population, by the early 1990s they earned 15.7 percent of the nation's yearly income and owned 37.2 percent of all privately held wealth, including 49.6 percent of all corporate stocks and 62.4 percent of all bonds. Due to their wealth and the lifestyle it makes possible, these owners and managers draw closer as a common social group. They belong to the same exclusive social clubs, frequent the same summer and winter resorts, and send their children to a relative handful of private schools. Members of the corporate community thereby become a *corporate rich* who create a nationwide *social upper class* through their social interaction.... Members of the growth coalitions, on the other hand, are *place entrepreneurs,* people who sell locations and buildings. They come together as local upper classes in their respective cities and sometimes mingle with the corporate rich in educational or resort settings.

The corporate rich and the growth entrepreneurs supplement their small numbers by developing and directing a wide variety of nonprofit organizations, the most important of which are a set of tax-free charitable foundations, think tanks, and policy-discussion groups. These specialized nonprofit groups constitute a *policy-formation network* at the national level. Chambers of commerce and policy groups affiliated with them form similar policy-formation networks at the local level, aided by a few national-level city development organizations that are available for local consulting.

Those corporate owners who have the interest and ability to take part in general governance join with top-level executives in the corporate community and the policy-formation network to form the *power elite*, which is the leadership group for the corporate rich as a whole. The concept of a power elite makes clear that not all members of the upper class are involved in governance; some of them simply enjoy the lifestyle that their great wealth affords them. At the same time, the focus on a leadership group allows for the fact that not all those in the power elite are members of the upper class; many of them are high-level employees in profit and nonprofit organizations controlled by the corporate rich. . . .

The power elite is not united on all issues because it includes both moderate conservatives and ultraconservatives. Although both factions favor minimal reliance on government on all domestic issues, the moderate conservatives sometimes agree to legislation advocated by liberal elements of the society, especially in times of social upheaval like the Great Depression of the 1930s and the Civil Rights Movement of the early 1960s. Except on defense spending, ultraconservatives are characterized by a complete distaste for any kind of government programs under any circumstances—even to the point of opposing government support for corporations on some issues.

Moderate conservatives often favor foreign aid, working through the United Nations, and making attempts to win over foreign enemies through patient diplomacy, treaties, and trade agreements. Historically, ultraconservatives have opposed most forms of foreign involvement, although they have become more tolerant of foreign trade agreements over the past thirty or forty years. At the same time, their hostility to the United Nations continues unabated.

Members of the power elite enter into the electoral arena as the leaders within a *corporate-conservative coalition*, where they are aided by a wide variety of patriotic, antitax, and other single-issue organizations. These conservative advocacy organizations are funded in varying degrees by the corporate rich, direct-mail appeals, and middle-class conservatives. This coalition has played a large role in both political parties at the presidential level and usually succeeds in electing a conservative majority to both houses of Congress. Historically, the conservative majority in Congress was made up of most Northern Republicans and most Southern Democrats, but that arrangement has been changing gradually since the 1960s as the conservative Democrats of the South are replaced by even more conservative Southern Republicans. The corporate-conservative coalition also has access to the federal government in Washington through lobbying and the appointment of its members to top positions in the executive branch. . . .

Despite their preponderant power within the federal government and the many useful policies it carries out for them, members of the power elite are constantly critical of government as an alleged enemy of freedom and economic growth. Although their wariness toward government is expressed in terms of a dislike for taxes and government regulations, I believe their underlying concern is that government could change the power relations in the private sphere by aiding average Americans through a number of different avenues: (1) creating government jobs for the unemployed; (2) making health, unemployment, and welfare benefits more generous; (3) helping employees gain greater workplace rights and protections; and (4) helping workers organize unions. All of these initiatives are opposed by members of the power elite because they would increase wages and taxes, but the deepest opposition is toward any government support for unions because unions are a potential organizational base for advocating the whole range of issues opposed by the corporate rich. . . .

Where Does Democracy Fit In?

. . .[T]o claim that the corporate rich have enough power to be considered a dominant class does not imply that lower social classes are totally powerless. *Domination* means the power to set the terms under which other groups and classes must operate, not total control. Highly trained professionals with an interest in environmental and consumer issues have been able to couple their technical information and their understanding of the legislative and judicial processes with well-timed publicity, lobbying, and lawsuits to win governmental restrictions on some corporate practices. Wage and salary employees, when they are organized into unions and have the right to strike, have been able to gain pay increases, shorter hours, better working conditions, and social benefits such as health insurance. Even the most powerless of people—the very poor and those discriminated against—sometimes develop the capacity to influence the power structure through sit-ins, demonstrations, social movements, and other forms of social disruption, and there is evidence that such activities do bring about some redress of grievances, at least for a short time.

More generally, the various challengers to the power elite sometimes work together on policy issues as a *liberal-labor coalition* that is based in unions, local environmental organizations, some minority group communities, university and arts communities, liberal churches, and small newspapers and magazines. Despite a decline in membership over the past twenty years, unions are the largest and best-financed part of the coalition, and the largest organized social force in the country (aside from churches). They also cut across racial and ethnic lines more than any other institutionalized sector of American society. . . .

The policy conflicts between the corporate-conservative and liberal-labor coalitions are best described as *class conflicts* because they primarily concern the distribution of profits and wages, the rate and progressivity of taxation, the usefulness of labor unions, and the degree to which business should be regulated by government. The liberal-labor coalition wants corporations to pay higher wages to employees and higher taxes to government. It wants government to regulate a wide range of business practices, including many that are related to the environment, and help employees to organize unions. The corporate-conservative coalition resists all these policy objectives to a greater or lesser degree, claiming they endanger the freedom of individuals and the efficient workings of the economic marketplace. The conflicts these disagreements generate can manifest themselves in many different ways: workplace protests, industrywide boycotts, massive demonstrations in cities, pressure on Congress, and the outcome of elections.

Neither the corporate-conservative nor the liberal-labor coalition includes a very large percentage of the American population, although each has the regular support of about 25–30 percent of the voters. Both coalitions are made up primarily of financial donors, policy experts, political consultants, and party activists....

Pluralism

The main alternative theory [I] address ... claims that power is more widely dispersed among groups and classes than a class-dominance theory allows. This general perspective is usually called *pluralism*, meaning there is no one dominant power group. It is the theory most favored by social scientists. In its strongest version, pluralism holds that power is held by the general public through the pressure that public opinion and voting put on elected officials. According to this version, citizens form voluntary groups and pressure groups that shape public opinion, lobby elected officials, and back sympathetic political candidates in the electoral process....

The second version of pluralism sees power as rooted in a wide range of well-organized "interest groups" that are often based in economic interests (e.g., industrialists, bankers, labor unions), but also in other interests as well (e.g., environmental, consumer, and civil rights groups). These interest groups join together in different coalitions depending on the specific issues. Proponents of this version of pluralism sometimes concede that public opinion and voting have only a minimal or indirect influence, but they see business groups as too fragmented and antagonistic to form a cohesive dominant class. They also claim that some business interest groups occasionally join coalitions with liberal or labor groups on specific issues, and that business-dominated coalitions sometimes lose. Furthermore, some proponents of this version of pluralism believe that the Democratic Party is responsive to the wishes of liberal and labor interest groups.

In contrast, I argue that the business interest groups are part of a tightly knit corporate community that is able to develop classwide cohesion on the issues of greatest concern to it: opposition to unions, high taxes, and government regulation. When a business group loses on a specific issue, it is often because other business groups have been opposed; in other words, there are arguments within the corporate community, and these arguments are usually settled within the governmental arena. I also claim that liberal and labor groups are rarely part of coalitions with business groups and that for most of its history the Democratic Party has been dominated by corporate and agribusiness interests in the Southern states, in partnership with the growth coalitions in large urban areas outside the South. Finally, I show that business interests rarely lose on labor and regulatory issues except in times of extreme social disruption like the 1930s and 1960s, when differences of opinion between Northern and Southern corporate leaders made victories for the liberal-labor coalition possible....

HOW THE POWER ELITE DOMINATES GOVERNMENT

This [section] shows how the power elite builds on the ideas developed in the policy-formation process and its success in the electoral arena to dominate the federal government. Lobbyists from corporations, law firms, and trade associations play a key role in shaping government on narrow issues of concern to specific corporations or business sectors, but their importance should not be overestimated because a majority of those elected to Congress are predisposed to agree with them. The corporate community and the policy-formation network supply top-level governmental appointees and new policy directions on major issues.

Once again, as seen in the battles for public opinion and electoral success, the power elite faces opposition from a minority of elected officials and their supporters in labor unions and liberal advocacy groups. These opponents are sometimes successful in blocking ultra-conservative initiatives, but most of the victories for the liberal-labor coalition are the result of support from moderate conservatives....

Appointees to Government
The first way to test a class-dominance view of the federal government is to study the social and occupational backgrounds of the people who are appointed to manage the major departments of the executive branch, such as state, treasury, defense, and justice. If pluralists are correct, these appointees should come from a wide range of interest groups. If the state autonomy theorists are correct, they should be disproportionately former elected officials or longtime government employees. If the class-dominance

view is correct, they should come disproportionately from the upper class, the corporate community, and the policy-formation network.

There have been numerous studies over the years of major governmental appointees under both Republican and Democratic administrations, usually focusing on the top appointees in the departments that are represented in the president's cabinet. These studies are unanimous in their conclusion that most top appointees in both Republican and Democratic administrations are corporate executives and corporate lawyers—and hence members of the power elite....

Conclusion
This [section] has demonstrated the power elite's wide-ranging access to government through the interest-group and policy-formation processes, as well as through its ability to influence appointments to major government positions. When coupled with the several different kinds of power discussed in earlier [sections] this access and involvement add up to power elite domination of the federal government.

By *domination,* as stated in the first [section], social scientists mean the ability of a class or group to set the terms under which other classes or groups within a social system must operate. By this definition, domination does not mean control on each and every issue, and it does not rest solely on involvement in government. Influence over government is only the final and most visible aspect of power elite domination, which has its roots in the class structure, the corporate control of the investment function, and the operation of the policy-formation network. If government officials did not have to wait for corporate leaders to decide where and when they will invest, and if government officials were not further limited by the general public's acceptance of policy recommendations from the policy-formation network, then power elite involvement in elections and government would count for a lot less than they do under present conditions.

Domination by the power elite does not negate the reality of continuing conflict over government policies, but few conflicts, it has been shown, involve challenges to the rules that create privileges for the upper class and domination by the power elite. Most of the numerous battles within the interest-group process, for example, are only over specific spoils and favors; they often involve disagreements among competing business interests.

Similarly, conflicts within the policy-making process of government often involve differences between the moderate conservative and ultraconservative segments of the dominant class. At other times they involve issues in which the needs of the corporate community as a whole come into conflict with the needs of specific industries, which is what happens to some extent on tariff policies and also on some environmental legislation. In neither case does the nature of the conflict call into question the domination of government by the power elite.

...Contrary to what pluralists claim, there is not a single case study on any issue of any significance that shows a liberal-labor victory over a united corporate-conservative coalition, which is strong evidence for a class-domination theory on the "Who wins?" power indicator. The classic case studies frequently cited by pluralists have been shown to be gravely deficient as evidence for their views. Most of these studies reveal either conflicts among rival groups within

the power elite or situations in which the moderate conservatives have decided for their own reasons to side with the liberal-labor coalition....

More generally, it now can be concluded that all four indicators of power introduced in [the first section] point to the corporate rich and their power elite as the dominant organizational structure in American society. First, the wealth and income distributions are skewed in their favor more than in any other industrialized democracy. They are clearly the most powerful group in American society in terms of "Who benefits?" Second, the appointees to government come overwhelmingly from the corporate community and its associated policy-formation network. Thus, the power elite is clearly the most powerful in terms of "Who sits?"

Third, the power elite wins far more often than it loses on policy issues resolved in the federal government. Thus, it is the most powerful in terms of "Who wins?" Finally, as shown in reputational studies in the 1950s and 1970s,... corporate leaders are the most powerful group in terms of "Who shines?" By the usual rules of evidence in a social science investigation using multiple indicators, the owners and managers of large income-producing properties are the dominant class in the United States.

Still, as noted at the end of the first [section], power structures are not immutable. Societies change and power structures evolve or crumble from time to unpredictable time, especially in the face of challenge. When it is added that the liberal-labor coalition persists in the face of its numerous defeats, and that free speech and free elections are not at risk, there remains the possibility that class domination could be replaced by a greater sharing of power in the future.

NO

Jeffrey M. Berry

CITIZEN GROUPS AND THE CHANGING NATURE OF INTEREST GROUP POLITICS IN AMERICA

ABSTRACT: The rise of liberal citizen groups that began in the 1960s has had a strong impact on the evolution of interest group advocacy. The success of these liberal organizations was critical in catalyzing the broader explosion in the numbers of interest groups and in causing the collapse of many subgovernments. New means of resolving policy conflicts had to be established to allow for the participation of broader, more diverse policy communities. Citizen groups have been particularly important in pushing policymakers to create new means of structuring negotiations between large numbers of interest group actors. The greater participation of citizen groups, the increased numbers of all kinds of interest groups, and change in the way policy is made may be making the policymaking process more democratic.

Many protest movements have arisen in the course of American history, each affecting the political system in its own way. The social movements that took hold in the 1960s had their own unique set of roots but seemed to follow a conventional life span. The civil rights and antiwar groups that arose to protest the injustices they saw were classic social movements. Their views were eventually absorbed by one of the political parties, and, after achieving their immediate goals, their vitality was sapped. The antiwar movement disappeared, and black civil rights organizations declined in power. The most enduring and vital citizen groups born in this era of protest were never protest oriented. Consumer groups, environmental groups, and many other kinds of citizen lobbies have enjoyed unprecedented prosperity in the last 25 years. Never before have citizen groups been so prevalent in American politics, and never before have they been so firmly institutionalized into the policymaking process.

The rise of citizen groups has not only empowered many important constituencies, but it has altered the policymaking process as well. This article

From Jeffrey M. Berry, "Citizen Groups and the Changing Nature of Interest Group Politics in America," *The Annals of the American Academy of Political and Social Science*, vol. 528 (July 1993). Copyright © 1993 by The American Academy of Political and Social Science. Reprinted by permission of Sage Publications, Inc. Notes omitted.

focuses on how citizen groups have affected interest group politics in general and how these organizations have contributed to the changing nature of public policymaking. A first step is to examine the initial success of liberal advocacy organizations as well as the conservative response to this challenge. Next, I will look at the impact of this growth of citizen group politics on the policymaking process. Then I will turn to how Congress and the executive branch have tried to cope with a dense population of citizen groups and the complex policymaking environment that now envelops government.

Finally, I will speculate as to how all of this has affected policymaking in terms of how democratic it is. The popular perception is that the rise of interest groups along with the decline of political parties has had a very negative impact on American politics. Analysis of the decline of parties will be left to others, but a central point here is that the growth in the numbers of citizen groups and of other lobbying organizations has not endangered the political system. There are some unfortunate developments, such as the increasing role of political action committees in campaign financing, but the rise of citizen groups in particular has had a beneficial impact on the way policy is formulated. The overall argument may be stated succinctly: the rise of liberal citizen groups was largely responsible for catalyzing an explosion in the growth of all types of interest groups. Efforts to limit the impact of liberal citizen groups failed, and the policymaking process became more open and more participatory. Expanded access and the growth in the numbers of competing interest groups created the potential for gridlock, if not chaos. The government responded, in turn, with in-

stitutional changes that have helped to rationalize policymaking in environments with a large number of independent actors.

THE RISE OF CITIZEN GROUPS

The lobbying organizations that emerged out of the era of protest in the 1960s are tied to the civil rights and antiwar movements in two basic ways. First, activism was stimulated by the same broad ideological dissatisfaction with government and the two-party system. There was the same feeling that government was unresponsive, that it was unconcerned about important issues, and that business was far too dominant a force in policymaking. Second, the rise of liberal citizen groups was facilitated by success of the civil rights and antiwar movements. More specifically, future organizers learned from these social movements. They learned that aggressive behavior could get results, and they saw that government could be influenced by liberal advocacy organizations. Some activists who later led Washington-based citizen lobbies cut their teeth as volunteers in these earlier movements.

For liberal consumer and environmental groups, an important lesson of this era was that they should not follow the protest-oriented behavior of the civil rights and antiwar movements. There was a collective realization that lasting influence would come from more conventional lobbying inside the political system. For consumer and environmental organizers, "power to the people" was rejected in favor of staff-run organizations that placed little emphasis on participatory democracy. This is not to say that these new organizations were simply copies of business lobbies; leaders of these groups like Ralph Nader and John Gardner placed themselves above politics-as-usual with their moralistic rhetoric and their attacks against the established political order.

While there was significant support for these groups from middle-class liberals, a major impetus behind their success was financial backing from large philanthropic foundations. The foundations wanted to support social change during a time of political upheaval, but at the same time they wanted responsible activism. This early support, most notably from the Ford Foundation's program in public interest law, was largely directed at supporting groups relying on litigation and administrative lobbying. The seed money for these organizations enabled them to flourish and provided them with time to establish a track record so that they could appeal to individual donors when the foundation money ran out. Other groups emerged without the help of foundations, drawing on a combination of large donors, dues-paying memberships, and government grants. Citizen lobbies proved remarkably effective at raising money and at shifting funding strategies as the times warranted.

Citizen groups emerged in a variety of areas. In addition to consumer and environmental groups, there were organizations interested in hunger and poverty, governmental reform, corporate responsibility, and many other issues. A number of new women's organizations soon followed in the wake of the success of the first wave of citizen groups, and new civil rights groups arose to defend other groups such as Hispanics and gays. As has been well documented, the rise of citizen groups was the beginning of an era of explosive growth in interest groups in national politics. No precise baseline exists, so exact measurement of this growth is impossible. Yet the mobilization of interests is unmistakable. One analysis of organizations represented in Washington in 1980 found that 40 percent of the groups had been started since 1960, and 25 percent had begun after 1970.

The liberal citizen groups that were established in the 1960s and 1970s were not simply the first ripples of a new wave of interest groups; rather, they played a primary role in catalyzing the formation of many of the groups that followed. New business groups, which were by far the most numerous of all the groups started since 1960, were directly stimulated to organize by the success of consumer and environmental groups. There were other reasons why business mobilized, but much of their hostility toward the expanded regulatory state was directed at agencies strongly supported by liberal citizen groups. These organizations had seemingly seized control of the political agenda, and the new social regulation demanded increased business mobilization. New conservative citizen lobbies, many focusing on family issues such as abortion and the Equal Rights Amendment, were also begun to counter the perceived success of the liberal groups.

The swing of the ideological pendulum that led to a conservative takeover of the White House in 1980 led subsequently to efforts to limit the impact of liberal citizen groups. The Reagan administration believed that the election of 1980 was a mandate to eliminate impediments to economic growth. Environmental and consumer groups were seen as organizations that cared little about the faltering American economy; President Reagan referred to liberal public interest lawyers as "a bunch of ideological ambulance chasers." Wherever possible, liberal citizen groups were to be removed from the governmental process....

The Reagan administration certainly succeeded in reducing the liberal groups' access to the executive branch. On a broader level, however, the conservative counterattack against the liberal groups was a failure. The reasons go far beyond the more accommodating stance of the Bush administration or the attitude of any conservative administrations that may follow. These organizations have proved to be remarkably resilient, and they are a strong and stable force in American politics. Most fundamentally, though, the Reagan attempt failed because the transformation of interest group politics led to large-scale structural changes in the public policymaking process.

CONSEQUENCES

The rise of citizen groups and the rapid expansion of interest group advocacy in general have had many important long-term consequences for the way policy is formulated by the national government. Most important, policymaking moved away from closed subgovernments, each involving a relatively stable and restricted group of lobbyists and key government officials, to much broader policymaking communities. Policymaking in earlier years is typically described as the product of consensual negotiations between a small number of backscratching participants.

Policymaking is now best described as taking place within issue networks rather than in subgovernments. An issue network is a set of organizations that share expertise in a policy area and interact with each other over time as relevant issues are debated. As sociologist Barry Wellman states, "The world is composed of networks, not groups." This is certainly descriptive of Washington policymaking. Policy formulation cannot be portrayed in terms of what a particular group wanted and how officials responded to those demands. The coalitions within networks, often involving scores of groups, define the divisions over issues and drive the policymaking process forward. Alliances are composed of both old friends and strange bedfellows; relationships are built on immediate need as well as on familiarity and trust. Organizations that do not normally work in a particular issue network can easily move into a policymaking community to work on a single issue. The only thing constant in issue networks is the changing nature of the coalitions.

The result of issue network politics is that policymaking has become more open, more conflictual, and more broadly participatory. What is crucial about the role of citizen groups is that they were instrumental in breaking down the barriers to participation in subgovernments. Building upon their own constituency support and working with allies in Congress, citizen groups made themselves players. They have not been outsiders, left to protest policies and a system that excluded them. Rather, they built opposition right into the policymaking communities that had previously operated with some commonality of interest. Even conservative administrators who would prefer to exclude these liberal advocacy groups have recognized that they have to deal with their opponents in one arena or another. The Nuclear Regulatory Commission, the epitome of an agency hostile to liberal advocacy groups, cannot get away with ignoring groups like the Union of Concerned Scientists. The consensus over nuclear power has long been broken. Critics and advocacy groups like the Union of Concerned Scientists have the technical expertise to involve themselves in agency proceedings, and they have the political know-how to get themselves heard on Capitol Hill and in the news media.

Issue networks are not simply divided between citizen groups on one side and business groups on another. Organizations representing business usually encompass a variety of interests, many of which are opposed to each other. As various business markets have undergone rapid change and become increasingly competitive, issue networks have found themselves divided by efforts of one sector of groups to use the policymaking process to try to gain market share from another sector of the network. Citizen groups, rather than simply being the enemy of business, are potential coalition partners for different business sectors. A characteristic of the culture of interest group politics in Washington is that there are no permanent allies and no permanent enemies.

Citizen groups are especially attractive as coalition partners because they have such a high level of credibility with the public and the news media. All groups claim to represent the public interest because they sincerely believe that the course of action they are advocating would be the most beneficial to the country. Since they do not represent any vocational or business interest, citizen groups may be perceived by some to be less biased—though certainly not unbiased—in their approach to public policy problems. This credibility is also built around the high-quality research that many citizen groups produce and distribute to journalists and policymakers in Washington. Reports from advocacy organiza-

tions such as Citizens for Tax Justice or the Center for Budget and Policy Priorities are quickly picked up by the media and disseminated across the country. Most business groups would love to have the respect that these citizen groups command in the press. For all the financial strength at the disposal of oil lobbyists, no representative of the oil industry has as much credibility with the public as a lobbyist for the Natural Resources Defense Council.

Despite the growth and stability of citizen groups in national politics, their reach does not extend into every significant policymaking domain. In the broad area of financial services, for example, citizen groups have played a minor role at best. There are some consumer groups that have been marginally active when specific issues involving banks, insurance companies, and securities firms arise, but they have demonstrated little influence or staying power. There is, however, a vital consumer interest at stake as public policymakers grapple with the crumbling walls that have traditionally divided different segments of the financial services market. Defense policy is another area where citizen groups have been relatively minor actors. But if citizen groups are conspicuous by their absence in some important areas, their overall reach is surprisingly broad. They have become major actors in policy areas where they previously had no presence at all. In negotiations over a free trade agreement with Mexico, for example, environmental groups became central players in the bargaining. These groups were concerned that increased U.S. investment in Mexico would result in increased pollution there from unregulated manufacturing, depleted groundwater supplies, and other forms of environmental degradation. To its dismay, the Bush White House found that the only practical course was to negotiate with the groups.

The increasing prominence of citizen groups and the expanding size of issue networks change our conception of the policymaking process. The basic structural attribute of a subgovernment was that it was relatively bounded with a stable set of participants. Even if there was some conflict in that subgovernment, there were predictable divisions and relatively clear expectations of what kind of conciliation between interest groups was possible. In contrast, issue networks seem like free-for-alls. In the health care field alone, 741 organizations have offices in Washington or employ a representative there. Where subgovernments suggested control over public policy by a limited number of participants, issue networks suggest no control whatsoever. Citizen groups make policymaking all the more difficult because they frequently sharpen the ideological debate; they have different organizational incentive systems from those of the corporations and trade groups with which they are often in conflict; and they place little emphasis on the need for economic growth, an assumption shared by most other actors.

This picture of contemporary interest group politics may make it seem impossible to accomplish anything in Washington. Indeed, it is a popular perception that Congress has become unproductive and that we are subject to some sort of national gridlock. Yet the policymaking system is adaptable, and the relationship between citizen groups and other actors in issue networks suggests that there are a number of productive paths for resolving complicated policy issues.

COMPLEX POLICYMAKING

The growth of issue networks is not, of course, the only reason why the policymaking process has become more complex. The increasingly technical nature of policy problems has obviously put an ever higher premium on expertise. Structural changes are critical, too. The decentralization of the House of Representatives that took place in the mid-1970s dispersed power and reduced the autonomy of leaders. Today, in the House, jurisdictions between committees frequently overlap and multiple referrals of bills are common. When an omnibus trade bill passed by both houses in 1987 was sent to conference, the House and the Senate appointed 200 conferees, who broke up into 17 subconferences. The growth of the executive branch has produced a similar problem of overlapping jurisdictions. In recent deliberations on proposed changes in wetlands policy, executive branch participants included the Soil Conservation Service in the Agriculture Department, the Fish and Wildlife Service in Interior, the Army Corps of Engineers, the Environmental Protection Agency (EPA), the Office of Management and Budget, the Council on Competitiveness, and the President's Domestic Policy Council.

Nevertheless, even though the roots of complex policymaking are multifaceted, the rise of citizen groups has been a critical factor in forcing the Congress and the executive branch to focus more closely on developing procedures to negotiate settlements of policy disputes. The quiet bargaining of traditional subgovernment politics was not an adequate mechanism for handling negotiations between scores of interest groups, congressional committees, and executive branch agencies.

Citizen groups have been particularly important in prompting more structured negotiations for a number of reasons. First, in many policy areas, citizen groups upset long-standing working arrangements between policymakers and other interest groups. Citizen groups were often the reason subgovernments crumbled; under pressure from congressional allies and public opinion, they were included in the bargaining and negotiating at some stage in the policymaking process.

Second, citizen groups could not be easily accommodated in basic negotiating patterns. It was not a matter of simply placing a few more chairs at the table. These groups' entrance into a policymaking community usually created a new dividing line between participants. The basic ideological cleavage that exists between consumer and environmental interests and business is not easy to bridge, and, consequently, considerable effort has been expended to devise ways of getting mutual antagonists to negotiate over an extended period. As argued above, once accepted at the bargaining table, citizen groups could be attractive coalition partners for business organizations.

Third, . . . citizen groups typically have a great deal of credibility with the press. Thus, in negotiating, they often have had more to gain by going public to gain leverage with other bargainers. This adds increased uncertainty and instability to the structure of negotiations.

Fourth, citizen groups are often more unified than their business adversaries. The business interests in an issue network may consist of large producers, small producers, foreign producers, and companies from other industries trying to expand into new markets. All these business interests may be fiercely divided as each tries to defend or encroach upon established market patterns. The environmentalists in the same network, while each may have its own niche in terms of issue specialization, are likely to present a united front on major policy disputes. In a perverse way, then, the position of citizen groups has been aided by the proliferation of business groups. (Even without the intrusion of citizen lobbies, this sharp rise in the number of business groups would have irretrievably changed the nature of subgovernments.) . . .

CONCLUSION

Citizen groups have changed the policymaking process in valuable and enduring ways. Most important, they have broadened representation in our political system. Many previously unrepresented or underrepresented constituencies now have a powerful voice in Washington politics. The expanding numbers of liberal citizen groups and their apparent success helped to stimulate a broad mobilization on the part of business. The skyrocketing increase in the numbers of interest groups worked to break down subgovernments and led to the rise of issue networks.

Issue networks are more fragmented, less predictable policymaking environments. Both Congress and the executive branch have taken steps to bring about greater centralized control and coherence to policymaking. Some of these institutional changes seem aimed directly at citizen groups. Negotiated regulations, for example, are seen as a way of getting around the impasse that often develops between liberal citizen groups and business organizations. Centralized regulatory review has been used by Republican administrations as a means of ensuring that business interests are given primacy; regulators are seen as too sympathetic to the citizen groups that are clients of their agencies.

Although government has established these and other institutional mechanisms for coping with complex policymaking environments, the American public does not seem to feel that the government copes very well at all. Congress has been portrayed as unproductive and spineless, unwilling to tackle the tough problems that require discipline or sacrifice. At the core of this criticism is that interest groups are the culprit. Washington lobbies, representing every conceivable interest and showering legislators with the political action committee donations they crave, are said to be responsible for this country's inability to solve its problems.

Although it is counterintuitive, it may be that the increasing number of interest groups coupled with the rise of citizen groups has actually improved the policymaking system in some important ways. More specifically, our policymaking process may be more democratic today because of these developments. Expanded interest group participation has helped to make the policymaking process more open and visible. The closed nature of subgovernment politics meant not only that participation was restricted but that public scrutiny was minimal. The proliferation of interest groups, Washington media that are more aggressive, and the willingness and ability of citizen groups in particular to go public as part of their advocacy strategy have worked to open up policymaking to the public eye.

The end result of expanded citizen group advocacy is policy communities that are highly participatory and more broadly representative of the public. One can argue that this more democratic policymaking process is also one that is less capable of concerted action; yet there is no reliable evidence that American government is any more or less responsive to pressing policy problems than it has ever been. There are, of course, difficult problems that remain unresolved, but that is surely true of every era. Democracy requires adequate representation of interests as well as institutions capable of addressing difficult policy problems. For policymakers who must balance the demand for representation with the need for results, the key is thinking creatively about how to build coalitions and structure negotiations between large groups of actors.

POSTSCRIPT

Is Government Dominated by Big Business?

One of the problems for any pluralist is the danger that many people may not be properly represented. Suppose, for example, that business and environmental groups in Washington compromise their differences by supporting environmental legislation but passing the costs along to consumers. The legislation may be good, even necessary, but have the consumer's interests been taken into account? There are, of course, self-styled consumer groups, but it is hard to determine whether or not they really speak for the average consumer. The same is true of other activist organizations that claim to represent different groups in our society. The challenge for pluralists is to make their system as inclusive as possible.

Social science literature contains a number of works on the issues of pluralism and corporate power. Political scientist Charles E. Lindblom supported pluralism in the 1950s, but he later changed his mind and concluded that big business dominates American policy making. Lindblom takes the pluralist perspective in his early book *Politics, Economics, and Welfare* (Harper, 1953), written with Robert A. Dahl. His repudiation of pluralism was complete by the time he published *Politics and Markets: The World's Political-Economic Systems* (Basic Books, 1977). Ever since the obvious demonstration of corporate influence in the elections of 1980, Lindblom's view has been dominant. More recent works arguing that corporate elites possess inordinate power in American society are Michael Schwartz, ed., *The Structure of Power in America* (Holmes & Meier, 1987); G. William Domhoff, *The Power Elite and the State* (Aldine de Gruyter, 1990) and *Who Rules America Now?* (Prentice Hall, 1983); Michael Useem, *The Inner Circle* (Oxford University Press, 1984); Beth Mintz and Michael Schwartz, *The Power Structure of American Business* (University of Chicago Press, 1985); Robert R. Alford and Roger Friedland, *Powers of Theory: Capitalism, the State, and Democracy* (Cambridge University Press, 1985); Dan Clawson et al., *Money Talks: Corporate PACs and Political Influence* (Basic Books, 1992); and Mark S. Mizruchi, *The Structure of Corporate Political Action: Interfirm Relations and Their Consequences* (Harvard University Press, 1992). For an analysis of the changes taking place in the organization of corporate power, see Michael Useem, *Investor Capitalism: How Money Managers Are Changing the Face of Corporate America* (Basic Books, 1996).

For some pluralist arguments, see Andrew M. Greeley, *Building Coalitions* (Franklin Watts, 1974); David Vogel, *Fluctuating Fortunes: The Political Power of Business in America* (Basic Books, 1989) and *Kindred Strangers: The Uneasy Relationship Between Politics and Business in America* (Princeton University

Press, 1996); John P. Heinz, Edward O. Laumann, Robert L. Nelson, and Robert H. Salisbury, *The Hollow Core: Private Interests in National Policy Making* (Harvard University Press, 1993); Lawrence S. Rothenberg, *Linking Citizens to Government: Interest Group Politics at Common Cause* (Cambridge University Press, 1992); and Susan Herbst, *Numbered Voices: How Opinion Polls Shape American Politics* (University of Chicago Press, 1993).

ISSUE 12

Should Government Intervene in a Capitalist Economy?

YES: Ernest Erber, from "Virtues and Vices of the Market: Balanced Correctives to a Current Craze," *Dissent* (Summer 1990)

NO: Milton and Rose Friedman, from *Free to Choose: A Personal Statement* (Harcourt Brace Jovanovich, 1980)

ISSUE SUMMARY

YES: Author Ernest Erber argues that capitalism creates serious social problems that need to be redressed by an activist government.

NO: Economists Milton and Rose Friedman maintain that market competition, when permitted to work unimpeded, protects citizens better than government regulations intended to correct for failures of the market.

The expression "That government is best which governs least" sums up a deeply rooted attitude of many Americans. From early presidents Thomas Jefferson and Andrew Jackson to America's most recent leaders, Ronald Reagan, George Bush, and Bill Clinton, American politicians have often echoed the popular view that there are certain areas of life best left to the private actions of citizens.

One such area is the economic sphere, where people make their living by buying, selling, and producing goods and services. The tendency of most Americans is to regard direct government involvement in the economic sphere as both unnecessary and dangerous. The purest expression of this view is the economic theory of *laissez-faire,* a French term meaning "let be" or "let alone." The seminal formulation of *laissez-faire* theory was the work of eighteenth-century Scottish philosopher Adam Smith, whose treatise *The Wealth of Nations* appeared in 1776. Smith's thesis was that each individual, pursuing his or her own selfish interests in a competitive market, will be "led by an invisible hand to promote an end which was no part of his intention." In other words, when people single-mindedly seek profit, they actually serve the community because sellers must keep prices down and quality up if they are to meet the competition of other sellers.

Laissez-faire economics was much honored (in theory, if not always in practice) during the nineteenth and early twentieth centuries. But as the nineteenth century drew to a close, the Populist Party sprang up. The Populists denounced eastern bankers, Wall Street stock manipulators, and rich "moneyed interests," and they called for government ownership of railroads, a progressive income tax, and other forms of state intervention. The Populist Party died out early in the twentieth century, but the Populist message was not forgotten. In fact, it was given new life after 1929, when the stock market collapsed and the United States was plunged into the worst economic depression in its history.

By 1932 a quarter of the nation's workforce was unemployed, and most Americans were finding it hard to believe that the "invisible hand" would set things right. Some Americans totally repudiated the idea of a free market and embraced socialism, the belief that the state (or "the community") should run all major industries. Most stopped short of supporting socialism, but they were now prepared to welcome some forms of state intervention in the economy. President Franklin D. Roosevelt, elected in 1932, spoke to this mood when he pledged a "New Deal" to the American people. "New Deal" has come to stand for a variety of programs that were enacted during the first eight years of Roosevelt's presidency, including business and banking regulations, government pension programs, federal aid to the disabled, unemployment compensation, and government-sponsored work programs. Side by side with the "invisible hand" of the marketplace was now the very visible hand of an activist government.

Government intervention in the economic sphere increased during World War II as the government fixed prices, rationed goods, and put millions to work in government-subsidized war industries. Activist government continued during the 1950s, but the biggest leap forward occurred during the late 1960s and early 1970s, when the federal government launched a variety of new welfare and regulatory programs: the multibillion-dollar War on Poverty, new civil rights and affirmative action mandates, and new laws protecting consumers, workers, disabled people, and the environment. These, in turn, led to a proliferation of new government agencies and bureaus, as well as shelves and shelves of published regulations. Proponents of the new activism conceded that it was expensive, but they insisted that activist government was necessary to protect Americans against pollution, discrimination, dangerous products, and other effects of the modern marketplace. Critics of government involvement called attention not only to its direct costs but also to its effect on business activity and individual freedom.

In the following selections, Ernest Erber argues that although competitive markets are very productive, they bring about a variety of negative consequences, and he concludes that business regulation and other forms of government intervention are necessary to counter some of the harmful effects of the marketplace. Milton and Rose Friedman argue that the "invisible hand" of the market will work effectively if it is allowed to do so without government interference.

YES

Ernest Erber

VIRTUES AND VICES OF THE MARKET: BALANCED CORRECTIVES TO A CURRENT CRAZE

Not since they encountered it in nursery rhymes have references to the market so intruded into the consciousness of Americans as in recent months. There is now a virtual consensus that the market is the natural state of economic affairs, and its creation in nations not yet blessed with it is the prescription for every economic ailment. This makes vague good sense to most Americans, for whom the market has pleasant associations. Not surprisingly, for the market has long since come to determine their tastes and values, their very lives....

This worldwide consensus would not exist if it did not reflect a body of evidence that links the market with economic growth, increased productivity, and improved living standards. That this historical progress has been facilitated by the market's competitive and entrepreneurial incentives cannot be contested. Neither can the beliefs that the market's function as a pricing mechanism has historically contributed to economic stability conducive to growth, even if plagued by a persistent tendency toward inflation in recent years, nor that the market's negative, even self-destructive, side effects have been largely diminished by state intervention through regulation, credit-budget-tax policies, price supports, and social welfare programs....

NATURE OF THE MARKET

... The market as we know it today is the historically specific product of industrial capitalism and can only be understood if perceived as such....

The Market is, essentially, an economic decision-making process that determines the allocation of society's resources by deciding what and how much is produced and how and to whom it is distributed. Those who participate in this process are buyers and sellers who "meet" in the "marketplace," though they are not only individuals, since buyers and sellers also include businesses of all sizes, farmers and professionals as groups, governments at all levels.

As an alternative to the Market, society's resources can also be directly allocated by political decisions of government (that is, by "command"). Gov-

From Ernest Erber, "Virtues and Vices of the Market: Balanced Correctives to a Current Craze," *Dissent* (Summer 1990). Copyright © 1990 by The Foundation for the Study of Independent Social Ideas, Inc. Reprinted by permission.

ernment can also act deliberately to influence indirectly how the Market functions indirectly. Those who determine a government's economic role are citizens, governing officials, and administrators (including, sometimes, planners, though every governmental impact upon the economy should not be called "planning" and, in the United States, it almost never is that). Within capitalist economies, the purpose of governmental intervention in the Market is twofold: (1) to facilitate the functioning of the Market by protecting it from its shortcomings, including tendencies toward self-destructiveness; (2) to supplement the Market by providing those goods and services that the Market has no incentive to supply because they do not entail a profit (public schools, social welfare, low-cost housing, infrastructure, and so on).

The extent to which government should influence the economy is an issue that has been fought over for a very long time. Charles E. Lindblom begins his definitive *Politics and Markets* by observing that "the greatest distinction between one government and another is in the degree to which market replaces government or government replaces market. Both Adam Smith and Karl Marx knew this."

* * *

The word "degree" is used by Lindblom deliberately, for neither the market nor government replaces the other completely. Thus all economies are a mix of the Market and political decision making. Even the totally mad Stalinist effort to eliminate the Market in Soviet-type societies fell short of complete success, for these societies had to tolerate market operations in corners of the economy, either by compromise, as in permitted sales from garden plots of collective farmers and *kolkhoz* "surplus" production, or through black market sales of scarce commodities, tolerated because they were considered helpful to the economy.

Another variant of madness, though largely rhetorical, is the Thatcherite and Reaganite pronouncements about getting government out of the economy and "letting the market decide." After a decade of such huffing and puffing, the role of government vis-à-vis the economy, both in Great Britain and in the United States, remains essentially unchanged, some privatizations notwithstanding....

* * *

A final aspect of the Market's historical context is the largely forgotten role played by the state in getting market-based economies off the ground in various parts of the world. Japan, Prussia, and Czarist Russia are outstanding examples of the state's role in "jump starting" both capitalist production and market relations through generous credit, subsidies, enactment of special rights, licenses, and so on. Government construction of infrastructure often played a key role.

What we can conclude is that the prevailing view that attributes the material progress of human societies during the last century or two *solely* to the Market is fallacious, because the Market's contribution cannot be sufficiently separated from that of the Industrial Revolution, the capitalist mode of production, or the nourishing role of the state. To the extent that references to the Market are euphemistic in order to advocate capitalism under another name, there is an implied admission that the market cannot be separated from capitalism, that is, private property in the means of production, labor as a commodity, unearned income, accumulation, and so forth. But insofar as there now exists an effort to utilize the Market's virtues, while straining out its vices, in order to serve the common welfare, an assessment of its feasibility cannot be made until we have clearer insights into how it would resolve a number of contradictions that seem to make this objective unworkable.

THE MARKET'S SIDE EFFECTS AND POLITICAL REMEDIES

The following descriptions of the Market's side effects are valid, on the whole, though in some cases not entirely separable from other causes. The rationale of the Market is competition—for survival and gain. It pits each against all in social Darwinian "survival of the fittest": worker against worker and entrepreneur against entrepreneur, capital against labor and producer against consumer. The weak are eliminated and the strong survive, resulting in the trend toward concentration and monopolies. Businesses live by the "bottom line," with an incentive toward price gouging, adulteration, misrepresentation, environmental degradation. Product or service promotion caters to every human weakness. Advertising seduces consumers to develop endless wants. The central effect is to subvert human solidarity and civic responsibility.

The multitudinous buy/sell decisions that drive the market process are made in total ignorance of their collective impact, as expressed in Adam Smith's now hoary "unseen hand." Its social impact causes society to "fly blind," as when millions of individually bought automobiles collectively spell traffic gridlock and death-dealing air pollution. Government seeks to overcome these destructive results by regulating the manufacture of automobiles and gasoline. If this fails, as is likely,

government will have to turn to long-range planning of alternate transportation, replacing private automobile trips with public conveyances. This will be a political decision to allocate resources from the private sector's automobile solution to the public sector's rail and bus solution. This is only one example of the choices between decisions by the Market and by the political process (made with or without planning).

The nineteenth-century laissez-faire market process, almost total economic determination by consumer demand, eventually proved unworkable. This was capitalism as Karl Marx knew it, and unworkable as he had predicted. During the course of the twentieth century, laissez-faire gave way to large-scale political intervention, resulting in state-guided and, increasingly, state-managed capitalism, with the state's control of money flow through central banks (Federal Reserve in the United States), credit control, tariffs and quotas, subsidies, tax policy, industrial and agricultural loans, price supports, wages policy, loan guarantees, savings incentives, marketing assistance, stockpiling, and various regulatory controls. This continuing transformation of market-based economies, which has come to be known as the Keynesian Revolution, is likely to be viewed by historians as of greater significance than the Soviet Revolution.

* * *

The proportions of market vs. political decision making in economic affairs does not necessarily reflect the proportions of private vs. state ownership of the economy. State-owned industries in countries such as Austria, Italy, and France, where they form a high proportion of the economy, are largely indistinguishable from the private sector in operating by the rules of the Market to produce in response to consumer demand. On the other hand, despite a relatively small nationalized sector, the state in Sweden is omnipresent in managing economic affairs. *The current widespread tilt toward privatization does not, therefore, diminish the trend toward an increased role of the state in economic affairs.*

The Market process demands that those who wish to participate pay admission. Those who cannot afford to get in—or who drop out—fall through the cracks; if lucky, into a social safety net. As the burden increased beyond private charities' resources, government was forced to assume it and the twentieth century's "welfare state" emerged. Its "transfer" programs of public goods and services exist outside the Market for those who cannot make it within.

The insecurity of various categories of entrepreneurs (such as farmers, oil drillers, ship owners, owners of small businesses, bank depositors), caused by the instability and unpredictability of the market process, led these entrepreneurs to use their political power to seek public assistance through subsidies, loans, insurance, "bailouts," and so forth, eventually becoming entitlements. The latter, together with welfare state transfer payments, proliferated and grew enormously, in part because they reflected the universal transition within affluent societies from satisfying needs to meeting wants. Adding these to the cost of traditional categories of public goods and services (such as national defense, public schools, parks, libraries, streets and roads) resulted in ballooning governmental budgets and the diversion through taxation of increasing proportions of the GNPs of industrial nations to their public sectors.

This had the effect of cutting into the availability of accumulated capital for investment in direct wealth-producing enterprise. Government response differed sharply, depending upon whether it followed a national economic policy or relied upon the Market. Sweden, an example of the former, tapped its Supplementary Pension Program to create the so-called fourth fund for targeted industrial investment, creating and sustaining employment that yielded a flow of payroll deductions back into the fund. The United States, on the other hand, permitted Market forces to drive up interest rates, bringing an inflow of foreign capital and an outflow of dividends and interest.

But, regardless of how the problem is managed, there are political limits to the diversion of funds from the private sector to the public sector via taxation. This can be seen in the "tax revolts" in Europe and the United States in the last two decades, which also had repercussions in the Scandinavian countries, including Sweden. This diversion also triggered the resurgence of laissez-faire ideology and right-wing politics.

Even for those countries in which the Market successfully accumulates the "wealth of nations," there results a lopsided inequality of distribution within the population, resulting in recurring economic instability and social confrontation. (Brazil, a country with the eighth largest Market-based economy in the world, leads all others in polarization between rich and poor.) The Market process generates cyclical and chronic unemployment, bankruptcies, mass layoffs, over- and underproduction, strikes and lockouts, and many other kinds of economic warfare and social tension. There is good reason to believe that the sharp shift in income from earned to unearned during the 1980s will be reflected in rising class conflict in the 1990s.

The Market is not a surefire prescription for the "wealth of nations" because its acclaimed incentives, acting as a spur to economic development, are also historically specific. Just because eighteenth-century England used the Market process to turn itself into a "nation of shop-keepers" and nineteenth-century England used it to lead the way in the Industrial Revolution to become the "world's workshop," is no assurance that, at any other time in history, people of any other culture and level of development can similarly use the Market to the same end—notwithstanding the examples of Western Europe, the United States, Canada, and Japan. (South Korea and Taiwan, judged by their per capita incomes, have not yet made it.)

Internationally, the Market has resulted in hierarchical ranking of nations by wealth, grouping a fortunate few as the rich nations and the rest as relatively or absolutely poor. Market-process relations between the industrially developed nations and the rest take the form of the developed responding to the consumer-driven demands of the underdeveloped for investments, loans, goods, and services, thereby aggravating their dependency, and frustrating their ability to accumulate enough capital to significantly improve their productivity (Argentina, Brazil, Mexico, Egypt, India, to name some).

* * *

In summarizing the Market's negative side effects we have noted that it flies blindly; that its growth becomes destruc-tive of communitarian values and institutions and of the natural environment; that its "work ethic" becomes exploitation, even of children (child labor is again on the rise in the United States according to the Department of Labor); that it reduces the cost of production but also triggers inflation; that it produces a cornucopia of goods but also mountains of waste; that its pharmaceutical research lengthens lifespans, but its chemicals (pesticides and herbicides) shorten them; that it makes feverish use of humankind's growing power over nature, born of scientific and technological progress, but puts profits above ecology and market share above the need to conserve natural resources; that it provides conveniences, comforts, and luxuries for an increasing number but shows no ability to close the widening gap between haves and have nots, neither within nor between nations. But, above all, the Market, despite Keynesianism, operates in cycles of boom and bust, victimizing businesses, large and small, farmers, professionals, and wage workers. Left to its own devices, the Market is inherently self-destructive.

Though the Market's negative side effects can be countered through government intervention and largely have been, such countering tends to be ameliora-tive rather than curative, and often raises new problems requiring additional intervention, thus reinforcing the overall tendency for the state to backstop the Market. But, despite this, Market economies still move blindly, though increasingly within broad channels marked out by government. The Market economy still overheats and runs out of fuel, but government now acts to cool it and then to fuel it (and even attempts to "fine tune" it). Will it prove a viable arrangement in the long term for government to treat the

Market as if it were an elemental force of nature?

The people seem to want the benefits of the Market, but look to government to minimize the dreadful side effects that come with it. But one person's "dreadful side effects" are another person's sweet accumulation of capital. Translated into social relations, this conflict of interests expresses itself as interest-group confrontations and social-class struggles. And as decision making in economic affairs continues to shift from the Market to the political process, an ever fiercer political resistance is mounted by the interest groups and classes whose power is far greater and more direct in the Market than in the political arena—for instance, the resurgence of the new right in waging ideological and political warfare on behalf of laissez-faire policies.

THE MARKET'S THRUST VS. SOCIETAL GUIDANCE

Understanding the direction in which the Market is likely to move in the next few decades is critically important to an assessment of its capacity to accommodate solutions for outstanding problems. In the past, especially since World War II, the Market's contribution to easing the great problems of civilization has been in the form of economic growth. The nature of the problems that now loom, however, makes them less subject to solution through economic growth. The rising tide that once raised all boats now leaves many stuck on muddy bottoms.

Market-based growth has not demonstrated an ability to reduce the glaring inequality in living standards and in educational/cultural levels within and between nations. In the United States during the last decade the gap between the bottom and the top of the income quintiles has widened. And growth solutions now generate new problems: the degradation of the natural environment on earth and in space; the exhaustion of natural resources; the emergence of *social* limits to growth, caused by the level at which acquisition of goods, services, and facilities by enough people spoils the advantages of possessing them; the puzzle of insatiable wants after basic needs have been satisfied (when is enough enough?). There are also the growth of private affluence and public squalor; an individualistic society's reluctance to resort to collective solutions (national health care) before first going through the agony of postponing the inevitable, and other looming problems sensed but seemingly too elusively complex to articulate. These problems join a long list of old problems that go unsolved to become a leaden weight on progress.

* * *

Is there reason to believe that the Market's failure to cope with these problems will (or can) be remedied in the future? Is there anything in the nature and function of the Market that is likely to redirect its performance to be able to solve these problems? Are any of its negative side effects going to be eliminated, except insofar as governmentally applied correctives can curb them without altering the overall thrust of the Market? Left to its own devices, the Market's current trends are likely to expand and exacerbate problems. Are any countervailing forces in view? Yes.

One is the sharpening competition in the world market. The latter is being badly misread. True, a coded message on a computer or fax machine can transfer billions of dollars overseas at the end of the business day and retrieve it first thing in the morning—with earnings added. True, multinationals no longer fly a single flag. But national interests are as sharply defined as ever. And waging war with economic weapons has not reduced competitiveness and aggressiveness. The competitors are dividing into several major blocs: North America (the United States plus Canada and Mexico), Japan (plus the Asian rim countries) and a united Europe. The goal: market share. As Japan has shown (and also Europe to a lesser extent), this warfare requires maximum mobilization of economic resources: capital, management, knowledge-industry, and labor. Japan has shown that the way to bring these together is by making them all part of the corporate state. The power of Japan, Inc. is recognized in all American boardrooms, though a much smaller nation, Sweden, has also used the corporate strategy brilliantly. The striking similarity of Japanese and Swedish economic strategies, though for different social ends, is largely overlooked because the former is dominated by corporations and the latter by organized labor acting through the Social Democratic party.

The corporate state strategy has anti-market overtones. Rather than letting the market decide, it operates through strategic planning and a national industrial (investment) policy. If global market share is the goal, the nation's consumers had better not be permitted to decide on the allocation of resources. Laissez-faire America illustrates why not. The consumers opt for second homes, third cars, snowmobiles, Jacuzzis, and Torneau watches, thereby short-changing education at all levels, skill retraining of the labor force, housing, and health care—all essential ingredients in mobilizing resources to fight for market share.

The last thing any nation needs or will ever want after the debacle of the Stalinist model is an administrative-command economy (misnamed "planning"). Let the Market process determine the number, style, size, and color of shoes. And similarly for other basic needs and reasonable wants. But the nation also has collective needs, and the polity should determine the allocation of resources to supply them. Because this cannot be determined by the blind outcomes of the Market, the latter must be subordinated to strategically planned priorities designed to serve an overriding common purpose.

If coping with the major problems facing humankind in both its social and natural environments requires societal guidance, it necessitates setting goals and choosing strategies to achieve them; in short, strategic planning. This calls for conscious, deliberate, and coordinated measures to mobilize a nation's resources. The American people with its Market-instilled value system is decidedly averse to this (except in time of war, when by political decision a goal-oriented government controlled wages, employment, prices, profits, manufacturing, and construction).

The twenty-first is not likely to be an American Century. Clinging to the Market, the negation of societal guidance, we might not even come in second. More likely we will be third, after a united Europe and an Asian-rim dominant Japan operating with strategic planning. Americans are more likely to be content with nursery reveries of

To market, to market, to buy a fat pig,
Home again, home again, to dance a fast
 jig.

NO

Milton and Rose Friedman

FREE TO CHOOSE

THE POWER OF THE MARKET

The Role of Prices

The key insight of Adam Smith's *Wealth of Nations* is misleadingly simple: if an exchange between two parties is voluntary, it will not take place unless both believe they will benefit from it. Most economic fallacies derive from the neglect of this simple insight, from the tendency to assume that there is a fixed pie, that one party can gain only at the expense of another.

This key insight is obvious for a simple exchange between two individuals. It is far more difficult to understand how it can enable people living all over the world to cooperate to promote their separate interests.

The price system is the mechanism that performs this task without central direction, without requiring people to speak to one another or to like one another. When you buy your pencil or your daily bread, you don't know whether the pencil was made or the wheat was grown by a white man or a black man, by a Chinese or an Indian. As a result, the price system enables people to cooperate peacefully in one phase of their life while each one goes about his own business in respect of everything else.

Adam Smith's flash of genius was his recognition that the prices that emerged from voluntary transactions between buyers and sellers—for short, in a free market—could coordinate the activity of millions of people, each seeking his own interest, in such a way as to make everyone better off. It was a startling idea then, and it remains one today, that economic order can emerge as the unintended consequence of the actions of many people, each seeking his own interest.

The price system works so well, so efficiently, that we are not aware of it most of the time. We never realize how well it functions until it is prevented from functioning, and even then we seldom recognize the source of the trouble.

The long gasoline lines that suddenly emerged in 1974 after the OPEC oil embargo, and again in the spring and summer of 1979 after the revolution in Iran, are a striking recent example. On both occasions there was a sharp disturbance in the supply of crude oil from abroad. But that did not lead to gasoline lines in Germany or Japan, which are wholly dependent on imported oil. It led to long gasoline lines in the United States, even though we produce much of our own oil, for one reason and one reason only: because legislation, administered by a government agency, did not permit the price system to function. Prices in some areas were kept by command below the level that would have equated the amount of gasoline available at the gas stations to the amount consumers wanted to buy at that price. Supplies were allocated to different areas of the country by command, rather than in response to the pressures of demand as reflected in price. The result was surpluses in some areas and shortages plus long gasoline lines in others. The smooth operation of the price system —which for many decades had assured every consumer that he could buy gasoline at any of a large number of service stations at his convenience and with a minimal wait—was replaced by bureaucratic improvisation....

The Role of Government

Where does government enter into the picture?...

[W]hat role should be assigned to government?

It is not easy to improve on the answer that Adam Smith gave to this question two hundred years ago:

... According to the system of natural liberty, the sovereign has only three duties to attend to; three duties of great importance, indeed, but plain and intelligible to common understandings: first, the duty of protecting the society from the violence and invasion of other independent societies; secondly, the duty of protecting, as far as possible, every member of the society from the injustice or oppression of every other member of it, or the duty of establishing an exact administration of justice; and thirdly, the duty of erecting and maintaining certain public works and certain public institutions, which it can never be for the interest of any individual, or small number of individuals, to erect and maintain; because the profit could never repay the expence to any individual or small number of individuals, though it may frequently do much more than repay it to a great society.

... A fourth duty of government that Adam Smith did not explicitly mention is the duty to protect members of the community who cannot be regarded as "responsible" individuals. Like Adam Smith's third duty, this one, too, is susceptible of great abuse. Yet it cannot be avoided....

Adam Smith's three duties, or our four duties of government, are indeed "of great importance," but they are far less "plain and intelligible to common understandings" than he supposed. Though we cannot decide the desirability or undesirability of any actual or proposed government intervention by mechanical reference to one or another of them, they provide a set of principles that we can use in casting up a balance sheet of pros and cons. Even on the loosest interpretation, they rule out much existing government intervention—all those "systems either of preference or of restraint" that Adam Smith fought against, that were subsequently destroyed, but have since reappeared in the form of today's tariffs, governmentally fixed prices and wages, restrictions on entry into various occupations, and numerous other departures from his "simple system of natural liberty." ...

CRADLE TO GRAVE

... At the end of the war [World War II] it looked as if central economic planning was the wave of the future. That outcome was passionately welcomed by some who saw it as the dawn of a world of plenty shared equally. It was just as passionately feared by others, including us, who saw it as a turn to tyranny and misery. So far, neither the hopes of the one nor the fears of the other have been realized.

Government has expanded greatly. However, that expansion has not taken the form of detailed central economic planning accompanied by ever widening nationalization of industry, finance, and commerce, as so many of us feared it would. Experience put an end to detailed economic planning, partly because it was not successful in achieving the announced objectives, but also because it conflicted with freedom. ...

The failure of planning and nationalization has not eliminated pressure for an ever bigger government. It has simply altered its direction. The expansion of government now takes the form of welfare programs and of regulatory activities. As W. Allen Wallis put it in a somewhat different context, socialism, "intellectually bankrupt after more than a century of seeing one after another of its arguments for socializing the *means* of production demolished—now seeks to socialize the *results* of production."

In the welfare area the change of direction has led to an explosion in recent decades, especially after President Lyndon Johnson declared a "War on Poverty" in 1964. New Deal programs of Social Security, unemployment insurance, and direct relief were all expanded to cover new groups; payments were increased; and Medicare, Medicaid, food stamps, and numerous other programs were added. Public housing and urban renewal programs were enlarged. By now there are literally hundreds of government welfare and income transfer programs. The Department of Health, Education and Welfare, established in 1953 to consolidate the scattered welfare programs, began with a budget of $2 billion, less than 5 percent of expenditures on national defense. Twenty-five years later, in 1978, its budget was $160 billion, one and a half times as much as total spending on the army, the navy, and the air force. It had the third largest budget in the world, exceeded only by the entire budget of the U.S. government and of the Soviet Union. ...

No one can dispute two superficially contradictory phenomena: widespread dissatisfaction with the results of this explosion in welfare activities; continued pressure for further expansion.

The objectives have all been noble; the results, disappointing. Social Security expenditures have skyrocketed, and the system is in deep financial trouble. Public housing and urban renewal programs have subtracted from rather than added to the housing available to the poor. Public assistance rolls mount despite growing employment. By general agreement, the welfare program is a "mess" saturated with fraud and corruption. As government has paid a larger share of the nation's medical bills, both patients and physicians complain of rocketing costs and of the increasing impersonality of medicine. In education, student performance has dropped as federal intervention has expanded. . . .

The repeated failure of well-intentioned programs is not an accident. It is not simply the result of mistakes of execution. The failure is deeply rooted in the use of bad means to achieve good objectives.

Despite the failure of these programs, the pressure to expand them grows. Failures are attributed to the miserliness of Congress in appropriating funds, and so are met with a cry for still bigger programs. Special interests that benefit from specific programs press for their expansion—foremost among them the massive bureaucracy spawned by the programs. . . .

CREATED EQUAL

Capitalism and Equality
Everywhere in the world there are gross inequities of income and wealth. They offend most of us. Few can fail to be moved by the contrast between the luxury enjoyed by some and the grinding poverty suffered by others.

In the past century a myth has grown up that free market capitalism—equality of opportunity as we have interpreted that term—increases such inequalities, that it is a system under which the rich exploit the poor.

Nothing could be further from the truth. Wherever the free market has been permitted to operate, wherever anything approaching equality of opportunity has existed, the ordinary man has been able to attain levels of living never dreamed of before. Nowhere is the gap between rich and poor wider, nowhere are the rich richer and the poor poorer, than in those societies that do not permit

the free market to operate. That is true of feudal societies like medieval Europe, India before independence, and much of modern South America, where inherited status determines position. It is equally true of centrally planned societies, like Russia or China or India since independence, where access to government determines position. It is true even where central planning was introduced, as in all three of these countries, in the name of equality. . . .

WHO PROTECTS THE CONSUMER?

. . . The pace of intervention quickened greatly after the New Deal—half of the thirty-two agencies in existence in 1966 were created after FDR's election in 1932. Yet intervention remained fairly moderate and continued in the single-industry mold. The *Federal Register*, established in 1936 to record all the regulations, hearings, and other matters connected with the regulatory agencies, grew, at first rather slowly, then more rapidly. Three volumes, containing 2,599 pages and taking six inches of shelf space, sufficed for 1936; twelve volumes, containing 10,528 pages and taking twenty-six inches of shelf space, for 1956; and thirteen volumes, containing 16,850 pages and taking thirty-six inches of shelf space, for 1966.

Then a veritable explosion in government regulatory activity occurred. No fewer than twenty-one new agencies were established in the next decade. Instead of being concerned with specific industries, they covered the waterfront: the environment, the production and distribution of energy, product safety, occupational safety, and so on. In addition to concern with the consumer's pocketbook, with protecting him from exploitation by sellers, recent agencies are primarily concerned with things like the consumer's safety and well-being, with protecting him not only from sellers but also from himself.

Government expenditures on both older and newer agencies skyrocketed —from less than $1 billion in 1970 to roughly $5 billion estimated for 1979. Prices in general roughly doubled, but these expenditures more than quintupled. The number of government bureaucrats employed in regulatory activities tripled, going from 28,000 in 1970 to 81,000 in 1979; the number of pages in the *Federal Register*, from 17,660 in 1970 to 36,487 in 1978, taking 127 inches of shelf space—a veritable ten-foot shelf....

This revolution in the role of government has been accompanied, and largely produced, by an achievement in public persuasion that must have few rivals. Ask yourself what products are currently least satisfactory and have shown the least improvement over time. Postal service, elementary and secondary schooling, railroad passenger transport would surely be high on the list. Ask yourself which products are most satisfactory and have improved the most. Household appliances, television and radio sets, hi-fi equipment, computers, and, we would add, supermarkets and shopping centers would surely come high on that list.

The shoddy products are all produced by government or government-regulated industries. The outstanding products are all produced by private enterprise with little or no government involvement. Yet the public—or a large part of it—has been persuaded that private enterprises produce shoddy products, that we need ever vigilant government employees to keep business from foisting off unsafe, meretricious products at outrageous prices on ignorant, unsuspecting, vulnerable customers. That public relations campaign has succeeded so well that we are in the process of turning over to the kind of people who bring us our postal service the far more critical task of producing and distributing energy....

Government intervention in the marketplace is subject to laws of its own, not legislated laws, but scientific laws. It obeys forces and goes in directions that may have little relationship to the intentions or desires of its initiators or supporters. We have already examined this process in connection with welfare activity. It is present equally when government intervenes in the marketplace, whether to protect consumers against high prices or shoddy goods, to promote their safety, or to preserve the environment. Every act of intervention establishes positions of power. How that power will be used and for what purposes depends far more on the people who are in the best position to get control of that power and what their purposes are than on the aims and objectives of the initial sponsors of the intervention....

Environment

The environmental movement is responsible for one of the most rapidly growing areas of federal intervention. The Environmental Protection Agency, established in 1970 "to protect and enhance the physical environment," has been granted increasing power and authority. Its budget has multiplied sevenfold from 1970 to 1978 and is now more than half a billion dollars. It has a staff of about 7,000. It has imposed costs on industry and local and state governments to meet its standards that total in the tens of billions of dollars a year. Something between a tenth and a quarter of total net investment in new capital equipment by business now goes for antipollution purposes. And this does not count the costs of requirements imposed by other agencies, such as those designed to control emissions of motor vehicles, or the costs of land-use planning or wilderness preservation or a host of other federal, state, and local government activities undertaken in the name of protecting the environment.

The preservation of the environment and the avoidance of undue pollution are real problems and they are problems concerning which the government has an important role to play. When all the costs and benefits of any action, and the people hurt or benefited, are readily identifiable, the market provides an excellent means for assuring that only those actions are undertaken for which the benefits exceed the costs for all participants. But when the costs and benefits or the people affected cannot be identified, there is a market failure. . . .

Government is one means through which we can try to compensate for "market failure," try to use our resources more effectively to produce the amount of clean air, water, and land that we are willing to pay for. Unfortunately, the very factors that produce the market failure also make it difficult for government to achieve a satisfactory solution. Generally, it is no easier for government to identify the specific persons who are hurt and benefited than for market participants, no easier for government to assess the amount of harm or benefit to each. Attempts to use government to correct market failure have often simply substituted government failure for market failure.

Public discussion of the environmental issue is frequently characterized more by emotion than reason. Much of it proceeds as if the issue is pollution versus no pollution, as if it were desirable and possible to have a world without pollution. That is clearly nonsense. No one who contemplates the problem seriously will regard zero pollution as either a desirable or a possible state of affairs. We could have zero pollution from automobiles, for example, by simply abolishing all automobiles. That would also make the kind of agricultural and industrial productivity we now enjoy impossible, and so condemn most of us to a drastically lower standard of living, perhaps many even to death. One source of atmospheric pollution is the carbon dioxide that we all exhale. We could stop that very simply. But the cost would clearly exceed the gain.

It costs something to have clean air, just as it costs something to have other good things we want. Our resources are limited and we must weigh the gains from reducing pollution against the costs. Moreover, "pollution" is not an objective phenomenon. One person's pollution may be another's pleasure. To some of us rock music is noise pollution; to others of us it is pleasure.

The real problem is not "eliminating pollution," but trying to establish arrangements that will yield the "right" amount of pollution: an amount such that the gain from reducing pollution a bit more just balances the sacrifice of the other good things—houses, shoes, coats, and so on—that would have to be given up in order to reduce the pollution. If we go farther than that, we sacrifice more than we gain. . . .

The Market
Perfection is not of this world. There will always be shoddy products, quacks, con artists. But on the whole, market competition, when it is permitted to work, protects the consumer better than do the

alternative government mechanisms that have been increasingly superimposed on the market.

As Adam Smith said..., competition does not protect the consumer because businessmen are more soft-hearted than the bureaucrats or because they are more altruistic or generous, or even because they are more competent, but only because it is in the self-interest of the businessman to serve the consumer.

If one storekeeper offers you goods of lower quality or of higher price than another, you're not going to continue to patronize his store. If he buys goods to sell that don't serve your needs, you're not going to buy them. The merchants therefore search out all over the world the products that might meet your needs and might appeal to you. And they stand back of them because if they don't, they're going to go out of business. When you enter a store, no one forces you to buy. You are free to do so or go elsewhere. That is the basic difference between the market and a political agency. You are free to choose. There is no policeman to take the money out of your pocket to pay for something you do not want or to make you do something you do not want to do.

But, the advocate of government regulation will say, suppose the FDA weren't there, what would prevent business from distributing adulterated or dangerous products? It would be a very expensive thing to do.... It is very poor business practice—not a way to develop a loyal and faithful clientele. Of course, mistakes and accidents occur—but ... government regulation doesn't prevent them. The difference is that a private firm that makes a serious blunder may go out of business. A government agency is likely to get a bigger budget.

Cases will arise where adverse effects develop that could not have been foreseen—but government has no better means of predicting such developments than private enterprise. The only way to prevent all such developments would be to stop progress, which would also eliminate the possibility of unforeseen favorable developments....

What about the danger of monopoly that led to the antitrust laws? That is a real danger. The most effective way to counter it is not through a bigger antitrust division at the Department of Justice or a larger budget for the Federal Trade Commission, but through removing existing barriers to international trade. That would permit competition from all over the world to be even more effective than it is now in undermining monopoly at home. Freddie Laker of Britain needed no help from the Department of Justice to crack the airline cartel. Japanese and German automobile manufacturers forced American manufacturers to introduce smaller cars.

The great danger to the consumer is monopoly—whether private or governmental. His most effective protection is free competition at home and free trade throughout the world. The consumer is protected from being exploited by one seller by the existence of another seller from whom he can buy and who is eager to sell to him. Alternative sources of supply protect the consumer far more effectively than all the Ralph Naders of the world.

Conclusion

... [T]he reaction of the public to the more extreme attempts to control our behavior —to the requirement of an interlock system on automobiles or the proposed ban of saccharin—is ample evidence that we want no part of it. Insofar as the government has information not generally available about the merits or demerits of the items we ingest or the activities we engage in, let it give us the information. But let it leave us free to choose what chances we want to take with our own lives.

POSTSCRIPT

Should Government Intervene in a Capitalist Economy?

Erber concedes that the market should not be abolished. He writes that a "body of evidence . . . links the market with economic growth, increased productivity, and improved living standards," and that this linkage "cannot be contested." Nevertheless, he calls for an activist government to subordinate the market to "planned priorities designed to serve an overriding common purpose." The Friedmans believe that such subordination can only destroy the market. The question, then, is whether or not we can successfully graft the market's "invisible hand" to the arm of the state. Would the graft take? Has the experiment perhaps already proven successful in post–New Deal America? Or is the American government in the process of destroying what gave the nation its growth, prosperity, and living standards?

Erber calls the market a "blind" force. The Friedmans seem to agree that the market in itself is amoral, though they feel that it produces good results. But philosopher Michael Novak goes further, contending that the ethic of capitalism transcends mere moneymaking and is (or can be made) compatible with Judeo-Christian morality. See *The Spirit of Democratic Capitalism* (Madison Books, 1991) and *The Catholic Ethic and the Spirit of Capitalism* (Free Press, 1993). No such claim is made by the Friedmans in *Free to Choose* or in Milton Friedman's earlier *Capitalism and Freedom* (University of Chicago Press, 1962), which portrays capitalism as supportive of democracy and freedom. Another broad-based defense of capitalism is Peter L. Berger's *The Capitalist Revolution: Fifty Propositions About Prosperity, Equality and Liberty* (Basic Books, 1988). For an attack on capitalism, see Victor Perlo, *Superprofits and Crisis: Modern U.S. Capitalism* (International Publishers, 1988). For a mixed view of capitalism, see Charles Wolf, Jr., *Markets or Governments: Choosing Between Imperfect Alternatives* (MIT Press, 1993). Andrew Shonfield's *In Defense of the Mixed Economy* (Oxford University Press, 1984) takes a similar position to Erber and commends Japan for steering the right course between *laissez-faire* and socialism. Ralph Miliband, in *Socialism for a Skeptical Age* (Verso, 1995), argues that socialism is still applicable today. Two works that attack government interventions in the market are William C. Mitchell and Randy T. Simmons, *Beyond Politics: Markets, Welfare, and the Failure of Bureaucracy* (Westview, 1994) and Jonathan Rauch, *Demosclerosis: The Silent Killer of American Government* (Times Books, 1994). For a discussion of capitalism in the future, see *The Future of Capitalism* by Lester C. Thurow (William Morrow, 1996).

ISSUE 13

Will Welfare Reform Benefit the Poor?

YES: Daniel Casse, from "Why Welfare Reform Is Working," *Commentary* (September 1997)

NO: David Stoesz, from "Welfare Behaviorism," *Society* (March/April 1997)

ISSUE SUMMARY

YES: Daniel Casse, a former senior director of the White House Writers Group, asserts that 1.2 million people came off the welfare rolls since the 1996 welfare reform legislation was passed, without noticeable signs of increased misery as opponents of the reform had predicted.

NO: Social work professor David Stoesz surveys state welfare programs and sees in them little to support optimism about the full impact of welfare reform.

In his 1984 book *Losing Ground* (Basic Books), Charles Murray dared to recommend abolishing Aid to Families with Dependent Children (AFDC), the program at the heart of the welfare debate. At the time this suggestion struck almost everyone as incredible and as just a dramatic way for Murray to make some of his points. However, what most people thought was a wild and even irresponsible idea became the dominant idea in Congress only 14 years later. In 1996 Bill Clinton signed into law the Work Opportunity Reconciliation Act and fulfilled his 1992 campaign pledge to "end welfare as we know it." Perhaps even more remarkable is the fact that many who supported this bill claim that it was the compassionate thing to do. Murray's thesis that welfare hurt the poor had become widely accepted. In "What to Do About Welfare," *Commentary* (December 1994), Murray argued that welfare contributes to dependency, illegitimacy, and absent fathers, which in turn have terrible effects on the children involved. He claimed that workfare, enforced child support, and the abolition of welfare would greatly reduce these problems. Now that his view has become law, we need to determine if he was right.

One reason why Congress ended AFDC was the emergence of a widespread backlash against welfare recipients, often voiced in mean-spirited jibes, such as "Make the loafers work" and "I'm tired of paying them to breed." Such attitudes ignore the fact that most people on welfare are not professional loafers but women with dependent children who have intermittent periods of work or are elderly or disabled persons. Petty fraud may be common since welfare payments are insufficient to live on in many cities, but "welfare queens" who cheat the system for spectacular sums are so rare that they should not be part of any serious debate on welfare issues. The majority of people on welfare are those whose condition would become desperate if payments were cut off. Although many people believe that women on welfare commonly bear children in order to increase their benefits, there is no conclusive evidence that child support payments have anything to do with conception; the costs of raising children far exceed the payments. Also, payments to families with dependent children have eroded considerably relative to the cost of living over the last two decades, so the incentive to get off welfare has increased.

Not all objections to AFDC can be dismissed. There does seem to be evidence that in some cases AFDC reduces work incentives and increases the likelihood of family breakups. However, there is also a positive side to AFDC: it has helped many needy people get back on their feet. But now these facts are water under the bridge; AFDC is over. AFDC-type programs will continue for a few years to allow welfare mothers time to be trained for jobs or to complete their schooling. Meanwhile, many have started work or are actively looking for work. This does not end the story, however, because job retention is a major problem for many of these women.

On July 1, 1997, the Work Opportunity Reconciliation Act went into effect. It is too soon to obtain an accurate assessment of the impacts of the act. Nevertheless, AFDC rolls have dramatically declined since the act was passed, so it is easy to believe that it is a success rather than a failure. Of course, the early leavers are the ones with the best prospects of succeeding in the work world; the welfare-to-work transition gets harder as the program works with the more difficult cases. The crucial question is whether or not the reform will benefit those it affects. Already many working former welfare recipients are better off. But what about the average or more vulnerable recipient?

Daniel Casse, in the following selection, finds the effects of welfare reform overwhelmingly positive but admits that the strong economy has greatly helped many programs succeed. One factor that he feels may cause some failures in the short run but greater success in the long run is the high level of experimentation resulting from the decentralization of the program from the federal government to the states. David Stoesz, in the second selection, denies that the reform is a big success. Since the welfare reform was instituted too recently for careful evaluation, Stoesz bases his analysis on longer-standing state programs of a similar character. Their results are not promising. Moreover, says Stoesz, the research indicates that the reform is based on false assumptions about the motivations and behaviors of welfare mothers.

YES

Daniel Casse

WHY WELFARE REFORM IS WORKING

On July 1, [1997], the "end of welfare as we know it" began in earnest. On that day, the federal legislation that President Clinton had signed nearly a year earlier went into effect, terminating a 62-year-old federal entitlement and creating, for the first time, a limit on how long one can receive federal welfare assistance.

... The welfare-reform legislation that went into effect on July 1 is the most far-reaching policy move of the Clinton presidency—and also, to date, the most successful. Not surprisingly, the President used his July 4 national radio address to crow about it. Since he took office in January 1993, he announced, three million fewer people were on the welfare rolls. Even more impressive was the fact that an astonishing 1.2 million had come off the rolls in the first nine months since the welfare-reform legislation passed Congress and before it formally went into effect. Using rhetoric that was once the preserve of conservative polemicists, the President told the nation on July 4 that "we have begun to put an end to the culture of dependency, and to elevate our values of family, work, and responsibility."

In truth, the legislation itself deserves only part of the credit. Earlier this year, the President's own Council of Economic Advisers concluded that the drop in the number of people on welfare was due in some measure to the healthy economy and also to the wide variety of initiatives that had emerged over the last few years at the state level. We have, indeed, never witnessed such a fertile period of experimentation, with dozens of state legislatures trying new ways to move people off government assistance and onto a path of self-sufficiency. Most of these former recipients have gone successfully into full- or part-time jobs, while others, recognizing the new demands the local welfare office will soon place on them, have voluntarily dropped out of the system. With the more comprehensive measures of the federal law now taking effect—and notwithstanding the deleterious changes introduced in the balanced-budget negotiations—we have every reason to expect that these trends will continue. ...

Quite obviously, no one knows at this early stage what the ultimate effect of welfare reform will be. But the critics, having lost the legislative battle, now seem determined to convince us that without a massive infusion of new federal funds, the nation's poor are headed pell-mell toward cruel deprivation and suffering. Fortunately for the country, the facts suggest otherwise.

* * *

The Personal Responsibility and Work Opportunity Reconciliation Act of 1996 passed both Houses of Congress with considerable bipartisan support. Like all such sweeping pieces of legislation, it makes changes to numerous federal laws and regulations. But the bulk of the legislation is directed at Aid to Families with Dependent Children (AFDC), the Roosevelt-era assistance program that was the target of most of the growing public dissatisfaction with welfare. The new law effectively repeals AFDC and replaces it with a new program known as Temporary Assistance for Needy Families (TANF). In addition, the law introduces four fundamental changes that distinguish it from every attempt at welfare reform that has come before.

First, it ends the federal entitlement to cash assistance. In the past, eligibility for this assistance was means-tested: anyone meeting the income requirements was automatically qualified. Under the new law, each state determines eligibility. Second, the new law gives a block grant to each of the 50 states, permitting it to design a cash-assistance program as it sees fit. Third, the law establishes a five-year lifetime limit on cash assistance and a two-year limit on receiving assistance without working, thus ensuring that welfare cannot become a way of life. Finally, the law requires each state to craft work requirements as part of its welfare program. By the year 2002, states will need to show that at least 50 percent

of those receiving welfare are involved in some form of work or training in exchange for benefits.

These changes all come with a catalogue of exemptions, qualifications, and alternative requirements in special cases —a flexibility that guarantees that the actual programs will vary considerably from state to state. The law will not, for example, "throw a million children into poverty." States can exempt 20 percent of their caseload from the time limit, and also convert block-grant money into vouchers for children after their families have reached the limit. Even when the federal limits are triggered, states can continue to spend their own money helping poor families (as they do now). And states may exempt parents of infants from all work requirements, while single parents with children under six will be asked to work only part-time.

Although one would never know it from the critics, left untouched by this reform are a host of poverty-assistance programs. Medicaid, a program still in need of reform, continues to provide health coverage to all poor families under the new welfare law. Public-housing programs remain in effect, as do child-nutrition programs and the Earned Income Tax Credit. The food-stamp program will continue to grow, if at a slower rate. Again contrary to what has been charged, children with serious long-term medical conditions and disabilities will *not* lose their Supplemental Security Income aid; the new law merely narrows the definition of "disability" to exclude some purely behavioral problems....

* * *

But most confounding of all to critics of the bill, and most heartening to its supporters, is the fact that welfare reform, in its embryonic stages, has wildly surpassed expectations. In April of [1997], eleven million people were on welfare, the lowest share of the U.S. population since 1970. Nor have any of the widely predicted nightmare scenarios materialized. Even in cities like Milwaukee, where thousands of welfare recipients have dropped off the rolls in the last two years, local shelters and food banks have reported no new surges in demand for their services.

What accounts for these early signs of success? Following the lead of the Council of Economic Advisers, some have suggested that the drop in caseloads is traceable entirely to the current strength of the economy. But this cannot be right. The economy has indeed been strong; yet previous cycles of prosperity have failed to produce anything close to the reduction we see today.

What is different, clearly, is that the *rules* governing welfare dependence have started to change. Indeed, they started to change well before the federal law was passed last year. Impatient with Washington's habitual inaction, both Democratic and Republican governors began introducing time limits, work requirements, and rules designed to promote responsibility in their own state systems. The burgeoning economy has made their work easier, but there is no denying that in states where the rules have changed, the lives and behavior of welfare recipients have also changed, and for the better.

Wisconsin's much-touted reforms are a case in point. In a detailed study published in *Policy Review*, Robert Rector has shown how two new programs in that state, Self-Sufficiency First and Pay for Performance, fundamentally altered the relationship between welfare recipients and government. Implemented in April 1996, the programs required recipients to work in the private sector or perform community service, attend remedial-education classes, or participate in a supervised job search in exchange for AFDC payments or food stamps. Those who did not want to work, take classes, or look for a job were no longer eligible for payments. Seven months after the program began, the AFDC caseload had dropped 33 percent.

Recent experience in Tennessee, though less widely reported, is no less impressive. As it happens, Tennessee is not subject to the provisions of the new federal law, having won prior approval for an equally comprehensive program of its own. Like the federal law, the Tennessee plan, known as Families First, replaces AFDC with a cash-assistance program that requires recipients to work, go to school, or train while working part-time. Tennessee exempts almost a third of its welfare recipients from the time limits (and from some of the work requirements), and in that respect its plan is even more flexible than the federal law. On the other hand, Tennessee imposes a tighter restriction on the number of consecutive months welfare recipients can receive cash benefits. Finally, everyone eligible for benefits, even if exempt from the work requirements and the time limits, must sign a "personal-responsibility contract" outlining the steps to be taken toward self-sufficiency.

In the first six months of the program, 19,000 Tennesseans left the welfare rolls —a 21-percent drop, unprecedented in the state's history. What makes this reduction more remarkable still is that during these early months no one was being forcibly removed from the rolls by an arbitrary cutoff date. Instead, social-service officials in Tennessee discovered that the mere requirements to show up at a welfare office, sign a statement of personal responsibility, and participate in a work or educational program had a dramatic impact on the lives of people accustomed to receiving a government check without anything being asked of them at all.

Tennessee officials broke down the declining caseload to understand what was taking place. The results are revealing: 5,800 recipients asked that their cases be closed within the first month ("I don't want to be bothered," was a common response). Another 5,500 found work and earned enough money to make them ineligible. Almost a third either refused to sign the personal-responsibility contract, or failed to comply with its terms, or refused to attend classes or begin a job search. The rest moved out of the state. As for those still receiving cash assistance, many appear to be enthusiastically pursuing a route to independence. In the first six months of Families First, 18 percent of this group had found full-time employment; 22 percent were in training or were looking for a job; 19 percent were pursuing adult education; 6 percent had gotten some form of employment mixed with training.

Tennessee's record so far vividly contradicts the most prevalent and long-standing liberal criticism of a decentralized welfare system: that it will spur a "race to the bottom" among the states. Harvard's David Ellwood, who served as an assistant secretary of Health and Human Services and was a point man for the administration's welfare-reform plans before quitting in frustration, has made this criticism most explicitly:

History is filled with examples of states choosing to ignore poor families or ignoring racial minorities, regions, or types of families. Moreover, if one state's rules differ markedly from those of another, there will be an incentive for migration. It is a lot easier to move poor people from welfare to the state border than from welfare to work. Needs and resources also differ widely across states. The states with the smallest tax base are usually the states with the greatest proportion of poor children and families. Fearful of becoming "welfare magnets," some states may cut benefits and impose more punitive measures than they would otherwise prefer.

On almost every point, the Tennessee example has disproved Ellwood and those who repeat his arguments....

* * *

As for the risks, no one knows how states will manage if regional economies start to fizzle, depriving former welfare recipients of their jobs. Nor can we be sure state programs will discourage *new* entrants to the welfare system as successfully as they have been moving people off. There is also reason to question whether work requirements will deter out-of-wedlock births, which is bound to be a major criterion in judging their success.

Still, the early stages of state reform have already told us volumes about the American welfare population itself, and this will be of inestimable value in addressing the dilemmas of the future. Over the decades, as the evidence of a crisis mounted, it had become customary to speak of this population as if it were a single class of people exhibiting a uniform set of behaviors, motivations, and responses to public policy. If the last few months have taught us anything, it is that welfare recipients are a varied lot.

At one end of the spectrum are those who are unlikely ever to find or hold a job, or to lead a life free of government support. They are the disabled, the chronically ill, and those with severe learning problems or long-term histories of drug and alcohol abuse. They have often been on AFDC without interruption for many years, even decades; their families may have been on AFDC for generations. No mix of carrots and sticks is likely to move such people from welfare to independence. In virtually every state they will be exempt from welfare requirements—quite sensibly so—and continue to depend on government support.

Then there is the opposite end of the spectrum: the considerable portion of the welfare population, perhaps as many as 30 percent, who are easily moved off the rolls at the slightest prompting. Many may have already been in the workforce at some point or other (or may have been defrauding the system by working and collecting welfare simultaneously); when compelled to comply with tighter rules, they simply stop showing up for their check. Others move readily into the workforce when they need to. Still others, as we have seen in Tennessee, would rather drop out of the system than be held accountable for their daily activities. Although some of these welfare recipients may find themselves falling back onto government assistance after a short period of time, they are among those best-equipped to move off welfare permanently, and a well-designed program may be all the motivation they need for long-term self-reliance.

* * *

Between these two groups are those who are neither highly motivated nor completely incapable of self-sufficiency. Almost all the major efforts in the months ahead will be focused on this group. But consider how much more doable the task has become. To critics, most of the success so far is attributable to "cherry picking." As the *New Republic* put it dramatically on the cover of its August 4 issue: "Welfare Reform Has Moved More Than a Million People Off the Rolls. But Those Were the Easy Cases." This, however, is wide of the mark; the fact that the states have a significantly smaller caseload to work with means they can devote more money to each family struggling to get off welfare. Policy-makers have never enjoyed this luxury before.

How should the money be spent? There is, unfortunately, no proven formula. Many states will no doubt invest millions of dollars in job training and preparedness programs. But the evidence that these can lead to success is, at best, mixed. Thus, the Job Training Partnership Act, one of the largest government-funded training programs, has led to some improvement in women's earnings but very little in men's. Similarly unencouraging is a recent study of New Chance, a program operating in twelve U.S. cities and designed to help teenage mothers gain self-sufficiency. Although New Chance spent approximately $9,000 per mother on education, training, child care, parenting skills, and health care, the study (conducted by the same corporation that designed the program) found that these young mothers were no more likely than before to find a job, leave welfare, or delay future pregnancies.

More hopeful are initiatives to replace training and counseling with real work, or at least rigorous preparation for work. In a recent book, *It Takes a Nation*, Rebecca Blank, an intelligent critic of the legislation passed by Congress, concedes that for welfare recipients with minimal job experience, some time at work often proves far more effective than months of training or classroom education. The work environment introduces into their lives a higher level of accountability and stimulates them to acquire more training if they want to move up the ladder. Most important, job placement and work programs shift the relationship between welfare recipients and their local social-service agency. Putting someone in a job is an entirely different mandate from merely certifying his eligibility for cash benefits, and the change is beneficial to both sides.

The most frequent question raised by skeptics is how welfare recipients will find employment. Following the lead of critics like Christopher Jencks, liberals now propose the creation of thousands of public-sector jobs as the only way to absorb the welfare population into the workforce. States that heed their advice, however, will quickly discover that these programs are expensive and extraordinarily difficult to manage. The history of similar efforts at the federal level —most notoriously, the Comprehensive Employment and Training Act (CETA)— confirms the folly of replacing one welfare system with another that goes by a different name.

Nevertheless, there may be a virtue in putting people in some form of *temporary* public-sector workfare or community service. As Robert Rector has pointed out, Wisconsin has created thousands of such jobs, not for make-work but to establish the principle of pay for performance. The same model is now to be seen in other states and cities, including New York, where more than half of the public-park workers are welfare recipients earning their benefits. Ironically, though, this quintessential New Deal-style program has also enraged liberals. In July, a coalition of New York churches, synagogues, and nonprofit groups, evidently oblivious to the social destruction the city's *existing* welfare system has wrought, announced that its members would not offer workfare positions to welfare recipients, on the grounds that the program is tantamount to slavery.

Such moral posturing aside, it is true mandatory public-work programs are not always ideal: under them, many older, laid-off skilled workers may be forced to do menial labor in order to gain temporary cash assistance while seeking a new job. But the vast majority of welfare recipients do not have the skills or wherewithal to enter the job market on their own—they are predominantly young women who have never held a full- *or* part-time job—and for them, programs that demand work in exchange for cash harbor a twofold benefit. First, they habituate a welfare recipient to the norms of the workplace: arriving on time, following instructions, working with others, and so on. Second, by transforming welfare itself, they make it a far less attractive option for a young woman who might once have seen AFDC as a way out of the world of adult responsibility....

* * *

[W]hat distinguishes the current reform is that it has forced both federal and state governments to take seriously the idea that welfare policy can deter, or encourage, behavior. The fact that Tennessee will increase welfare spending this year tells us nothing in itself. But the fact that Tennessee now holds parents accountable for their children's immunizations and school attendance; that it forces teen parents to stay in school and live at home or with a guardian; and that it provides no additional benefits for single mothers who have additional children while on welfare, means that government is no longer indifferent to the way welfare recipients live and raise their children. All this represents a stark departure from the liberalism that has dominated government policy toward the poor for the last three decades.

Changing the way the poor behave may not make them prosperous, and there will always be critics to insist that until poverty is eradicated, no program can claim success. But by eliminating the certainty that one will be paid whether or not one works or seeks work, we have already taken the most important step on the road toward the end of welfare—and of liberalism—as we have known them.

NO

David Stoesz

WELFARE BEHAVIORISM

On August 22, 1996, President Bill Clinton signed the Personal Responsibility and Work Opportunity Act (PRWOA) that ends the welfare entitlement to poor families through the Aid to Families with Dependent Children (AFDC) program, devolving responsibility to the states in the form of a block grant, Temporary Assistance to Needy Families (TANF). That welfare should come under the aegis of the states is ironic. The last social program that was block-granted and devolved to the states, the Title XX Social Services Block Grant, has been so mismanaged that it is implicated in the deaths of the two thousand American children who die of abuse and neglect annually—almost half of such deaths are of children whose cases are known to state children's agencies that are unable or unwilling to protect them. States have proven so inept at protecting children that courts have assumed management of child welfare agencies in twenty-one states and the District of Columbia. Experience notwithstanding, congressional leaders were eager to bluff the president with a welfare reform proposal that he could not veto without risk of public disapproval. Conveniently, the most punitive part of the plan—the institution of a five-year lifetime limit to receipt of welfare—will not take effect until President Clinton leaves the White House.

Welfare Behaviorism
Yet as an attempt to reprogram the behavior of the poor, Republican-inspired welfare reform is unlikely to deliver on its sponsors' promises. Evidence accumulating from the multitude of state welfare demonstrations indicates that the imposition of conditions for receipt of welfare yields modest results at best; at worst, the consequences are downright perverse. Despite data demonstrating the marginal economic benefits of making welfare conditional, conservatives effectively leveraged a moral argument that public policy should change the behavior of the welfare poor. In so doing, "welfare behaviorism" represented a change in the way that conservatives had come to understand poverty. On the eve of passage of the 1988 Family Support Act (FSA), conservative theorists had arrived at a "new consensus" on poverty: Although the liberally inspired public assistance programs, such as AFDC,

may have once been appropriate for the "cash poor," they were counterproductive with the "behaviorally poor." Rather than alleviating problems of the behaviorally poor, public welfare exacerbated the "culture of poverty." As poverty programs expanded, conservatives contended, the social dysfunctions of the behaviorally poor metastasized: Beginning as teen mothers, women dominated family life, ultimately becoming generationally dependent on welfare; young men dropped out of school, failed to pursue legitimate employment, and resorted to sexual escapades and repetitive crime to demonstrate prowess; children, lacking adult role models of effective parents at home and capable workers on the job, promised to further populate the underclass.

Symbolically, PRWOA is a radical departure in American social welfare, ending the sixty-year federal entitlement to an income floor for poor families. The political fallout has been extensive. Die-hard conservatives justified termination of welfare with George Gilder's contention that what the poor needed most was "the spur of their own poverty," while "bleeding heart" conservatives found a rationale in "tough love." Either way, welfare reformers conceded that terminating benefits would probably worsen deprivation but contended that that was necessary too. If making welfare conditional worsened poverty, that was the price for combating the underclass. As a manifestation of public policy, welfare behaviorism might not be pretty, but it was no less essential to restore social order. Liberals were aghast.... Senator Daniel Patrick Moynihan castigated President Clinton for endorsing a bill whose premise was that "the behavior of certain adults can be changed by making the lives of their children as miserable as possible." Liberal advocacy groups scrambled to convince the president to veto the legislation, but they failed....

If the politics of welfare reform were hyperbolic, the research on various welfare waivers scarcely mattered. By mid-1996, evaluation research revealed that the results of state welfare demonstrations were at best problematic. Yet regardless of what both liberal and conservative policy analysts were coming to conclude about making receipt of welfare contingent on specific behaviors, this seemed to accelerate the momentum behind welfare reform. Indeed, the contradictory evidence may well have fueled the palpable urgency that propelled welfare reform through the 104th Congress and on to the White House. Accumulating research on a range of welfare reform experiments—welfare-to-work, learnfare, teen pregnancy, paternity, and time limits—suggested caution in proceeding with major changes in public assistance programs. But data be damned, Congress and the White House were intent on reforming welfare in anticipation of the upcoming election.

Welfare-to-Work

By the early 1990s, the Manpower Demonstration Research Corporation (MDRC) had amassed considerable evidence about the performance of state welfare-to-work programs, and the results fell far short of what conservatives had promised in converting AFDC to an employment-based program. In the best of all welfare worlds, state welfare-to-work programs would show positive outcomes in three ways: Earnings of welfare participants would improve, optimally enough for them to become economically self-sufficient; welfare expenditures through AFDC would decrease; and states would recover the costs of putting in place welfare-to-work programs. Of thirteen welfare-to-work programs evaluated in 1991, most boosted participants' earnings little more than $700 per year. Most programs also experienced reductions in AFDC payments, but these too were modest, typically less than $400 per year. Significantly, in only two programs were AFDC payment reductions greater than the cost per welfare-to-work participant. In other words, in eleven of thirteen welfare-to-work programs, the cost of mounting the welfare-to-work program was not recovered initially in welfare savings.

As in most field research, there are important caveats to these findings. First, the welfare-to-work program that met the three requirements noted above most efficiently was the one implemented in Arkansas; for the first year of the program, earnings increased on average $167, and AFDC payments were reduced $145, enough to recover the additional cost of Arkansas's WORK program, $118 per participant. This explains much of presidential candidate Clinton's enthusiasm about "ending welfare as we know it." Second, two programs were noted for significantly higher annual earnings ($2,000+) as well as welfare savings (more than $700); but in both cases the cost per participant was also high ($5,000+). Thus, independence from welfare carries with it acute "sticker shock."

Yet such modest accomplishments were not to dampen the fervor of welfare-to-work zealots. Quickly, they pointed to the Riverside County, California, GAIN program (Greater Avenues for Independence, California's welfare-to-work program) as an exemplar. Culminating an eight-year investigation of Califor-

nia's GAIN program, the nation's largest welfare-to-work effort, Judith Gueron, head of MDRC, chronicled Riverside County's achievements: a 26 percent increase in AFDC parents working, an average earnings increase of 49 percent, and a 15 percent savings of welfare payments. Over three years, Riverside County GAIN participants' income increased $3,113; welfare savings for the same period were $1,983. In Gueron's words, these were "the most impressive [outcomes] measured to date anywhere." On an annual basis, of course, such figures diminish in significance. Earnings increases on the order of $1,000 per year are unlikely to vault the typical AFDC family off of the program; welfare savings of little more than $600 per year do not raise the specter of cashiering the welfare bureaucracy, either. Indeed, the Riverside experience led Randall Eberts of the Upjohn Institute for Employment Research to observe that only 23 percent of participants were still employed and off AFDC three years after beginning GAIN. Riverside County's vibrant economy probably accounted for much of this superior performance, raising the question of how representative it is of other American communities.

To welfare reform researchers, the welfare-to-work bandwagon was not the star-spangled apparatus that its proponents had made it out to be. Before his assignment to the Clinton working panel on welfare reform, Harvard's David Ellwood admitted as much, writing that the typical welfare-to-work program increased earnings between $250 and $750 per year. "Most work-welfare programs look like decent investments," he concluded, "but no carefully evaluated work-welfare programs have done more than put a tiny dent in the welfare caseloads, even though they have been received with enthusiasm."

But perhaps the modest returns in welfare-to-work programs would be amplified over a longer period, welfare reform proponents averred. If many AFDC recipients have been out of the labor force for so long, they suggested, a two- or three-year assessment of a welfare-to-work program's performance might not reveal more substantial, longer-term benefits. Fortunately, a five-year assessment of welfare-to-work programs in Virginia, Arkansas, Baltimore, and San Diego examines this possibility. At the end of five years, Virginia and Arkansas participants had increased their earnings by a little more than $1,000, while those in Baltimore and San Diego experienced an earnings increase of a little more than $2,000. Welfare savings, on the other hand, varied widely; Baltimore reduced welfare costs by $62, while San Diego reported the greatest savings, $1,930. Net program costs varied as well, from $118 per participant in Arkansas to $953 per participant in Baltimore. Once annualized, these figures confirm the shorter-term experience of welfare-to-work programs in other locales. Again, earnings increases are modest; welfare programs savings somewhat less; and the recovery of set-up costs iffy.

The long-term study of welfare-to-work provides additional insight that had not been available in previous research, however. Earnings of participants do not continue to increase with each additional year; rather, earnings tend to peak during the second or third year and then to fall back toward the range prior to enrollment in welfare-to-work. The only program in which earnings did not fall was in Baltimore, the program with the highest cost per participant. By definition, higher cost per participant is in-

consistent with welfare savings. Hence a trade-off appears: The objectives of increasing earnings in order to make families independent of welfare *and* reducing government welfare payments are contradictory.

Work and Welfare Reform

If the reality of welfare-to-work diverges from the rhetoric of welfare reform, it is because of the assumption that AFDC mothers are so welfare dependent that they have no experience with the labor market. In fact, many mothers have worked and have, as a result, come to see welfare benefits as a form of un- or underemployment assistance. To explain the relationship between work and welfare, labor economist Michael Piore split workers into primary and secondary labor markets. Workers in the primary labor market hold down salaried jobs that include health and vacation benefits, are full-time, and incorporate a career track. Workers in the secondary labor market work for hourly wages— often at the minimum wage—without benefits, in jobs that are part-time or seasonal, and are not part of a career track. Welfare program analysts, by way of illustration, hold jobs in the primary labor market, while working welfare recipients populate the secondary labor market.

Recent research has captured the erratic relationship between work and welfare for many mothers on AFDC. Findings of the Institute for Women's Policy Research reveal that 43 percent of AFDC mothers are either peripherally attached to the labor market, augmenting welfare with wages, or they drift on and off of welfare depending on the availability of work. Once AFDC mothers who are seeking work are coupled to those above, 66 percent of welfare mothers are either participating in the labor market or are trying to. But conditions of the secondary labor market, to say nothing of the machinations of the welfare bureaucracy, make this problematic. Thus, LaDonna Pavetti of the Urban Institute reports that 56 percent of women are off welfare within a year, and 70 percent within two years; however, 45 percent return to public assistance before the end of the first year off welfare, and 57 percent return by the end of two years.

Given the reality of the secondary labor market, the trick of welfare reform is to catapult AFDC mothers beyond the secondary labor market and into the primary labor market. If this could be done, earnings would increase enough to assure economic self-sufficiency, and welfare savings would be substantial since families would be unlikely to revert to public assistance in the future. The sticking point is that substantial investments are necessary to achieve such welfare-to-work program performance. But to do so creates two problems: First, a "moral hazard" emerges as welfare beneficiaries become recipients of benefits that are not available to the working poor who are not on welfare. Working stiffs not only grumble about the welfare-dependent obtaining benefits not available to them, but they also suspect that ample benefits induce those who should be working to apply for public assistance instead. Second, a "political hazard" is created for any elected or appointed official who states a willingness to support welfare recipients over working stiffs. In such circumstances, the prudent politician favors the least costly and most expedient option: push welfare recipients into the labor market and celebrate doing so with paeans to the work ethic. These moral and political hazards thus prescribe the boundaries of plausibility: Perforce, welfare reform is limited to elevating the welfare poor up to the strata of the working poor.

If welfare reform means modest work opportunities for AFDC recipients, it has come to mean something else for welfare program managers, however. Confronted with static, if not declining, revenues, welfare officials—both elected officials and appointed department heads—have come under increasing pressure to reform welfare, by whatever means. Exactly how this has come about is revealed in the five-year study noted above. From the perspective of welfare administrators, there are three primary ways to reduce welfare costs: trim monthly benefits to AFDC recipients who have found work (but who are not earning enough to escape reliance on welfare completely), sanction families who are not complying with work or other conditions attached to receipt of benefits, or simply terminate cases. Regarding these options, researchers found that reducing benefits in relation to earnings accounted for no more than 2 percent of savings, while sanctioning noncompliant recipients only produced a "very small *direct* effect." Most of the savings in welfare costs were generated by terminating cases, closing them as soon as possible. In Arkansas case closings reduced receipt of AFDC by three months on average, in San Diego by almost four months. Yet case closings did not alter recidivism (frequent cycling on and off welfare). Even those AFDC recipients who had found work and were terminated from public assistance were soon back on welfare. What is going on here?

The probable answer to this question can be found in the way welfare programs are administered. Welfare programs such as AFDC require a significant amount of paperwork to establish and maintain eligibility. Yet welfare departments are rarely adequately staffed to process the mountains of paperwork that program management dictates. The resultant quagmire is familiar to anyone who has spent time in a welfare department: Applicants for assistance spend hours waiting to be seen by eligibility workers, often only to be sent off in search of additional documentation to support an application. Until the application is complete, no aid will be forthcoming. Facing a lobby full of anxious and resentful applicants, eligibility workers exercise latitude in making decisions about the fate of those applying for benefits, occasionally expediting the application of someone in dire straits, often impeding the applications of those more troublesome. Sociologist Michael Lipsky coined the term "bureaucratic disentitlement" to describe those instances in which eligibility workers decline valid applications for capricious reasons. The prevalence of outright denial of benefits to those who are entitled is unknown, but probably approaches one in four cases in some welfare offices. Recognizing that administrative caprice is routine in public assistance, it requires little imagination for the ambitious welfare administrator to use welfare reform as an opportunity to accelerate the denial of benefits, thereby achieving significant welfare savings. Given the difficulty in reestablishing eligibility, any case termination realizes a three-to-four month dividend in benefit reductions simply because it takes that long for a recipient to reactivate a claim on public assistance. Thus, purging and churning the AFDC caseload generates savings, but not necessarily for the reasons claimed by proponents of welfare reform.

Learnfare

In the face of modest outcomes generated by welfare-to-work programs, reformers have redoubled their efforts at welfare behaviorism. Insofar as the underclass was the result of the isolation of the poor from the mainstream, conservatives ranked two social institutions as pivotal for social reintegration: Employment was addressed in welfare-to-work; the importance of education was reinforced through "learnfare." As introduced in Wisconsin in the fall of 1988, learnfare targeted teenagers who had more than two unexcused absences from school. Under learnfare "sanctions," the family's AFDC benefits for a dependent teen were reduced $77 per month; for an independent teen with a child, the penalty was $190 per month. Wisconsin officials contended that such sanctions would result in the return of 80 percent of teens on AFDC who had dropped out of school. Rhetoric notwithstanding, subsequent evaluation of the Milwaukee demonstration conducted by an independent agency "did not show improvement in student attendance that could be attributed to the Learnfare requirement." Undeterred, state officials wrote to the evaluators demanding that they suppress parts of the study that detailed the failure of Learnfare to enhance teen school attendance. When the researchers refused, Wisconsin officials canceled the contract, in the process impugning the professionalism of the evaluators.

Teen Parenthood

Meanwhile, Ohio promised teens a $62-per-month carrot for good school attendance, coupled with a $62-per-month stick for truancy through LEAP (Learning, Earning, and Parenting). Three years after [the] program's inception, LEAP was heralded as a major victory in the battle against teen profligacy. Pundits such as William Raspberry trumpeted LEAP's 20 percent increase in the rate that teens completed high school and a 40 percent increase in employment. Alas, a closer examination of the LEAP evaluation is less sanguine. The glowing results were reported only for those teens currently enrolled in school and excluded those who had dropped out, even though both groups were part of the study's population. If drop-outs are included, LEAP's successes plummet: The number completing high school is not 20 percent, but 6.5 percent; the number employed is not 40 percent, but 20 percent. By comparative measures LEAP *does* improve teen behavior, but only modestly. And although LEAP generated outcomes that were positive, it also produced negative results. For teens who had already dropped out of school—arguably, those most likely to join the underclass—LEAP produced no discernable effect. However, because the benefit reduction sanction was levied against all truant teens, a significant number of all mothers in the study reported "diminished spending on essentials for their families, especially clothing and food." In their concluding observations, evaluators conceded that changing adolescent behavior is difficult and admitted that LEAP produced some "perverse effects." ...

Paternity

... Whenever social engineering directed at the welfare poor produced ambiguous or contradictory outcomes, conservatives resorted to child support enforcement (CSE) as their penultimate strategy for welfare reform. Because each dollar paid in child support is a dollar saved in welfare expenditures, CSE is an ideal method for reducing welfare expenditures. Conservatives understood correctly that much of the AFDC program would be unnecessary if absent parents conscientiously paid child support. Whenever welfare behaviorism flagged, conservatives knew they could go to voters and demand that the least absent fathers could do was to support their offspring, and they knew that the public would heartily agree. As has been the case with making receipt of AFDC conditional on various virtues, CSE has yielded diminishing dividends on investment.

Having been incorporated in AFDC in 1975, CSE is the "oldest" of contemporary welfare reform initiatives. For 1993, $9.0 billion was collected through CSE, but this cost the government $2.2 billion. Having obtained collections from 2.8 million families removed 241,880 families, or about 10 percent, from AFDC. For that year, 12 percent of AFDC payments were retrieved through CSE. As a welfare prevention strategy, CSE is available to the nonpoor as well as to those on welfare, a feature that obscures the limited effectiveness of the program as a welfare reform measure. Thus, of the $9.0 billion in CSE collections, most—$6.5 billion—came for families not on AFDC; only $2.4 billion was collected for AFDC families. While CSE is a strong performer in overall collections, it barely breaks even with the welfare population, obtaining only $1.08 in collections for every dollar in program costs. In terms of its total impact on public revenues, CSE is actually a loser, in 1993 reporting a $278 million *loss*, so much of which was borne by the federal government that the states received a benefit of $462 million. ...

The most ambitious initiative to enhance child support payments to poor families is Parent's Fair Share (PFS), a pilot project operated from 1992 through 1993. PFS attempted to increase the child support payments of some 4,000 noncustodial parents (97 percent of whom were male) who had support orders for families on AFDC. Attributes of the noncustodial parents recruited for PFS suggested poor candidacy for full and regular payment of child support: Nearly two-thirds reported working three months or less during the previous year; almost three-fourths stated their most recent wage was less than $7 per hour; almost 40 percent stated they had gone hungry during the previous three months; nearly one-third had trouble paying rent during the past quarter; and three-fourths reported having been arrested at least once since their sixteenth birthday. Typically, the noncustodial parent was $4,252 in arrears for child support. PFS was a comprehensive program including employment and training services, peer support groups, enhanced support payment activities, and conflict mediation. Preliminary analysis indicated that the average monthly child support payment for noncustodial parents decreased from $22.95 for those four months before referral to PFS to $22.62 four months afterward. When those PFS participants who had made no previous support payments were excluded, the amount decreased from $63.80 to $62.89. Note that PFS not only failed to increase child support payments among participants, but it has yet to incorporate into its outcomes the costs of mounting the program.

Time Limits

The ultimate in welfare behaviorism is time-limited AFDC. During the presidential campaign, Bill Clinton won voters' approval for his pledge to "end welfare as we know it." As conceived during the campaign, Clinton's prescription for welfare reform included a two-year time limit on receipt of AFDC followed by government-provided employment in the event a private sector job could not be found. In the presidency, however, Clinton was confronted with the cost of his proposal: While the provision of a job for welfare recipients would increase welfare costs (perhaps $10 billion), the price-tag on making similar opportunities available to the working poor was simply unacceptable (between $45–$60 billion). The president's working group on welfare reform finally resolved the matter by applying the two-year time limit after which public employment would be available only to those AFDC recipients born after 1971 (at that time those under age twenty-five). This compromise was made moot by presidential dithering over health care reform, which delayed welfare reform so long that it could not be presented to a lame-duck Democratic Congress.

The Republican 104th Congress, under the leadership of Speaker Newt Gingrich, presented a much more strict time limit through the Personal Responsibility Act (PRA). In addition to a two-year time limit for any given episode of receipt of welfare, PRA imposed a five-year lifetime limit on receipt of public assistance. It was abundantly clear that President Clinton and Speaker Gingrich had tapped deep public resentment about welfare. As recently as 1996, Public Agenda, a nonprofit public opinion research organization, surveyed sentiment about welfare and found the public fuming. In response to a series of vignettes about families on welfare, respondents approved time limits in the 80 and 90 percentile ranges.

(The only exception was the vignette for a physically and mentally handicapped young man whose family could not support him.) Significantly, *even respondents who were welfare recipients approved of time limits,* although at just slightly lower percentages.

The clearest elucidation of time-limited welfare has been that of the Urban Institute's LaDonna Pavetti. Using a computer simulation, Pavetti programmed a number of scenarios constructed from the primary features of welfare reform proposals before Congress. Both two- and five-year time limits were simulated; in addition, a series of exemptions were incorporated, including having a child under eighteen months of age, being disabled, and already having a job. Pavetti then projected the consequences for families who were newly eligible for AFDC as well as those who were long-term dependents on public assistance. As might be expected, there are many permutations generated by so complex an analysis; however, the major findings are as follows:

- In the long run 58 percent of families receive AFDC longer than two years; more than one-third for longer than five years.
- Because the welfare rolls are populated by families who have been on AFDC for a long period, at any given time about 70 percent have *already* received AFDC for longer than two years, and 48 percent for longer than five years.
- By exempting a recipient because of a very young child at home, the number of families hitting a two-year time limit drops from 37 percent to 10 percent.
- By exempting a recipient who has a young or disabled child, or who is already working, the number of

families reaching a two-year time limit falls to 5 percent.

Time limits without exemptions would cut a swath through AFDC. Based on the number of AFDC recipients in 1993, a prospective two-year time limit would dump 2.07 million families out of the safety net into the underclass; a five-year limit, 1.42 million families. Thus, the two-year scenario would delete 3.07 million children from AFDC; the five-year scenario, 2.11 million children. If exemptions were granted for young children under Pavetti's scenarios, the AFDC termination rate for a two-year time limit would eliminate 207,000 families, including 307,000 children. A two-year time limit granting multiple exemptions would halve that. Yet Pavetti's numbers may underestimate the casualty rate. Subsequent to passage of PRWOA, the Center on Budget and Policy Priorities cited a Congressional Budget Office (CBO) report stating that "if all states were to adopt a two-year time limit, 5.5 million children would be denied aid by 2006, even assuming that states exempted 20 percent of their caseloads from these state time limits."

Time limited welfare is troubling in several respects. Because no state welfare experiment has yet reached that point (although several will in the near future), the consequences for poor families can only be guessed at. When Michigan terminated its General Assistance (GA) program in 1991, only 20 percent of former recipients held formal jobs two years later. If AFDC mothers are similar to Michigan GA recipients, only a minority will make the transition to employment; a substantial—and as yet unknown—number will be ejected from the safety net. There will be no incentives for the states to track the casualties of time limits since they will only highlight the more conspicuous failures of welfare reform. In order to dissuade poor families from moving to states with higher welfare benefits, states are induced to reduce benefits. The down-bidding of welfare benefits fuels a "race to the bottom" with states continually underpricing their neighbors to minimize welfare expenditures. . . .

Consequences of Welfare Reform

Several features of the PRWOA make its implementation, consistent with the aspirations of its proponents, unlikely. A fundamental question is the extent to which states can be expected to comply with the federal work requirements: States must have 25 percent of single parents working at least twenty hours per week by 1997 and 50 percent working at least thirty hours per week by 2002. To date only a few localities have even approached the first target, and by their performance the second seems unreachable. The CBO projects that over six years PRWOA will fall $12 billion short of what is required to provide the services and opportunities necessary to meet work requirements; yet the legislation penalizes states— from 5 percent up to 21 percent of federal funds—for noncompliance. This will produce an enormous compression effect on the states. Squeezed between static resources and increasing demands for job placement, the initial response will be to drop families from welfare. . . . [S]tates will be induced to reduce the number of cases out of compliance with work requirements. Given the difficulties in operationalizing the federal five-year lifetime limit, states will be induced to consider ever shorter limits of their own.

Terminating families as soon as possible on the basis of "noncompliance" will ultimately screen out those families least likely to become employed. Eventually, such families will cease seeking aid; to the extent large numbers of more disorganized families disappear from state welfare rolls, states will avoid federal penalties for failing to meet employment requirements.

What will happen to the families dumped from state welfare programs is open to conjecture. Conservative scholars, such as Marvin Olasky, have promised that private, especially religious, agencies will pick up the slack, but this is doubtful. Contributions to non-profit agencies, such as the United Way, have stagnated during the past few years, and PRWOA reduces federal contributions to states by cutting the Title XX Social Services block grant by 15 percent. Those states concerned about families terminated from the welfare block grant will be able to transfer no more than 10 percent of the TANF block grant to Title XX, but it is unlikely that many would choose to do so because of the underfunding of the work requirements. Ineligible for state aid and unable to get necessary assistance from the nonprofit sector, former welfare families will turn to metropolitan government as the last resort. Big-city mayors are already dreading the impact that such families will have on their precarious budgets. . . .

Given the track record of demonstration programs designed to prevent teen pregnancy and increase child support, stiff penalties directed at adolescents and "deadbeat dads" seem more likely to be of rhetorical value to elected officials than to save the public revenues now allocated to welfare programs. Regarding a larger issue, no one seems to have taken the trouble to calculate the ultimate cost of deploying a state-administered welfare apparatus with the sort of tracking, surveillance, and sanction capacity designed to reprogram the behavior of the 5 million or so families now on welfare. In this respect, it is probably just a matter of time until some pundit relabels PRWOA as the "Social Workers' Full-Employment Act." ...

The research legacy of state demonstrations in welfare reform does not bode well for welfare reform engineered by the 104th Congress and signed by President Clinton. Welfare behaviorism has been of modest benefit in select circumstances, but just as often it has proven to produce results contrary to the behaviors explicitly articulated in public policy. We may have put an "end to welfare as we know it," but the task of configuring a workable policy for poor families remains.

POSTSCRIPT

Will Welfare Reform Benefit the Poor?

There are several issues to sort out in this debate. First, what are welfare recipients like? Before we design policies for changing their circumstances and perhaps even their characters, we need to know what makes them tick and why they are in the situations that they are. Casse barely touches on this topic. He seems to presume that welfare recipients can be forced to change their behavior by making their welfare contingent on their taking steps to get off welfare. Stoesz, on the other hand, does focus on this issue. Instead of looking at all welfare mothers as work aversive, he sees two-thirds of them as work oriented prior to the reform. So their work problems are not due to an unwillingness to work.

The second issue is what incentive system could motivate welfare recipients to self-sufficiency. For example, how much would welfare recipients work if they were allowed to retain a portion of their earnings while on welfare? Would they work themselves off welfare? Some critics see the reform as using the threat of starvation—for welfare recipients and their children—as the motivator to self-sufficiency.

The third issue is the appropriate government structure for the administration of welfare programs. Will decentralizing the control of welfare programs from the federal government to the states improve their performance?

The fourth issue is what to do for those who cannot make it under the reform rules. What percentage of welfare recipients are essentially unemployable or cannot retain jobs for long? What combination of programs are needed to deal with them? Will the old system have to be re-created for them?

The fifth issue is what the states will do. The reform lumps AFDC and Emergency Aid to Families monies into block grants with virtually no oversight and with no requirement for the states to provide matching funds. Each state is motivated to pay as little welfare as possible so that poor people will not be attracted to the state. Will some of them allow the misery of the poor to increase greatly? For example, Michigan abolished its General Relief program during the 1991–1992 recession and cut off benefits for 82,000 recipients. This was one factor in the 50 percent increase of homelessness in Michigan at that time.

Michael B. Katz, in *The Undeserving Poor: From the War on Poverty to the War on Welfare* (Pantheon Books, 1989), traces the evolution of welfare policies in the United States from the 1960s through the 1980s. Charles Noble traces it into the late 1990s and argues that the structure of the political economy has greatly limited the welfare state in *Welfare as We Knew It: A Political History of the American Welfare State* (Oxford University Press, 1997). Critics of AFDC include Lawrence M. Mead, *The New Politics of Poverty* (Basic Books, 1992); Jack D. Douglas, *The Myth of the Welfare State* (Transaction, 1989); and Michael Tanner, *The End of Welfare* (Cato Institute, 1996). Mary Jo Bane and David T. Ellwood are critical of the organization and administration of welfare. See their *Welfare Realities: From Rhetoric to Reform* (Harvard University Press, 1994). Marvin Olasky is critical of big government welfare programs and advocates a return to welfare by faith-based groups or local organizations in *Tough Love: Renewing American Compassion* (Free Press, 1996). Mickey Kaus, in *The End of Equality* (Basic Books, 1992), reviews welfare's negative effects and advocates workfare as the best reform of welfare. Studies of the success of welfare-to-work programs include Daniel Friedlander and Gary Burtless, *Five Years After: The Long-Term Effects of Welfare-to-Work Programs* (Russell Sage Foundation, 1995) and Richard L. Koon, *Welfare Reform: Helping the Least Fortunate Become Less Dependent* (Garland Publishing, 1997). For a review of a range of views on welfare reform see *Welfare Reform* edited by Charles P. Cozic (Greenhaven Press, 1997). Fred Block and his colleagues respond to attacks on welfare in *The Mean Season: The Attack on the Welfare State* (Pantheon Books, 1987). Two works that offer explanations of why welfare provision is so minimal in the United States and that bring in race and gender factors are Linda Gordon, *Pitied but Not Entitled: Single Mothers and the History of Welfare* (Free Press, 1994) and Joel F. Handler and Yeheskel Hasenfeld, *The Moral Construction of Poverty: Welfare Reform in America* (Sage Publications, 1991). For sympathetic descriptions of people on welfare, see Kathryn Edin and Laura Lein, *Making Ends Meet: How Single Mothers Survive Welfare and Low-Wage Work* (Russell Sage Foundation, 1997) and David Zucchino, *The Myth of the Welfare Queen: A Pulitzer Prize-Winning Journalist's Portrait of Women on the Line* (Scribner's, 1997).

ISSUE 14

Are Vouchers the Solution to the Ills of Public Education?

YES: Kevin Walthers, from "Saying Yes to Vouchers: Perception, Choice, and the Educational Response," *NASSP Bulletin* (September 1995)

NO: Albert Shanker, from "Privatization: The Wrong Medicine for Public Schools" *Vital Speeches of the Day* (March 15, 1996)

ISSUE SUMMARY

YES: Teacher Kevin Walthers examines the criticisms of public education and argues that vouchers and choice are well suited to correct its deficiencies, which include a lack of professionalism among teachers and low academic standards.

NO: Albert Shanker, president of the American Federation of Teachers until his death in 1998, argues that there is no evidence that privatizing the public schools works or that the public wants vouchers. He maintains that the public wants discipline and academic standards, which can be provided by public schools modeled after those of countries with better primary and secondary education than the United States.

The quality of American public schooling has been criticized for several decades. Secretary of Education Richard Riley said in 1994 that some American schools are so bad that they "should never be called schools at all." The average school year in the United States is 180 days, while Japanese children attend school 240 days of the year. American schoolchildren score lower than the children of many other Western countries on certain standardized achievement tests. In 1983 the National Commission on Excellence in Education published *A Nation at Risk*, which argued that American education was a failure. Critics of *A Nation at Risk* maintain that the report produced very little evidence to support its thesis, but the public accepted it anyway. Now, 13 years and several reforms later, the public still thinks that the American school system is failing and needs to be fixed. The solution most frequently proposed today is school choice, usually involving a voucher system.

The U.S. educational system has a proud record of achievement over the last two centuries. The present system began to take shape in the nineteenth century, when the states set up locally controlled school districts providing free elementary and high school education. Over time the states also passed compulsory schooling laws, which usually were applicable through elementary school and later were raised to age 16. With free and compulsory education, America has always been and still is the world leader in providing mass education. In the twentieth century the expansion of mass education was phenomenal. Today 99 percent of children aged 6 to 13 are in school. In 1900 only about 7 percent of the appropriate age group graduated from high school, but in 1990, 86 percent did. Another success is the extraordinary improvement in the graduation rates for blacks since 1964, when it was 45 percent, to 1987, when it was 83 percent. Now this rate is almost at parity with white graduation rates. And over two-thirds of the present American population have a high school degree. No other nation comes close to these accomplishments.

American education reforms of the past 40 years have focused on quality and on what is taught. In the late 1950s the Soviet Union's launch of the first space satellite convinced the public of the need for more math and science in the curriculum. In the late 1960s and 1970s schools were criticized for rigid authoritarian teaching styles, and schools were made less structured. They became more open, participatory, and individualized in order to stimulate student involvement, creativity, and emotional growth. In the 1980s a crusade for the return to basics was triggered by the announcement that SAT scores had declined since the early 1960s. More recently, the continued problems of public schools have led many to call for their restructuring by means of school choice.

Two questions on the current situation in American schools serve as background for the voucher issue. First, is there really a school performance crisis? David C. Berliner and Bruce J. Biddle, in *The Manufactured Crisis: Myths, Fraud, and the Attack on America's Public Schools* (Addison-Wesley, 1995), argue that school performance has not declined. They point out that the decline in SAT scores since 1960 was due to the changing composition of the sample of students taking the tests, and better indicators of school performance over time show gains, not losses. Second, is the current structure of schools the main reason why schools seem to be failing? Many other trends have also affected school performance. For example, curricula changes away from basics, new unstructured teaching techniques, and the decline of discipline in the classroom have contributed to perceived problems. The relatively poor quality of teachers may be another factor. There is evidence that those who go into teaching score far lower on SATs than the average college student. In addition, societal trends outside the school may significantly impact on school performance. Increasing breakdown of the family, more permissive childrearing, the substantial decline in the amount of time that parents spend with children, and the increased exposure of children to television are trends that are affecting school performance.

In the following selections, Kevin Walthers promotes vouchers as a way to improve public education, while Albert Shanker attacks voucher systems as unnecessary, unwanted, and no better than public schools.

YES

Kevin Walthers

SAYING YES TO VOUCHERS: PERCEPTION, CHOICE, AND THE EDUCATIONAL RESPONSE

Critics of public education abound. Adults bemoan the lax standards of modern schools, industry leaders complain that students lack basic work skills, college professors decry the lack of logical reasoning in student writing, parents cry out for more and better programs, and taxpayers reject increased funding for schools that are retreating academically while expanding fiscally. . . .

Educators must take an objective look at the charges against them. . . . To accomplish this, educators must evaluate the three main areas of education that receive a majority of the criticism: lack of professional standards among educators; lack of appropriate academic standards for students; and the alienation of parents and taxpayers from the educational process.

BARRIERS TO PROFESSIONALISM

. . . The National Commission on Excellence in Education (1983) addressed the needs of education in *A Nation at Risk*. The commission offered several recommendations regarding teachers designed "to make teaching a more rewarding and respected profession" (National Commission on Excellence in Education [NCEE], 1983, p. 30). The commission stated that education colleges should require prospective teachers to meet high academic standards and that salaries should be market-sensitive and performance based. These are basic elements of professionalism, yet educational leaders have erected barriers to keep these elements out of the educational process.

The NCEE realized that a need existed for better qualified students to enter the field of education. Historically, students enrolled in colleges of education consistently scored below the national average on standardized tests such as the ACT, SAT, and GRE (Sowell, 1993). The brightest students entering universities were choosing not to enroll in colleges of education, depriving schools of a resource considered very valuable in the private sector: bright, young, educated talent. The NCEE recommended awarding grants and loans to attract outstanding students to the teaching profession (particularly in areas of critical shortage such as science and mathematics), as well as developing strategies such as an 11-month contract that would make teaching more attractive financially (NCEE, 1983).

Enhancing the financial aspect of teaching is a key to building professionalism. One characteristic that all professionals share is the right to negotiate contracts on their own behalf, based on their worth to the employer. Friedman notes that "[p]oor teachers are grossly overpaid and good teachers grossly underpaid" (1982, p. 94). The problem with teacher salaries, the economist/author claims, is not that they are too low but that they are too rigid (Friedman, 1982).

If they are to be considered professionals, teachers should be compensated based not only on their value to the school but also on their value to others who seek to employ them. A lack of market incentives for salaries and the penalizing effect of the certification system lead to critical shortages in education. For example, highly qualified scientists, mathematicians, and language specialists are lured away from teaching because of financial disincentives to enter the classroom, and prevented from entering the educational field by legal barriers requiring a teaching certificate. The teaching certificate is designed to ensure that all teachers meet professional standards, but it is rarely more than a "union card":

> Certification raises problems not just because it fails to screen out the mediocre and the bad. It also raises problems because it sets up formidable barriers to entry that keep many excellent prospects out of the job pool. People who are well educated, bright, enthusiastic, creative, and good with children cannot simply pursue a latent interest in education by simply giving it a try. Nor can talented people already working in other lines of endeavor shift into teaching, or perhaps move in and out of it, as they might in other jobs. Instead, potential teachers are asked by the state to foreclose other options, make a substantial investment of time and resources, and jump through formal hoops. Our society is full of people who could make excellent teachers, but burdensome certification requirements are the best way to ensure that most of them never teach (Chubb and Moe, 1990, p. 196).

ACADEMIC STANDARDS

While some question the professionalism of educators, others fear a lack of appropriate academic standards for students. Adults remember "how tough it was when I was in school," but growing evidence supports the public's position that school, while getting easier, ignores the increasing knowledge base needed to compete in a high tech marketplace. Parents and taxpayers see falling test scores, inclusion, affective learning, self-esteem training, and values clarification lessons as proof that schools are not teaching as much material as they used to. Furthermore, they believe the material being taught is not as difficult as it should be.

> 'Sex education' courses and textbooks, for example, seldom involve a mere conveying of biological or medical information. Far more often, the primary thrust is toward re-shaping of attitudes, not only toward sex, but also toward parents, toward society, and toward life. The same pattern is found in many other programs claiming to be about drug prevention,

smoking prevention, and many other worthy purposes (Sowell, 1993, p. 35).

Parents and taxpayers demand that "basic skills" regain the attention of educators. They wonder how a person who lacks the skill to complete an employment application managed to graduate from a public high school. This is a strong perception in the community, one educators would be unwise to dismiss as "hate-mongering from the radical right."

The lack of academic standards in the public school is profound. According to the U.S. Census Bureau, in 1930: "...most of the 1 million white illiterates and 2 million black illiterates were people over the age of 50 who had never been to school. By 1990, 30 to 35 million (American) citizens could not read. Most are people under 50 who have been to school for at least eight years" (Wood, 1992, p. 51)....

ALIENATION

A correlating factor to watered-down curricula is the feeling of alienation held by many taxpayers and parents. Educators cry out for parent and community involvement, then complain when these forces initiate change in school policy. Educators, when asked to identify their "customers, often respond that students or their parents are their clients. One overlooked public school client, however, is the taxpayer. Citizen funding of the educational process creates "a stable and democratic society (that) is impossible without a minimum degree of literacy and knowledge on the part of most citizens" (Friedman, 1982, p. 86) In refusing to acknowledge the role of the community in education, schools are alien-

ating the portion of the population that pays the bills. Therefore, "citizens everywhere, whether or not they have children in school and whether or not they live in the local school district or even the state, have a legitimate hand in governing each and every local school" (Chubb and Moe, 1990, p. 30).

Parents, of course, possess a natural right to be involved directly in the education of their children. The Family Educational Rights and Privacy Act of 1974 arms parents with the legal means to force educators to divulge information regarding course content, among other things. Even without federal law, parents have direct local access to principals, teachers, administrators, and even school board members. This close tie to the schools does not mean, however, that parents should have any more influence on school policy than any other tax-paying member of the community (Chubb and Moe, 1990). The community establishes the schools and sets policies in accordance with the public good, not the individual preference.

A WORKABLE SOLUTION

... Nobel Prize-winning economist Milton Friedman developed a plan that, though a radical departure from the status quo, would empower parents as well as quality educators. "Free market vouchers" embody the application of Friedman's plan for what Zerchykov (1987) calls "unregulated vouchers." If Friedman did not coin the term vouchers as it relates to school choice, he certainly may be credited with the universal acceptance of the term as it relates to educational policy.

Vouchers, according to Friedman, would provide a mechanism for equalizing educational opportunities: "Governments could require a minimum level of schooling financed by giving parents vouchers redeemable for a specified maximum sum per child per year if spent on approved educational services" (Friedman, 1982, p. 87).

He begins his argument by noting that while it is a responsibility of the government to provide funding for education (which promotes the common welfare), the government is not required to administer education. This could be done much more efficiently in the private sector, with only minimal regulations that would concern health and safety issues (Friedman, 1982). He does not advocate the abolition of the modern public school, but challenges them to compete for students with private and parochial schools.

Thomas Ascik, executive director of the Clearinghouse on Educational Choice, agrees that free market vouchers give parents the liberty to raise their children as they see fit: "Child rearing is the whole and schooling is only a part. Parents have the authority over the whole and, therefore, they should have the ultimate authority over the part" (Ascik, 1986, p. 109).

Ascik and Friedman also claim that free market vouchers will be a greater benefit to the poor than to the wealthy. Friedman explains that a parent in a low income job can save money and buy the same car that the wealthy drive. In like manner, the parent can work an extra job to send his child to private school so that he can get an education on a par with that of a child in a public school in a wealthy neighborhood. A voucher would enable the family to send the child to a better school and devote economic resources to other aspects of making

a better life such as home ownership or providing for otherwise unaffordable extracurricular activities.

Opponents of the free market voucher plan call this plan "welfare for the rich," asserting that private schools would merely raise the cost of tuition by the amount of the voucher, keeping the school as unreachable for the poor as it was before. They also claim that the poorest segments of our society are the least educated, so they would not know how to find the best school for their child. Ascik confronts the latter problem by comparing school funding to the food stamp program:

> Annually, governments invest as much in health as in education. Nutrition is a big part of health. Using the same rationale used to justify the status quo in public education, we may wonder why the government should not fund grocery stores directly rather than deliver food stamps to individuals (Ascik, 1986, p. 111).

In response to the first objection, the market theory used by Friedman to advocate free market vouchers holds that if private schools raise their tuition by the amount of the voucher, someone will fill the gap in the market and provide an alternative of equal quality for a lower price. This basic principal of economic efficiency will bring down the tuition price of the other schools as well, creating more educational opportunities for those on the lower end of the economic scale.

WHY SHOULD EDUCATORS SUPPORT CHOICE?

Educators claim to support choice. They point to alternative schools, open enrollment policies, magnet programs, and

GED classes as evidence. When students are restricted to choosing from the programs offered by a single entity (usually the local school district), the promise of choice remains unfulfilled. By implementing a true choice plan, educators would elevate the stature of their field, allow for specialized, relevant academic standards, and intimately involve parents in the education of their children.

Unfortunately, teacher associations and unions adamantly oppose any form of choice that would allow students to attend nonpublic schools. Unions cite student welfare as the reason for their opposition to choice, but self-serving political motives are the driving force against any plan that undermines the power of the unions, especially the National Education Association.

The NEA claims to be interested in student success, yet opposes allowing students to leave the monopolistic school district in search of better schools. Association president Keith Geiger asserted that "the solution to the funding and social inequities that condemn children in inner cities and other impoverished areas to inferior schools is not to encourage the flight of the most promising students" (Dunne, 1991, p. 14).

Geiger fails (or refuses) to see that all students would have access to better schools, not just the top prospects. There is a strong inverse link between economic disadvantage and educational achievement. For this reason, federal block grant funds are distributed based on the income level of the students attending a particular school or district. Wealthy districts get little while poor districts receive a substantial supplement.

This would continue under a voucher plan by giving financial incentives to schools that educate children from eco-nomically depressed areas. By increasing the financial value of the child's education, inner-city children would become highly desirable members of the student body (Rinehart and Jackson, 1991). Choice plans in Cambridge, Mass., have increased overall student achievement while closing the educational gap between white and black students. East Harlem, N.Y., has seen a five-fold increase in the rate of students reading at or above grade level since initiating a school choice plan (Nathan, 1990). One study of interdistrict choice plans shows that parents want better schools for their children, even if it means taking the student to a school in another district:

> It would be a mistake to dismiss interdistrict school choice as a phenomenon driven by family convenience. Enrollment patterns in districts where significant numbers of transfers occurred (20 students or more from one community to another) show a strong and unmistakable trend. Families enrolled their children in districts that had higher median family incomes and better educated adult populations than their home communities. They also went to districts that had better standardized test scores at the high school level, lower out-of-school suspension rates, lower dropout rates, and higher per-pupil funding (Fossey, 1994).

The plan that Geiger assails as damaging to the minority student has in fact, proved to work just as Milton Friedman said it would more than 30 years ago, even though the programs are limited in scope. Lower-income parents in Massachusetts choice districts are empowered to seek out an education for their children that is equal to that of families with higher income while the taxpayers are blessed with a young population that will have increased earning power due to an improving educational system.

Even if free market vouchers are not the best option, those who oppose choice refuse to engage in thoughtful debate. Many advocates of choice are intelligent, prominent, and eloquent. They count among their ranks politicians, professors, journalists, and at least one Nobel Laureate. Hurling invective at a group with these credentials, as the education associations continue to do, only strengthens the choice position.

The arguments presented by voucher supporters are solid, gaining widespread acceptance from lawmakers in both major parties (Lieberman 1990). Educators must look at the issue impartially, realizing that the best way to educate children may not be through a government-run monopoly. If educators are to be considered professionals, they must allow for dissent, innovation, and input from the community. Arrogantly claiming to be the sole possessors of educational knowledge and demanding ever-growing infusions of tax money to support public schools is no longer politically viable.

CONCLUSION

Vouchers hold the promise of elevating teaching to professional status, raising levels of student achievement, and restoring the confidence of the tax paying public. If teachers do not embrace this idea, they should at least develop thoughtful arguments that show why the plan is unworkable. Until educators and their associations agree that dissent is not only acceptable but encouraged, the public will continue to perceive education as just another in a long list of non-performing, over-bureaucratized, autocratic government programs that usurp individual liberty.

REFERENCES

Ascik, T. In *Content, Character, and Choice in Schooling*. Washington, D.C.: National Council on Educational Research, 1986.

Chubb, J., and Moe, T. *Politics, Markets, and America's Schools*. Washington, D.C.: The Brookings Institution, 1990.

Dunne, D. *School Choice: Pros, Cons, and Concerns*. Washington, D.C.: ASPIRA Issue Brief, 1991.

Fossey, R. "Open Enrollment in Massachusetts: Why Families Choose." *Educational Evaluation and Policy Analysis* 3(1994): 320–34.

Friedman, M. *Capitalism and Freedom*. Chicago, Ill.: University of Chicago Press, 1982.

———. *Public School Choice: Current Issues/Future Prospects*. Lancaster, Pa.: Technomic, 1990.

Nathan, J. "Progress, Problems, and Prospects of State Education Plans." In *Choice in Education: Potential and Problems*, edited by W. Boyd and H. Walberg. Berkeley, Calif.: McCutchan, 1990.

National Commission on Excellence in Education. *A Nation at Risk*. Washington, D.C.: U.S. Department of Education, 1983.

Rinehart, J., and Jackson, L., Jr. *American Education and the Dynamics of Choice*. New York: Praeger, 1991.

Sowell, T. *Inside American Education: The Decline, the Deception, the Dogmas*. New York: The Free Press, 1993.

Wood, R. "That's Right—They're Wrong." *National Review* 18(1992): 50–53.

Zerchykov, R. *Parent Choice: A Digest of Research*. Boston, Mass.: Institute for Responsive Education, 1987.

NO

Albert Shanker

PRIVATIZATION: THE WRONG MEDICINE FOR PUBLIC SCHOOLS

Delivered to the Joint Economic Committee of the U.S. Senate, Washington, D.C., February 5, 1996

Mr. Chairman and Members of the Committee: I am Albert Shanker, president of the American Federation of Teachers, AFL-CIO, which represents 885,000 teachers and school staff at all levels of the education system, as well as state and local government employees and healthcare professionals. I appreciate the chance to speak to you today about privatization in education.

What's the Real Problem with Schools?

Privatization is not a new idea for fixing public schools. It's been around for a long time. Proponents of privatization see public schools as a monopoly, and, it's always easy to get applause by knocking monopolies. The theory is that monopolies don't produce good results because there's no competition, and without competition, the monopoly has no incentive to strive for quality or efficiency. The obvious conclusion, then, is to inject some good, old-fashioned private-sector competition into the public school system.

There's only one problem with this theory, and that is that there is no evidence that it works. So I think it's important to start by taking a look at why people are dissatisfied with our public schools. Are parents and the public saying get rid of the public school monopoly? No. Are they clamoring for vouchers or private managers? No. In fact, the public—when given a chance to vote on it in California, Oregon, Colorado, and D.C.—has emphatically rejected vouchers.

What do parents and the public say they want? Two things: discipline and academic standards. They've been saying this for at least ten years, but politicians and would-be reformers haven't been listening. They're still not listening.

What parents and the public want are schools that are safe and orderly enough for learning to take place and that set high academic standards for all students. Recent polls, particularly two very interesting studies by the

From Albert Shanker, "Privatization: The Wrong Medicine for Public Schools," *Vital Speeches of the Day* (March 15, 1996). Copyright © 1996 by City News Publishing Company, Inc. Reprinted by permission.

nonpartisan research group Public Agenda, show overwhelming support for greater discipline and higher standards, including among minority parents and those who consider themselves "traditional Christians." Here are a few figures from "First Things First," the first Public Agenda Study:

Sixty-one percent of Americans said that academic standards are too low in their schools, with 70 percent of African-American parents with children in public schools agreeing.

Eighty-two percent supported setting up "very clear guidelines on what students should learn and teachers should teach in every major subject," with 92 percent of African-American parents and 91 percent of traditional Christian parents agreeing.

Seventy percent want to raise standards of promotion from grade school to junior high, letting students move ahead only when they pass a test showing they have met the standards.

Other polls show that these views are also widely supported by teachers and the business community. In a second study, called "Assignment Incomplete," Public Agenda further probed the public's views on school reform, asking a number of questions comparing public and private schools. What they found people liked about private schools was not competition or freedom from monopoly. They believe that private schools are more orderly and disciplined than public schools, and that they have higher academic standards.

When Public Agenda offered a series of proposed solutions for failing public schools, 48 percent of respondents said they wanted to "overhaul the public schools" and "increase the money public schools get," versus 10 percent who favored private management and 28 percent who wanted vouchers. A 1995 Gallup poll on education found that 65 percent of respondents opposed allowing students to attend private schools at public expense.

How should we respond? By giving the public what it doesn't want—vouchers and private management? Or by making the common-sense changes parents and the public are asking for in public schools: order, discipline, and high standards? Public schools can do these things. It's public policies that made them stop, and so it's public policies—not privatization—that can restore discipline and standards.

The Crucial Role of Standards

If I were a businessman and I saw someone else in the same business putting out a better product than mine, I'd sure want to know what the other guy was doing and maybe try to steal some of his ideas. So let's look at the school systems of OECD countries that do a better job with their students. What do we see? Monopolies. And, moreover, the most reviled sort of monopolies—*government* monopolies!

Other countries whose students routinely outperform ours all have education systems that are monopolies, centrally directed or coordinated by their national governments. Not a single one of these countries uses competition or private management or vouchers as an instrument of educational improvement. And not a single one has considered dismantling or selling off their public school systems, which is what some are advocating here.

What all of these countries have in common are a system of clear, common, and rigorous academic standards for all students, at least through their equivalent of our ninth or tenth grades, a set of national or nationally coordinated tests to see if students are meeting the standards, and incentives for students to work hard in school. In these other countries, unlike here, good advanced training or apprenticeships, good jobs, and university admission all depend on doing well in school. Students—and their parents and teachers—know what's expected of them in school, and they know that there will be serious consequences in their lives if they fail to meet the standards. Moreover, since the primary mission of schooling in these countries is academic, students who constantly disrupt classes are suspended or put in alternative placements, so that those who want to learn can do so.

A few of these other countries do subsidize private and religious schools. But the important point is that the state requires private and religious schools to operate according to the same standards as public schools. They must use the same curriculum and the same tests. They get roughly the same level of funding and pay the same teacher salaries as public schools. They are highly regulated within highly centralized education systems. To do that here would breach the wall of separation between church and state, destroy the independence of independent schools; and add to government regulation and costs. It's unthinkable here, given our traditions. Yet without doing these things to ensure accountability, quality and equity, we will further fragment a system that is already dangerously fragmented.

The main exception to these basic operating principles of OECD systems is England, which is actually trying some of the choice and competition experiments proposed here and finding mixed results.

Well, why am I beating the drum for standards again, when your topic is privatization? Because I believe that the effort to privatize schools is completely misguided and destructive. It will erode, not improve, the quality of education and student achievement. I'm arguing that discipline and a system of standards, assessments, and incentives for students are the most essential reforms our schools need right now, and they're standard operating procedure in other successful school systems.

We know that such standards-based systems work in other countries. And standards and discipline are what characterize good schools in this country, public and private. I believe that it is irresponsible and immoral for us to continue ignoring what works while pressing for unproved fads. It's time to stop fooling the public by promising them that privatization panaceas with no evidence of success behind them are the answer to the problems in our public schools. Let's do for all students what we now do only for some students, usually those in more affluent communities, and what other countries do for all their students.

The Promise of Privatization

A leading assumption behind privatization efforts is that competition and private-sector know-how will make public schools more efficient. But there is a large body of literature showing that the assumption is baseless. Here are a few examples.

One recent study found "only weak and inconsistent evidence" for the proposition that competition among schools increased efficiency and concluded that "reforms aimed solely at increasing competition among schools could be ineffectual." Others demonstrate that a voucher system would dramatically increase education costs and shift these costs from the private to the public sector. Yet another argues that "markets are not always more efficient than internal production, especially when the product in question —public benefits in one area or another— is hard to measure and control. The transaction costs involved in regulating private producers may well exceed any of the supposed gains in efficiency from a reduced public sector."

This last point about transaction costs is especially important because it is so often overlooked. Privatization and voucher schemes are more complex transactions than the market analogy suggests. There is a voluminous literature demonstrating that there are huge public costs involved in monitoring and evaluating the performance of private contractors and in running third party payment systems, which is what a voucher system is. And rather than reducing bureaucracy, they increase it. These transaction costs are rarely discussed with the public until a crisis, like healthcare or the Department of Defense contractor scandals, brings them to light.

A Case Study in Private Management: Education Alternatives, Inc.

Let's look briefly at the track record of the only private company that has tried to manage public schools, Education Alternatives, Inc. (EAI). In Baltimore, they promised a dramatic improvement in student achievement in the first year, and they promised to do it for less money. What happened? Test scores went down in EAI schools, while they went up in other Baltimore schools. What did the superintendent and school board do? Nothing, in part because

the superintendent was busy running around the country proselytizing for EAI.

What about the second year? EAI schools' test scores were still down. EAI came under investigation for violations of special education laws, and information from the school system showed that EAI increased class size, cut special education services, and took money away from classrooms to pay for corporate overhead. We learned that, not only was EAI failing to cut costs, it was getting about $500 more per student than other schools—money that was drained from other Baltimore schools and is a big part of their current budget shortfall. Meanwhile, the company took home $2.6 million in profits.

In the third year, some test scores in EAI schools started to inch back up, but students are still behind where they were before EAI arrived. An independent evaluation by the University of Maryland/Baltimore County showed that EAI failed to deliver on most of its promises. When they couldn't raise test scores, the company touted its success in cleaning up the schools and supplying computers. But the UMBC evaluation showed that they didn't even do a very good job at that. The evaluation found few differences between EAI schools and other Baltimore schools—and those schools didn't get any extra money.

EAI lied repeatedly about test scores and attendance figures, and when they were caught in their lies, claimed that they were simply "errors." They withheld financial information to the point that the Baltimore city council was forced to subpoena the company for its financial records. In Hartford, they booked the entire Hartford school district budget as revenue, even though they were managing only five schools and did not control the funds. This made the company look more successful on Wall Street than it really was, and city officials criticized the accounting maneuver as misleading and unethical. With no sense of irony, EAI is now claiming that the reason they failed in Hartford was that they didn't control the money they earlier claimed they controlled!

After three-and-a-half years, the Baltimore school board finally pulled the plug on EAI. Who gets to keep the computers is now the subject of a dispute, but there's no disputing the fact that Baltimore got less for more from EAI, not the reverse. The person who benefited most was EAI's executive, John Golle, who made lavish profits by taking public dollars out of Baltimore and trading his EAI stock in timely fashion.

EAI was recently kicked out of Hartford, as well, largely over a financial dispute. EAI is claiming millions of dollars in reimbursement, but the city says EAI agreed that they would only be paid if they could find savings in the school budget. Hartford taxpayers were outraged when EAI billed the city for thousands in first-class travel for EAI staff, public relations fees, and condominium rent. John Golle recently announced that he's now setting his sights on more affluent suburban districts.

The record of EAI demonstrates that private contractors can engineer profit through stock manipulation, inflated claims, and pocketing public funds taken from other schools—all before a single student has shown improvement. The record also shows that EAI knew no more—in fact, a lot less—than public schools about how to improve students achievement.

Behind the zeal to privatize public schools is the assumption that there's a lot of fat to cut out of school budgets. We hear repeatedly that public education costs have gone up, while achievement has remained flat. But as EAI learned, there isn't a lot of fat. Most of the increase in education expenditures over the last twenty years has gone to special education and other hard-to-educate youngsters. In Baltimore, EAI made its profits not from bureaucratic excess—in fact, no central office functions or staff were cut —but by cutting special education and remedial services to disadvantaged students and by increasing class size, that is, by taking money out of classrooms. In Hartford, they didn't get paid because they couldn't identify any savings.

In sum, the case for privatization in education rests only on theory or ideology, not on facts. The facts, with respect to EAI, earlier privatization experiments called "performance contracting," and the Milwaukee voucher program, show that privatization is, at worst, a scandal and a disaster, and, at best, no improvement over the status quo. It has produced no improvement in student achievement, and, in some cases, has depressed it. And student achievement, after all, is our main problem in education. Privatization is a hope and a prayer, when what we need are reliable answers to our problem.

The Role of Public Education
In a Democracy

Privatization arguments rest on the argument that education is primarily a private benefit and so best left to parent and private discretion. But in a democracy, education is, first and foremost, a public good. All taxpayers support education, not just the small number of families (somewhere around 27 percent) who actually have children in public schools. Why? Because in a democracy, all citizens have a stake in a well-educated populace and suffer from one that is ill educated. In a diverse and pluralistic country like ours, public schools are the glue that helps hold society together. If we privatize our education system, we would become the only nation on earth to abdicate our responsibility for socializing our young into the common values of our society and the shared duties of citizenship. The Founding Fathers had it right. Only with public education can you have both the unfettered pursuit of individual private interests and a free society.

Despite their dissatisfaction, Americans remain fiercely attached to their public schools. All the polls tell us they want them fixed, not abandoned. In a democracy, when you think the public is wrong, you need to make the case for why they're wrong. If you think they're right, you should give them what they want. The American Federation of Teachers believes that parents and the public are right, and that they should get what they want and what we know works, standards of conduct and achievement, not radical proposals for dismantling our public schools.

POSTSCRIPT

Are Vouchers the Solution to the Ills of Public Education?

With a great deal of public attention focused on school choice, the literature on it has mushroomed. The choice proposal first gained public attention in 1955 when Milton Friedman wrote about vouchers in "The Role of Government in Education," in Robert Solo, ed., *Economics and the Public Interest* (Rutgers University Press). More recent school choice advocates include David Harmer, *School Choice: Why We Need It, How We Get It* (Cato Institute, 1994); Bruce W. Wilkinson, *Educational Choice: Necessary but Not Sufficient* (Renouf Publishing, 1994); James R. Rinehart and Jackson F. Lee, Jr., *American Education and the Dynamics of Choice* (Praeger, 1991); Terry M. Moe, ed., *Private Vouchers* (Hoover Institution, 1995); Daniel McGroarty, *Break These Chains: The Battle for School Choice* (Forum, 1996); and Myron Lieberman, *Public Education: An Autopsy* (Harvard University Press, 1993). Some advocates of choice would limit the choices in major ways. Timothy W. Young and Evans Clinchy, in *Choice in Public Education* (Teachers College Press, 1992), contend that there is already considerable choice in public education in that there are alternative and magnet schools, intradistrict choice plans, "second chance" options, postsecondary options, and interdistrict choice plans. Research shows that these options work well, so the authors recommend that they be expanded. They argue against a voucher system, which they feel will divert badly needed financial resources from the public schools to give further support to parents who can already afford private schools. In the end they promote a limited choice plan rather than a fully free market plan. For another proposal of a limited choice plan, see Peter W. Cookson, Jr., *School Choice: The Struggle for the Soul of American Education* (Yale University Press, 1994).

Important critiques of school choice include Albert Shanker and Bella Rosenberg, *Politics, Markets, and America's Schools: The Fallacies of Private School Choice* (American Federation of Teachers, 1991); Jeffrey R. Henig, *Rethinking School Choice: Limits of the Market Metaphor* (Princeton University Press, 1994); Kevin B. Smith and Kenneth J. Meier, *The Case Against School Choice: Politics, Markets, and Fools* (M. E. Sharpe, 1995); and Judith Pearson, *Myths of Educational Choice* (Praeger, 1993). Three works that cover the issue broadly or from several points of view are William L. Boyd and Herbert J. Walberg, eds., *Choice in Education: Potential and Problems* (McCutchan, 1990); Ruth Randall and Keith Geiger, *School Choice: Issues and Answers* (National Educational Service, 1991); and Simon Hakim et al., *Privatizing Education and Educational Choice: Concepts, Plans, and Experiences* (Praeger, 1994). Jerome J. Hanus and Peter W. Cookson, Jr., debate the issue of vouchers in *Choosing Schools: Vouch-*

ers and American Education (American University Press, 1996). On the issue of the impact of choice on the equalization of opportunity, see Stanley C. Trent, "School Choice for African-American Children Who Live in Poverty: A Commitment to Equality or More of the Same?" *Urban Education* (October 1992) and Charles V. Willie, "Controlled Choice: An Alternative Desegregation Plan for Minorities Who Feel Betrayed," *Education and Urban Society* (February 1991).

ISSUE 15

Should Doctor-Assisted Suicide Be Legalized for the Terminally Ill?

YES: Marcia Angell, from "The Supreme Court and Physician-Assisted Suicide: The Ultimate Right," *The New England Journal of Medicine* (January 2, 1997)

NO: Paul R. McHugh, from "The Kevorkian Epidemic," *The American Scholar* (Winter 1997)

ISSUE SUMMARY

YES: Marcia Angell, executive editor of *The New England Journal of Medicine*, presents medical and ethical reasons justifying doctor-assisted suicide, including that it honors the autonomy of the patient and is merciful in cases when pain cannot be adequately relieved.

NO: Paul R. McHugh, director of the Department of Psychiatry and Behavioral Sciences at the Johns Hopkins University School of Medicine, argues that sick people who wish to kill themselves suffer from verifiable mental illness and that, since they can be treated for their pain and depressed state, physicians cannot be allowed to kill them.

According to a recent anonymous survey of almost 2,000 doctors who regularly care for dying patients, 6 percent of physicians say they have assisted patient suicides. Only 18 percent had received such requests, and one-third of these had given the requested help. Most physicians who admitted assisting in patients' deaths said they did it only once or twice, so the practice seems to be fairly uncommon. One-third of all doctors surveyed said that they would write prescriptions for deadly doses of drugs in certain cases if the law allowed, and one-quarter would give lethal injections if it were legal. *Officially* the medical community is adamantly opposed to doctor-assisted suicide.

The issue of doctor-assisted suicide is quite complex and confusing. Part of the confusion relates to definitions. Doctor-assisted suicide does not refer to a doctor injecting a patient with a lethal drug nor assisting the suicide of someone who is not terminally ill. The most common method of doctor-assisted suicide is for the doctor to prescribe a drug and then telling the patient how much of it would be lethal. The patient then administers the drug himself or herself. Doctor-assisted suicide lies between letting patients die by removing life-support systems at their request and euthanasia. The first is legal according to the Supreme Court's 1990 decision in *Cruzan v.*

Director, Missouri Department of Health, and the latter is considered murder. So the question arises whether doctor-assisted suicide is more like the legal removal of life-support systems or the illegal euthanasia.

The legal, social, and moral issues involved add to the complexity and confusion. First, doctor-assisted suicide is a hotly contested legal issue governed by laws and court decisions. The legal issue was somewhat clarified by the Supreme Court on June 26, 1997, when it unanimously decided that terminally ill people have no constitutional right to die and, therefore, no right to doctor-assisted suicide. Thus, the Supreme Court will not declare invalid state laws that prohibit this practice.

Second, doctor-assisted suicide is a complex social issue with very active groups championing both sides of the debate. Medical technologies have advanced to the point that death can be postponed for a long time after the mind has ceased to function or after the quality of life has declined deeply into the negative. This produces countless situations in which people should not go on living in the judgment of most people. But what should be done for them? The situation for some may suggest that they should be helped to die. How should such a decision be made and how should it be carried out? The patient, of course, should make such decisions, if such decisions are even allowed. Painful ambiguity still remains for those who cannot make intelligent decisions and for those who have chosen to die but may not be competent to make that decision. Furthermore, what are loved ones to do when consulted by the patient or when the patient is no longer capable of making these decisions? The high medical costs for prolonging the lives of some of these very ill people may affect loved ones' decisions regarding the care or life extension of the patient and make the purity of their motives questionable. But costs cannot be totally ignored either.

Third, doctor-assisted suicide is a divisive moral issue. There is no consensus on the norms that should apply to these situations. A strong norm against euthanasia is the belief that stopping someone's life is murder even if that person wants to die. Some people apply the same norm to assisted suicide because they see little difference between injecting a patient with a lethal drug and supplying the patient with the drug to ingest. On the other side, many believe that love and mercy demand assisted suicide or even euthanasia for the terminally ill when great suffering accompanies all other options.

The following selections provide strong arguments for and against doctor-assisted suicide. Marcia Angell contends that the relieving of suffering and honoring the patient's wishes are the overriding concerns, which fully justify the practice in light of the absence of compelling arguments to the contrary. Paul R. McHugh, citing the case of Dr. Jack Kevorkian, maintains that the patients that Kevorkian helped to die were all suffering from depression and that Kevorkian should have advised them to get competent psychological help, which would have restored their desire to live.

YES

Marcia Angell

THE SUPREME COURT AND PHYSICIAN-ASSISTED SUICIDE— THE ULTIMATE RIGHT

The U.S. Supreme Court will decide later this year whether to let stand decisions by two appeals courts permitting doctors to help terminally ill patients commit suicide. The Ninth and Second Circuit Courts of Appeals last spring held that state laws in Washington and New York that ban assistance in suicide were unconstitutional as applied to doctors and their dying patients. If the Supreme Court lets the decisions stand, physicians in 12 states, which include about half the population of the United States, would be allowed to provide the means for terminally ill patients to take their own lives, and the remaining states would rapidly follow suit. Not since *Roe* v. *Wade* has a Supreme Court decision been so fateful.

The decision will culminate several years of intense national debate, fueled by a number of highly publicized events. Perhaps most important among them is Dr. Jack Kevorkian's defiant assistance in some 44 suicides since 1990, to the dismay of many in the medical and legal establishments, but with substantial public support, as evidenced by the fact that three juries refused to convict him even in the face of a Michigan statute enacted for that purpose. Also since 1990, voters in three states have considered ballot initiatives that would legalize some form of physician-assisted dying, and in 1994 Oregon became the first state to approve such a measure. (The Oregon law was stayed pending a court challenge.) Several surveys indicate that roughly two thirds of the American public now support physician-assisted suicide, as do more than half the doctors in the United States, despite the fact that influential physicians' organizations are opposed. It seems clear that many Americans are now so concerned about the possibility of a lingering, high-technology death that they are receptive to the idea of doctors' being allowed to help them die.

In this editorial I will explain why I believe the appeals courts were right and why I hope the Supreme Court will uphold their decisions. I am aware that this is a highly contentious issue, with good people and strong arguments on both sides. The American Medical Association (AMA) filed an amicus brief opposing the legalization of physician-assisted suicide, and the Massachusetts Medical Society, which owns the *Journal*, was a signatory to it. But here I speak for myself, not the *Journal* or the Massachusetts Medical Society. The legal aspects of the case have been well discussed elsewhere, to me most compellingly in Ronald Dworkin's essay in the *New York Review of Books*. I will focus primarily on the medical and ethical aspects.

I begin with the generally accepted premise that one of the most important ethical principles in medicine is respect for each patient's autonomy, and that when this principle conflicts with others, it should almost always take precedence. This premise is incorporated into our laws governing medical practice and research, including the requirement of informed consent to any treatment. In medicine, patients exercise their self-determination most dramatically when they ask that life-sustaining treatment be withdrawn. Although others may sometimes consider the request ill-founded, we are bound to honor it if the patient is mentally competent—that is, if the patient can understand the nature of the decision and its consequences.

A second starting point is the recognition that death is not fair and is often cruel. Some people die quickly, and others die slowly but peacefully. Some find personal or religious meaning in the process, as well as an opportunity for a final reconciliation with loved ones. But others, especially those with cancer, AIDS, or progressive neurologic disorders, may die by inches and in great anguish, despite every effort of their doctors and nurses. Although nearly all pain can be relieved, some cannot, and other

symptoms, such as dyspnea, nausea, and weakness, are even more difficult to control. In addition, dying sometimes holds great indignities and existential suffering. Patients who happen to require some treatment to sustain their lives, such as assisted ventilation or dialysis, can hasten death by having the life-sustaining treatment withdrawn, but those who are not receiving life-sustaining treatment may desperately need help they cannot now get.

If the decisions of the appeals courts are upheld, states will not be able to prohibit doctors from helping such patients to die by prescribing a lethal dose of a drug and advising them on its use for suicide. State laws barring euthanasia (the administration of a lethal drug by a doctor) and assisted suicide for patients who are not terminally ill would not be affected. Furthermore, doctors would not be *required* to assist in suicide; they would simply have that option. Both appeals courts based their decisions on constitutional questions. This is important, because it shifted the focus of the debate from what the majority would approve through the political process, as exemplified by the Oregon initiative, to a matter of fundamental rights, which are largely immune from the political process. Indeed, the Ninth Circuit Court drew an explicit analogy between suicide and abortion, saying that both were personal choices protected by the Constitution and that forbidding doctors to assist would in effect nullify these rights. Although states could regulate assisted suicide, as they do abortion, they would not be permitted to regulate it out of existence.

It is hard to quarrel with the desire of a greatly suffering, dying patient for a quicker, more humane death or to disagree that it may be merciful to help bring that about. In those circumstances, loved ones are often relieved when death finally comes, as are the attending doctors and nurses. As the Second Circuit Court said, the state has no interest in prolonging such a life. Why, then, do so many people oppose legalizing physician-assisted suicide in these cases? There are a number of arguments against it, some stronger than others, but I believe none of them can offset the overriding duties of doctors to relieve suffering and to respect their patients' autonomy. Below I list several of the more important arguments against physician-assisted suicide and discuss why I believe they are in the last analysis unpersuasive.

Assisted suicide is a form of killing, which is always wrong. In contrast, withdrawing life-sustaining treatment simply allows the disease to take its course. There are three methods of hastening the death of a dying patient: withdrawing life-sustaining treatment, assisting suicide, and euthanasia. The right to stop treatment has been recognized repeatedly since the 1976 case of Karen Ann Quinlan and was affirmed by the U.S. Supreme Court in the 1990 *Cruzan* decision and the U.S. Congress in its 1990 Patient Self-Determination Act. Although the legal underpinning is the right to be free of unwanted bodily invasion, the purpose of hastening death was explicitly acknowledged. In contrast, assisted suicide and euthanasia have not been accepted; euthanasia is illegal in all states, and assisted suicide is illegal in most of them.

Why the distinctions? Most would say they turn on the doctor's role: whether it is passive or active. When life-sustaining treatment is withdrawn, the doctor's role is considered passive and the cause of death is the underlying disease, despite the fact that switching off the ventilator of a patient dependent on it looks anything but passive and would be considered homicide if done without the consent of the patient or a proxy. In contrast, euthanasia by the injection of a lethal drug is active and directly causes the patient's death. Assisting suicide by supplying the necessary drugs is considered somewhere in between, more active than switching off a ventilator but less active than injecting drugs, hence morally and legally more ambiguous.

I believe, however, that these distinctions are too doctor-centered and not sufficiently patient-centered. We should ask ourselves not so much whether the doctor's role is passive or active but whether the *patient's* role is passive or active. From that perspective, the three methods of hastening death line up quite differently. When life-sustaining treatment is withdrawn from an incompetent patient at the request of a proxy or when euthanasia is performed, the patient may be utterly passive. Indeed, either act can be performed even if the patient is unaware of the decision. In sharp contrast, assisted suicide, by definition, cannot occur without the patient's knowledge and participation. Therefore, it must be active—that is to say, voluntary. That is a crucial distinction, because it provides an inherent safeguard against abuse that is not present with the other two methods of hastening death. If the loaded term "kill" is to be used, it is not the doctor who kills, but the patient. Primarily because euthanasia can be performed without the patient's participation, I oppose its legalization in this country.

Assisted suicide is not necessary. All suffering can be relieved if care givers are sufficiently skillful and compassionate, as illustrated by the hospice movement. I have no doubt that if expert palliative care were available to everyone who needed it, there would be few requests for assisted suicide. Even under the best of circumstances, however, there will always be a few patients whose suffering simply cannot be adequately alleviated. And there will be some who would prefer suicide to any other measures available, including the withdrawal of life-sustaining treatment or the use of heavy sedation. Surely, every effort should be made to improve palliative care, as I argued 15 years ago, but when those efforts are unavailing and suffering patients desperately long to end their lives, physician-assisted suicide should be allowed. The argument that permitting it would divert us from redoubling our commitment to comfort care asks these patients to pay the penalty for our failings. It is also illogical. Good comfort care and the availability of physician-assisted suicide are no more mutually exclusive than good cardiologic care and the availability of heart transplantation.

Permitting assisted suicide would put us on a moral "slippery slope." Although in itself assisted suicide might be acceptable, it would lead inexorably to involuntary euthanasia. It is impossible to avoid slippery slopes in medicine (or in any aspect of life). The issue is how and where to find a purchase. For example, we accept the right of proxies to terminate life-sustaining treatment, despite the obvious potential for abuse, because the reasons for doing so outweigh the risks. We hope our procedures will safeguard patients. In the case of assisted suicide, its voluntary nature is the best protection against sliding down a slippery slope, but we also need to ensure that the request is thoughtful and freely made. Although it is possible that we may someday decide to legalize voluntary eu-

thanasia under certain circumstances or assisted suicide for patients who are not terminally ill, legalizing assisted suicide for the dying does not in itself make these other decisions inevitable. Interestingly, recent reports from the Netherlands, where both euthanasia and physician-assisted suicide are permitted, indicate that fears about a slippery slope there have not been borne out.

Assisted suicide would be a threat to the economically and socially vulnerable. The poor disabled, and elderly might be coerced to request it. Admittedly, overburdened families or cost-conscious doctors might pressure vulnerable patients to request suicide, but similar wrongdoing is at least as likely in the case of withdrawing life-sustaining treatment, since that decision can be made by proxy. Yet, there is no evidence of widespread abuse. The Ninth Circuit Court recalled that it was feared *Roe* v. *Wade* would lead to coercion of poor and uneducated women to request abortions, but that did not happen. The concern that coercion is more likely in this era of managed care, although understandable, would hold suffering patients hostage to the deficiencies of our health care system. Unfortunately, no human endeavor is immune to abuses. The question is not whether a perfect system can be devised, but whether abuses are likely to be sufficiently rare to be offset by the benefits to patients who otherwise would be condemned to face the end of their lives in protracted agony.

Depressed patients would seek physician-assisted suicide rather than help for their depression. Even in the terminally ill, a request for assisted suicide might signify treatable depression, not irreversible suffering. Patients suffering greatly at the end of life may also be depressed, but the depression does not necessarily explain their decision to commit suicide or make it irrational. Nor is it simple to diagnose depression in terminally ill patients. Sadness is to be expected, and some of the vegetative symptoms of depression are similar to the symptoms of terminal illness. The success of antidepressant treatment in these circumstances is also not ensured. Although there are anecdotes about patients who changed their minds about suicide after treatment, we do not have good studies of how often that happens or the relation to antidepressant treatment. Dying patients who request assisted suicide and seem depressed should certainly be strongly encouraged to accept psychiatric treatment, but I do not believe that competent patients should be *required* to accept it as a condition of receiving assistance with suicide. On the other hand, doctors would not be required to comply with all requests; they would be expected to use their judgment, just as they do in so many other types of life-and-death decisions in medical practice.

Doctors should never participate in taking life. If there is to be assisted suicide, doctor must not be involved. Although most doctors favor permitting assisted suicide under certain circumstances, many who favor it believe that doctors should not provide the assistance. To them, doctors should be unambiguously committed to life (although most doctors who hold this view would readily honor a patient's decision to have life-sustaining treatment withdrawn). The AMA, too, seems to object to physician-assisted suicide primarily because it violates the profession's mission. Like others, I find that position too abstract. The highest ethical imperative of doctors should be to provide care in whatever way best serves patients' interests, in accord with each patient's wishes, not with a theoretical commitment to preserve life no matter what the cost in suffering. If a patient requests help with suicide and the doctor believes the request is appropriate, requiring someone else to provide the assistance would be a form of abandonment. Doctors who are opposed in principle need not assist, but they should make their patients aware of their position early in the relationship so that a patient who chooses to select another doctor can do so. The greatest harm we can do is to consign a desperate patient to unbearable suffering —or force the patient to seek out a stranger like Dr. Kevorkian. Contrary to the frequent assertion that permitting physician-assisted suicide would lead patients to distrust their doctors, I believe distrust is more likely to arise from uncertainty about whether a doctor will honor a patient's wishes.

Physician-assisted suicide may occasionally be warranted, but it should remain illegal. If doctors risk prosecution, they will think twice before assisting with suicide. This argument wrongly shifts the focus from the patient to the doctor. Instead of reflecting the condition and wishes of patients, assisted suicide would reflect the courage and compassion of their doctors. Thus, patients with doctors like Timothy Quill, who described in a 1991 *Journal* article how he helped a patient take her life, would get the help they need and want, but similar patients with less steadfast doctors would not. That makes no sense.

People do not need assistance to commit suicide. With enough determination, they can do it themselves. This is perhaps the cruelest of the arguments against physician-assisted suicide. Many patients at the end of life are, in fact, physically unable to commit suicide on their own. Others lack the resources to do so. It has sometimes been suggested that they can simply stop eating and drinking and kill themselves that way. Although this method has been described as peaceful under certain conditions, no one should count on that. The fact is that this argument leaves most patients to their suffering. Some, usually men, manage to commit suicide using violent methods. Percy Bridgman, a Nobel laureate in physics who in 1961 shot himself rather than die of metastatic cancer, said in his suicide note, "It is not decent for Society to make a man do this to himself."

My father, who knew nothing of Percy Bridgman, committed suicide under similar circumstances. He was 81 and had metastatic prostate cancer. The night before he was scheduled to be admitted to the hospital, he shot himself. Like Bridgman, he thought it might be his last chance. At the time, he was not in extreme pain, nor was he close to death (his life expectancy was probably longer than six months). But he was suffering nonetheless—from nausea and the side effects of antiemetic agents, weakness, incontinence, and hopelessness. Was he depressed? He would probably have freely admitted that he was, but he would have thought it beside the point. In any case, he was an intensely private man who would have refused psychiatric care. Was he overly concerned with maintaining control of the circumstances of his life and death? Many people would say so, but that was the way he was. It is the job of medicine to deal with patients as they are, not as we would like them to be.

I tell my father's story here because it makes an abstract issue very concrete. If physician-assisted suicide had been available, I have no doubt my father would have chosen it. He was protective of his family, and if he had felt he had the choice, he would have spared my mother the shock of finding his body. He did not tell her what he planned to do, because he knew she would stop him. I also believe my father would have waited if physician-assisted suicide had been available. If patients have access to drugs they can take when they choose, they will not feel they must commit suicide early, while they are still able to do it on their own. They would probably live longer and certainly more peacefully, and they might not even use the drugs.

Long before my father's death, I believed that physician-assisted suicide ought to be permissible under some circumstances, but his death strengthened my conviction that it is simply a part of good medical care—something to be done reluctantly and sadly, as a last resort, but done nonetheless. There should be safeguards to ensure that the decision is well considered and consistent, but they should not be so daunting or violative of privacy that they become obstacles instead of protections. In particular, they should be directed not toward reviewing the reasons for an autonomous decision, but only toward ensuring that the decision is indeed autonomous. If the Supreme Court upholds the decisions of the appeals courts, assisted suicide will not be forced on either patients or doctors, but it will be a choice for those patients who need it and those doctors willing to help. If, on the other hand, the Supreme Court overturns the lower courts' decisions, the issue will continue to be grappled with state by state, through the political process. But sooner or later, given the need and the widespread public support, physician-assisted suicide will be demanded of a compassionate profession.

NO
Paul R. McHugh

THE KEVORKIAN EPIDEMIC

Dr. Jack Kevorkian of Detroit has been in the papers most days this past summer and autumn [1997] helping sick people kill themselves. He is said to receive hundreds of calls a week. Although his acts are illegal by statute and common law in Michigan, no one stops him. Many citizens, including members of three juries, believe he means well, perhaps thinking: Who knows? Just maybe, we ourselves shall need his services some day.

To me it looks like madness from every quarter. The patients are mad by definition in that they are suicidally depressed and demoralized; Dr. Kevorkian is "certifiable" in that his passions render him, as the state code specifies, "dangerous to others"; and the usually reliable people of Michigan are confused and anxious to the point of incoherence by terrors of choice that are everyday issues for doctors. These three disordered parties have converged as a triad of host-agent-environment to interact synergistically in provoking a local epidemic of premature death.

Let me begin with the injured hosts of this epidemic, the patients mad by definition. At this writing, more than forty, as best we know, have submitted to Dr. Kevorkian's deadly charms. They came to him with a variety of medical conditions: Alzheimer's disease, multiple sclerosis, chronic pain, amyotrophic lateral sclerosis, cancer, drug addiction, and more. These are certainly disorders from which anyone might seek relief. But what kind of relief do patients with these conditions usually seek when they do not have a Dr. Kevorkian to extinguish their pain?

Both clinical experience and research on this question are extensive—and telling. A search for death does not accompany most terminal or progressive diseases. Pain-ridden patients customarily call doctors for remedies, not for termination of life. Physical incapacity, as with advanced arthritis, does not generate suicide. Even amyotrophic lateral sclerosis, or Lou Gehrig's disease, a harrowing condition I shall describe presently, is not associated with increased suicide amongst its sufferers. Most doctors learn these facts as they help patients and their families burdened by these conditions.

But we don't have to rely solely upon the testimonies of experienced physicians. Recently cancer patients in New England were asked about their attitudes toward death. The investigators—apparently surprised to discover a

From Paul R. McHugh, "The Kevorkian Epidemic," *The American Scholar*, vol. 66, no. 1 (Winter 1997). Copyright © 1996 by Paul R. McHugh. Reprinted by permission of *The American Scholar*.

will to live when they expected to find an urge to die—reported in the *Lancet* (vol. 347, pp. 1805–1810, 1996) two striking findings. First, that cancer patients enduring pain were not inclined to want euthanasia or physician-assisted suicide. In fact, "patients actually experiencing pain were more likely to find euthanasia or physician-assisted suicide unacceptable." Second, those patients inclined toward suicide—whether in pain or not—were suffering from depression. As the investigators noted: "These data indicate a conflict between attitudes and possible practices related to euthanasia and physician-assisted suicide. These *interventions* were approved of for terminally ill patients with unremitting pain, but these are not the patients most likely to request such *interventions*.... There is *some* concern that with legislation of euthanasia or physician-assisted suicide non-psychiatric physicians, who generally have a poor ability to detect and treat depression, may allow life-ending *interventions* when treatment of depression may be more appropriate." (Italics added to identify mealymouthed expressions: *interventions* means homicides, and *some* means that we investigators should stay cool in our concerns—after all, it's not we who are dying.)

None of this is news to psychiatrists who have studied suicides associated with medical illnesses. Depression, the driving force in most cases, comes in two varieties: symptomatic depression found as a feature of particular diseases—that is, as one of the several symptoms of that disease; and demoralization, the common state of mind of people in need of guidance for facing discouraging circumstances alone. Both forms of depression render patients vulnerable to feelings of hopelessness that, if not adequately confronted, may lead to suicide.

Let me first concentrate on the symptomatic depressions because an understanding of them illuminates much of the problem. By the term *symptomatic*, psychiatrists mean that with some physical diseases suicidal depression is one of the condition's characteristic features. Careful students of these diseases come to appreciate that this variety of depression is not to be accepted as a natural feeling of discouragement provoked by bad circumstances—that is, similar to the downhearted state of, say, a bankrupt man or a grief-stricken widow. Instead the depression we are talking about here, with its beclouding of judgment, sense of misery, and suicidal inclinations, is a symptom identical in nature to the fevers, pains, or loss of energy that are signs of the disease itself....

The problematic nature of symptomatic depression goes beyond the painful state of mind of the patient. Other observers—such as family members and physicians—may well take the depressive's disturbed, indeed insane, point of view as a proper assessment of his or her situation. It was this point that Huntington, long before the time of modern anti-depressant treatment, wished to emphasize by identifying it as an insanity. He knew that failure to diagnose this feature will lead to the neglect of efforts to treat the patient properly and to protect him or her from suicide until the symptom remits.

Such neglect is a crucial blunder, because, whether the underlying condition is Huntington's disease, Alzheimer's disease, MS, or something else, modern anti-depressant treatment is usually effective at relieving the mood disorder and restoring the patient's emotional equilibrium. In Michigan and in Holland, where physician-assisted suicide also takes place, these actions to hasten death are the ultimate neglect of patients with symptomatic depression; they are, really, a form of collusion with insanity.

The diagnosis of symptomatic depression is not overly difficult if its existence is remembered and its features systematically sought. But many of its characteristics—such as its capacity to provoke bodily pains—are not known to all physicians. The fact that such depression occurs in dire conditions, such as Huntington's disease, may weigh against its prompt diagnosis and treatment. Again and again, kindly intended physicians presume that a depression "makes sense"—given the patient's situation—and overlook the stereotypic signs of the insanity. They presume justifiable demoralization and forget the pharmacologically treatable depressions.

Over the last decade, at least among psychiatrists, the reality of symptomatic depressions has become familiar and treatment readiness has become the rule. Yet not all sick patients with life-threatening depression have symptomatic depressions. Many physically ill patients are depressed for perfectly understandable reasons, given the grueling circumstances of their progressive and intractable disease. Just as any misfortune can provoke grief and anxiety, so can awareness of loss of health and of a closed future.

Well-titled *demoralization*, this depression, too, has a number of attributes. It waxes and wanes with experiences and events, comes in waves, and is worse at certain times—such as during the night, when contemplating future discomforts and burdens, and when the patient is alone or uninstructed about the benefits that modern treatments can bring him.

In contrast to the symptomatic depressions that run their own course almost independent of events, demoralization is sensitive to circumstances and especially to the conduct of doctors toward the patient. Companionship, especially that which provides understanding and clear explanations of the actions to be taken in opposing disease and disability, can be immensely helpful in overcoming this state and sustaining the patient in a hopeful frame of mind....

This is the point: Depression, both in the form of a symptomatic mental state and in the form of demoralization, is the result of illness and circumstances combined and is treatable just as are other effects of illness. These treatments are the everyday skills of many physicians, but particularly of those physicians who are specialists in these disorders and can advance the treatments most confidently.

Most suicidally depressed patients are not rational individuals who have weighed the balance sheet of their lives and discovered more red than black ink. They are victims of altered attitudes about themselves and their situation, which cause powerful feelings of hopelessness to abound. Doctors can protect them from these attitudes by providing information, guidance, and support all along the way. Dr. Kevorkian, however, trades upon the vulnerabilities and mental disorders of these patients and in so doing makes a mockery of medicine as a discipline of informed concern for patients.

Let us turn to Dr. Kevorkian, the agent of this epidemic in Michigan, and consider why I think that he is "certifiably" insane, by which I mean that he suffers from a mental condition rendering him dangerous to others.

Without question, Dr. Kevorkian has proven himself dangerous, having participated in killing more than forty people already, with no end in sight. . . .

The question is whether his behavior is a product of a mental disorder. Not everyone agrees on an answer. Indeed the *British Medical Journal (BMJ)* described Dr. Kevorkian as a "hero."

His champions see no discernible motive for Dr. Kevorkian other than that he believes his work is fitting. The *BMJ* notes that greed for money or fame or some sadistic urge does not motivate Dr. Kevorkian. They make much of the fact that he does not charge a fee for killing.

Because of the absence of such motives, the editors presume that he is a hero among doctors since it is only a "personal code of honor that admits of no qualification" that leads him into action.

But let us look rather more closely at "personal codes that admit no qualification." We have seen a few of them before and not all were admirable. As Dr. Kevorkian motors around Michigan carrying cylinders of carbon monoxide or bottles of potassium chloride to dispatch the sick, his is the motivation of a person with an "overvalued idea," a diagnostic formulation first spelled out by the psychiatrist Carl Wernicke in 1906. Wernicke differentiated overvalued ideas from obsessions and delusions. Overvalued ideas are often at the motivational heart of "personal codes that admit no qualification" and certainly provide a drive as powerful as that of hunger for money, fame, or sexual gratification.

An individual with an overvalued idea is someone who has taken up an idea shared by others in his milieu or culture and transformed it into a ruling passion or "monomania" for himself. It becomes the goal of all his efforts and he is prepared to sacrifice everything—family, reputation, health, even life itself—for it. He presumes that what he does in its service is right regardless of any losses that he or others suffer for it. He sees all opposition as at best misguided and at worst malevolent.

For Dr. Kevorkian, people may die before their time and the fabric of their families may be torn apart, but it's all for the good if he can presume they were "suffering pain unnecessarily" and he has eliminated it. He scorns all opposition —in particular constitutional democratic opposition—as resting on bad faith or ignorance. Empowered by his idea, he feels free to disregard the law and any of its officers.

An overvalued idea has three characteristics: (1) it is a self-dominating but not idiosyncratic opinion, given great importance by (2) intense emotional feelings over its significance, and evoking (3) persistent behavior in its service. For Dr. Kevorkian, thinking about how to terminate the sick has become his exclusive concern. His belief in the justice of his ideas is intense enough for him to starve himself if thwarted by law.

Dr. Kevorkian thinks that all opposition to him is "bad faith" and thus worthy of contempt—a contempt he expresses with no reservation. He is fond of saying that the judicial system of our country is "corrupt," the religious members of our society are "irrational," the medical profession is "insane," the press is "meretricious."

He considers his own behavior "humanitarian." Dr. Kevorkian holds himself beyond reproach, even after killing one patient he believed had multiple sclerosis but whose autopsy revealed no evidence of that disease and another patient with the vague condition of "chronic fatigue syndrome" in whom no pathological process could be found at autopsy—only Kevorkian's poison. He acts without taking a careful medical history, trying alternative treatments, or reflecting on how his actions affect such people as surviving family members.

Dr. Kevorkian's is a confident business. As the news reports flow out of Michigan, it appears that his threshold for medicide is getting lower. Physician-assisted suicide that had previously demanded an incurable disease such as Alzheimer's is now practiced upon patients with such chronic complaints as pelvic pain and emphysema, whose life expectancy cannot be specified. He can justify the active termination of anyone with an ailment—which is just what might be expected once the boundary against active killing by doctors has been breached. What's to stop him now that juries have found his actions to be de facto legal in Michigan?

A crucial aspect of overvalued ideas is that, in contrast to delusions, they are not idiosyncratic. They are ideas that can be found in a proportion of the public —often an influential proportion. It is from such reservoirs of opinion that the particular individual harnesses and amplifies an idea with the disproportionate zeal characteristic of a ruling passion. That Dr. Kevorkian can find people in the highest places—even within the medical profession—to support his ideas and say that they see heroism in his actions is not surprising, given the passion of the contemporary debate over euthanasia. In this way the person with the overvalued idea may be seen, by those who share his opinion but not his self-sacrificing zeal, as giving expression to their hopes —disregarding the slower processes of democracy, filled with prejudice against all who resist, and pumped up with a sense of a higher purpose and justice.

People such as Dr. Kevorkian have found a place in history. With some, with the passage of time, we come to agree with the idea if not the method by which the idea was first expressed. Such was John Brown, the abolitionist, ready to hack five anonymous farmers to death in the Pottowatomi massacre to advance his cause. With others we may come to tolerate some aspect of the idea but see its expression in actual behavior as ludicrous. Such was Carry Nation, the scourge of Kansas barkeeps and boozers, who went to jail hundreds of times for chopping up saloons with a small hatchet in the cause of temperance. Finally, for some, we come to recognize the potential for horror in an overvalued idea held by a person in high authority. Such was Adolf Hitler.

But how is it that anxieties and confusions about medical practice and death can so afflict the judicious people of Michigan as to paralyze them before the outrageous behavior of Dr. Kevorkian and thus generate an environment for this epidemic? In Michigan these states of mind derive from conflicting concerns over medical decisions. The citizens—like any inexpert group—are relatively uninformed about what doctors can do for patients, even in extreme situations. Conflicting goals and unfamiliar practices—common enough around medical decisions—produce anxiety and confusion every time.

No one thinks happily about dying, especially dying in pain. Death is bad; dying can be worse. Anyone who says he does not fear dying—and all the pain and suffering tied to it—has probably not experienced much in life.

This concern, though, certainly has been exaggerated in our times, even though now much can be done to relieve the heaviest burdens of terminally ill patients. Yet through a variety of sources —such as movies, newspapers, and essays—all the negative aspects of dying have been emphasized, the agonies embellished, and the loss of control represented by disease accentuated. Horror stories feed upon one another, and rumors of medical lack of interest grow into opinions that doctors both neglect the dying and hold back relief. Doctors are regularly accused of surrendering to professional taboos or to legal advice to avoid risk of malpractice or prosecution—and in this way are presumed ready to sacrifice their patients out of selfish fear for themselves.

On the contrary, most doctors try to collaborate with patients and do listen to their wishes, especially when treatments that carry painful burdens are contemplated. As Dr. Kevorkian can demonstrate—with videotapes, no less—the patients he killed asked him repeatedly for help in dying rather than for help in living. Do not they have some right to die at their own hands steadied by Dr. Kevorkian? Is not the matter of assisted suicide simply a matter of rights and wants to which any citizen of Michigan is entitled?

The idea of a right to suicide provokes most psychiatrists. Psychiatry has worked to teach everyone that suicide is not an uncomplicated, voluntary act to which rights attach. It has shown that suicide is an act provoked, indeed compelled, by mental disorder—such as a disorienting depression or a set of misdirected, even delusionary, ideas. In that sense psychiatry taught that suicidal people were not "responsible" for this behavior—no matter what they said or wrote in final letters or testaments—any more than they would be for epileptic seizures.

This idea—generated from the careful study of the clinical circumstances and past histories of suicidal patients— gradually prevailed in civil law and even in the canon law of churches. As a result, laws against suicide were repealed—not to make suicide a "right" but to remove it from the status of a crime.

We psychiatrists thought we had done a worthy thing for our society, for families of patients, and even for patients themselves. We were not saying, not for a moment, that we approved of suicide. Far from it. We knew such deaths to be ugly and misguided—misguided in particular because the disposition to die, the wish for suicide, was, on inspection, often a symptom of the very mental disorders that psychiatry treats. Suicide in almost all cases is as far from a rational choice based on a weighing of the balance books of life as is responding to hallucinated voices or succumbing to the paranoid ideas of a charismatic madman such as Jim Jones, who at Jonestown directed a gruesome exhibition of mass assisted suicide.

Psychiatrists were united in their views about suicide and shook their heads when contemplating past traditions when suicides were considered scandalous. We did not think too deeply into the consequences of our actions. For, after suicide ceased to be a crime, it soon became a right and, conceivably under some circumstances, such as when costs of care grow onerous, an obligation. Psychiatrists, who had worked for decades demonstrating that suicides were insane acts, are now recruited in Holland to assure that requests for suicide made by patients offered "no hope of cure" by their doctors are "rational."

What had begun as an effort at explanation and understanding of the tragic act of suicide has developed into complicity in the seduction of vulnerable people into that very behavior. The patients are seduced just as the victims in Jonestown were—by isolating them, sustaining their despair, revoking alternatives, stressing examples of others choosing to die, and sweetening the deadly poison by speaking of death with dignity. If even psychiatrists succumb to this complicity with death, what can be expected of the lay public in Michigan? . . .

One can think of ways to combat the deadly convergence of madnesses in Michigan and to deter the spread of this local epidemic to other regions of our country. The suicidal patients certainly should be treated for their depressive vulnerabilities by doctors able to assist them with their underlying illnesses. Dr. Kevorkian, the agent of their extinction, should be stopped by whatever means the state has at its disposal to stay dangerous men. And the people of Michigan should be taught about the capacities of modern medicine. With this information, the hope is, they will emerge from their anxious confusions, accept mortality for what it is rather than for what they imagine, and, at last, end their support for this insanity.

POSTSCRIPT

Should Doctor-Assisted Suicide Be Legalized for the Terminally Ill?

Angell tells the story of her father's suicide because he seemed to be a perfect candidate for doctor-assisted suicide. Since it was not available to him, he shot himself before being hospitalized for his cancer. Like any case this one allows for various interpretations, but it points up the problem of a blanket rule for all cases. What if we were to come to the conclusion that doctor-assisted suicide is wrong in most cases when patients request it but right in a minority of cases? Maybe both sides are right at times and wrong at other times. The problem is that it is difficult to make laws that apply only sometimes. Most laws provide too little leeway to be adjusted to the peculiarities of individual cases. For example, if a man goes over the speed limit, he breaks the law, even if he is driving his wife to the hospital to deliver a baby. Fortunately, most policemen would not write this man a ticket but rather turn on their siren and escort him to the hospital. For many laws the discretion of judges and juries, like that of the policeman, provides some badly needed flexibility, but problems will always remain.

The literature on doctor-assisted suicide and the larger issue of euthanasia has mushroomed in the last decade. For arguments against these practices, see Robert Laurence Barry, *Breaking the Thread of Life: On Rational Suicide* (Transaction Publishers, 1994); Tom Beauchamp, *Ethical Issues in Death and Dying* (Prentice Hall, 1996); Herbert Hendin, *Seduced by Death: Doctors, Patients and the Dutch Cure* (W. W. Norton, 1996); and Wesley J. Smith, *Forced Exit: The Slippery Slope from Assisted Suicide to Legalized Murder* (Times Books, 1997).

For works that favor doctor-assisted suicide or euthanasia or that contain various viewpoints, see Ira Byock, *Dying Well: The Prospect for Growth at the End of Life* (Thorndike Press, 1997); Timothy E. Quill, *A Midwife Through the Dying Process* (Johns Hopkins University Press, 1996); and Marylin Webb, *The Good Death: The New American Search to Reshape the End of Life* (Bantam Books, 1997). For works that present or analyze the issues as debates, see Michael M. Uhlman, ed., *Last Rights? Assisted Suicide and Euthanasia Debated* (William B. Eerdmans, 1998); Tamara Roleff, ed., *Suicide: Opposing Viewpoints* (Greenhaven Press, 1998); and Carol Wedesser, ed., *Euthanasia: Opposing Viewpoints* (Greenhaven Press, 1995). For multiple views on doctor-assisted suicide and euthanasia, see Melvin I. Urafsky and Philip E. Urofsky, eds., *The Right to Die: A Two-Volume Anthology of Scholarly Articles* (Garland, 1996) and Robert F. Weir et al., *Physician-Assisted Suicide* (Indiana University Press, 1997).

On the Internet . . .

http://www.dushkin.com

American Society of Criminology

An excellent starting point for studying all aspects of criminology and criminal justice, this page provides links to sites on criminal justice in general, international criminal justice, juvenile justice, courts, the police, and the government. *http://www.bsos.umd.edu/asc/four.html*

Crime-Free America

Crime-Free America is a grassroots, nonprofit group dedicated to ending the crime epidemic that it feels has gripped the United States over the last four decades. This site has links to the Bureau of Justice Statistics, forums, and crime watch profiles. *http://www.announce.com/cfa/*

Crime Times

This site lists research reviews and other information regarding the causes of criminal and violent behavior. It is provided by the nonprofit Wacker Foundation, publishers of *Crime Times*. *http://www.crime-times.org/titles.htm*

Justice Information Center (JIC)

Provided by the National Criminal Justice Reference Service, the JIC site connects to information about corrections, courts, crime prevention, criminal justice, statistics, drugs and crime, law enforcement, and victims, among other topics. *http://www.ncjrs.org/*

Sociology Library

This site provides a number of indexes of culture and ethnic studies, criminology, population and demographics, and statistical sources. *http://www.library.upenn.edu/resources/social/sociology/sociology.html*

PART 5

Crime and Social Control

All societies label certain hurtful actions as crimes and punish those who commit the crimes. Other harmful actions, however, are not defined as crimes, and the perpetrators are not punished. Today the definition of crime and the appropriate treatment of criminals is widely debated. Some of the major questions are: Does street crime pose more of a threat to the public's well-being than white-collar crime? Billions of dollars have been spent on the "war on drugs," but who is winning? Would decriminalizing some drugs free up money that could be directed to other types of social welfare programs, such as the rehabilitation of addicts? And is imprisonment an effective means of reducing crime by removing criminals from the streets, or is it, in the long run, costly and inhumane?

■ Is Street Crime More Harmful Than White-Collar Crime?

■ Should Drug Use Be Decriminalized?

■ Is Incapacitation the Answer to the Crime Problem?

ISSUE 16

Is Street Crime More Harmful Than White-Collar Crime?

YES: John J. DiIulio, Jr., from "The Impact of Inner-City Crime," *The Public Interest* (Summer 1989)

NO: Jeffrey Reiman, from *The Rich Get Richer and the Poor Get Prison: Ideology, Class, and Criminal Justice,* 5th ed. (Allyn & Bacon, 1998)

ISSUE SUMMARY

YES: John J. DiIulio, Jr., a professor of politics and public affairs, analyzes the enormous harm done—especially to the urban poor and, by extension, to all of society—by street criminals and their activities.

NO: Professor of philosophy Jeffrey Reiman argues that the dangers posed by negligent corporations and white-collar criminals are a greater menace to society than are the activities of typical street criminals.

The word *crime* entered the English language (from the Old French) around A.D. 1250, when it was identified with "sinfulness." Later, the meaning of the word was modified: crime became the kind of sinfulness that was rightly punishable by law. Even medieval writers, who did not distinguish very sharply between church and state, recognized that there were some sins for which punishment was best left to God; the laws should punish only those that cause harm to the community. Of course, their concept of harm was a very broad one, embracing such offenses as witchcraft and blasphemy. Modern jurists, even those who deplore such practices, would say that the state has no business punishing the perpetrators of these types of offenses.

What, then, should the laws punish? The answer depends in part on our notion of harm. We usually limit the term to the kind of harm that is tangible and obvious: taking a life, causing bodily injury or psychological trauma, and destroying property. For most Americans today, particularly those who live in cities, the word *crime* is practically synonymous with street crime. Anyone who has ever been robbed or beaten by street criminals will never forget the experience. The harm that these criminals cause is tangible, and the connection between the harm and the perpetrator is very direct.

But suppose the connection is not so direct. Suppose, for example, that A hires B to shoot C. Is that any less a crime? B is the actual shooter, but is A any less guilty? Of course not, we say; he may even be more guilty, since he is the ultimate mover behind the crime. A would be guilty even if the chain of command were much longer, involving A's orders to B, and B's to C, then on to D, E, and F to kill G. Organized crime kingpins go to jail even when they are far removed from the people who carry out their orders. High officials of the Nixon administration, even though they were not directly involved in the burglary attempt at the Democratic National Committee headquarters at the Watergate Hotel complex in 1972, were imprisoned.

This brings us to the topic of white-collar crime. The burglars at the Watergate Hotel were acting on orders that trickled down from the highest reaches of political power in the United States. Other white-collar criminals are as varied as the occupations from which they come. They include stockbrokers who make millions through insider trading, as Ivan Boesky did; members of Congress who take payoffs; and people who cheat on their income taxes, like hotel owner and billionaire Leona Helmsley. Some, like Helmsley, get stiff prison sentences when convicted, though many others (like most of the officials in the Watergate scandal) do little or no time in prison. Do they deserve stiffer punishment, or are their crimes less harmful than the crimes of street criminals?

Although white-collar criminals do not directly cause physical harm or relieve people of their wallets, they can still end up doing considerable harm. The harm done by Nixon's aides threatened the integrity of the U.S. electoral system. Every embezzler, corrupt politician, and tax cheat exacts a toll on our society. Individuals can be hurt in more tangible ways by decisions made in corporate boardrooms: Auto executives, for example, have approved design features that have caused fatalities. Managers of chemical companies have allowed practices that have polluted the environment with cancer-causing agents. And heads of corporations have presided over industries wherein workers have been needlessly killed or maimed.

Whether or not these decisions should be considered crimes is debatable. A crime must always involve "malicious intent," or what the legal system calls *mens rea*. This certainly applies to street crime—the mugger obviously has sinister designs—but does it apply to every decision made in a boardroom that ends up causing harm? And does that harm match or exceed the harm caused by street criminals? In the following selections, John J. DiIulio, Jr., focuses on the enormous harm done—especially to the poor—by street criminals. Not only does street crime cause loss, injury, terror, and death for individuals, he argues, but it also causes neighborhood decline, community disintegration, loss of pride, business decline and failure, hampered schools, and middle-class flight to the suburbs. According to Jeffrey Reiman, white-collar crime also does more harm than is commonly recognized. By his count, white-collar crime causes far more deaths, injuries, illnesses, and financial loss than street crime. In light of this, he argues, we must redefine our ideas about what crime is and who the criminals are.

YES

John J. DiIulio, Jr.

THE IMPACT OF INNER-CITY CRIME

My grandmother, an Italian immigrant, lived in the same Philadelphia row house from 1921 till her death in 1986. When she moved there, and for the four decades thereafter, most of her neighbors were Irish and Italian. When she died, virtually all of her neighbors were black. Like the whites who fled, the first blacks who moved in were mostly working-class people living just above the poverty level.

Until around 1970, the neighborhood changed little. The houses were well-maintained. The children played in the streets and were polite. The teenagers hung out on the street corners in the evenings, sometimes doing mischief, but rarely—if ever—doing anything worse. The local grocers and other small businesspeople (both blacks and the few remaining whites) stayed open well past dark. Day or night, my grandmother journeyed the streets just as she had during the days of the Great Depression, taking the bus to visit her friends and relatives, going shopping, attending church, and so on.

She was a conspicuous and popular figure in this black community. She was conspicuous for her race, accent, and advanced age; she was popular for the homespun advice (and home-baked goods) she dispensed freely to the teenagers hanging out on the corners, to the youngsters playing ball in the street in front of her house, and to their parents (many of them mothers living without a husband).

Like the generations of ethnics who had lived there before them, these people were near the bottom of the socioeconomic ladder. I often heard my grandmother say that her new neighbors were "just like us," by which she meant that they were honest, decent, law-abiding people working hard to advance themselves and to make a better life for their children.

But in the early 1970s, the neighborhood began to change. Some, though by no means all, of the black families my grandmother had come to know moved out of the neighborhood. The new neighbors kept to themselves. The exteriors of the houses started to look ratty. The streets grew dirty. The grocery and variety stores closed or did business only during daylight hours. The children played in the schoolyard but not in front of their homes. The teenagers on the corners were replaced by adult drug dealers and their "runners." Vandalism

Excerpted from John J. DiIulio, Jr., "The Impact of Inner-City Crime," *The Public Interest*, no. 96 (Summer 1989), pp. 28–46. Copyright © 1989 by National Affairs, Inc. Reprinted by permission of *The Public Interest* and the author.

and graffiti became commonplace. My grandmother was mugged twice, both times by black teenagers; once she was severely beaten in broad daylight.

In the few years before she died at age eighty-four, and after years of pleading by her children and dozens of grandchildren, she stopped going out and kept her doors and windows locked at all times. On drives to visit her, when I got within four blocks of her home, I instinctively checked to make sure that my car doors were locked. Her house, where I myself had been raised, was in a "bad neighborhood," and it did not make sense to take any chances. I have not returned to the area since the day of her funeral.

My old ethnic and ghetto neighborhood had become an underclass neighborhood. Why is it that most readers of this article avoid, and advise their friends and relatives to avoid, walking or driving through such neighborhoods? Obviously we are not worried about being infected somehow by the extremely high levels of poverty, joblessness, illiteracy, welfare dependency, or drug abuse that characterize these places. Instead we shun these places because we suppose them to contain exceedingly high numbers of predatory street criminals, who hit, rape, rob, deal drugs, burglarize, and murder.

This supposition is absolutely correct. The underclass problem, contrary to the leading academic and journalistic understandings, is mainly a crime problem. It is a crime problem, moreover, that can be reduced dramatically (although not eliminated) with the human and financial resources already at hand.

Only two things are required: common sense and compassion. Once we understand the underclass problem as a crime problem, neither of those two qualities should be scarce. Until we understand the underclass problem as a crime problem, policymakers and others will continue to fiddle while the underclass ghettos of Philadelphia, Newark, Chicago, Los Angeles, Miami, Washington, D.C., and other cities burn....

THE TRULY DEVIANT

Liberals... have understood the worsening of ghetto conditions mainly as the by-product of a complex process of economic and social change. One of the latest and most influential statements of this view is William Julius Wilson's *The Truly Disadvantaged: The Inner City, the Underclass, and Public Policy* (1987).

Wilson argues that over the last two decades a new and socially destructive class structure has emerged in the ghetto. As he sees it, the main culprit is deindustrialization. As plants have closed, urban areas, especially black urban areas, have lost entry-level jobs. To survive economically, or to enjoy their material success, ghetto residents in a position to do so have moved out, leaving behind them an immobilized "underclass."...

Wilson has focused our attention on the socioeconomic straits of the truly disadvantaged with an elegance and rhetorical force that is truly admirable.[1] But despite its many strengths, his often subtle analysis of the underclass problem wrongly deemphasizes one obvious possibility: "The truly disadvantaged" exist mainly because of the activities of "the truly deviant"—the large numbers of chronic and predatory street criminals—in their midst. One in every nine adult black males in this country is under some form of correctional supervision (prison, jail, probation, or parole).[2] Criminals come disproportionately from underclass neighborhoods. They victimize their neighbors directly through crime, and indirectly by creating or worsening the multiple social and economic ills that define the sad lot of today's ghetto dwellers.

PREDATORY GHETTO CRIMINALS

I propose [another] way of thinking about the underclass problem. The members of the underclass are, overwhelmingly, decent and law-abiding residents of America's most distressed inner cities. Fundamentally, what makes them different from the rest of us is not only their higher than normal levels of welfare dependency and the like, but their far higher than normal levels of victimization by predatory criminals.

This victimization by criminals takes several forms. There is *direct victimization* —being mugged, raped, or murdered; being threatened and extorted; living in fear about whether you can send your children to school or let them go out and play without their being bothered by dope dealers, pressured by gang members, or even struck by a stray bullet. And there is *indirect victimization*—dampened neighborhood economic development, loss of a sizable fraction of the neighborhood's male population to prison or jail, the undue influence on young people exercised by criminal "role models" like the cash-rich drug lords who rule the streets, and so on.

Baldly stated, my hypothesis is that this victimization causes and perpetuates the other ills of our underclass neighborhoods. Schools in these neighborhoods are unable to function effectively because of their disorderly atmosphere and because of the violent behavior of the criminals (especially gang members) who hang around their classrooms. The truly deviant are responsible for a high percentage of teen pregnancies, rapes, and sexual assaults. Similarly, many of the chronically welfare-dependent, female-headed households in these neighborhoods owe their plights to the fact that the men involved are either unable (because they are under some form of correctional supervision) or unwilling (because it does not jibe well with their criminal lifestyles) to seek and secure gainful employment and live with their families. And much of the poverty and joblessness in these neighborhoods can be laid at the door of criminals whose presence deters local business activity, including the development of residential real estate.

Blacks are victims of violent crimes at much higher rates than whites. Most lone-offender crime against blacks is committed by blacks, while most such crimes against whites are committed by whites; in 1986, for instance, 83.5 percent of violent crimes against blacks were committed by blacks, while 80.3 percent of violent crimes against whites were committed by whites. This monochrome picture of victim-offender relationships also holds for multiple-offender crimes. In 1986, for example, 79.6 percent of multiple-offender violent crimes against blacks were committed by blacks; the "white-on-white" figure was 59.4 percent.

Criminals are most likely to commit crimes against people of their own race. The main reason is presumably their physical proximity to potential victims. If so, then it is not hard to understand why underclass neighborhoods, which have more than their share of would-be criminals, have more than their share of crime.

Prison is the most costly form of correctional supervision, and it is normally reserved for the most dangerous felons —violent or repeat offenders. Most of my readers do not personally know anyone in prison; most ghetto dwellers of a decade or two ago probably would not have known anyone in prison either. But most of today's underclass citizens do; the convicted felons were their relatives and neighbors—and often their victimizers.

For example, in 1980 Newark was the street-crime capital of New Jersey. In the Newark area, there were more than 920 violent crimes (murders, nonnegligent manslaughters, forcible rapes, robberies, and aggravated assaults) per 100,000 residents; in the rest of the state the figure was under 500, and in affluent towns like Princeton it was virtually nil. In the same year, New Jersey prisons held 5,866 criminals, 2,697 of them from the Newark area.[3] In virtually all of the most distressed parts of this distressed city, at least one of every two hundred residents was an imprisoned felon.[4] The same basic picture holds for other big cities.[5]

Correlation, however, is not causation, and we could extend and refine this sort of crude, exploratory analysis of the relationship between crime rates, concentrations of correctional supervisees, and the underclass neighborhoods from which they disproportionately come. But except to satisfy curiosity, I see no commanding need for such studies. For much the same picture emerges from the anecdotal accounts of people who have actually spent years wrestling with—as opposed to merely researching —the problem.

For example, in 1988 the nation's capital became its murder capital. Washington, D.C., had 372 killings, 82 percent of them committed on the streets by young black males against other young black males. The city vied with Detroit for the highest juvenile homicide rate in America. Here is part of the eloquent testimony on this development given by Isaac Fulwood, a native Washingtonian and the city's police-chief designate:

> The murder statistics don't capture what these people are doing. We've had in excess of 1,260 drug-related shootings.... People are scared of these kids. Someone can get shot in broad daylight, and nobody saw anything.... Nobody talks. And that's so different from the way it was in my childhood.

The same thing can be said about the underclass neighborhoods of other major cities. In Detroit, for instance, most of the hundreds of ghetto residents murdered over the last six years were killed within blocks of their homes by their truly deviant neighbors.

To devise meaningful law-enforcement and correctional responses to the underclass problem, we need to understand why concentrations of crime and criminals are so high in these neighborhoods, and to change our government's criminal-justice policies and practices accordingly.

UNDERSTANDING THE PROBLEM

We begin with a chicken-and-egg question: Does urban decay cause crime, or does crime cause urban decay?

In conventional criminology, which derives mainly from sociology, ghettos are portrayed as "breeding grounds" for predatory street crime. Poverty, joblessness, broken homes, single-parent families, and similar factors are identified as the "underlying causes" of crime.[6] These conditions cause crime, the argument goes; as they worsen—as the ghetto community becomes the underclass neighborhood—crime worsens. This remains the dominant academic perspective on the subject, one that is shared implicitly by most public officials who are close to the problem.

Beginning in the mid-1970s, however, a number of influential studies appeared that challenged this conventional criminological wisdom.[7] Almost without exception, these studies have cast grave doubts on the classic sociological explanation of crime, suggesting that the actual relationships between such variables as poverty, illiteracy, and unemployment, on the one hand, and criminality, on the other, are far more ambiguous than most analysts freely assumed only a decade or so ago....

LOCKS, COPS, AND STUDIES

Camden, New Jersey, is directly across the bridge from Philadelphia. Once-decent areas have become just like my grandmother's old neighborhood: isolated, crime-torn urban war zones. In February 1989 a priest doing social work in Camden was ordered off the streets by drug dealers and threatened with death if he did not obey. The police chief of Camden sent some extra men into the area, but the violent drug dealers remained the real rulers of the city's streets.

The month before the incident in Camden, the Rockefeller Foundation announced that it was going to devote some of its annual budget (which exceeds $100 million) to researching the underclass problem. Other foundations, big and small, have already spent (or misspent) much money on the problem. But Rockefeller's president was quoted as follows: "Nobody knows who they are, what they do.... The underclass is not a topic to pursue from the library. You get out and look for them."

His statement was heartening, but it revealed a deep misunderstanding of the problem. Rather than intimating that the underclass was somehow hard to locate, he would have done better to declare that his charity would purchase deadbolt locks for the homes of ghetto dwellers in New York City who lacked them, and subsidize policing and private-security services in the easily identifiable neighborhoods where these poor people are concentrated.

More street-level research would be nice, especially for the networks of policy intellectuals (liberal and conservative) who benefit directly from such endeavors. But more locks, cops, and corrections officers would make a more positive, tangible, and lasting difference in the lives of today's ghetto dwellers.

NOTES

1. In addition, he has canvassed competing academic perspectives on the underclass; see William Julius Wilson, ed., "The Ghetto Underclass: Social Science Perspectives," *Annals of the American Academy of Political and Social Science* (January 1989). It should also be noted that he is directing a $2.7 million research project on poverty in Chicago that promises to be the most comprehensive study of its kind yet undertaken.

2. According to the Bureau of Justice Statistics, in 1986 there were 234,430 adult black males in prison, 101,000 in jail, an estimated 512,000 on probation, and 133,300 on parole. There were 8,985,000 adult black males in the national residential population. I am grateful to Larry Greenfeld for his assistance in compiling these figures.

3. I am grateful to Hank Pierre, Stan Repko, and Commissioner William H. Fauver of the New Jersey

Department of Corrections for granting me access to these figures and to related data on density of prisoner residence; to Andy Ripps for his heroic efforts in organizing them; and to my Princeton colleague Mark Alan Hughes for his expert help in analyzing the data.

4. Ten of the thirteen most distressed Newark census tracts were places where the density of prisoner residence was that high. In other words, 76.9 percent of the worst underclass areas of Newark had such extremely high concentrations of hardcore offenders. In most of the rest of Newark, and throughout the rest of the state, such concentrations were virtually nonexistent.

5. In 1980 in the Chicago area, for example, in 182 of the 1,521 census tracts at least one of every two hundred residents was an imprisoned felon. Fully twenty of the thirty-five worst underclass tracts had such extraordinary concentrations of serious criminals; in several of them, more than one of every hundred residents was behind prison bars. I am grateful to Wayne Carroll and Commissioner Michael Lane of the Illinois Department of Corrections for helping me with these data.

6. For example, see the classic statement by Edwin H. Sutherland and Donald R. Cressey, *Principles of Criminology*, 7th rev. ed. (Philadelphia: J. P. Lippincott, 1966).

7. See, for example, James Q. Wilson, *Thinking About Crime* (New York: Basic Books, 1975), especially the third chapter.

NO

Jeffrey Reiman

A CRIME BY ANY OTHER NAME...

If one individual inflicts a bodily injury upon another which leads to the death of the person attacked we call it manslaughter; on the other hand, if the attacker knows beforehand that the blow will be fatal we call it murder. Murder has also been committed if society places hundreds of workers in such a position that they inevitably come to premature and unnatural ends. Their death is as violent as if they had been stabbed or shot.... Murder has been committed if society knows perfectly well that thousands of workers cannot avoid being sacrificed so long as these conditions are allowed to continue. Murder of this sort is just as culpable as the murder committed by an individual.

—Frederick Engels
The Condition of the Working Class in England

WHAT'S IN A NAME?

If it takes you an hour to read this chapter, by the time you reach the last page, three of your fellow citizens will have been murdered. *During that same time, at least four Americans will die as a result of unhealthy or unsafe conditions in the workplace!* Although these work-related deaths could have been prevented, they are not called murders. Why not? Doesn't a crime by any other name still cause misery and suffering? What's in a name?

The fact is that the label "crime" is not used in America to name all or the worst of the actions that cause misery and suffering to Americans. It is primarily reserved for the dangerous actions of the poor.

In the February 21, 1993, edition of the *New York Times*, an article appears with the headline: "Company in Mine Deaths Set to Pay Big Fine." It describes an agreement by the owners of a Kentucky mine to pay a fine for safety misconduct that may have led to "the worst American mining accident in nearly a decade." Ten workers died in a methane explosion, and the company pleaded guilty to "a pattern of safety misconduct" that included falsifying reports of methane levels and requiring miners to work under unsupported roofs. The company was fined $3.75 million. The acting foreman at the mine was the only individual charged by the federal government, and for his cooperation with the investigation, prosecutors were recommending that he receive the minimum sentence: probation to six months in prison. The company's president expressed regret for the tragedy that occurred. And the U.S. attorney said he hoped the case "sent a clear message that violations of Federal safety and health regulations that endanger the lives of our citizens will not be tolerated."

Compare this with the story of Colin Ferguson, who prompted an editorial in the *New York Times* of December 10, 1993, with the headline: "Mass Murder on the 5:33." A few days earlier, Colin had boarded a commuter train in Garden City, Long Island, and methodically shot passengers with a 9-millimeter pistol, killing 5 and wounding 18. Colin Ferguson was surely a murderer, maybe a mass murderer. My question is, Why wasn't the death of the miners also murder? Why weren't those responsible for subjecting ten miners to deadly conditions also "mass murderers"?

Why do ten dead miners amount to an "accident," a "tragedy," and five dead commuters a "mass murder"? "Murder" suggests a murderer, whereas "accident" and "tragedy" suggest the work of impersonal forces. But the charge against the company that owned the mine said that they "repeatedly exposed the mine's work crews to danger and that such conditions were frequently concealed from Federal inspectors responsible for enforcing the mine safety act." And the acting foreman admitted to falsifying records of methane levels only two months before the fatal blast. Someone was responsible for the conditions that led to the death of ten miners. Is that person not a murderer, perhaps even a *mass murderer*?

These questions are at this point rhetorical. My aim is not to discuss this case but rather to point to the blinders we wear when we look at such an "accident." There was an investigation. One person, the acting foreman, was held responsible for falsifying records. He is to be sentenced to six months in prison (at most). The company was fined. But no one will be tried for *murder*. No one will be thought of as a murderer. *Why not?* ...

Didn't those miners have a right to protection from the violence that took their lives? *And if not, why not?*

Once we are ready to ask this question seriously, we are in a position to see that the reality of crime—that is, the acts we label crime, the acts we think of as crime, the actors and actions we treat as criminal—is *created:* It is an image shaped by decisions as to *what* will be called crime and *who* will be treated as a criminal.

THE CARNIVAL MIRROR

... The American criminal justice system is a mirror that shows a distorted image of the dangers that threaten us—an image created more by the shape of the mirror than by the reality reflected. What do we see when we look in the criminal justice mirror? ...

He is, first of all, a *he*. Out of 2,012,906 persons arrested for FBI Index crimes [which are criminal homicide, forcible rape, robbery, aggravated assault, burglary, larceny, and motor vehicle theft] in 1991, 1,572,591, or 78 percent, were males. Second, he is a *youth*.... Third, he is predominantly *urban*.... Fourth, he is disproportionately *black*—blacks are arrested for Index crimes at a rate three times that of their percentage in the national population.... Finally, he is *poor:* Among state prisoners in 1991, 33 percent were unemployed prior to being arrested —a rate nearly four times that of males in the general population....

This is the Typical Criminal feared by most law-abiding Americans. Poor, young, urban, (disproportionately) black males make up the core of the enemy forces in the war against crime. They are the heart of a vicious, unorganized guerrilla army, threatening the lives, limbs, and possessions of the law-abiding members of society—necessitating recourse to the ultimate weapons of force and detention in our common defense.

... The acts of the Typical Criminal are not the only acts that endanger us, nor are they the acts that endanger us the most. As I shall show ..., we have as great or sometimes even a greater chance of being killed or disabled by an occupational injury or disease, by unnecessary surgery, or by shoddy emergency medical services than by aggravated assault or even homicide! Yet even though these threats to our well-being are graver than those posed by our poor young criminals, they do not show up in the FBI's Index of serious crimes. The individuals responsible for them do not turn up in arrest records or prison statistics. *They never become part of the reality reflected in the criminal justice mirror, although the danger they pose is at least as great and often greater than the danger posed by those who do!*

Similarly, the general public loses more money *by far* ... from price-fixing and monopolistic practices and from consumer deception and embezzlement than from all the property crimes in the FBI's Index combined. Yet these far more costly acts are either not criminal, or if technically criminal, not prosecuted, or if prosecuted, not punished, or if punished, only mildly.... *Their faces rarely appear in the criminal justice mirror, although the*

danger they pose is at least as great and often greater than that of those who do....

The criminal justice system is like a mirror in which society can see the face of the evil in its midst. Because the system deals with some evil and not with others, because it treats some evils as the gravest and treats some of the gravest evils as minor, the image it throws back is distorted like the image in a carnival mirror. Thus, the image cast back is false not because it is invented out of thin air but because the proportions of the real are distorted....

If criminal justice really gives us a carnival-mirror of "crime," we are doubly deceived. First, we are led to believe that the criminal justice system is protecting us against the gravest threats to our well-being when, in fact, the system is protecting us against only some threats and not necessarily the gravest ones. We are deceived about how much protection we are receiving and thus left vulnerable. The second deception is just the other side of this one. If people believe that the carnival mirror is a true mirror— that is, if they believe the criminal justice system simply *reacts* to the gravest threats to their well-being—they come to believe that whatever is the target of the criminal justice system must be the greatest threat to their well-being....

A CRIME BY ANY OTHER NAME...

Think of a crime, any crime. Picture the first "crime" that comes into your mind. What do you see? The odds are you are not imagining a mining company executive sitting at his desk, calculating the costs of proper safety precautions and deciding not to invest in them. Probably what you do see with your mind's eye is one person physically attacking another or robbing something from another via the threat of physical attack. Look more closely. What does the attacker look like? It's a safe bet he (and it is a *he*, of course) is not wearing a suit and tie. In fact, my hunch is that you—like me, like almost anyone else in America—picture a young, tough lower-class male when the thought of crime first pops into your head. You (we) picture someone like the Typical Criminal described above. The crime itself is one in which the Typical Criminal sets out to attack or rob some specific person....

It is important to identify this model of the Typical Crime because it functions like a set of blinders. It keeps us from calling a mine disaster a mass murder even if ten men are killed, even if someone is responsible for the unsafe conditions in which they worked and died. I contend that this particular piece of mental furniture so blocks our view that it keeps us from using the criminal justice system to protect ourselves from the greatest threats to our persons and possessions.

What keeps a mine disaster from being a mass murder in our eyes is that it is not a one-on-one harm. What is important in one-on-one harm is not the numbers but the *desire of someone (or ones) to harm someone (or ones) else.* An attack by a gang on one or more persons or an attack by one individual on several fits the model of one-on-one harm; that is, for each person harmed there is at least one individual who wanted to harm that person. Once he selects his victim, the rapist, the mugger, the murderer all want this person they have selected to suffer. A mine executive, on the other hand, does not want his employees to be harmed. He would truly prefer that there be no accident, no injured or dead miners. What he does want is something legitimate. It is what

he has been hired to get: maximum profits at minimum costs. If he cuts corners to save a buck, he is just doing his job. If ten men die because he cut corners on safety, we may think him crude or callous but not a murderer. He is, at most, responsible for an *indirect harm,* not a one-on-one harm. For this, he may even be criminally indictable for violating safety regulations —but not for murder. The ten men are dead as an unwanted consequence of his (perhaps overzealous or undercautious) pursuit of a legitimate goal. So, unlike the Typical Criminal, he has not committed the Typical Crime—or so we generally believe. As a result, ten men are dead who might be alive now if cutting corners of the kind that leads to loss of life, whether suffering is specifically aimed at or not, were treated as murder.

This is my point. Because we accept the belief... that the model for crime is one person specifically trying to harm another, we accept a legal system that leaves us unprotected against much greater dangers to our lives and well-being than those threatened by the Typical Criminal....

According to the FBI's *Uniform Crime Reports,* in 1991, there were 24,703 murders and nonnegligent manslaughters, and 1,092,739 aggravated assaults. In 1992, there were 23,760 murders and non-negligent manslaughters, and 1,126,970 aggravated assaults.... Thus, as a measure of the physical harm done by crime in the beginning of the 1990s, we can say that reported crimes lead to roughly 24,000 deaths and 1,000,000 instances of serious bodily injury short of death a year. As a measure of monetary loss due to property crime, we can use $15.1 billion —the total estimated dollar losses due to property crime in 1992 according to the UCR. Whatever the shortcomings of these reported crime statistics, they are the statistics upon which public policy has traditionally been based. Thus, I will consider any actions that lead to loss of life, physical harm, and property loss comparable to the figures in the UCR as actions that pose grave dangers to the community comparable to the threats posed by crimes....

In testimony before the Senate Committee on Labor and Human Resources, Dr. Philip Landrigan, director of the Division of Environmental and Occupational Medicine at the Mount Sinai School of Medicine in New York City, stated that

... [I]t may be calculated that occupational disease is responsible each year in the United States for 50,000 to 70,000 deaths, and for approximately 350,000 new cases of illness.

... The BLS estimate of 330,000 job-related illnesses for 1990 roughly matches Dr. Landrigan's estimates. For 1991, BLS estimates 368,000 job-related illnesses. These illnesses are of varying severity.... Because I want to compare these occupational harms with those resulting from aggravated assault, I shall stay on the conservative side here too, as with deaths from occupational diseases, and say that there are annually in the United States approximately 150,000 job-related serious illnesses. Taken together with 25,000 deaths from occupational diseases, how does this compare with the threat posed by crime?

Before jumping to any conclusions, note that the risk of occupational disease and death falls only on members of the labor force, whereas the risk of crime falls on the whole population, from infants to the elderly. Because the labor force is about half the total population (124,810,000 in 1990, out of a total population of 249,900,000), to get a true picture of the *relative* threat posed by occupational diseases compared with that posed by crimes, we should *halve* the crime statistics when comparing them with the figures for industrial disease and death. Using the crime figures for the first years of the 1990s,... we note that the *comparable* figures would be

	Occupational Disease	Crime (halved)
Death	25,000	12,000
Other physical harm	150,000	500,000

... Note... that the estimates in the last chart are *only* for occupational *diseases* and deaths from those diseases. They do not include death and disability from work-related injuries. Here, too, the statistics are gruesome. The National Safety Council reported that in 1991, work-related accidents caused 9,600 deaths and 1.7 million disabling work injuries, a total cost to the economy of $63.3 billion. This brings the number of occupation-related deaths to 34,600 a year and other physical harms to 1,850,000. If, on the basis of these additional figures, we recalculated our chart comparing occupational harms from both disease and accident with criminal harms, it would look like this:

	Occupational Hazard	Crime (halved)
Death	34,600	12,000
Other physical harm	1,850,000	500,000

Can there be any doubt that workers are more likely to stay alive and healthy in the face of the danger from the underworld than in the work-world?...

To say that some of these workers died from accidents due to their own carelessness is about as helpful as saying that some of those who died at the hands of murderers asked for it. It overlooks the fact that where workers are careless, it is not because they love to live dangerously. They have production quotas to meet, quotas that they themselves do not set. If quotas were set with an eye to keeping work at a safe pace rather than to keeping the production-to-wages ratio as high as possible, it might be more reasonable to expect workers to take the time to be careful. Beyond this, we should bear in mind that the vast majority of occupational deaths result from disease, not accident, and disease is generally a function of conditions outside a worker's control. Examples of such conditions are the level of coal dust in the air ("260,000 miners receive benefits for [black lung] disease, and perhaps as many as 4,000 retired miners die from the illness or its complications each year"; about 10,000 currently working miners "have X-ray evidence of the beginnings of the crippling and often fatal disease") or textile dust... or asbestos fibers... or coal tars...; (coke oven workers develop cancer of the scrotum at a rate five times that of the general population). Also, some 800,000 people suffer from occupationally related skin disease each year....

To blame the workers for occupational disease and deaths is to ignore the history of governmental attempts to compel industrial firms to meet safety standards that would keep dangers (such as chemicals or fibers or dust particles in the air) that are outside the worker's control down to a safe level. This has been a continual struggle, with firms using everything from their own "independent" research institutes to more direct and often questionable forms of political pressure to influence government in the direction of loose standards and lax enforcement. So far, industry has been winning because OSHA [Occupational Safety and Health Administration] has been given neither the personnel nor the mandate to fulfill its purpose. It is so understaffed that, in 1973, when 1,500 federal sky marshals guarded the nation's airplanes from hijackers, only 500 OSHA inspectors toured the nation's workplaces. By 1980, OSHA employed 1,581 compliance safety and health officers, but this still enabled inspection of only roughly 2 percent of the 2.5 million establishments covered by OSHA. The *New York Times* reports that in 1987 the number of OSHA inspectors was down to 1,044. As might be expected, the agency performs fewer inspections that it did a dozen years ago....

According to a report issued by the AFL-CIO [American Federation of Labor and Congress of Industrial Organizations] in 1992, "The median penalty paid by an employer during the years 1972–1990 following an incident resulting in death or serious injury of a worker was just $480." The same report claims that the federal government spends $1.1 billion a year to protect fish and wildlife and only $300 million a year to protect workers from health and safety hazards on the job....

Is a person who kills another in a bar brawl a greater threat to society than a business executive who refuses to cut into his profits to make his plant a safe place to work? By any measure of death and suffering the latter is by far a greater danger than the former. Because he wishes his workers no harm, because he is only indirectly responsible for death and disability while pursuing legitimate economic goals, his acts are not called "crimes." Once we free our imagination from the blinders of the one-on-one model of crime, can there be any doubt that the criminal justice system does *not* protect us from the gravest threats to life and limb? It seeks to protect us when danger comes from a young, lower-class male in the inner city. When a threat comes from an upper-class business executive in an office, the criminal justice system looks the other way. This is in the face of growing evidence that for every three American citizens murdered by thugs, at least four American workers are killed by the recklessness of their bosses and the indifference of their government.

Health Care May Be Dangerous to Your Health

... On July 15, 1975, Dr. Sidney Wolfe of Ralph Nader's Public Interest Health Research Group testified before the House Commerce Oversight and Investigations Subcommittee that there "were 3.2 million cases of unnecessary surgery performed each year in the United States." These unneeded operations, Wolfe added, "cost close to $5 billion a year and kill as many as 16,000 Americans." ...

In an article on an experimental program by Blue Cross and Blue Shield aimed at curbing unnecessary surgery, *Newsweek* reports that

a Congressional committee earlier this year [1976] estimated that more than 2 million of the elective operations performed in 1974 were not only unnecessary—but also killed about 12,000 patients and cost nearly $4 billion.

Because the number of surgical operations performed in the United States rose from 16.7 million in 1975 to 22.4 million in 1991, there is reason to believe that at least somewhere between... 12,000 and ... 16,000 people a year still die from unnecessary surgery. In 1991, the FBI reported that 3,405 murders were committed by a "cutting or stabbing instrument." Obviously, the FBI does not include the scalpel as a cutting or stabbing instrument. If they did, they would have had to report that between 15,405 and 19,405 persons were killed by "cutting or stabbing" in 1991.... No matter how you slice it, the scalpel may be more dangerous than the switchblade....

Waging Chemical Warfare Against America

One in 4 Americans can expect to contract cancer during their lifetimes. The American Cancer Society estimated that 420,000 Americans would die of cancer in 1981. The National Cancer Institute's estimate for 1993 is 526,000 deaths from cancer. "A 1978 report issued by the President's Council on Environmental Quality (CEQ) unequivocally states that 'most researchers agree that 70 to 90 percent of cancers are caused by environmental influences and are hence theoretically preventable.'" This means that a concerted national effort could result in saving 350,000 or more lives a year and reducing each individual's chances of getting cancer in his or her lifetime from 1 in 4 to 1 in 12 or fewer. If you think this would require a massive effort in terms of money and personnel, you are right. How much of an effort, though, would the nation make to stop a foreign invader who was killing a thousand people and bent on capturing one-quarter of the present population?

In face of this "invasion" that is already under way, the U.S. government has allocated $1.9 billion to the National Cancer Institute (NCI) for fiscal year 1992, and NCI has allocated $219 million to the study of the physical and chemical (i.e., environmental) causes of cancer. Compare this with the (at least) $45 billion spent to fight the Persian Gulf War. The simple truth is that the government that strove so mightily to protect the borders of a small, undemocratic nation 7,000 miles away is doing next to nothing to protect us against the chemical war in our midst. This war is being waged against us on three fronts:

- Pollution
- Cigarette smoking
- Food additives

... The evidence linking *air pollution* and cancer, as well as other serious and often fatal diseases, has been rapidly accumulating in recent years. In 1993, the *Journal of the American Medical Association* reported on research that found " 'robust' associations between premature mortality and air pollution levels." They estimate that pollutants cause about 2 percent of all cancer deaths (at least 10,000 a year)....

A ... recent study ... concluded that air pollution at 1988 levels was responsible for 60,000 deaths a year. The Natural Resources Defense Council sued the EPA [Environmental Protection Agency] for its foot-dragging in implementation of the Clean Air Act, charging that "One hundred million people live in areas of unhealthy air."

This chemical war is not limited to the air. The National Cancer Institute has identified as carcinogens or suspected carcinogens 23 of the chemicals commonly found in our drinking water.

Moreover, according to one observer, we are now facing a "new plague—toxic exposure." ...

The evidence linking *cigarette smoking* and cancer is overwhelming and need not be repeated here. The Centers for Disease Control estimates that cigarettes cause 87 percent of lung cancers—approximately 146,000 in 1992. Tobacco continues to kill an estimated 400,000 Americans a year. Cigarettes are widely estimated to cause 30 percent of all cancer deaths....

This is enough to expose the hypocrisy of running a full-scale war against heroin (which produces no degenerative disease) while allowing cigarette sales and advertising to flourish. It also should be enough to underscore the point that once again there are threats to our lives much greater than criminal homicide. The legal order does not protect us against them. Indeed, not only does our government fail to protect us against this threat, it promotes it! ...

Based on the knowledge we have, there can be no doubt that air pollution, tobacco, and food additives amount to a chemical war that makes the crime wave look like a football scrimmage. Even with the most conservative estimates, it is clear that *the death toll in this war is far higher than the number of people killed by criminal homicide!* ...

SUMMARY

Once again, our investigations lead to the same result. The criminal justice system does not protect us against the gravest threats to life, limb, or possessions. Its definitions of crime are not simply a reflection of the objective dangers that threaten us. The workplace, the medical profession, the air we breathe, and the poverty we refuse to rectify lead to far more human suffering, far more death and disability, and take far more dollars from our pockets than the murders, aggravated assaults, and thefts reported annually by the FBI. What is more, this human suffering is preventable. A government really intent on protecting our well-being could enforce work safety regulations, police the medical profession, require that clean air standards be met, and funnel sufficient money to the poor to alleviate the major disabilities of poverty—but it does not. Instead we hear a lot of cant about law and order and a lot of rant about crime in the streets. It is as if our leaders were not only refusing to protect us from the major threats to our well-being but trying to cover up this refusal by diverting our attention to crime—as if this were the only real threat.

POSTSCRIPT

Is Street Crime More Harmful Than White-Collar Crime?

It is important to consider both the suffering and the wider ramifications caused by crimes. DiIulio captures many of these dimensions and gives a full account of the harms of street crime. Today the public is very concerned about street crime, especially wanton violence. However, it seems relatively unconcerned about white-collar crime. Reiman tries to change that perception. By defining many harmful actions by managers and professionals as crimes, he argues that white-collar crime is worse than street crime. He says that more people are killed and injured by "occupational injury or disease, by unnecessary surgery, and by shoddy emergency medical services than by aggravated assault or even homicide!" But are shoddy medical services a crime? In the end, the questions remain: What is a crime? Who are the criminals?

A set of readings that support Reiman's viewpoint is *Corporate Violence: Injury and Death for Profit* edited by Stuart L. Hills (Rowman & Littlefield, 1987). Further support is provided by Marshall B. Clinard, *Corporate Corruption: The Abuse of Power* (Praeger, 1990). *White-Collar Crime* edited by Gilbert Geis and Robert F. Meier (Free Press, 1977) is a useful compilation of essays on corporate and political crime, as is Gary Green's *Occupational Crime* (Nelson-Hall, 1990). Four other books that focus on crime in high places are J. Douglas and J. M. Johnson, *Official Deviance* (J. B. Lippincott, 1977); J. Anthony Lukas, *Nightmare: The Underside of the Nixon Years* (Viking Press, 1976); Marshall B. Clinard, *Corporate Elites and Crime* (Sage Publications, 1983); and David R. Simon and Stanley Eitzen, *Elite Deviance* (Allyn & Bacon, 1982). A work that deals with the prevalence and fear of street crime is Elliott Currie, *Confronting Crime: An American Challenge* (Pantheon Books, 1985). Two works on gangs, which are often connected with violent street crime, are Martin Sanchez Jankowski, *Islands in the Street: Gangs and American Urban Society* (University of California Press, 1991) and Felix M. Padilla, *The Gang as an American Enterprise* (Rutgers University Press, 1992). William J. Bennett, John J. DiIulio, and John P. Walters, in *Body Count: Moral Poverty—and How to Win America's War Against Crime and Drugs* (Simon & Schuster, 1996), argue that moral poverty is the root cause of crime (meaning street crime). How applicable is this thesis to white-collar crime? One interesting aspect of many corporate, or white-collar, crimes is that they involve crimes of obedience, as discussed in Herman C. Kelman and V. Lee Hamilton, *Crimes of Obedience: Toward a Social Psychology of Authority and Responsibility* (Yale University Press, 1989).

ISSUE 17

Should Drug Use Be Decriminalized?

YES: Ethan A. Nadelmann, from "Commonsense Drug Policy," *Foreign Affairs* (January/February 1998)

NO: James A. Inciardi and Christine A. Saum, from "Legalization Madness," *The Public Interest* (Spring 1996)

ISSUE SUMMARY

YES: Ethan A. Nadelmann, director of the Lindesmith Center, a drug policy research institute, argues that history shows that drug prohibition is costly and futile. Examining the drug policies in other countries, he finds that decriminalization plus sane and humane drug policies and treatment programs can greatly reduce the harms from drugs.

NO: James A. Inciardi, director of the Center for Drug and Alcohol Studies at the University of Delaware, and his associate Christine A. Saum argue that legalizing drugs would not eliminate drug-related criminal activity and would greatly increase drug use. Therefore, the government should continue the war against drugs.

A century ago, drugs of every kind were freely available to Americans. Laudanum, a mixture of opium and alcohol, was popularly used as a painkiller. One drug company even claimed that it was a very useful substance for calming hyperactive children, and the company called it Mother's Helper. Morphine came into common use during the Civil War. Heroin, developed as a supposedly less addictive substitute for morphine, began to be marketed at the end of the nineteenth century. By that time, drug paraphernalia could be ordered through Sears and Roebuck catalogues, and Coca-Cola, which contained small quantities of cocaine, had become a popular drink.

Public concerns about addiction and dangerous patent medicines, and an active campaign for drug laws waged by Dr. Harvey Wiley, a chemist in the U.S. Department of Agriculture, led Congress to pass the first national drug regulation act in 1906. The Pure Food and Drug Act required that medicines containing certain drugs, such as opium, must say so on their labels. The Harrison Narcotic Act of 1914 went much further and cut off completely the supply of legal opiates to addicts. Since then, ever stricter drug laws have been passed by Congress and by state legislatures.

Drug abuse in America again came to the forefront of public discourse during the 1960s, when heroin addiction started growing rapidly in inner-city neighborhoods. Also, by the end of the decade, drug experimentation had spread to the middle-class, affluent baby boomers who were then attending college. Indeed, certain types of drugs began to be celebrated by some of the leaders of the counterculture. Heroin was still taboo, but other drugs, notably marijuana and LSD (a psychedelic drug), were regarded as harmless and even spiritually transforming. At music festivals like Woodstock in 1969, marijuana and LSD were used openly and associated with love, peace, and heightened sensitivity. Much of this enthusiasm cooled over the next 20 years as baby boomers entered the workforce full-time and began their careers. But even among the careerists, certain types of drugs enjoyed high status. Cocaine, noted for its highly stimulating effects, became the drug of choice for many hard-driving young lawyers, television writers, and Wall Street bond traders.

The high price of cocaine put it out of reach for many people, but in the early 1980s, cheap substitutes began to appear on the streets and to overtake poor urban communities. Crack cocaine, a potent, highly addictive, smokable form of cocaine, came into widespread use. By the end of the 1980s, the drug known as "ice," or as it is called on the West Coast, "L.A. glass," a smokable form of amphetamine, had hit the streets. These stimulants tend to produce very violent, disorderly behavior. Moreover, the street gangs who sell them are frequently at war with one another and are well armed. Not only gang members but also many innocent people have become victims of contract killings, street battles, and drive-by shootings.

This new drug epidemic prompted President George Bush to declare a "war on drugs," and in 1989 he asked Congress to appropriate $10.6 billion for the fight. Although most Americans support such measures against illegal drugs, some say that in the years since Bush made his declaration, the drug situation has not showed any signs of improvement. Some believe that legalization would be the best way to fight the drug problem.

The drug decriminalization issue is especially interesting to sociologists because it raises basic questions about what should be socially sanctioned or approved, what is illegal or legal, and what is immoral or moral. An aspect of the basic value system of America is under review. The process of value change may be taking place in front of our eyes. As part of this debate, Ethan A. Nadelmann argues that the present policy does not work and that it is counterproductive. Legalization, he contends, would stop much of the disease, violence, and crime associated with illegal drugs. Although Nadelmann concedes that it may increase the use of lower-potency drugs, he believes that legalization would reduce the use of the worst drugs. James A. Inciardi and Christine A. Saum argue that legalization would be madness because "drug prohibition seems to be having some very positive effects and . . . legalizing drugs would not necessarily have a depressant effect on violent crime."

YES

Ethan A. Nadelmann

COMMONSENSE DRUG POLICY

FIRST, REDUCE HARM

In 1988 Congress passed a resolution proclaiming its goal of "a drug-free America by 1995." U.S. drug policy has failed persistently over the decades because it has preferred such rhetoric to reality, and moralism to pragmatism. Politicians confess their youthful indiscretions, then call for tougher drug laws. Drug control officials make assertions with no basis in fact or science. Police officers, generals, politicians, and guardians of public morals qualify as drug czars—but not, to date, a single doctor or public health figure. Independent commissions are appointed to evaluate drug policies, only to see their recommendations ignored as politically risky. And drug policies are designed, implemented, and enforced with virtually no input from the millions of Americans they affect most: drug users. Drug abuse is a serious problem, both for individual citizens and society at large, but the "war on drugs" has made matters worse, not better.

Drug warriors often point to the 1980s as a time in which the drug war really worked. Illicit drug use by teenagers peaked around 1980, then fell more than 50 percent over the next 12 years. During the 1996 presidential campaign, Republican challenger Bob Dole made much of the recent rise in teenagers' use of illicit drugs, contrasting it with the sharp drop during the Reagan and Bush administrations. President Clinton's response was tepid, in part because he accepted the notion that teen drug use is the principal measure of drug policy's success or failure; at best, he could point out that the level was still barely half what it had been in 1980.

In 1980, however, no one had ever heard of the cheap, smokable form of cocaine called crack, or drug-related HIV infection or AIDS. By the 1990s, both had reached epidemic proportions in American cities, largely driven by prohibitionist economics and morals indifferent to the human consequences of the drug war. In 1980, the federal budget for drug control was about $1 billion, and state and local budgets were perhaps two or three times that. By 1997, the federal drug control budget had ballooned to $16 billion, two-thirds of it for law enforcement agencies, and state and local funding to

From Ethan A. Nadelmann, "Commonsense Drug Policy," *Foreign Affairs*, vol. 77, no. 1 (January/February 1998). Copyright © 1998 by The Council on Foreign Relations, Inc. Reprinted by permission of *Foreign Affairs*. Notes omitted.

at least that. On any day in 1980, approximately 50,000 people were behind bars for violating a drug law. By 1997, the number had increased eightfold, to about 400,000. These are the results of a drug policy overreliant on criminal justice "solutions," ideologically wedded to abstinence-only treatment, and insulated from cost-benefit analysis.

Imagine instead a policy that starts by acknowledging that drugs are here to stay, and that we have no choice but to learn how to live with them so that they cause the least possible harm. Imagine a policy that focuses on reducing not illicit drug use per se but the crime and misery caused by both drug abuse and prohibitionist policies. And imagine a drug policy based not on the fear, prejudice, and ignorance that drive America's current approach but rather on common sense, science, public health concerns, and human rights. Such a policy is possible in the United States, especially if Americans are willing to learn from the experiences of other countries where such policies are emerging.

ATTITUDES ABROAD

Americans are not averse to looking abroad for solutions to the nation's drug problems. Unfortunately, they have been looking in the wrong places: Asia and Latin America, where much of the world's heroin and cocaine originates. Decades of U.S. efforts to keep drugs from being produced abroad and exported to American markets have failed. Illicit drug production is bigger business than ever before. The opium poppy, source of morphine and heroin, and *cannabis sativa*, from which marijuana and hashish are prepared, grow readily around the world; the coca plant, from whose leaves cocaine

is extracted, can be cultivated far from its native environment in the Andes. Crop substitution programs designed to persuade Third World peasants to grow legal crops cannot compete with the profits that drug prohibition makes inevitable. Crop eradication campaigns occasionally reduce production in one country, but new suppliers pop up elsewhere. International law enforcement efforts can disrupt drug trafficking organizations and routes, but they rarely have much impact on U.S. drug markets....

While looking to Latin America and Asia for supply-reduction solutions to America's drug problems is futile, the harm-reduction approaches spreading throughout Europe and Australia and even into corners of North America show promise. These approaches start by acknowledging that supply-reduction initiatives are inherently limited, that criminal justice responses can be costly and counterproductive, and that single-minded pursuit of a "drug-free society" is dangerously quixotic. Demand-reduction efforts to prevent drug abuse among children and adults are important, but so are harm-reduction efforts to lessen the damage to those unable or unwilling to stop using drugs immediately, and to those around them.

Most proponents of harm reduction do not favor legalization. They recognize that prohibition has failed to curtail drug abuse, that it is responsible for much of the crime, corruption, disease, and death associated with drugs, and that its costs mount every year. But they also see legalization as politically unwise and as risking increased drug use. The challenge is thus making drug prohibition work better, but with a focus on reducing the negative consequences of both drug use and prohibitionist policies....

Harm-reduction innovations include efforts to stem the spread of HIV by making sterile syringes readily available and collecting used syringes; allowing doctors to prescribe oral methadone for heroin addiction treatment, as well as heroin and other drugs for addicts who would otherwise buy them on the black market; establishing "safe injection rooms" so addicts do not congregate in public places or dangerous "shooting galleries"; employing drug analysis units at the large dance parties called raves to test the quality and potency of MDMA, known as Ecstasy, and other drugs that patrons buy and consume there; decriminalizing (but not legalizing) possession and retail sale of cannabis and, in some cases, possession of small amounts of "hard" drugs; and integrating harm-reduction policies and principles into community policing strategies. Some of these measures are under way or under consideration in parts of the United States, but rarely to the extent found in growing numbers of foreign countries.

STOPPING HIV WITH STERILE SYRINGES

The spread of HIV, the virus that causes AIDS, among people who inject drugs illegally was what prompted governments in Europe and Australia to experiment with harm-reduction policies. During the early 1980s public health officials realized that infected users were spreading HIV by sharing needles. Having already experienced a hepatitis epidemic attributed to the same mode of transmission, the Dutch were the first to tell drug users about the risks of needle sharing and to make sterile syringes available and collect dirty needles through pharmacies,

needle exchange and methadone programs, and public health services. Governments elsewhere in Europe and in Australia soon followed suit. The few countries in which a prescription was necessary to obtain a syringe dropped the requirement. Local authorities in Germany, Switzerland, and other European countries authorized needle exchange machines to ensure 24-hour access. In some European cities, addicts can exchange used syringes for clean ones at local police stations without fear of prosecution or harassment. Prisons are instituting similar policies to help discourage the spread of HIV among inmates, recognizing that illegal drug injecting cannot be eliminated even behind bars.

These initiatives were not adopted without controversy. Conservative politicians argued that needle exchange programs condoned illicit and immoral behavior and that government policies should focus on punishing drug users or making them drug-free. But by the late 1980s, the consensus in most of Western Europe, Oceania, and Canada was that while drug abuse was a serious problem, AIDS was worse. Slowing the spread of a fatal disease for which no cure exists was the greater moral imperative. There was also a fiscal imperative. Needle exchange programs' costs are minuscule compared with those of treating people who would otherwise become infected with HIV.

Only in the United States has this logic not prevailed, even though AIDS was the leading killer of Americans ages 25 to 44 for most of the 1990s and is now No. 2. The Centers for Disease Control (CDC) estimates that half of new HIV infections in the country stem from injection drug use. Yet both the White House and Congress block allocation of AIDS or drug-abuse prevention funds for needle exchange, and virtually all state governments retain drug paraphernalia laws, pharmacy regulations, and other restrictions on access to sterile syringes. During the 1980s, AIDS activists engaging in civil disobedience set up more syringe exchange programs than state and local governments. There are now more than 100 such programs in 28 states, Washington, D.C., and Puerto Rico, but they reach only an estimated 10 percent of injection drug users.

Governments at all levels in the United States refuse to fund needle exchange for political reasons, even though dozens of scientific studies, domestic and foreign, have found that needle exchange and other distribution programs reduce needle sharing, bring hard-to-reach drug users into contact with health care systems, and inform addicts about treatment programs, yet do not increase illegal drug use. In 1991 the National AIDS Commission appointed by President Bush called the lack of federal support for such programs "bewildering and tragic." In 1993 a CDC-sponsored review of research on needle exchange recommended federal funding, but top officials in the Clinton administration suppressed a favorable evaluation of the report within the Department of Health and Human Services. In July 1996 President Clinton's Advisory Council on HIV/AIDS criticized the administration for its failure to heed the National Academy of Sciences' recommendation that it authorize the use of federal money to support needle exchange programs. An independent panel convened by the National Institute[s] of Health reached the same conclusion in February 1997. Last summer, the American Medical Association, the American Bar Association, and even the politicized U.S. Conference of Mayors endorsed the concept of needle exchange. In the fall,

an endorsement followed from the World Bank.

To date, America's failure in this regard is conservatively estimated to have resulted in the infection of up to 10,000 people with HIV. Mounting scientific evidence and the stark reality of the continuing AIDS crisis have convinced the public, if not politicians, that needle exchange saves lives; polls consistently find that a majority of Americans support needle exchange, with approval highest among those most familiar with the notion. Prejudice and political cowardice are poor excuses for allowing more citizens to suffer from and die of AIDS, especially when effective interventions are cheap, safe, and easy.

METHADONE AND OTHER ALTERNATIVES

The United States pioneered the use of the synthetic opiate methadone to treat heroin addiction in the 1960s and 1970s, but now lags behind much of Europe and Australia in making methadone accessible and effective. Methadone is the best available treatment in terms of reducing illicit heroin use and associated crime, disease, and death. In the early 1990s the National Academy of Sciences' Institute of Medicine stated that of all forms of drug treatment, "methadone maintenance has been the most rigorously studied modality and has yielded the most incontrovertibly positive results.... Consumption of all illicit drugs, especially heroin, declines. Crime is reduced, fewer individuals become HIV positive, and individual functioning is improved." However, the institute went on to declare, "Current policy ... puts too much emphasis on protecting society from methadone, and not enough on protecting society from the epidemics of addiction, violence, and infectious diseases that methadone can help reduce."

Methadone is to street heroin what nicotine skin patches and chewing gum are to cigarettes—with the added benefit of legality. Taken orally, methadone has little of injected heroin's effect on mood or cognition. It can be consumed for decades with few if any negative health consequences, and its purity and concentration, unlike street heroin's, are assured. Like other opiates, it can create physical dependence if taken regularly, but the "addiction" is more like a diabetic's "addiction" to insulin than a heroin addict's to product brought on the street. Methadone patients can and do drive safely, hold good jobs, and care for their children. When prescribed adequate doses, they can be indistinguishable from people who have never used heroin or methadone.

Popular misconceptions and prejudice, however, have all but prevented any expansion of methadone treatment in the United States. The 115,000 Americans receiving methadone today represent only a small increase over the number 20 years ago. For every ten heroin addicts, there are only one or two methadone treatment slots. Methadone is the most tightly controlled drug in the pharmacopoeia, subject to unique federal and state restrictions. Doctors cannot prescribe it for addiction treatment outside designated programs. Regulations dictate not only security, documentation, and staffing requirements but maximum doses, admission criteria, time spent in the program, and a host of other specifics, none of which has much to do with quality of treatment. Moreover, the regulations do not prevent poor treatment; many clinics provide insufficient doses, prematurely detoxify clients, expel clients for offensive behavior, and engage in other practices that would be regarded as unethical in any other field of medicine. Attempts to open new clinics tend to be blocked by residents who don't want addicts in their neighborhood....

The Swiss government began a nationwide trial in 1994 to determine whether prescribing heroin, morphine, or injectable methadone could reduce crime, disease, and other drug-related ills. Some 1,000 volunteers—only heroin addicts with at least two unsuccessful experiences in methadone or other conventional treatment programs were considered—took part in the experiment. The trial quickly determined that virtually all participants preferred heroin, and doctors subsequently prescribed it for them. Last July the government reported the results so far: criminal offenses and the number of criminal offenders dropped 60 percent, the percentage of income from illegal and semilegal activities fell from 69 to 10 percent, illegal heroin *and* cocaine use declined dramatically (although use of alcohol, cannabis, and tranquilizers like Valium remained fairly constant), stable employment increased from 14 to 32 percent, physical health improved enormously, and most participants greatly reduced their contact with the drug scene. There were no deaths from overdoses, and no prescribed drugs were diverted to the black market. More than half those who dropped out of the study switched to another form of drug treatment, including 83 who began abstinence therapy. A cost-benefit analysis of the program found a net economic benefit of $30 per patient per day, mostly because of reduced criminal justice and health care costs.

The Swiss study has undermined several myths about heroin and its habitual users. The results to date demonstrate that, given relatively unlimited availability, heroin users will voluntarily stabilize or reduce their dosage and some will even choose abstinence; that long-addicted users can lead relatively normal, stable lives if provided legal access to their drug of choice; and that ordinary citizens will support such initiatives. In recent referendums in Zurich, Basel, and Zug, substantial majorities voted to continue funding local arms of the experiment. And last September, a nationwide referendum to end the government's heroin maintenance and other harm-reduction initiatives was rejected by 71 percent of Swiss voters, including majorities in all 26 cantons....

REEFER SANITY

Cannabis, in the form of marijuana and hashish, is by far the most popular illicit drug in the United States. More than a quarter of Americans admit to having tried it. Marijuana's popularity peaked in 1980, dropped steadily until the early 1990s, and is now on the rise again. Although it is not entirely safe, especially when consumed by children, smoked heavily, or used when driving, it is clearly among the least dangerous psychoactive drugs in common use. In 1988 the administrative law judge for the Drug Enforcement Administration, Francis Young, reviewed the evidence and concluded that "marihuana, in its natural form, is one of the safest therapeutically active substances known to man."

As with needle exchange and methadone treatment, American politicians have ignored or spurned the findings of government commissions and scientific organizations concerning marijuana policy. In 1972 the National Commission on Marihuana and Drug Abuse—created by President Nixon and chaired by a former Republican governor, Raymond Shafer—recommended that possession of up to one ounce of marijuana be decriminalized. Nixon rejected the recommendation. In 1982 a panel appointed by the National Academy of Sciences reached the same conclusions as the Shafer Commission.

Between 1973 and 1978, with attitudes changing, 11 states approved decriminalization statutes that reclassified marijuana possession as a misdemeanor, petty offense, or civil violation punishable by no more than a $100 fine. Consumption trends in those states and in states that retained stricter sanctions were indistinguishable. A 1988 scholarly evaluation of the Moscone Act, California's 1976 decriminalization law, estimated that the state had saved half a billion dollars in arrest costs since the law's passage. Nonetheless, public opinion began to shift in 1978. No other states decriminalized marijuana, and some eventually recriminalized it.

Between 1973 and 1989, annual arrests on marijuana charges by state and local police ranged between 360,000 and 460,000. The annual total fell to 283,700 in 1991, but has since more than doubled. In 1996, 641,642 people were arrested for marijuana, 85 percent of them for possession, not sale, of the drug. Prompted by concern over rising marijuana use among adolescents and fears of being labeled soft on drugs, the Clinton administration launched its own anti-marijuana campaign in 1995. But the administration's claims to have identified new risks of marijuana consumption

—including a purported link between marijuana and violent behavior—have not withstood scrutiny. Neither Congress nor the White House seems likely to put the issue of marijuana policy before a truly independent advisory commission, given the consistency with which such commissions have reached politically unacceptable conclusions. . . .

WILL IT WORK?

Both at home and abroad, the U.S. government has attempted to block resolutions supporting harm reduction, suppress scientific studies that reached politically inconvenient conclusions, and silence critics of official drug policy. In May 1994, the State Department forced the last-minute cancellation of a World Bank conference on drug trafficking to which critics of U.S. drug policy had been invited. That December the U.S. delegation to an international meeting of the U.N. Drug Control Program refused to sign any statement incorporating the phrase "harm reduction." In early 1995 the State Department successfully pressured the World Health Organization to scuttle the release of a report it had commissioned from a panel that included many of the world's leading experts on cocaine because it included the scientifically incontrovertible observations that traditional use of coca leaf in the Andes causes little harm to users and that most consumers of cocaine use the drug in moderation with few detrimental effects. Hundreds of congressional hearings have addressed multitudinous aspects of the drug problem, but few have inquired into the European harm-reduction policies described above. When former Secretary of State George Shultz, then–Surgeon General M. Joyce-

lyn Elders, and Baltimore Mayor Kurt Schmoke pointed to the failure of current policies and called for new approaches, they were mocked, fired, and ignored, respectively—and thereafter mischaracterized as advocating the outright legalization of drugs.

In Europe, in contrast, informed, public debate about drug policy is increasingly common in government, even at the EU level. In June 1995 the European Parliament issued a report acknowledging that "there will always be a demand for drugs in our societies... the policies followed so far have not been able to prevent the illegal drug trade from flourishing." The EU called for serious consideration of the Frankfurt Resolution, a statement of harm-reduction principles supported by a transnational coalition of 31 cities and regions. In October 1996 Emma Bonino, the European commissioner for consumer policy, advocated decriminalizing soft drugs and initiating a broad prescription program for hard drugs. Greece's minister for European affairs, George Papandreou, seconded her. Last February the monarch of Liechtenstein, Prince Hans Adam, spoke out in favor of controlled drug legalization. Even Raymond Kendall, secretary general of Interpol, was quoted in the August 20, 1994, *Guardian* as saying, "The prosecution of thousands of otherwise law-abiding citizens every year is both hypocritical and an affront to individual, civil and human rights.... Drug use should no longer be a criminal offense. I am totally against legalization, but in favor of decriminalization for the user." . . .

The lessons from Europe and Australia are compelling. Drug control policies should focus on reducing drug-related crime, disease, and death, not the number of casual drug users. Stopping the spread of HIV by and among drug users by making sterile syringes and methadone readily available must be the first priority. American politicians need to explore, not ignore or automatically condemn, promising policy options such as cannabis decriminalization, heroin prescription, and the integration of harm-reduction principles into community policing strategies. Central governments must back, or at least not hinder, the efforts of municipal officials and citizens to devise pragmatic approaches to local drug problems. Like citizens in Europe, the American public has supported such innovations when they are adequately explained and allowed to prove themselves. As the evidence comes in, what works is increasingly apparent. All that remains is mustering the political courage.

NO

James A. Inciardi and
Christine A. Saum

LEGALIZATION MADNESS

Frustrated by the government's apparent inability to reduce the supply of illegal drugs on the streets of America, and disquieted by media accounts of innocents victimized by drug-related violence, some policy makers are convinced that the "war on drugs" has failed. In an attempt to find a better solution to the "drug crisis" or, at the very least, to try an alternative strategy, they have proposed legalizing drugs.

They argue that, if marijuana, cocaine, heroin, and other drugs were legalized, several positive things would probably occur: (1) drug prices would fall; (2) users would obtain their drugs at low, government-regulated prices, and they would no longer be forced to resort to crime in order to support their habits; (3) levels of drug-related crime, and particularly violent crime, would significantly decline, resulting in less crowded courts, jails, and prisons (this would allow law-enforcement personnel to focus their energies on the "real criminals" in society); and (4) drug production, distribution, and sale would no longer be controlled by organized crime, and thus such criminal syndicates as the Colombian cocaine "cartels," the Jamaican "posses," and the various "mafias" around the country and the world would be decapitalized, and the violence associated with drug distribution rivalries would be eliminated.

By contrast, the anti-legalization camp argues that violent crime would not necessarily decline in a legalized drug market. In fact, there are three reasons why it might actually increase. First, removing the criminal sanctions against the possession and distribution of illegal drugs would make them more available and attractive and, hence, would create large numbers of new users. Second, an increase in use would lead to a greater number of dysfunctional addicts who could not support themselves, their habits, or their lifestyles through legitimate means. Hence crime would be their only alternative. Third, more users would mean more of the violence associated with the ingestion of drugs.

These divergent points of view tend to persist because the relationships between drugs and crime are quite complex and because the possible outcomes of a legalized drug market are based primarily on speculation. However, it is possible, from a careful review of the existing empirical literature on drugs and violence, to make some educated inferences.

CONSIDERING "LEGALIZATION"

Yet much depends upon what we mean by "legalizing drugs." Would all currently illicit drugs be legalized or would the experiment be limited to just certain ones? True legalization would be akin to selling such drugs as heroin and cocaine on the open market, much like alcohol and tobacco, with a few age-related restrictions. In contrast, there are "medicalization" and "decriminalization" alternatives. Medicalization approaches are of many types, but, in essence, they would allow users to obtain prescriptions for some, or all, currently illegal substances. Decriminalization removes the criminal penalties associated with the possession of small amounts of illegal drugs for personal use, while leaving intact the sanctions for trafficking, distribution, and sale.

But what about crack-cocaine? A quick review of the literature reveals that the legalizers, the decriminalizers, and the medicalizers avoid talking about this particular form of cocaine. Perhaps they do not want to legalize crack out of fear of the drug itself, or of public outrage. Arnold S. Trebach, a professor of law at American University and president of the Drug Policy Foundation, is one of the very few who argues for the full legalization of all drugs, including crack. He explains, however, that most

are reluctant to discuss the legalization of crack-cocaine because, "it is a very dangerous drug. . . . I know that for many people the very thought of making crack legal destroys any inclination they might have had for even thinking about drug-law reform."

There is a related concern associated with the legalization of cocaine. Because crack is easily manufactured from powder cocaine (just add water and baking soda and cook on a stove or in a microwave), many drug-policy reformers hold that no form of cocaine should be legalized. But this weakens the argument that legalization will reduce drug-related violence; for much of this violence would appear to be in the cocaine- and crack-distribution markets.

To better understand the complex relationship between drugs and violence, we will discuss the data in the context of three models developed by Paul J. Goldstein of the University of Illinois at Chicago. They are the "psychopharmacological," "economically compulsive," and "systemic" explanations of violence. The first model holds, correctly in our view, that some individuals may become excitable, irrational, and even violent due to the ingestion of specific drugs. In contrast, taking a more economic approach to the behavior of drug users, the second holds that some drug users engage in violent crime mainly for the sake of supporting their drug use. The third model maintains that drug-related violent crime is simply the result of the drug market under a regime of illegality.

PSYCHOPHARMACOLOGICAL VIOLENCE

The case for legalization rests in part upon the faulty assumption that drugs themselves do not cause violence; rather, so goes the argument, violence is the result of depriving drug addicts of drugs or of the "criminal" trafficking in drugs. But, as researcher Barry Spunt points out, "Users of drugs do get violent when they get high."

Research has documented that chronic users of amphetamines, methamphetamine, and cocaine in particular tend to exhibit hostile and aggressive behaviors. Psychopharmacological violence can also be a product of what is known as "cocaine psychosis." As dose and duration of cocaine use increase, the development of cocaine-related psychopathology is not uncommon. Cocaine psychosis is generally preceded by a transitional period characterized by increased suspiciousness, compulsive behavior, fault finding, and eventually paranoia. When the psychotic state is reached, individuals may experience visual, as well as auditory, hallucinations, with persecutory voices commonly heard. Many believe that they are being followed by police or that family, friends, and others are plotting against them.

Moreover, everyday events are sometimes misinterpreted by cocaine users in ways that support delusional beliefs. When coupled with the irritability and hyperactivity that cocaine tends to generate in almost all of its users, the cocaine-induced paranoia may lead to violent behavior as a means of "self-defense" against imagined persecutors. The violence associated with cocaine psychosis is a common feature in many crack houses across the United States. Violence may also result from the irritability associated with drug-withdrawal syndromes. In addition, some users ingest drugs before committing crimes to both loosen inhibitions and bolster their resolve to break the law....

AND ALCOHOL ABUSE

A point that needs emphasizing is that alcohol, because it is legal, accessible, and inexpensive, is linked to violence to a far greater extent than any illegal drug. For example, in the study just cited, it was found that an impressive 64 percent of those women who eventually killed their abusers were alcohol users (44 percent of those who did not kill their abusers were alcohol users). Indeed, the extent to which alcohol is responsible for violent crimes in comparison with other drugs is apparent from the statistics. For example, Carolyn Block and her colleagues at the Criminal Justice Information Authority in Chicago found that, between 1982 and 1989, the use of alcohol by offenders or victims in local homicides ranged from 18 percent to 32 percent.

Alcohol has, in fact, been consistently linked to homicide. Spunt and his colleagues interviewed 268 homicide offenders incarcerated in New York State correctional facilities to determine the role of alcohol in their crimes: Thirty-one percent of the respondents reported being drunk at the time of the crime and 19 percent believed that the homicide was related to their drinking. More generally, Douglass Murdoch of Quebec's McGill University found that in some 9,000 criminal cases drawn from a multinational sample, 62 percent of violent offenders were drinking shortly before, or at the time of, the offense.

It appears that alcohol reduces the inhibitory control of threat, making it more likely that a person will exhibit violent behaviors normally suppressed by fear. In turn, this reduction of inhibition heightens the probability that intoxicated persons will perpetrate, or become victims of, aggressive behavior.

When analyzing the psychopharmacological model of drugs and violence, most of the discussions focus on the offender and the role of drugs in causing or facilitating crime. But what about the victims? Are the victims of drug- and alcohol-related homicides simply casualties of someone else's substance abuse? In addressing these questions, the data demonstrates that victims are likely to be drug users as well. For example, in an analysis of the 4,298 homicides that occurred in New York City during 1990 and 1991, Kenneth Tardiff of Cornell University Medical College found that the victims of these offenses were 10 to 50 times more likely to be cocaine users than were members of the general population. Of the white female victims, 60 percent in the 25- to 34-year age group had cocaine in their systems; for black females, the figure was 72 percent. Tardiff speculated that the classic symptoms of cocaine use—irritability, paranoia, aggressiveness—may have instigated the violence. In another study of cocaine users in New York City, female high-volume users were found to be victims of violence far more frequently than low-volume and nonusers of cocaine. Studies in numerous other cities and countries have yielded the same general findings —that a great many of the victims of homicide and other forms of violence are drinkers and drug users themselves.

ECONOMICALLY COMPULSIVE VIOLENCE

Supporters of the economically compulsive model of violence argue that in a legalized market, the prices of "expensive drugs" would decline to more affordable levels, and, hence, predatory crimes would become unnecessary. This argument is based on several specious assumptions. First, it assumes that there is empirical support for what has been referred to as the "enslavement theory of addiction." Second, it assumes that people addicted to drugs commit crimes only for the purpose of supporting their habits. Third, it assumes that, in a legalized market, users could obtain as much of the drugs as they wanted whenever they wanted. Finally, it assumes that, if drugs are inexpensive, they will be affordable, and thus crime would be unnecessary.

With respect to the first premise, there has been for the better part of this century a concerted belief among many in the drug-policy field that addicts commit crimes because they are "enslaved" to drugs, and further that, because of the high price of heroin, cocaine, and other illicit chemicals on the black market, users are forced to commit crimes in order to support their drug habits. However, there is no solid empirical evidence to support this contention. From the 1920s through the end of the 1960s, hundreds of studies of the relationship between crime and addiction were conducted. Invariably, when one analysis would support the posture of "enslavement theory," the next would affirm the view that addicts were criminals first and that their drug use was but one more manifestation of their deviant lifestyles. In retrospect, the difficulty lay in the ways that many of the studies had been conducted: Biases and deficiencies in research designs and sampling had rendered their findings of little value.

Studies since the mid 1970s of active drug users on the streets of New

York, Miami, Baltimore, and elsewhere have demonstrated that the "enslavement theory" has little basis in reality. All of these studies of the criminal careers of drug users have convincingly documented that, while drug use tends to intensify and perpetuate criminal behavior, it usually does not initiate criminal careers....

Looking at the second premise, a variety of studies show that addicts commit crimes for reasons other than supporting their drug habit. They do so also for daily living expenses....

With respect to the third premise, that in a legalized market users could obtain as much of the drugs as they wanted whenever they wanted, only speculation is possible. More than likely, however, there would be some sort of regulation, and hence black markets for drugs would persist for those whose addictions were beyond the medicalized or legalized allotments. In a decriminalized market, levels of drug-related violence would likely either remain unchanged or increase (if drug use increased).

As for the last premise, that cheap drugs preclude the need to commit crimes to obtain them, the evidence emphatically suggests that this is not the case. Consider crack-cocaine: Although crack "rocks" are available on the illegal market for as little as two dollars in some locales, users are still involved in crime-driven endeavors to support their addictions. For example, researchers Norman S. Miller and Mark S. Gold surveyed 200 consecutive callers to the 1-800-COCAINE hotline who considered themselves to have a problem with crack. They found that, despite the low cost of crack, 63 percent of daily users and 40 percent of non-daily users spent more than $200 per week on the drug....

SYSTEMIC VIOLENCE

It is the supposed systemic violence associated with trafficking in cocaine and crack in America's inner cities that has recently received the attention of drug-policy critics interested in legalizing drugs. Certainly it might appear that, if heroin and cocaine were legal substances, systemic drug-related violence would decline. However, there are two very important questions in this regard: First, is drug-related violence more often psychopharmacological or systemic? Second, is the great bulk of systemic violence related to the distribution of crack? If most of the drug-related violence is psychopharmacological in nature, and if systemic violence is typically related to crack —the drug generally excluded from consideration when legalization is recommended—then legalizing drugs would probably *not* reduce violent crime.

Regarding the first question, several recent studies conducted in New York City tend to contradict, or at least not support, the notion that legalizing drugs would reduce violent systemic-related crime. For example, Paul J. Goldstein's ethnographic studies of male and female drug users during the late 1980s found that cocaine-related violence was more often psychopharmacological than systemic. Similarly, Kenneth Tardiff's study of 4,298 New York City homicides found that 31 percent of the victims had used cocaine in the 24-hour period prior to their deaths....

Regarding the second question, the illegal drug most associated with systemic violence is crack-cocaine. Of all illicit drugs, crack is the one now responsible for the most homicides....

DON'T JUST SAY NO

The issue of whether or not legalization would create a multitude of new users also needs to be addressed. It has been shown that many people do not use drugs simply because drugs are illegal. As Mark A.R. Kleiman, author of *Against Excess: Drug Policy for Results,* recently put it: "Illegality by itself tends to suppress consumption, independent of its effect on price, both because some consumers are reluctant to disobey the law and because illegal products are harder to find and less reliable as to quality and labeling than legal ones."

Although there is no way of accurately estimating how many new users there would be if drugs were legalized, there would probably be many. To begin with, there is the historical example of Prohibition. During Prohibition, there was a decrease of 20 percent to 50 percent in the number of alcoholics. These estimates were calculated based on a decline in cirrhosis and other alcohol-related deaths; after Prohibition ended, both of these indicators increased.

Currently, relatively few people are steady users of drugs. The University of Michigan's *Monitoring the Future* study reported in 1995 that only two-tenths of 1 percent of high-school seniors are daily users of either hallucinogens, cocaine, heroin, sedatives, or inhalants. It is the addicts who overwhelmingly consume the bulk of the drug supply—80 percent of all alcohol and almost 100 percent of all heroin. In other words, there are significantly large numbers of non-users who have yet to even try drugs, let alone use them regularly. Of those who begin to use drugs "recreationally," researchers estimate that approximately 10 percent go on to serious, heavy, chronic, compulsive use. Herbert Kleber, the former deputy director of the Office of National Drug Control Policy, recently estimated that cocaine legalization might multiply the number of addicts from the current 2 million to between 18 and 50 million (which are the estimated numbers of problem drinkers and nicotine addicts).

This suggests that drug prohibition seems to be having some very positive effects and that legalizing drugs would not necessarily have a depressant effect on violent crime. With legalization, violent crime would likely escalate; or perhaps some types of systemic violence would decline at the expense of greatly increasing the overall rate of violent crime. Moreover, legalizing drugs would likely increase physical illnesses and compound any existing psychiatric problems among users and their family members. And finally, legalizing drugs would not eliminate the effects of unemployment, inadequate housing, deficient job skills, economic worries, and physical abuse that typically contribute to the use of drugs.

POSTSCRIPT

Should Drug Use Be Decriminalized?

The analogy often cited by proponents of drug legalization is the ill-fated attempt to ban the sale of liquor in the United States, which lasted from 1919 to 1933. Prohibition has been called "an experiment noble in purpose," but it was an experiment that greatly contributed to the rise of organized crime. The repeal of Prohibition brought about an increase in liquor consumption and alcoholism, but it also deprived organized crime of an important source of income. Would drug decriminalization similarly strike a blow at the drug dealers? Possibly, and such a prospect is obviously appealing. But would drug decriminalization also exacerbate some of the ills associated with drugs? Would there be more violence, more severe addiction, and more crack babies born to addicted mothers?

There are a variety of publications and theories pertaining to drug use and society. Ronald L. Akers, in *Drugs, Alcohol, and Society* (Wadsworth, 1992), relates drug patterns to social structure. For a comprehensive overview of the history, effects, and prevention of drug use, see Weldon L. Witters, Peter J. Venturelli, and Glen R. Hanson, *Drugs and Society*, 3rd ed. (Jones & Bartlett, 1992) and Mike Gray, *Drug Crazy: How We Got into This Mess and How We Can Get Out* (Random House, 1998). Terry Williams describes the goings-on in a crackhouse in *Crackhouse: Notes from the End of the Zone* (Addison-Wesley, 1992). James A. Inciardi, Ruth Horowitz, and Anne El Pottieger focus on street kids and drugs in *Street Kids, Street Drugs, Street Crime: An Examination of Drug Use and Serious Delinquency in Miami* (Wadsworth, 1993). For an excellent study of how users of the drug ecstasy perceive the experience, see Jerome Beck and Marsha Rosenbaum, *Pursuit of Ecstasy: The MDMA Experience* (SUNY Press, 1994). For studies of female drug-using groups, see Carl S. Taylor, *Girls, Gangs, Women and Drugs* (Michigan State University Press, 1993) and Avril Taylor, *Women Drug Users: An Ethnography of a Female Injecting Community* (Clarendon Press, 1993). For a relatively balanced yet innovative set of drug policies, see Elliott Carrie, *Reckoning: Drugs, the Cities, and the American Future* (Hill & Wang, 1993). William O. Walker III, ed., *Drug Control Policy* (Pennsylvania State University Press, 1992) critically evaluates drug policies from historical and comparative perspectives. On the legalization debate, see Eric Goode, *Between Politics and Reason: The Drug Legalization Debate* (St. Martin's Press, 1997) and Arnold Trebach and James A. Inciardi, *Legalize It? Debating American Drug Policy* (American University Press, 1993). For criticism of the current drug policies, see Dan Baum, *Smoke and Mirrors: The War on Drugs and the Politics of Failure* (Little, Brown, 1996) and Leif Rosenberger, *America's Drug War Debacle* (Avebury, 1996).

ISSUE 18

Is Incapacitation the Answer to the Crime Problem?

YES: Morgan O. Reynolds, from "Crime Pays, But So Does Imprisonment,"
Journal of Social, Political, and Economic Studies (Fall 1990)

NO: D. Stanley Eitzen, from "Violent Crime: Myths, Facts, and Solutions,"
Vital Speeches of the Day (May 15, 1995)

ISSUE SUMMARY

YES: Professor of economics Morgan O. Reynolds argues that the decline in
the cost of crime for criminals has contributed greatly to the increase in crime
and that catching, convicting, and imprisoning more criminals would greatly
reduce the crime rate.

NO: Professor emeritus of sociology D. Stanley Eitzen argues that the "get
tough with criminals" approach to reducing crime does not work, costs too
much, keeps many people who would otherwise go straight imprisoned, and
does not deal with the fundamental causes of crime.

Not a day passes in America without reports of murders, rapes, or other
violent crimes. As crime has increasingly captured the headlines, public in-
dignation has intensified—particularly when spectacular cases have been
brought to light about paroled convicts committing new felonies, light sentences being handed down for serious crimes, and cases being thrown out of
court on legal technicalities. The perception that Michael Dukakis was soft
on criminals seriously hurt his bid for the presidency in 1988. (As governor of
Massachusetts, Dukakis approved a prison furlough program that released a
convict named Willie Horton, who subsequently went on to commit a widely
publicized violent crime in another state.) Over the past three decades, there
has been a dramatic increase in the number of Americans who think that the
authorities should be tougher on criminals. For example, while a majority of
Americans in the 1960s favored the abolition of the death penalty, today more
than 70 percent favor its use for certain crimes.

Even in the intellectual community there has been a turnaround. When
the southern Democrat and presidential candidate George Wallace and other
politicians raised the issue of "law and order" at the end of the 1960s, the
term was called "a code word for racism" in academic and literary circles.
This is understandable because Wallace *had* previously identified himself
with white racism. The attitude toward crime that was popular in academic

circles during the 1960s might be briefly summarized under two headings: the prevention of crime and the treatment of criminals.

To prevent crime, some academics argued, government must do more than rely upon police, courts, and jails. It must do something about the underlying social roots of crime, especially poverty and racism. It was assumed that, once these roots were severed, crime would begin to fade away or at least cease to be a major social problem.

The prescription for treating criminals followed much the same logic. The word *punishment* was avoided in favor of *treatment* or *rehabilitation,* for the purpose was not to inflict pain or to "pay back" the criminal but to bring about a change in his behavior. If that could be done by lenient treatment—short prison terms, education, counseling, and, above all, understanding—then so much the better.

By the late 1970s the intellectual community itself showed signs that it was reassessing its outlook toward crime. Criminologist and political scientist James Q. Wilson's views on crime became widely respected in universities and in the mass media. He argued that society's attempts to change social conditions had met with little success and that locking up criminals remained the best way to deal with the crime problem in the short term. Wilson's view is carried forward by Morgan O. Reynolds, who, after examining data collected on crimes and time in prison, has found that "crime pays" because most crimes do not result in significant jail time for the criminal. According to Reynolds, the way to reverse the increasing crime rate is to increase deterrence to at least the level of the 1950s, and this requires more prisons. Because the main objection is the high costs of imprisoning criminals, he discusses a number of ways to reduce these costs.

D. Stanley Eitzen argues that America already puts too many people in prison at too high a cost. The answer, he claims, is not cost reduction policies such as those that Reynolds recommends but to change the social conditions that are known to contribute greatly to violent crimes. We must break the cycle of poverty, strengthen the family, improve employment opportunities, and improve education for poor children. These are long-term solutions that even he admits are difficult to achieve. In the short run Eitzen recommends imprisoning the predatory sociopaths but otherwise imprisoning fewer criminals, enforcing stringent gun control laws and keeping guns away from juveniles, making laws more fair, rehabilitating criminals, and legalizing drugs.

YES

Morgan O. Reynolds

CRIME PAYS, BUT SO DOES IMPRISONMENT

America is burdened by an appalling amount of crime. Even though the crime rate is not soaring as it did during the 1960s and 1970s, we still have more crimes per capita than any other developed country.

- Every year nearly 6 million people are victims of violent crimes—murder, rape, robbery or assault.
- Another 29 million Americans each year are victims of property crimes— arson, burglary and larceny-theft.
- There is a murder every 25 minutes, a rape every six minutes, a robbery every minute and an aggravated assault every 35 seconds.
- There is a motor vehicle theft every 22 seconds, a burglary every ten seconds, and a larceny-theft every four seconds.

Although the number of crimes reported to the police each year has leveled off somewhat in the 1980s, our crime rate today is still enormously high— 411 percent higher, for example, than it was in 1960.

Why is there so much crime?

THE EXPECTED PUNISHMENT FOR COMMITTING A CRIME

The economic theory of crime is a relatively new field of social science. According to this theory, most crimes are not irrational acts. Instead, crimes are freely committed by people who compare the expected benefits of crime with the expected costs. The reason we have so much crime is that, for many people, the benefits outweigh the costs. For some people, a criminal career is more attractive than their other career options. Put another way, the reason we have so much crime is that crime pays.

Because criminals and potential criminals rarely have accurate information about the probabilities of arrest, conviction and imprisonment, a great deal of uncertainty is involved in the personal assessment of the expected punishment from committing crimes. Individuals differ in skill and intellect. The more skillful and more intelligent criminals have better odds of commit-

From Morgan O. Reynolds, "Crime Pays, But So Does Imprisonment," *Journal of Social, Political, and Economic Studies* (Fall 1990). Copyright © 1990 by The Council for Social and Economic Studies, P.O. Box 35070, NW Washington, DC 20043. Reprinted by permission. Notes omitted.

ting successful crimes. Some people overestimate their probability of success, while others underestimate theirs.

Despite the element of subjectivity, the economic theory of crime makes one clear prediction: Crime will increase if the expected cost of crime to criminals declines. This is true for "crimes of passion" as well as economic crimes such as burglary or auto theft. The less costly crime becomes, the more often people fail to control their passions.

The economic theory of crime is consistent with public opinion, and with the perceptions of potential criminals. It is supported by considerable statistical research. According to the theory, the amount of crime is inversely related to expected punishment. What follows is a brief summary of the punishment criminals can expect.

EXPECTED TIME IN PRISON

What is the expected punishment for committing major types of serious crime in the United States today?... [T]he expected punishment is shockingly low.

- Even for committing the most serious crime—murder—an individual can expect to spend only 2.3 years in prison.
- On the average, an individual who commits an act of burglary can expect to spend only 7.1 days in prison.
- Someone considering an auto theft can expect to spend only 6.3 days in prison.

THE DECLINE IN EXPECTED IMPRISONMENT AND THE RISE IN CRIME

... On the average, those crimes with the longest expected prison terms (murder, rape, robbery and assault) are the crimes

Figure 1

Crime and Punishment

*Median prison sentence for all serious crimes, weighted by probabilities of arrest, prosecution, conviction, and imprisonment.

least frequently committed, comprising only about 10 percent of all serious crime. The remaining 90 percent carry an expected prison term of only a few days. When expected punishment is weighted by the frequency of types of crimes, the picture is even more shocking: On the average, a perpetrator of a serious crime in the United States can expect to spend about eight days in prison.... [T]his overall expectation has changed over time.

- Since the early 1950s, the expected punishment for committing a serious crime in the United States (measured in terms of expected time in prison) has been reduced by two-thirds.

- Over the same period, the total number of serious crimes committed has increased sevenfold.

THE "PRICES" WE CHARGE FOR CRIME

It is virtually impossible to prevent people from committing crimes. The most that the criminal justice system can do is impose punishment after the crime has been committed. People are largely free to commit almost any crime they choose. What the criminal justice system does is construct a list of prices (expected punishments) for various criminal acts. People commit crimes so long as they are willing to pay the prices society charges, just as many of us might risk parking or speeding tickets.

Viewed in this way, the expected prison sentences . . . are the prices we charge for various crimes. Thus, the price of murder is about 2.3 years in prison; the price of burglary is 7.7 days; the price for stealing a car is 4.2 days. Since these prices are so low, it is small wonder so many people are willing to pay them.

CALCULATING THE EXPECTED PUNISHMENT FOR CRIME

Five adverse events must occur before a criminal actually ends up in prison. The criminal must be arrested, indicted, prosecuted, convicted and sent to prison. As a result, the expected punishment for crime depends upon a number of probabilities: The probability of being arrested, given that a crime is committed; the probability of being prosecuted, given an arrest; the probability of conviction, given prosecution; and the probability of being sent to prison, given a conviction. As Table 1 shows, the overall probability of being punished is the result of multiplying four probabilities.

Even if each of the separate probabilities is reasonably high, their product can be quite low. For example, suppose that each of these probabilities were 0.5. That is, one-half of crimes result in an arrest, one-half of arrests lead to prosecution, one-half of prosecutions lead to a conviction, and one-half of convictions lead to a prison term. In this case, the overall probability that a criminal will spend time in prison is only 6.25 percent.

Table 1 also depicts recent probabilities in the case of burglary. Note that burglars who are sent to prison stay there for about 17 months, on the average. . . . But someone considering an act of burglary will surely be influenced by the fact that the probability of being arrested is only 14 percent. Although the probabilities of prosecution and conviction following an arrest are high, the criminal's probability of going to prison is less than one in three after being convicted. When all factors are taken into account (including the probability that the crime will never be reported), the overall probability that a burglar will end up in prison is less than one percent. The expected punishment prior to committing the crime is only 7.1 days.

PROBABILITY OF ARREST

. . . The striking fact . . . is the degree to which arrest rates have declined over the past 40 years, even for the most serious crimes. For example:

- Since 1950, the probability of being arrested after committing a murder has fallen by 25 percent.
- The probability of arrest for rapists has fallen 35 percent, for robbers 42 percent and for burglars 53 percent.

On the average, during the 1980s, only about 21 percent of all crimes in the United States were cleared by arrest.

Table 1

Calculating the Expected Punishment for Potential Criminals

Expected Time in Prison	=	Probability of arrest	×	Probability of prosecution, given arrest
	×	Probability of conviction, given prosecution	×	Probability of imprisonment, given conviction
	×	median sentence		

Example: Expected punishment for burglary

Expected Time in Prison	=	14% (Probability of arrest)	×	88% (Probability of prosecution, given arrest)
	×	81% (Probability of conviction, given prosecution)	×	28% (Probability of imprisonment, given conviction)
	×	1/2 (Adjustment for unreported crimes)*	×	17 months (median sentence)
	=	7.1 days		

* Approximately one-half of all burglaries are not reported to the police. Law enforcement agencies "clear" (or solve) an offense when at least one person is arrested, charged with the offense, and turned over for prosecution.

In Japan, by contrast, the clearance-by-arrest rate is 50 percent. Moreover, Japan with a population of 122 million has fewer murders each year than New York City with a population of seven million.

PROBABILITY OF PROSECUTION, CONVICTION AND IMPRISONMENT

Although there are 13 million arrests each year in the United States, including 2.8 million for serious (Index) crimes, annual admissions to prison only topped 200,000 in 1986. In other words, only eight of every 100 arrests for Index crimes results in imprisonment after defense attorneys, prosecutors and courts complete their work.

OVERALL PROBABILITY OF GOING TO PRISON

A criminal's overall probability of imprisonment has fallen dramatically since 1950....

- Since 1950, the percent of crimes resulting in a prison sentence has declined by at least 60 percent for every major category of crime.

- This includes a 60 percent drop for murder, a 79 percent decrease for rape, an 83 percent reduction for robbery and a 94 percent plunge for auto theft.

UNREPORTED CRIMES

Based on the number of crimes reported to the police, 1.66 percent of all serious crimes are punished by imprisonment; therefore 98.34 percent of serious crimes are not. According to the National Crime Survey, however, only 37 percent of serious crimes are actually reported. If there are two unreported crimes for every one reported, then the overall probability of going to prison for the commission of a serious crime falls to about 0.61 percent (.37 × 1.66%). This amounts to one prison term for every 164 felonies committed.

A POSSIBLE EXPLANATION: THE ROLE OF THE WARREN COURT

The main factor in the decline in expected punishment over the last three decades was a virtual collapse in the probability of imprisonment. Why? We cannot point to a shrinkage in law enforcement personnel as an explanation.... [T]he number of full-time police employees has risen steadily over the past three decades. Further, total employment in the criminal justice sector increased from 600,000 in 1965 to nearly 1.5 million in 1986. Government spending on the criminal justice sector doubled as a share of GNP, rising from less than 0.6 percent to nearly 1.2 percent. During the same period, private employment in detective and protection services grew rapidly, reaching half a million persons by the end of 1989. Apparently, more people now produce less justice.

The 1960s was a turbulent decade—the Vietnam War, the counterculture, urban riots. But one policy change that lasted well into the 1970s and 1980s was the change in the criminal justice system caused by the Supreme Court. Influenced by sociologists and other intellectuals, there was a growing reluctance to apprehend and punish criminals during the 1960s. In particular, 1961 brought the first landmark decision of the U.S. Supreme Court expanding the rights of criminal defendants and making it more costly for police and prosecutors to obtain criminal convictions.

Mapp v. Ohio (1961) declared that illegally obtained evidence could not be admitted in any state criminal prosecution, imposing the so-called "exclusionary rule" on all state judicial systems. A series of related decisions followed: *Gideon v. Wainwright* (1963) required taxpayer-funded counsel for defendants; *Escobedo v. Illinois* (1964) and *Malloy v. Hogan* (1964) expanded privileges against self-incrimination, thereby impeding interrogation by the police; and *Miranda v. Arizona* (1966) went further and made confessions, even if voluntary, inadmissible as evidence unless the suspect had been advised of certain rights.

The enforcement system was transformed by these decisions. Under the exclusionary rule, according to Justice Cardozo, "The criminal is to go free because the constable has blundered." Justice White, dissenting in the *Miranda* case, warned that the decision would have "a corrosive effect on the criminal laws as an effective device to prevent crime." It appears that the "pursuit of perfect justice," as Judge Macklin put it, changed the rules and increased the time and effort required to apprehend, convict and punish the guilty....

THE COST OF CRIME DETERRENCE

If America is to succeed in lowering the crime rate to, say, the level that prevailed in the 1950s, we must create at least as much crime deterrence as existed in the 1950s. For example, [there are] three ways of raising the expected prison sentence for burglary to its 1950 level. Since the probabilities of prosecution and conviction, given an arrest, are already high, the options are:

- Increase the proportion of burglaries cleared by arrest from 14 to 42 percent; or
- Increase the percent of convicted burglars sent to prison from 28 to 84 percent; or
- Increase the median prison sentence for burglars from 17 to 51 months.

All three alternatives are expensive. A higher arrest rate requires that more money be spent on criminal investigation. A higher sentencing rate requires more court and litigation costs. All three alternatives require more prison space. Unless prison space can be expanded, little else in the way of deterrence will be of much value.

America is in the midst of the biggest prison building boom in its history. On December 30, 1989, prisons held 673,565 convicts, up from 438,830 prisoners at the beginning of 1984 and at 110 percent of design capacity. In 1988 the system added 42,967 inmates, or enough to fill 86 new 500-bed prisons.

- Today, one out of every 364 Americans is in prison—not jail, probation or parole but in prison.
- With an additional 296,000 in local jails, 362,000 on parole and 2.4 million on probation, one out of every 69 Americans is under the supervision of the corrections establishment, or one of every 52 adults.

At an annual cost exceeding $20,000 per prisoner, the total prison tab is more than $15 billion a year. That cost will surely rise. Thirty-five states are under court orders to relieve prison overcrowding and others face litigation. To increase capacity, more than 100 new state and federal prisons currently are under construction around the country. California alone is spending $3.5 billion on new prison beds and has added 21,000 beds since 1984. State governments spent some $9 billion in 1989 on new prisons. In most cases, the construction cost per prison bed exceeds $50,000.

HOW TO REDUCE PRISON COSTS

Much could be done to reduce the high costs of constructing and operating prisons. The most promising ways to reduce taxpayer costs exploit private sector competition and efficiency in constructing and operating prisons and employing prisoners. Contracting out construction and remodeling is a proven economizer. Short of full privatization, government-operated correctional facilities should be corporatized and required to operate like private businesses, with profit and loss statements. Even within the existing system, economies are possible. What follows is a brief summary of ways to economize.

OPPORTUNITIES FOR REDUCING COSTS WITHIN THE PUBLIC SECTOR

Better Management Practices. Although entrepreneurship in the public sector is rare, opportunities for innovation in prison construction abound. For example:

- Florida expanded an existing facility by 336 beds for only $16,000 per cell.
- South Carolina used inmate labor to reduce construction costs by an estimated 50 percent with no quality loss and some delay.
- New York City has begun using renovated troop barges and a ferry boat for detention facilities.

Early Release of Elderly Prisoners. Although the recidivism rate is about 22 percent for prisoners age 18 to 24, among prisoners over 45 years old the recidivism rate is only 2.1 percent. Nationwide, there are at least 20,000 inmates over the age of 55. Moreover, the average maintenance cost of an elderly prisoner is about $69,000—three times the cost of a younger prisoner. Early release of elderly prisoners to make room for younger criminals makes sense and would improve crime deterrence.

Boot Camp Therapy for Young Prisoners. Called "shock incarceration" by federal drug Czar William Bennett, boot camp therapy as an alternative to prison for youngsters (not yet hardened criminals) is being used in Georgia, Alabama, Florida, Louisiana, Mississippi, New York, Oklahoma, South Carolina and Texas. Costs are lower, although the recidivism rate is about the same as for the prison system as a whole.

Electronic Ankle Bracelets. The cost of punishment would be greatly reduced if ways were found of punishing criminals without imprisonment. Few people would deny that imprisonment is necessary and desirable for violent crimes such as homicide, rape, robbery and assault. But less than half of U.S. prisoners have been incarcerated for such crimes. A mid-1980s survey found that:

- One-third of the prisoners were imprisoned for property offenses and another 20 percent for crimes against public order (including drug offenses).
- In Arkansas, nonviolent offenders outnumbered violent ones by a ratio of three to one.
- In Mississippi, Kentucky, Missouri and Wyoming the ratio was two to one.

A recent alternative to imprisonment is the electronic monitoring device that is worn by parolees. Judges can impose conditions of parole, including restrictions on the range and timing of activities, and they can be enforced by monitoring companies....

PRODUCTIVE WORK FOR PRISONERS

A recent survey commissioned by the National Institute of Justice identified more than 70 companies which employ inmates in 16 states in manufacturing, service and light assembly operations. Prisoners work as reservations clerks for TWA and Best Western, sew leisure wear, manufacture water-bed mattresses, and assemble electronic components. PRIDE, a state-sponsored private corporation that runs Florida's 46 prison industries from furniture-making to optical glass grinding, made a $4 million profit in 1987. This work benefits nearly everyone. It enables prisoners to earn wages, acquire skills, and subtly learn individual responsibility and the value of productive labor. It also insures that they can contribute to victim compensation, and to their own and their families' support....

THE COST OF NOT BUILDING PRISONS

Although the cost of building and maintaining prisons is high, the cost of not creating more prisons appears to be much higher. A study by the National Institute of Justice concluded that the "typical" offender let loose in society will engage in a one-man crime wave, creating damage to society more than 17 times as costly than imprisonment. Specifically:

- Sending someone to prison for one year costs the government about $25,000.

- A Rand Corporation survey of 2190 professional criminals found that the average criminal committed 187 to 287 crimes a year, at an average cost per crime of $2,300.

- On the average, then, a professional criminal out of prison costs society $430,000 per year, or $405,000 more than the cost of a year in prison.

The failure to keep offenders in prison once they are there is also a hazard of too little prison space, and early release often leads to much more crime. A Rand Corporation survey of former inmates found that:

- In California, 76 percent were arrested within three years of their release and 60 percent were convicted of new crimes.

- In Texas, 60 percent of former inmates were arrested within three years and 40 percent were reconvicted.

- A survey of 11 states showed that 62.5 percent of all released prisoners were arrested within 3 years, 46.8 percent were reconvicted and 41.1 percent were reincarcerated.

In California, a comparison between ex-convicts and criminals who received probation rather than a prison sentence showed a disheartening rate of failure for both. Each ex-convict committed an estimated 20 crimes. Each probationer committed 25 crimes.

A Bureau of Justice Statistics study of 22 states found that 69 percent of young adults (ages 17 to 22) released from prison in 1978 were arrested within six years— each committing an average of 13 new crimes.

CONCLUSION

While crime continues on the high plateau, there are grounds for optimism. The number of young males began to decline in the 1980s and will continue to do so through the 1990s. Further, the odds of imprisonment for a serious offense increased in the 1980s as legislators responded to the public's "get tough" attitude. Yet we remained plagued with crime rates (per capita) triple those of the 1950s.

What can be done to build on this relatively promising recent trend? At a minimum the analysis in this report suggests three things. First, the U.S. Supreme Court should continue to reestablish the rule of law by restricting application of the exclusionary rule and other expansions of criminal privileges inherited from the Warren Court. Second, the public sector must continue raising the odds of imprisonment toward those of the 1950s in order to improve personal security. Deterrence of criminals implies building prisons and reducing prison costs by privatization. Third, the laws hampering productive employment of prisoners must be relaxed to take full advantage of the benefits of privatization.

ACKNOWLEDGMENT

My thanks to Dr. John Goodman, President, National Center for Policy Analysis, Dallas, Texas, for his help on this paper and his permission to reprint material from NCPA Report No. 149. Author.

NO
D. Stanley Eitzen

VIOLENT CRIME: MYTHS, FACTS, AND SOLUTIONS

My remarks are limited to violent street crimes (assault, robbery, rape, and murder). We should not forget that there are other types of violent crimes that are just as violent and actually greater in magnitude than street crimes: corporate, political, organized, and white collar. But that is another subject for another time. Our attention this morning is on violent street crime, which has made our cities unsafe and our citizens extremely fearful. What are the facts about violent crime and violent criminals and what do we, as a society, do about them?

I am going to critique the prevailing thought about violent crime and its control because our perceptions about violent crime and much of what our government officials do about it is wrong. My discipline—sociology—knows a lot about crime but what we know does not seem to affect public perceptions and public policies. Not all of the answers, however, are always crystal clear. There are disagreements among reasonable and thoughtful people, coming from different theoretical and ideological perspectives. You may, difficult as it seems to me, actually disagree with my analysis. That's all right. The key is for us to address this serious problem, determine the facts, engage in dialogue, and then work toward logical and just solutions.

What do criminologists know about violent crime? Much of what we know is counter intuitive; it flies in the face of the public's understanding. So, let me begin with some demythologizing.

Myth 1: As a Christian nation with high moral principles, we rank relatively low in the amount of violent crime. Compared with the other industrialized nations of the world, we rank number one in belief in God, "the importance of God in our lives," and church attendance. We also rank first in murder rates, robbery rates, and rape rates. Take homicide, for example: the U.S. rate of 10 per 100,000 is three times that of Finland, five times that of Canada, and nine times greater than found in Norway, the Netherlands, Germany, and Great Britain. In 1992, for example, Chicago, a city about one-fifth the population

From D. Stanley Eitzen, "Violent Crime: Myths, Facts, and Solutions," *Vital Speeches of the Day* (May 15, 1995). Copyright © 1995 by *Vital Speeches of the Day*. Reprinted by permission.

of the Netherlands had nine times more gun-related deaths than occurred in the Netherlands.

Myth 2: We are in the midst of a crime wave. When it comes to crime rates we are misled by our politicians, and the media. Government data indicate that between 1960 and 1970 crime rates doubled, then continued to climb through the 1970s. From 1970 to 1990 the rates remained about the same. The problem is with violent crime by youth, which has increased dramatically. Despite the rise in violent crime among youth, however, the *overall* violent crime rate actually has decreased in the 1990s.

Our perceptions are affected especially by the media. While crime rates have leveled and slightly declined during the 1990s, the media have given us a different picture. In 1993, for example, the three major networks doubled their crime stories and tripled their coverage of murders. This distortion of reality results, of course, in a general perception that we are in the midst of a crime wave.

Myth 3: Serious violent crime is found throughout the age structure. Crime is mainly a problem of male youths. Violent criminal behaviors peak at age 17 and by age 24 it is one-half the rate. Young males have always posed a special crime problem. There are some differences now, however. Most significant, young males and the gangs to which they often belong now have much greater firepower. Alienated and angry youth once used clubs, knives, brass knuckles, and fists but now they use Uzis, AK47s, and "streetsweepers." The result is that since 1985, the murder rate for 18–24 year-olds has risen 65 percent while the rate for 14–17 year-olds has increased 165 percent.

The frightening demographic fact is that between now and the year 2005, the number of teenagers in the U.S. will grow by 23 percent. During the next ten years, black teenagers will increase by 28 percent and the Hispanic teenage population will grow by about 50 percent. The obvious prediction is that violent crime will increase dramatically over this period.

Myth 4: The most dangerous place in America is in the streets where strangers threaten, hit, stab, or shoot each other. The streets in our urban places are dangerous, as rival gangs fight, and drive-by shootings occur. But, statistically, the most dangerous place is in your own home, or when you are with a boyfriend or girlfriend, family member, or acquaintance.

Myth 5: Violent criminals are born with certain predispositions toward violence. Criminals are not born with a criminal gene. If crime were just a function of biology, then we would expect crime rates to be more or less the same for all social categories, times, and places. In fact, violent crime rates vary considerably by social class, race, unemployment, poverty, geographical place, and other social variables. Research on these variables is the special contribution of sociology to the understanding of criminal behavior.

Let's elaborate on these social variables because these have so much to do with solutions. Here is what we know about these social variables:

1. The more people in poverty, the higher the rate of street crime.

2. The higher the unemployment rate in an area, the higher the crime rate. Sociologist William J. Wilson says that black and white youths at age 11 are equally likely to commit violent crimes

but by their late 20s, blacks are four times more likely to be violent offenders. However, when blacks and whites in their late 20s are employed, they differ hardly at all in violent behavior.

3. The greater the racial segregation in an area, the higher the crime rate. Sociologist Doug Massey argues that urban poverty and urban crime are the consequences of extremely high levels of black residential segregation and racial discrimination. Massey says,

"Take a group of people, segregate them, cut off their capital and guess what? The neighborhoods go downhill. There's no other outcome possible."

As these neighborhoods go downhill and economic opportunities evaporate, crime rates go up.

4. The greater the family instability, the higher the probability of crimes by juveniles. Research is sketchy, but it appears that the following conditions are related to delinquent behaviors: (a) intense parental conflict; (b) lack of parental supervision; (c) parental neglect and abuse; and (d) failure of parents to discipline their children.

5. The greater the inequality in a neighborhood, city, region, or society, the higher the crime rate. In other words, the greater the disparities between rich and poor, the greater the probability of crime. Of all the industrialized nations, the U.S. has the greatest degree of inequality. For example, one percent of Americans own 40 percent of all the wealth. At the other extreme, $14\frac{1}{2}$ percent of all Americans live below the poverty line and 5 percent of all Americans live below *one-half* of the poverty line.

When these social variables converge, they interact to increase crime rates. Thus, there is a relatively high probability of

criminal behavior—violent criminal behavior—among young, black, impoverished males in inner cities where poverty, unemployment, and racial segregation are concentrated. There are about 5 million of these high-risk young men. In addition, we have other problem people. What do we do? How do we create a safer America?

To oversimplify a difficult and contentious debate, there are two answers —the conservative and progressive answers. The conservative answer has been to get tough with criminals. This involves mandatory sentences, longer sentences, putting more people in prison, and greater use of the death penalty. This strategy has accelerated with laws such as "three strikes and you're out (actually in)," and the passage of expensive prison building programs to house the new prisoners.

In my view, this approach is wrongheaded. Of course, some individuals must be put in prison to protect the members of society. Our policies, however, indiscriminately put too many people in prison at too high a cost. Here are some facts about prisons:

1. Our current incarceration rate is 455 per 100,000 (in 1971 it was 96 per 100,000). The rate in Japan and the Netherlands is one-tenth ours. Currently, there are 1.2 million Americans in prisons and jails (equivalent to the population of Philadelphia).

2. The cost is prohibitive, taking huge amounts of money that could be spent on other programs. It costs about $60,000 to build a prison cell and $20,000 to keep a prisoner for a year. Currently the overall cost of prisons and jails (federal, state, and local) is $29 billion annually. The willingness to spend for punishment reduces money that could be

spent to alleviate other social problems. For example, eight years ago Texas spent $7 dollars on education for every dollar spent on prisons. Now the ratio is 4 to 1. Meanwhile, Texas ranks 37th among the states in per pupil spending.

3. As mentioned earlier, violent crimes tend to occur in the teenage years with a rapid drop off afterwards. Often, for example, imprisonment under "3 strikes and you're out" laws gives life imprisonment to many who are in the twilight of their criminal careers. We, and they, would be better off if we found alternatives to prison for them.

4. Prisons do not rehabilitate. Actually, prisons have the opposite effect. The prison experience tends to increase the likelihood of further criminal behavior. Prisons are overcrowded, mean, gloomy, brutal places that change people, but usually for the worse, not the better. Moreover, prisoners usually believe that their confinement is unjust because of the bias in the criminal justice system toward the poor and racial minorities. Finally, prisoners do not ever pay their debt to society. Rather they are forever stigmatized as "ex-cons" and, therefore, considered unreliable and dangerous by their neighbors, employers, fellow workers, and acquaintances. Also, they are harassed by the police as "likely suspects." The result is that they are often driven into a deviant subculture and eventually caught—about two-thirds are arrested within three years of leaving prison.

Progressives argue that conservative crime control measures are fundamentally flawed because they are "after the fact" solutions. Like a janitor mopping up the floor while the sink continues to overflow; he or she may even redouble the effort with some success but the source of the flooding has not been addressed. If I might mix metaphors here (although keeping with the aquatic theme), the obvious place to begin the attack on crime is *upstream*, before the criminal has been formed and the crimes have been committed.

We must concentrate our efforts on high-risk individuals before they become criminals (in particular, impoverished young inner city males). These prevention proposals take time, are very costly, and out-of-favor politically but they are the only realistic solutions to reduce violent street crime.

The problem with the conservative "after the fact" crime fighting proposals is that while promoting criminal justice, these programs dismantle social justice. Thus, they enhance a criminogenic climate. During the Reagan years, for example, $51 billion dollars were removed from various poverty programs. Now, under the "Contract for America" the Republicans in Congress propose to reduce subsidized housing, to eliminate nutrition programs through WIC (Women, Infants, and Children), to let the states take care of subsidized school lunches, and to eliminate welfare for unmarried mothers under 18 who do not live with their parents or a responsible guardian.

Progressives argue that we abandon these children at our own peril. The current Republican proposals forsake the 26 percent of American children under six who live in poverty including 54 percent of all African American children and 44 percent of all Latino children under the age of six. Will we be safer as these millions of children in poverty grow to physical maturity?

Before I address specific solutions, I want to emphasize that sociologists examine the structural reasons for crime.

This focus on factors outside the individual does not excuse criminal behavior, it tries to understand how certain structural factors *increase* the proportion of people who choose criminal options.

Knowing what we know about crime, the implications for policy are clear. These proposals, as you will note, are easy to suggest but they are very difficult to implement. I will divide my proposals into immediate actions to deal with crime now and long-term preventive measure:

Measures to protect society immediately:

1. The first step is to protect society from predatory sociopaths. This does not mean imprisoning more people. We should, rather, only imprison the truly dangerous. The criminal law should be redrawn so that the list of crimes reflects the real dangers that individuals pose to society. Since prison does more harm than good, we should provide reasonable alternatives such as house arrest, half-way houses, boot camps, electronic surveillance, job corps, and drug/alcohol treatment.

2. We must reduce the number of handguns and assault weapons by enacting and vigorously enforcing stringent gun controls at the federal level. The United States is an armed camp with 210 million guns in circulation. Jeffrey Reiman has put it this way:

> "Trying to fight crime while allowing such easy access to guns is like trying to teach a child to walk and tripping him each time he stands up. In its most charitable light, it is hypocrisy. Less charitably, it is complicity in murder."

3. We must make a special effort to get guns out of the hands of juveniles. Research by James Wright and his colleagues at Tulane University found that juveniles are much more likely to have guns for protection than for status and power. They suggest that we must restore order in the inner cities so that fewer young people do not feel the need to provide their own protection. They argue that a perceived sense of security by youth can be accomplished if there is a greater emphasis on community policing, more cooperation between police departments and inner city residents, and greater investment by businesses, banks, and cities in the inner city.

4. We must reinvent the criminal justice system so that it commands the respect of youth and adults. The obvious unfairness by race and social class must be addressed. Some laws are unfair. For example, the federal law requires a five-year, no-parole sentence for possession of five grams of crack cocaine, worth about $400. However, it takes 100 times as much powder cocaine—500 grams, worth $10,000—and a selling conviction to get the same sentence. Is this fair? Of course not. Is it racist? It is racist since crack is primarily used by African Americans while powder cocaine is more likely used by whites. There are also differences by race and social class in arrest patterns, plea bargain arrangements, sentencing, parole, and imposition of the death penalty. These differences provide convincing evidence that the poor and racial minorities are discriminated against in the criminal justice system. As long as the criminal justice system is perceived as unfair by the disadvantaged, that system will not exert any moral authority over them.

5. We must rehabilitate as many criminals as possible. Prisons should be more humane. Prisoners should leave prison with vocational skills useful in the real world. Prisoners should leave

prison literate and with a high school degree. And, society should formally adopt the concept of "forgiveness" saying to ex-prisoners, in effect, you have been punished for your crime, we want you to begin a new life with a "clean" record.

6. We must legalize the production and sale of "illicit drugs" and treat addiction as a medical problem rather than a criminal problem. If drugs were legalized or decriminalized, crimes would be reduced in several ways: (a) By eliminating drug use as a criminal problem, we would have 1.12 million *fewer* arrests each year. (b) There would be many *fewer* prisoners (currently about 60 percent of all federal prisoners and 25 percent of all state prisoners are incarcerated for drug offenses). (c) Money now spent on the drug war ($31 billion annually, not counting prison construction) could be spent for other crime control programs such as police patrols, treatment of drug users, and job programs. (d) Drugs could be regulated and taxed, generating revenues of about $5 billion a year. (e) It would end the illicit drug trade that provides tremendous profits to organized crime, violent gangs, and other traffickers. (f) It would eliminate considerable corruption of the police and other authorities. (g) There would be many fewer homicides. Somewhere between one-fourth and one-half of the killings in the inner cities are drug-related. (h) The lower cost of purchasing drugs reduces the need to commit crimes to pay for drug habits.

Long-term preventive measures to reduce violent crime:

1. The link between poverty and street crime is indisputable. In the long run, reducing poverty will be the most effective crime fighting tool. Thus, as a society, we need to intensify our efforts to break the cycle of poverty.

This means providing a universal and comprehensive health care system, low-cost housing, job training, and decent compensation for work. There must be pay equity for women. And, there must be an unwavering commitment to eradicate institutional sexism and racism. Among other benefits, such a strategy will strengthen families and give children resources, positive role models, and hope.

2. Families must be strengthened. Single-parent families and the working poor need subsidized child care, flexible work schedules, and leave for maternity and family emergencies at a reasonable proportion of their wages. Adolescent parents need the resources to stay in school. They need job training. We need to increase the commitment to family planning. This means providing contraceptives and birth control counseling to adolescents. This means using federal funds to pay for legal abortions when they are requested by poor women.

3. There must be a societal commitment to full and decent employment. Meaningful work at decent pay integrates individuals into society. It is a source of positive identity. Employed parents are respected by their children. Good paying jobs provide hope for the future. They also are essential to keep families together.

4. There must be a societal commitment to education. This requires two different programs. The first is to help at-risk children, beginning at an early age. As it is now, when poor children start school, they are already behind. As Sylvia Ann Hewlett has said:

> "At age five, poor children are often less alert, less curious, and less effective at interacting with their peers than are more privileged youngsters."

This means that they are doomed to be underachievers. To overcome this we need intervention programs that prepare children for school. Research shows that Head Start and other programs can raise IQ scores significantly. There are two problems with Head Start, however. First, the current funding only covers 40 percent of eligible youngsters. And second, the positive effects from the Head Start program are sometimes short-lived because the children then attend schools that are poorly staffed, overcrowded, and ill-equipped.

This brings us to the second education program to help at-risk children. The government must equalize the resources of school districts, rather than the current situation where the wealth of school districts determines the amount spent per pupil. Actually, equalization is not the answer. I believe that there should be special commitment to invest *extra* resources in at-risk children. If we do, we will have a safer society in the long run.

These proposals seem laughable in the current political climate, where politicians—Republicans *and* Democrats—try to outdo each other in their toughness on crime and their disdain for preven-

tive programs. They are wrong, however, and society is going to pay in higher crime rates in the future. I am convinced that the political agenda of the conservatives is absolutely heading us in the wrong direction—toward more violent crime rather than less.

The proposals that I have suggested are based on what we sociologists know about crime. They should be taken seriously, but they are not. The proposals are also based on the assumption that if we can give at-risk young people hope, they will become a part of the community rather than alienated from it. My premise is this: Everyone needs a dream. Without a dream, we become apathetic. Without a dream, we become fatalistic. Without a dream, and the hope of attaining it, society becomes our enemy. Many young people act in antisocial ways because they have lost their dream. These troubled and troublesome people are society's creations because we have not given them the opportunity to achieve their dreams —instead society has structured the situation so that they will fail. Until they feel that they have a stake in society, they will fail, and so will we.

POSTSCRIPT

Is Incapacitation the Answer to the Crime Problem?

Many have complained that America has become lax on crime. Reynolds backs this statement up with statistics showing the dramatic drop in the average expected number of days in prison for serious crimes from 22.5 days in 1954 to 5.5 days in 1974. Since the number of crimes has increased more than fourfold during the time that expected days in prison shrank a similar amount, it is easy to assume that the declining punishment produced the increasing crime. During this period, however, many other changes occurred in the United States that would affect the crime rate, so the relationship of imprisonment to crime reduction may not be as clear as Reynolds's statistics suggest. The real debate is whether or not current policies overemphasize imprisonment and underemphasize alternative crime reduction strategies, as Eitzen maintains. But are Eitzen's proposals of breaking the cycle of poverty, strengthening the family, improving employment opportunities and wages, and improving education for the poor feasible? Society is already trying to do these things, but success is elusive. Some of Eitzen's other suggestions, such as legalizing drugs and imposing tighter bans on guns, will confront tough opposition. Is it realistic, therefore, to emphasize imprisonment?

In *Crime in America* (Simon & Schuster, 1971), former attorney general Ramsey Clark takes a position that is in many ways similar to Eitzen's. Hans Zeisel, in *The Limits of Law Enforcement* (University of Chicago Press, 1983), argues that the criminal justice system can do little to effectively reduce crime. He emphasizes increasing protection from crime and attacking its root causes, which he believes lie in the conditions of poverty. This approach is also advocated by Elliott Currie, in *Crime and Punishment in America* (Henry Holt, 1998), who points out that America has tried the punishment route and it has failed. See also John Irwin and James Austin, *It Is About Time: America's Imprisonment Binge*, 2d ed. (Wadsworth, 1997). The opposite view on the effectiveness of imprisonment is presented by Franklin E. Zimring in *Incapacitation: Penal Confinement and the Restraint of Crime* (Oxford University Press, 1995). For debates on this and other issues about imprisonment, see Charles P. Cozic, *America's Prisons: Opposing Viewpoints* (Greenhaven Press, 1997). The importance of the community in crime control is brought out by Robert J. Bursik, Jr., and Harold G. Grasmick in *Neighborhoods and Crime: The Dimensions of Effective Community Control* (Free Press, 1993). In a similar vein, Robert J. Sampson and John H. Laub show the importance of informal social control at home and at school in restraining juvenile delinquency in *Crime in the Making: Pathways and Turning Points Through Life* (Harvard University

Press, 1993). On the other side, Andrew Von Hirsch's *Doing Justice* (Hill & Wang, 1976) is critical of Eitzen's philosophy, and Mark Tunick provides a defense of the use of punishment for retribution in *Punishment: Theory and Practice* (University of California Press, 1992).

The issue of deterrence is hotly debated by Ernest van den Haag and John P. Conrad in their book on the ultimate in deterrence punishment, *The Death Penalty: A Debate* (Plenum Press, 1983). Graeme Newman presents an extreme position on punishment—advocating electric shocks and whippings—in *Just and Painful: A Case for the Corporal Punishment of Criminals* (Macmillan, 1983). A history of punishment choices other than prison is presented in *Alternatives to Prison: Punishment, Custody and the Community* (Sage Publications, 1990). Norval Morris and Michael Tonry advocate establishing a range of alternatives to prison in *Between Prison and Probation: Intermediate Punishments in a Rational Sentencing System* (Oxford University Press, 1993). Ulla V. Bondeson analyzes probation and other alternatives to imprisonment in *Alternatives to Imprisonment: Intentions and Reality* (Westview Press, 1994). She finds that lenient treatments produce lower recidivism rates. For a thorough and historical examination of parole, see Jonathan Simon, *Poor Discipline: Parole and the Social Control of the Underclass, 1890–1990* (University of Chicago Press, 1993). Many observers are appalled by the conditions in current American prisons. Nils Christie, a Norwegian criminologist, severely criticizes American prisons in *Crime Control as Industry: Towards Gulags, Western Style* (Routledge, 1993). Human Rights Watch has produced a report that is highly critical of the widespread abuse of human rights, which its investigations found in American prisons. Wilbert Rideau and Ron Wikberg's *Life Sentences: Rage and Survival Behind Bars* (Random House, 1992) presents a sympathetic insider's view of prison life that might soften the tough sentencing view of many.

On the Internet . . .

IISDnet
This site of the International Institute for Sustainable Development, a Canadian organization, presents information and links regarding sustainable development and society.
http://iisd1.iisd.ca/

SocioSite: Sociological Subject Areas
This large sociological site from the University of Amsterdam provides many discussions and references of interest to students regarding the environment.
http://www.pscw.uva.nl/sociosite/TOPICS/

United Nations Environment Program (UNEP)
The UNEP offers links to environmental topics of critical concern to sociologists. The site will direct you to useful databases and global resource information.
http://www.unep.ch/

William Davidson Institute
The William Davidson Institute at the University of Michigan Business School is dedicated to the understanding and promotion of economic transition. Consult this site for discussions of topics related to the changing global economy and the effects of globalization on society.
http://www.wdi.bus.umich.edu/

Worldwatch Institute
The Worldwatch Institute is dedicated to fostering the evolution of an environmentally sustainable society in which human needs are met without threatening the health of the natural environment. This site provides access to *World Watch Magazine* and *State of the World 1998.*
http://www.worldwatch.org/worldwatch/index.html

WWW Virtual Library: Demography and Population Studies
This is a definitive guide to demography and population studies. A multitude of important links to information about global poverty and hunger can be found at this site.
http://coombs.anu.edu.au/ResFacilities/DemographyPage.html

PART 6

The Future: Population/ Environment/Society

Can a world with limited resources support an unlimited population? This question has taken on new dimensions as we approach the start of a new century. Technology has increased enormously in the last 100 years, as have worldwide population growth and new forms of pollution that threaten to undermine the world's fragile ecological support system. Will technology itself be the key to controlling or accommodating an increased population growth along with the resulting increase in waste production? All nations have a stake in the health of the planet and the world economy. Is America in a political and economic position to meet these global challenges?

■ Does Population Growth Threaten Humanity?

■ Are Standards of Living in the United States Improving?

ISSUE 19

Does Population Growth Threaten Humanity?

YES: Lester Brown, from "Food Scarcity: An Environmental Wakeup Call," *The Futurist* (January–February 1998)

NO: Julian L. Simon, from "The State of Humanity: Steadily Improving," *Cato Policy Report* (September/October 1995)

ISSUE SUMMARY

YES: Lester Brown, president of the Worldwatch Institute, argues that the environment is deteriorating and that nature's limits are being exceeded due to population growth.

NO: Julian L. Simon, a professor of economics and business administration, asserts that "all aspects of material human welfare are improving in the aggregate," so population and economic growth are benefiting, not threatening, humanity.

Much of the literature on socioeconomic development in the 1960s was premised on the assumption of inevitable material progress for all. It largely ignored the impacts of development on the environment and presumed that the availability of raw materials would not be a problem. The belief was that all societies would get richer because all societies were investing in new equipment and technologies that would increase productivity and wealth. Theorists recognized that some poor countries were having trouble developing, but they blamed those problems on the deficiencies of the values and attitudes of those countries and on inefficient organizations.

Nevertheless, progress was thought possible even in the least developed countries. If certain social and psychological defects could be overcome by a modernizing elite, and if 10 percent of the gross national product could be devoted to capital formation for at least three decades, then poor countries would take off into self-sustained growth, just as industrial societies had done decades earlier. See Walt W. Rostow's *The Stages of Economic Growth* (Cambridge University Press, 1960) for a review of this. After take-off, growth would be self-sustaining and would continue for the foreseeable future.

In the late 1960s and early 1970s an intellectual revolution occurred. Environmentalists had criticized the growth paradigm throughout the 1960s, but they were not taken very seriously at first. By the end of the 1960s, however, marine scientist Rachel Carson's book *Silent Spring* (Alfred A. Knopf, 1962) had worked its way into the public's consciousness. Carson's book traced the noticeable loss of birds to the use of pesticides. Her book made the middle and upper classes in the United States realize that pollution affected complex ecological systems in ways that put even the wealthy at risk.

In 1968 Paul Ehrlich, a professor of population studies, published *The Population Bomb* (Ballantine Books), which stated that overpopulation was the major problem facing mankind. This meant that population had to be controlled or the human race might cause the collapse of the global ecosystem and its own destruction. Ehrlich explained why he thought the death of the world was imminent:

> Because the human population of the planet is about five times too large, and we're managing to support all these people—at today's level of misery—only by spending our capital, burning our fossil fuels, dispersing our mineral resources and turning our fresh water into salt water. We have not only overpopulated but overstretched our environment. We are poisoning the ecological systems of the earth—systems upon which we are ultimately dependent for all of our food, for all of our oxygen and for all of our waste disposal.

In 1973 *The Limits to Growth* (Universe) by Donella H. Meadows et al. was published. It presented a dynamic systems computer model for world economic, demographic, and environmental trends. When the computer model projected trends into the future, it predicted that the world would experience ecological collapse and population die-off unless population growth and economic activity were greatly reduced. This study was both attacked and defended, and the debate about the health of the world has been heated ever since.

Let us examine the population growth rates past, present, and future. At about A.D. 0, the world had about one-quarter billion people. It took about 1,650 years to double this number to one-half billion and 200 years to double the world population again to 1 billion by 1850. The next doubling took only about 80 years, and the last doubling took about 45 years (from 2 billion in 1930 to about 4 billion in 1975). The world population may double again to 8 billion sometime between 2010 and 2020. Is population growth and the increased economic activity that it requires diminishing the carrying capacity of the planet and jeopardizing the prospects for future generations?

In the following selections, Lester R. Brown answers this question affirmatively and argues that we need to control population growth and to quickly reverse the dangerous deterioration of the environment that is occurring throughout the world. Julian L. Simon, the major proponent of the optimistic view of further economic development without serious environmental consequences until his death in 1998, argues that the environment is becoming more beneficent for human beings because pollution is decreasing, resources are becoming more available and inexpensive, people are living longer, and population growth has largely positive economic and social impacts.

YES

FOOD SCARCITY: AN ENVIRONMENTAL WAKEUP CALL

The environmental deterioration of the last few decades cannot continue indefinitely without eventually affecting the world economy. Until now, most of the economic effects of environmental damage have been local: the collapse of a fishery here or there from overfishing, the loss of timber exports by a tropical country because of deforestation, or the abandonment of cropland because of soil erosion. But as the scale of environmental damage expands, it threatens to affect the global economy as well.

The consequences of environmental degradation are becoming more clear. We cannot continue to deforest the earth without experiencing more rainfall runoff, accelerated soil erosion, and more destructive flooding. If we continue to discharge excessive amounts of carbon into the atmosphere, we will eventually face economically disruptive climate change. If we continue to overpump the earth's aquifers, we will one day face acute water scarcity.

If we continue to overfish, still more fisheries will collapse. If over-grazing continues, so, too, will the conversion of rangeland into desert. Continuing soil erosion at the current rate will slowly drain the earth of its productivity. If the loss of plant and animal species continues at the rate of recent decades, we will one day face ecosystem collapse.

Everyone agrees that these trends cannot continue indefinitely, but will they stop because we finally do what we know we should do, or because the economic expansion that is causing environmental decline begins to be disrupted?

AGRICULTURE: THE MISSING LINK

The food system is likely to be the sector through which environmental deterioration eventually translates into economic decline. This should not come as a surprise. Archaeological evidence indicates that agriculture has often been the link between environmental deterioration and economic decline. The decline of the early Mesopotamian civilization was tied to the waterlogging and salting of its irrigated land. Soil erosion converted into desert the

From Lester Brown, "Food Scarcity: An Environmental Wakeup Call," *The Futurist* (January–February 1998). Copyright © 1998 by The World Future Society. Reprinted by permission of The World Future Society, 7910 Woodmont Avenue, Bethesda, MD 20814. http://www.wfs.org/wfs

fertile wheatlands of North Africa that once supplied the Roman Empire with grain.

Rising grain prices will be the first global economic indicator to tell us that we are on an economic and demographic path that is environmentally unsustainable. Unimpeded environmental damage will seriously impair the capacity of fishers and farmers to keep up with the growth in demand, leading to rising food prices. The social consequences of rising grain prices will become unacceptable to more and more people, leading to political instability. What begins as environmental degradation eventually translates into political instability.

A doubling of grain prices, such as occurred briefly for wheat and corn in early 1996, would not have a major immediate effect on the world's affluent, both because they spend only a small share of their income for food and because their food expenditures are dominated more by processing costs than by commodity prices. But for the 1.3 billion in the world who live on a dollar a day or less, a prolonged period of higher grain prices would quickly become life-threatening.

Heads of households unable to buy enough food to keep their families alive would hold their governments responsible and take to the streets. The resulting bread or rice riots could disrupt economic activity in many countries. If the world could not get inflated food prices back down to traditional levels, this could negatively affect the earnings of multinational corporations, the performance of stock markets, and the stability of the international monetary system. In a world economy more integrated than ever before, the problems of the poor would then become the problems of the rich.

The consequences of environmental abuse that scientists have warned about can be seen everywhere:

- In the European Union, the allowable fish catch has had to be reduced by 20% or more in an effort to avert the collapse of the region's fisheries.

- In Saudi Arabia, overreliance on a fossil aquifer to expand grain production contributed to an abrupt 62% drop in the grain harvest between 1994 and 1996.

- The soil degradation and resulting cropland abandonment that invariably follows the burning off of the Amazon rain forest for agriculture has helped make Brazil the largest grain importer in the Western Hemisphere.

As the number of such situations multiplies, it becomes more and more difficult to feed a world population that is expanding by 80 million people per year. Even without further environmental degradation, we approach the new millennium with 800 million hungry and malnourished people.

These 800 million are hungry because they are too poor to buy enough food to satisfy their basic nutritional needs. If the price of grain were to double, as it already has for some types of seafood, it could impoverish hundreds of millions more almost overnight. In short, a steep rise in grain prices could impoverish more people than any event in history, including the ill-fated Great Leap Forward in China that starved 30 million people to death between 1959 and 1961.

IN SEARCH OF LAND

As the world's population, now approaching 5.8 billion, continues to expand, both the area of cropland and the amount of irrigation water per person are shrinking, threatening to drop below the amount needed to provide minimal levels of food security.

Over time, farmers have used ingenious methods to expand the area used to produce crops. These include irrigation, terracing, drainage, fallowing, and even, for the Dutch, reclaiming land from the sea. Terracing let farmers cultivate steeply sloping land on a sustainable basis, quite literally enabling them to farm the mountains as well as the plains. Drainage of wetlands opened fertile bottomlands for cultivation. Alternate-year fallowing to accumulate moisture helped farmers extend cropping into semiarid regions.

By the middle of this century, the frontiers of agricultural settlement had largely disappeared, contributing to a dramatic slowdown in the growth in area planted to grain. Between 1950 and 1981, the area in grain increased from 587 million to 732 million hectares, a gain of nearly 25%. After reaching a record high in 1981, the area in grain declined, drooping to 683 million hectares in 1993. It has turned upward since then, increasing to 696 million hectares in 1996 as idled cropland was returned to production and as record grain prices in the spring of 1996 led farmers to shift land out of soybeans and other oilseeds.

While the world grain harvested area expanded from 1950 until it peaked in 1981, the growth was quite slow compared with that of population. As a result, the grainland area per person has been declining steadily since mid-century, shrinking from 0.23 hectares in 1950 to 0.12 hectares in 1996. If grainland gains and losses continue to offset each other in the decades ahead, the area will remain stable at roughly 700 million hectares. But with population projected to grow at some 80 million a year over the next few decades, the amount of cropland available to produce grain will continue to decline, shrinking to 0.08 hectares per person in 2030.

IN SEARCH OF WATER

The world's farmers are also facing water scarcity. The expanding demand for water is pushing beyond the sustainable yield of aquifers in many countries and is draining some of the world's major rivers dry before they reach the sea. As the demand for water for irrigation and for industrial and residential uses continues to expand, the competition between countryside and city for available water supplies intensifies. In some parts of the world, meeting growing urban needs is possible only by diverting water from irrigation.

One of the keys to the near tripling of the world grain harvest from 1950 to 1990 was a 2.5-fold expansion of irrigation, a development that extended agriculture into arid regions with little rainfall, intensified production in low-rainfall areas, and increased dry-season cropping in countries with monsoonal climates. Most of the world's rice and much of its wheat is produced on irrigated land.

A critical irrigation threshold was crossed in 1979. From 1950 until then, irrigation expanded faster than population, increasing the irrigated area per person by nearly one-third. This was closely associated with the worldwide rise in grain production per person of one-third. But since 1979, the growth in irrigation has fallen behind that of population, shrinking the irrigated area per person by some 7%. This trend, now well established, will undoubtedly continue as the demand for water presses ever more tightly against available supplies.

As countries and regions begin to press against the limits of water supplies, the competition between cities and the countryside intensifies. And the cities almost always win. As water is pulled away from agriculture, production often drops, forcing the country to import grain. Importing a ton of grain is, in effect, importing thousands of tons of water. For countries with water shortages, importing grain is the most efficient way to import water. Just as land scarcity has shaped international grain trade patterns historically, water scarcity is now beginning to do the same.

The bottom line is that the world's farmers face a steady shrinkage in both grainland and irrigation water per person. As cropland and irrigation water become ever more scarce, prices of both are likely to rise, pushing grain prices upward.

Aquifer depletion and the future cutbacks in water supplies that will eventually follow may pose a far greater threat to economic progress than most people realize. If aquifer depletion were simply a matter of a few isolated instances, it would be one thing, but it is now in evidence in scores of countries. Among those suffering from extensive aquifer depletion are China, India, and the United States—the three countries that collectively account for about half of the world grain harvest.

THE ONSET OF FOOD SCARCITY

Evidence that the degradation of the earth is leading to food scarcity has been accumulating for many years. The oceanic fish catch, for example, plagued by overfishing and pollution, has grown little after increasing from 19 million tons in 1950 to 89 million tons in 1989. Grainland productivity increased by more than 2% a year from 1950 to 1990, but dropped to scarcely 1% a year from 1990 to 1995—well below the growth in demand.

All the key food-security indicators signal a shift from surplus to scarcity. During the mid-1990s, the United States began using again all the cropland that had been idled under commodity programs in an effort to offset the slower rise in land productivity. Even so, in 1996 world carryover stocks of grain, perhaps the most sensitive indicator of food security, dropped to the lowest level on record—a mere 52 days of consumption. Even with the exceptional harvest of 1996, stocks were rebuilt to only 57 days of consumption, far below the 70 days needed to provide a minimal buffer against a poor harvest. If grain stocks cannot be rebuilt with an outstanding harvest, when can they be?

During the late spring and early summer of 1996, world wheat and corn prices set record highs under pressure from a 1995 harvest reduced by heat waves in the U.S. Corn Belt and from China's emergence as the world's second-largest grain importer. Wheat traded at over $7 a bushel, more than double the price in early 1995. In mid-July, corn traded at an all-time high of $5.54 a bushel, also double the level of a year earlier.

In the summer of 1996, the government of Jordan, suffering from higher prices for imported wheat and a growing fiscal deficit, was forced to eliminate the bread subsidy. The resulting bread riots lasted several days and threatened to bring down the government.

Food scarcity may provide the environmental wakeup call the world has long needed. Rising food prices may indicate the urgency of reversing the trends of environmental degradation before resulting political instability reaches the point where economic progress is no longer possible.

AN UNPRECEDENTED CHALLENGE

Making sure that the next generation has enough food is no longer merely an agricultural matter. Achieving an acceptable balance between food and people depends as much on family planners as on farmers. Decisions made in the ministries of energy that will affect future climate stability may have as much effect on the food security of the next generation as those made in agricultural ministries.

The two most difficult components of the effort to secure future food supplies and build an environmentally sustainable economy are stabilizing population and climate. The former depends on a revolution in human reproductive behavior; the latter, on a restructuring of the global energy economy. Either would thoroughly challenge a single generation, but our generation must attempt both simultaneously. In addition, building an environmentally sustainable economy depends on reversing deforestation, arresting the loss of plant and animal species, and stabilizing fisheries, aquifers, and soils.

In a world where both the seafood catch and the grain harvest per person are declining, it may be time to reassess population policy. For example, some governments, facing a deterioration in their food situation, may have to ask if couples are morally justified in having more than two children, the number needed to replace themselves.

The world has taken one small step in the right direction with the stabilization of population in some 32 countries—all of which, except Japan, are in Europe. These countries, home to some 14% of the world's people, clearly demonstrate that population stabilization is possible.

Stabilizing climate means reducing carbon emissions and, hence, fossil-fuel burning—not an easy undertaking given that 85% of all commercial energy comes from fossil fuels. The outline of a solar/hydrogen economy that is likely to replace the fossil-fuel-based economy of today is beginning to emerge. Both the technology and the economics of harnessing solar and wind energy on a massive scale are beginning to fall into place. Although still small compared with fossil-fuel use, wind-generated electricity is expanding by more than 20% a year, and the use of solar cells is growing almost as fast.

The second major opportunity for reducing carbon emissions is raising the efficiency of energy use. The impressive gains in boosting energy efficiency following the oil price shocks of the 1970s have waned in recent years. Adoption of a carbon tax (offset by a reduction in income taxes) that even partly reflected the costs of air pollution, acid rain, and climate disruption from burning fossil fuels would accelerate investment in solar and wind energy as well as in energy efficiency.

The shift from surplus to scarcity will affect land-use policy. During the last half century, when the world was plagued with farm surpluses and farmers were paid to idle cropland, there seemed little need to worry about the conversion of cropland to nonfarm uses. Cropland was a surplus commodity. But in a world of food scarcity, land use suddenly emerges as a central issue. Already, a group of leading scientists in China has issued a white paper challenging the decision by the Ministry of Heavy Industry to develop an auto-centered transport system, arguing that the country does not have enough land both to provide roads, highways, and parking lots and to feed its people. They argue instead for a state-of-the-art rail passenger system augmented by bicycles.

Perhaps the best model of successful cropland protection is Japan. The determination to protect its riceland with land-use zoning can be seen in the hundreds of small rice fields within the city boundaries of Tokyo. By tenaciously protecting the land needed for rice, Japan remains self-sufficient in staple food.

In addition to protecting cropland from conversion to nonfarm uses, either through zoning or through a stiff tax on conversion, future food security depends on reducing the loss of topsoil from wind and water erosion. In a world facing food scarcity, every ton of topsoil lost from erosion today threatens the food security of the next generation. Here, the United States has emerged as a leader, with its Conservation Reserve Program. Among other things, it promotes the conversion of highly erodible cropland into grass, transforming it to grazing land before it becomes wasteland. This program also denies the benefits of any government programs to farmers with excessive soil erosion on their land if they do not adopt an approved soil conservation management program.

Like land, water is also being diverted to nonfarm uses. With water scarcity now constraining efforts to expand food production in many countries, raising the efficiency of water use is emerging as a key to expanding food production. A shift to water markets, requiring users to pay the full cost of water, would lead to substantial investments in efficiency. The common practice of supplying water either free of charge or at a nominal cost to farmers, industries, and urban dwellers leads to water waste.

Stretching water supplies enough to satisfy future food needs means boosting the efficiency of water use, emulating the achievements of Israel—the pacesetter in this field. *Land productivity* has long been part of our vocabulary, an indicator that we measure in yield per hectare. But the term *water productivity* is rarely heard. Until it, too, becomes part of our everyday lexicon, water scarcity will cloud our future.

FEEDING THE FUTURE

Securing future food supplies will affect every facet of human existence—from land-use policy to water-use policy to how we use leisure time. If food security is the goal, then the dream of some of having a car in every garage, a swimming pool in every backyard, and a golf course in every community may remain simply a dream.

Until recently, the world had three reserves it could call on in the event of a poor harvest—cropland idled under farm programs, surplus stocks of grain in storage, and the one-third of the world grain harvest that is fed to livestock, poultry, and fish. By 1997, the first two of these reserves had largely disappeared. The only one remaining that can be tapped in a world food emergency is the grain used as feed. This is much more difficult to draw on. Higher prices, of course, will encourage the world's affluent to eat less grain-intensive livestock products, but prices high enough to have this effect would also threaten the survival of the world's low-income consumers.

In the event of a world food emergency, one way to restrict the rise in grain prices and restore market stability would be to level a tax on the consumption of livestock products, offsetting it with a reduction in income taxes. Lowering the demand for grain would also lower its price. Unpopular though it would be, such a tax might be acceptable if it were the key to maintaining political stability and sustaining economic progress in low-income countries. Such a step would not solve the food problem, but as a temporary measure it would buy some additional time to stabilize population.

It appears that future food security depends on creating an environmentally sustainable economy. Simply put, if political leaders do manage to secure food supplies for the next generation, it will be because they have moved the world economy off the current path of environmental deterioration and eventual economic disruption and onto an economic and demographic path that is environmentally sustainable.

NO

Julian L. Simon

THE STATE OF HUMANITY: STEADILY IMPROVING

The 1980 *Global 2000 Report to the President* began by stating that "if present trends continue, the world in 2000 will be more crowded, more polluted, less stable ecologically, and more vulnerable to disruption than the world we live in now." In the Introduction to *The Resourceful Earth,* which I edited in 1984 with the late Herman Kahn, we rewrote that passage, stating, "If present trends continue, the world in 2000 will be *less crowded* (though more populated), *less polluted, more stable ecologically,* and *less vulnerable to resource-supply disruption* that the world we live in now."

The years have been kind to our forecasts—or more important, the years have been good for humanity. The benign trends we then observed have continued. Our species is better off in just about every measurable material way. And there is stronger reason than ever to believe that progressive trends will continue past the year 2000, past the year 2100, and indefinitely.

When we widen our scope beyond such physical matters as natural resources and the environment—to mortality, the standard of living, slavery and freedom, housing, and the like—we find that the trends pertaining to economic welfare are heartening also. Please notice that this benign assessment does not imply that there will not be increases in *some* troubles—AIDS at present, for example, and other diseases in the future, as well as social and political upheavals. New problems always will arise. But the assessment refers to broad aggregate measures of effects upon people rather than the bad phenomena themselves—life expectancy rather than AIDS, skin cancers (or even better, lifetime healthy days) rather than a hole in the ozone layer (if that is indeed a problem), and agriculture rather than global warming.

We have seen extraordinary progress for the human enterprise, especially in the past two centuries. Yet many people believe that conditions of life are generally worse than in the past, rather than better. We must therefore begin by discussing that perception, because it affects a reader's reaction to the facts. Pessimism about the environment and resources is so universal that it needs no documentation. The comparison one chooses is always crucial. A premise of *The State of Humanity* is that it usually makes sense to compare

From Julian L. Simon, "The State of Humanity: Steadily Improving," *Cato Policy Report* (September/October 1995). Copyright © 1995 by *Cato Policy Report*. Reprinted by permission.

our present state of affairs with *how it was before*. That is the comparison that is usually relevant for policy purposes because it measures our progress. . . .

THE PATH OF MATERIAL HUMAN WELFARE

Let us distinguish three types of economic change: 1) Change that is *mainly absolute* rather than *relative*. An example is health improvement that benefits everyone worldwide. 2) Change that is *mainly relative* but also has an important overall effect. An example is a productivity improvement, due to people working smarter in one country, that allows that country to greatly increase its exports to the benefit of both exporters and importers but causes problems for some other exporting countries. 3) Change that is *wholly relative*. An example is a change in the price charged by one trading partner to another, or in the terms of trade between raw materials and consumer goods, or the dollar-yen exchange rate; in such zero-sum situations there is no on-balance change for bad or good. It is only the third category in which one finds bad news, and indeed bad news is inevitable for one party or the other.

This is my central assertion: Almost every absolute change, and the absolute component of almost every economic and social change or trend, points in a positive direction, as long as we view the matter over a reasonably long period of time. That is, all aspects of material human welfare are improving in the aggregate.

For proper understanding of the important aspects of an economy, we should look at the long-run movement. But short-run comparisons—between the sexes, age groups, races, political groups, which are usually purely relative—make more news.

Let's start with the longest and deepest trends. Surprising though they may be, these trends represent the uncontroversial settled findings of the economists and other experts who work in these fields.

LENGTH OF LIFE

The most important and amazing demographic fact—the greatest human achievement in history, in my view—is the decrease in the world's death rate. It took thousands of years to increase life expectancy at birth from just over 20 years to the high 20s. Then in just the past two centuries, the length of life one could expect for a newborn in the advanced countries jumped from less than 30 years to perhaps 75 years.

Starting in the 1950s, well after World War II, length of life in the poor countries leaped upward by perhaps 15 or even 20 years because of advances in agriculture, sanitation, and medicine. (China excelled in this respect before developing its economy, which is exceptional.)

The extraordinary decline in child mortality is an important element in increased life expectancy, for which every parent must give fervent thanks. But contrary to common belief, in the rich countries such as the United States the gains in life expectancy among the oldest cohorts have been particularly large in recent years. For example, among American males aged 65 to 74, mortality fell 26 percent from 1970 to 1988, and among females of that age, mortality fell 29 percent and 21 percent from 1960 and 1970 to 1988, respectively (*Statistical Abstract of the United States*, 1990, p. 75).

The decrease in the death rate is the root cause of there being a much larger world population nowadays than in former times. In the 19th century, the planet Earth could sustain only 1 billion people. Ten thousand years ago, only 4 million could keep themselves alive. Now, more than 5 billion people are living longer and more healthily than ever before, on average. This increase in the world's population represents humanity's victory against death.

The trends in health are more complex. The decline in mortality is the most important overall indicator of health, of course. But whether keeping more people alive to older ages is accompanied by better or poorer health, on average, in those older years is in doubt.

AGRICULTURAL LABOR FORCE

The best single measure of a country's standard of living is the proportion of the labor force devoted to agriculture. When everyone must work at farming, as was the case only two centuries ago, there can be little production of nonagricultural goods. In the advanced countries there has been an astonishing decline over the centuries in the proportion of the population working in agriculture, now only about 1 person in 50. That shift has enabled consumption per person to multiply by a factor of 20 or 40.

RAW MATERIALS

People have since antiquity worried about running out of natural resources —flint, game animals, what-have-you. Yet, amazingly, all the historical evidence shows that raw materials—all of them —have become less scarce rather than more. It is beyond any doubt that natural resource scarcity—as measured by the economically meaningful indicator of cost or price—has been decreasing rather than increasing in the long run for all raw materials, with only temporary and local exceptions. And there is no reason why this trend should not continue forever. The trend toward greater availability includes the most counterintuitive case of all—oil.

Food is an especially important resource. The evidence is particularly strong that the trend in nutrition is benign despite rising population. The long-run price of food is down sharply, even relative to consumer products, as a result of increased productivity. And per person food consumption is up over the last 30 years. The increase of height in the West is another mark of improved nutrition.

(Africa's food production per person is down, but in the 1990s, few people any longer claim that Africa's suffering has anything to do with a shortage of land or water or sun. Hunger in Africa clearly stems from civil wars and government interference with agriculture, which periodic droughts have made more murderous.)

Only one important resource has shown a trend of increasing scarcity rather than increasing abundance. It is the most important and valuable resource of all—human beings. Certainly, there are more people on earth now than ever before. But if we measure the scarcity of people the same way that we measure the scarcity of other economic goods—by how much we must pay to obtain their services—we see that wages and salaries have been going up all over the world, in poor countries as well as in rich countries. The amount that one must pay to obtain the services of a barber or a professor has risen in India, just as the price of a barber or professor has risen in the United States over the decades. That increase in the price of people's services is a clear indication that people are becoming more scarce even though there are more of us.

THE STANDARD OF LIVING

The data show unmistakably how the standard of living has increased in the world and in the United States through the recent centuries and decades, right up through the 1980s. Aggregate data always bring forth the question: But are not the gains mainly by the rich classes, and the expense of the poor? For a portion of U.S. history, income distribution did widen (though this is hardly proof that the rich were exploiting the poor). But there has been little or no such tendency during, say, the 20th century. And a widening gap does not negate the fact of a rising absolute standard of living for the poor. Nor is there evidence that an increasing proportion of the population lives below some fixed absolute poverty line. There have been extraordinary gains by the poor in America in consumption during this century, as well as a high standard of living by any historical and cross-national standards.

A related question concerns possible exploitation by the rich countries that might cause misery for the poor countries. But the distribution of the most important element of "real wealth"—life expectancy—has narrowed between rich and poor countries (as well as between the rich and poor segments of populations within countries) over previous decades—to wit, the extraordinary reduction in the gap between the mortality rate of China and those of the rich countries since World War II. The reduction in the gap between literacy rates and other measures of amount of education in rich and poor countries corroborates this con-vergence. The convergence in economic productivity in the rich countries, along with general growth, dovetails with the other measures of income distribution. Data on the *absolute* gap between yearly incomes of the rich and poor countries are beside the point; widening is inevitable if all get rich at the same proportional rate, and the absolute gap can increase even if the poor improve their incomes at a faster proportional rate than the rich. Here one should notice that increased life expectancy among the poor relative to the rich reduces the gap in lifetime income, which is a more meaningful measure than yearly income.

CLEANLINESS OF THE ENVIRONMENT

Ask an average roomful of people if our environment is becoming dirtier or cleaner, and most will say "dirtier." Yet the air in the United States and in other rich countries is irrefutably safer to breathe now than in decades past; the quantities of pollutants—especially particulates, which are the main threat to health—have been declining. And water quality has improved; the proportion of monitoring sites in the United States with water of good drinkability has increased since data collection began in 1961. More generally, the environment is increasingly healthy, with every prospect that this trend will continue.

When considering the state of the environment, we should think first of the terrible pollutions that were banished in the past century or so—the typhoid that polluted such rivers as the Hudson, smallpox that humanity has finally pursued to the ends of the earth and just about eradicated, the dysentery that distressed and killed people all over the world as it still does in India, the plagues and other epidemics that trouble us much less than in generations past, or not at all. Not only are we in the rich countries free of malaria (largely due to our intensive occupation of the land), but even the mosquitoes that do no more than cause itches with their bites are so absent from many urban areas that people no longer need screens for their homes and can have garden parties at dusk. It is a mark of our extraordinary success that these are no longer even thought of as pollutions.

The root cause of these victorious campaigns against the harshest pollutions was the nexus of increased technical capacity and increased affluence—wealth being the capacity to deal effectively with one's surroundings.

I am not saying that all is well everywhere, and I do not predict that all will be rosy in the future. Children are hungry, and sick people live out lives of physical or intellectual poverty and lack of opportunity; irrational war (not even for economic gain) or some new pollution may finish us off. For most relevant economic matters, however, the aggregate trends are improving.

CAN ALL THIS GOOD NEWS BE TRUE?

Readers of articles like this often ask, "But what about the other side's data?" There are no other data. Test for yourself the assertion that the physical conditions of humanity have gotten better. Pick up the U.S. Census Bureau's *Statistical Abstract of the United States* and *Historical Statistics of the United States* at the nearest library and consult the data on the measures of human welfare that depend on physical resources, for the United States or for the world as a whole. See the index for such topics as pollution, life expectancy, and the price indexes, plus the prices of the individual natural resources. While you're at it, check the amount of space per person in our homes and the presence of such amenities as inside toilets and telephones. You will find "official" data showing that just about every single measure of the quality of life shows improvement rather than the deterioration that the doomsayers claim has occurred.

WHAT IS THE MECHANISM THAT PRODUCES PROGRESS RATHER THAN INCREASING MISERY?

How can it be that economic welfare grows over time along with population, instead of humanity's being reduced to misery and poverty as population grows and we use more and more resources? We need some theory to explain this controversion of common sense.

The process operates as follows: More people and increased income cause problems in the short run—shortages and pollutions. Short-run scarcity raises prices and pollution causes outcries. Those problems present opportunity and prompt the search for solutions. In a free society solutions are eventually found, though many people seek and fail to find solutions at cost to themselves. In the long run the new developments leave us better off than if the problems had not arisen. This theory fits the facts of history.

Technology exists now to produce in virtually inexhaustible quantities just about all the products made by nature—foodstuffs, oil, even pearls and diamonds—and make them cheaper in most cases than the cost of gathering them in their natural state. And the standard of living of commoners is higher today than that of royalty only two centuries ago—especially their health and life expectancy, and their mobility to all parts of the world.

The extent to which the political-social-economic system provides personal freedom from government coercion is a crucial element in the economics of resources and population. Skilled persons require an appropriate social and economic framework that provides incentives for working hard and taking risks, enabling their talents to flower and come to fruition. The key elements of such a framework are economic liberty, respect for property, and fair and sensible rules of the market that are enforced equally for all.

We have in our hands now—actually, in our libraries—the technology to feed, clothe, and supply energy to an ever-growing population for the next 7 billion years. Most amazing is that most of this specific body of knowledge was developed within just the past two centuries or so, though it rests, of course, on basic knowledge that had accumulated for millennia.

Indeed, the last necessary additions to this body of technology—nuclear fission and space travel—occurred decades ago. Even if no new knowledge were ever gained after those advances, we would be able to go on increasing our population forever, while improving our standard of living and our control over our environment. The discovery of genetic manipulation certainly enhances our powers greatly, but even without it we could have continued our progress forever.

CONCLUSION

Progress toward a more abundant material life does not come like manna from heaven, however. My message certainly is not one of complacency. The ultimate resource is people—especially skilled, spirited, and hopeful young people endowed with liberty—who will exert their wills and imaginations for their own benefit and inevitably benefit the rest of us as well.

POSTSCRIPT

Does Population Growth Threaten Humanity?

The key issue of the debate is whether or not future technological improvements can continue to overcome the law of diminishing returns on investments and increasing costs for nonrenewable resources and environmentally benign waste disposal. Brown argues that some of nature's limits have been exceeded and that present consumption is harming the environment, depleting resources, and endangering future consumption. If Simon is right that mankind will solve environmental problems when it becomes necessary for survival, then, according to Brown, it is time to act because present trends are seriously threatening mankind. Simon asserts that the pessimists always underestimate humankind's ability to adapt to environmental problems. Although the pessimists can cite a long list of environmental problems, Simon is confident that they will be taken care of by human effort and inventiveness. He expects necessity to give birth to inventions because technological developments will reap substantial economic rewards as resources become scarce.

Paul R. Ehrlich and Anne H. Ehrlich wrote *Betrayal of Science and Reason: How Anti-Environmental Rhetoric Threatens Our Future* (Island Press, 1996) to refute many statements by optimists who attack the messages of the worried environmentalists. For a debate between a pessimist and an optimist, see Norman Myers and Julian L. Simon, *Scarcity or Abundance? A Debate on the Environment* (W. W. Norton, 1994).

Publications by some of the prominent optimists on the availability of resources and the health of the environment include Ronald Bailey, ed., *The True State of the Planet* (Free Press, 1995) and Gregg Easterbrook, *A Moment on the Earth: The Coming Age of Environmental Optimism* (Viking, 1995). Publications by some of the prominent pessimists include Joseph Wayne Smith, Graham Lyons, and Gary Sauer-Thompson, *Healing a Wounded World* (Praeger, 1997); Douglas E. Booth, *The Environmental Consequences of Growth* (Routledge, 1998); and Bill McKibben, *Hope, Human and Wild: True Stories of Living Lightly on the Earth* (Little, Brown, 1995).

Several works relate environmental problems to very severe political, social, and economic problems, including Michael Renner, *Fighting for Survival* (W. W. Norton, 1996) and Michael N. Dobkowski and Isidor Wallimann, eds., *The Coming Age of Scarcity: Preventing Mass Death and Genocide in the Twenty-First Century* (Syracuse University Press, 1998). An important series of publications on environmental problems are by the Worldwatch Institute, including two annuals: *State of the World* and *Vital Signs*.

ISSUE 20

Are Standards of Living in the United States Improving?

YES: W. Michael Cox and Richard Alm, from "The Good Old Days Are Now," *Reason* (December 1995)

NO: Beth A. Rubin, from *Shifts in the Social Contract: Understanding Change in American Society* (Pine Forge Press, 1996)

ISSUE SUMMARY

YES: Economist and banker W. Michael Cox and business journalist Richard Alm contend that U.S. living standards are improving. On average, they argue, Americans consume more, live better, live longer and healthier, achieve a higher net worth, enjoy more leisure time, and have more income per capita today than in 1970.

NO: Sociology professor Beth A. Rubin claims that Americans have not only lost income on average over the past 25 years, but they have also increasingly experienced insecurity and anxiety in their jobs and instability in their family relationships.

After World War II the United States emerged as the most powerful nation in the world. In part, this was because of the cumulative economic costs of two world wars for Germany, Great Britain, Japan, and the Soviet Union. America escaped the physical devastation that these nations suffered, and its economy boomed during and after the wars. With its unequalled prosperity and power, the United States assumed international leadership in armaments, investments, and aid.

Today that prosperity in terms of per capita income is equaled or surpassed by Japan and many European countries, and that leadership is in question. During the 1970s, 1980s, and early 1990s, Japan, Germany, Taiwan, South Korea, China, and other countries in Europe and Asia made enormous economic strides, while America was stuck in first gear. American stores were flooded with foreign-made goods—from shoes and textiles to cars and television sets. America went from winner to loser in many market competitions, resulting in large trade deficits. In the 1990s America's European and Asian competitors have experienced major difficulties and have been trying to climb out of serious recessions. The American economy looks good by comparison.

Because of recent, painful restructuring and downsizing, America now competes more equally with other industrial countries. American business is doing well, but workers are suffering. American workers have been laid off as industries have downsized or moved part of their operations offshore, where they can operate more cheaply than in the United States. Until 1997 the government continued to spend more than it received in revenue, resulting in America's national debt (the total of its accumulated annual budget deficits) growing to more than $5 trillion. Many Americans worry that future generations will be burdened with debts that will drive the nation deeper into economic malaise.

Despite a long stretch of modest economic growth with relatively low inflation and unemployment, Americans are anxious. Despite an endless array of new technological toys and gadgets, most Americans do not perceive life today as being better than it was a few decades ago. Visual signs of declining standards of living confront Americans in some of the grim aspects of daily life, particularly in its urban centers: homeless people sprawled on sidewalks, streets lined with boarded-up buildings, crumbling schools with metal detectors at the doors and peeling paint in the classrooms, bridges with chunks of concrete falling off them, and housing projects taken over by drug dealers. Statistical signs of declining standards of living are found in the decline in real wages and in the median income of individuals.

The above factors deal with material standards of living. But it has often been said that money does not buy happiness. In fact, many studies show that once people have enough money to satisfy their basic material needs, additional increments of wealth are not correlated with increasing happiness. Surveys indicate that family, relationships, and meaningful activities are the keys to happiness. What are indicators in these areas telling us? Since 1960 divorce rates have shot upward, fertility rates have plummeted downward, and the time parents devote to children has declined about 10 hours per week. On the other hand, these trends bottomed out in the mid-1980s, and family values are staging a small comeback. Furthermore, Robert Wuthnow, in *Sharing the Journey: Support Groups and America's New Quest for Community* (Free Press, 1994), reveals that more and more Americans participate in small groups and are thereby connecting with God and with other people in the process of dealing with their problems.

So where do we stand? Is the quality of life in America improving? W. Michael Cox and Richard Alm admit that average wages have declined slightly, but they assert that those smaller wages buy more than the slightly larger wages of several decades ago. They also observe that since more people are working, per capita income is increasing. And the fact that Americans are living healthier and longer leads them to conclude that the quality of life is improving. Beth A. Rubin argues that Americans are victims of the changes taking place in the economy, especially the shrinking commitment of employers to employees. The employers gain flexibility, while the employees, even professionals, lose security. She also sees trouble on the home front and concludes that the quality of life is suffering.

YES
W. Michael Cox and Richard Alm

THE GOOD OLD DAYS ARE NOW

Draw a six-inch line on a piece of paper. Make a dot at the right end, and label it *Knowledge*. Make another dot two inches from the line's other end. Label that point *Ignorance*. What's to the left of that dot might be called *Mythology*. It's what we think we know but what isn't really so.

Often the biggest stumbling block to accurate perceptions of our world is getting beyond the glib notions that nearly everyone takes for granted. We spend an awful lot of time stumbling about in the realm of mythology:

- U.S. living standards are falling, and Americans aren't as well off as they were 25 years ago.
- These days, it requires two workers for a typical family to maintain a middle-class lifestyle.
- Today's children are likely to become the first generation that won't live as well as their parents.
- The United States, once the world's undisputed leader, is falling behind as other nations grow faster.

These are the myths that plague discussion of what's happening to U.S. living standards. They have been repeated so often, and by such respected authorities, that few Americans even question the proposition that the economy is failing them. The message pours out of Washington, where Labor Secretary Robert Reich frets that American workers are getting stiffed by greedy corporations. It's the central theme of leading academics and think tanks, including Ray Marshall at the University of Texas, Frank Levy at the Massachusetts Institute of Technology, and the Progressive Policy Institute in Washington, D.C. Downward mobility has emerged as a staple of big-city newsrooms, where hard-luck stories make good copy.

Anecdotes, of course, can only illustrate, not prove. In good times and bad, individuals and families will move up and down in the social pecking order for a variety of reasons. Making the case, then, for slipping American living standards demands broad-based evidence. More often than not, the negativists point to falling real wages as their smoking gun.

And the trends do seem decidedly grim: After adjusting for inflation, average hourly wages rose by 2.1 percent a year from 1953 to 1973. After that, wages stagnated and then began a long slide, with an average annual decline of 0.8 percent since 1978. If Americans are making less, it stands to reason they're not going to be able to maintain their living standards.

The pessimists bolster their argument with other trends that seem to show lost dynamism: lackluster economic growth, less-than-stellar productivity gains, widening trade deficits, fewer manufacturing jobs, an inability to match the growth rates of Asia's fast-growing nations. All told, these statistics make for a rather bleak view of the U.S. economy. To make matters worse, the country seems plagued by crime, pollution, insecurity, homelessness, cynicism, and a host of other social pathologies always in a downward spiral toward deeper crisis.

In a society that's addicted to hand-wringing, in a country that accentuates the negative, all this gets plenty of repetition. There are problems in these United States—no doubt about it—but the conclusion that we're not living as well as we once did is pure mythology. There's abundant evidence, easily obtained but largely ignored, showing that economic progress is still on track in the United States. Today's Americans aren't orphans of history. Far from it, they are experiencing what previous generations worked so hard to achieve—rising living standards.

In fact, Americans never had it so good.

CONSUMING CONFIDENCE

At best, real wages and the other evidence of a faltering economy are indirect barometers of living standards. It's curious that the declinists spend so much time examining a bunch of proxies but can spare so little energy for direct measures of what's been happening to Americans' well-being. . . .

Living standards are best measured by what we *consume*, not by our earnings or income. Looked at this way, the available numbers don't lend any support to the view that the country isn't doing as well as it once did. Comparisons to the early 1970s are particularly relevant. After all, no one doubts that Americans are living better today than they did a century ago, or even 50 years ago. The past quarter century is when the declinists contend the country's living standards started to slip.

But many numbers say it isn't so. On average, for instance, Americans now live in bigger and better houses. From 1970 to 1992, a typical new home increased in size by the equivalent of two 15-foot by 20-foot rooms. While home ownership rates have remained roughly constant over the past two decades, the average age at which Americans buy their first home has moved by roughly three years —from 27.9 in 1970 to 31.0 in 1992. Doomsayers, of course, have been quick to chalk this up to deteriorating economic conditions, ignoring the marked change in Americans' lifestyles. The median age at which we first marry (an event that often precedes home buying) has increased from 21.5 in 1970 to 24.7 in 1992—again roughly three years. And nearly 12 percent more of us today also decide never to marry. Add to this the fact that the average number of children per family has declined—from 1.09 in 1970 to 0.67 today—and the story clearly changes from deteriorating economic conditions to lifestyle changes.

Then there are the homes themselves. New houses are much more likely to have central air conditioning and garages. About 45 percent of homes now have dishwashers, up from 26 percent two decades ago. Clothes washers were in three-quarters of homes in 1990, up from less than two-thirds in 1970. At the same time, households with dryers jumped from 45 percent to almost 70 percent. The average number of televisions in a household rose from 1.4 in 1970 to 2.1 in 1990. Comparing 1970 and 1990, the typical U.S. family owned 4.5 times more in audio and video equipment, 50 percent more in kitchen appliances, and 30 percent more in furniture. For fun and games, the household has twice as much gear for sports and hobbies.

Among those 15 years and older, passenger vehicles per 100,000 people increased from 61,400 in 1970 to 73,000 in 1991. Americans are enjoying more luxuries, too. The average amount spent on jewelry and watches, after adjusting for higher prices, more than doubled from 1970 to 1991. Per capita spending on overseas travel and tourism is three times greater than in the early 1970s.

Of course, we could be paying for our consumption by depleting our savings. The evidence, however, suggests it isn't so. Although Americans may not set aside as much as people in many other countries, the average American still has managed to gain net worth. Median real wealth per capita rose by 2 percent a year from 1970 to 1990. The Dow Jones Industrial Average jumped sixfold since the early 1970s. The nation has had the best of two worlds: consuming more in the present and setting aside more for the future—not a bad standard for "better off."

No catalog of higher living standards would be complete without products that didn't even exist for past generations. Twenty years ago, only a lucky few could show movies at home. Now, two of every three households own video-cassette recorders. When Elvis was king of rock 'n' roll, records succumbed to warps and scratches. Today's practically unbreakable compact discs offer concert-hall quality sound. Microwave ovens, answering machines, food processors, camcorders, home computers, exercise equipment, cable TV, Rollerblades, fax machines, and soft contact lenses are staples of the 1990s lifestyles. As important, many products from computers to clothing, have been getting higher in quality even as they drop in price.

A decade ago, most motorists had to search out a pay telephone to make a call. Now, cellular technology has put a phone in millions of cars. Companies served 11 million subscribers in 1992, up from 92,000 in 1984. The past 20 years brought many medical breakthroughs—new drugs, new treatments, new diagnostic tools—to enhance and prolong our lives. Today's cars go farther on a gallon of gas. They've been improved with anti-lock brakes, airbags, fuel injectors, turbochargers, cruise control, and sound systems that outperform even the best home stereos of 1970. Today's youth may gripe, but they're already benefiting from products their parents didn't get until later in life. What's more, there's a huge inventory of even more world-shaking technologies that will create new waves of convenient, innovative consumer products.

The first test of national well-being, the one that makes the most common sense, should be the material facts of life. If the average consumer owns more of everything, plus the bonus of new products, then it's hard to fathom how a nation could have lost ground over the past 20 years. (*See Table 1*.)

WISTFUL AS WE WORK?

At least some declinists will concede that Americans have more material goods than ever, but they contend that it's only because we're working harder. The two-income family, with both husband and wife holding jobs, is all that keeps the country from the consequences of the weakening of the economy.

What conclusion could be more backward? Both adults have always worked. Running a household entails a daunting list of chores—cooking, cleaning, gardening, child care, shopping, washing and ironing, financial management, ferrying family members to ballet lessons and soccer practice. The average work-week of yesterday's housewife, the stay-at-home mom of the 1950s, was 52 hours, a more exhausting schedule than the 39.8 hours typically put in at the office.

The idea that people at home don't work isn't just insulting to women, who do most of the housework. It also misses how specialization contributes to higher and higher living standards. At one time, both adults worked exclusively at home. The man constructed buildings, tilled the land, raised livestock. The woman prepared meals, preserved food, looked after the children. Living standards rarely rose above the subsistence level.

Over time, household tasks were turned over to the market. At first, only one adult went to work outside the home, gaining specialized skills and earning an income that allowed the family to buy what it didn't have the time, energy, or ability to make at home.

When men went to work outside the home, living standards rose. Why do we insist that the same transition for women results in a squeezing of the household's possibilities? What's good for the gander is good for the goose. It's more efficient for workers to spend time earning money doing what they do best on the job and then pay others to perform at least some household chores. It makes no sense to suggest that the economic rules flip-flop when a second adult takes a job. Working women make families better off.

As the United States grows richer, tasks once done by family members continue to move out of the home and into the market. To the extent they can afford it, households hire professionals to clean, paint, tend the yard, figure taxes, care for clothing, and perform other responsibilities once assigned to family members. In getting their daily bread, Americans are finding ways to ease the burden of cooking at home. In 1993, restaurants received 43 percent of the country's spending on food, a big gain from the 33 percent of 1972. Eating out, once an occasional luxury, has become a way of life. And, even when we eat at home, we often rely more on market goods—heat-and-serve products, microwave meals, and carry-out items.

The data show that home production—the market of all housework and related chores—fell steadily from 45 percent of GNP at the end of World War II to 33 percent in 1973. Since then, it has drifted slightly lower, and it's likely to continue a gradual ebbing. Turning to the marketplace for many of the time-consuming, dull chores of maintaining a household frees time for more valuable

Table 1

Living Standards Compared 1970 and 1990

	1970	1990
Average size of a new home (square feet)	1,500	2,080
New homes with central air conditioning	34%	76%
People using computers	<100,000	75.9 million
Households with color TV	33.9%	96.1%
Households with cable TV	4 million	55 million
Households with VCRs	0	67 million
Households with two or more vehicles	29.3%	54%
Median household net worth (real)	$24,217	$48,887
Housing units lacking complete plumbing	6.9%	1.1%
Homes lacking a telephone	13%	5.2%
Households owning a microwave oven	<1%	78.8%
Heart transplant procedures	<10	2,125*
Average work week	37.1 hours	34.5 hours
Average daily time working in the home	3.9 hours	3.5 hours
Work time to buy gas for 100-mile trip	49 minutes	31 minutes*
Annual paid vacation and paid holidays	15.5 days	22.5 days
Number of people retired from work	13.3 million	25.3 million
Women in the work force	31.5%	56.6%
Recreational boats owned	8.8 million	16 million
Manufacturers' shipments of RVs	30,300	226,500
Adult softball teams	29,000	188,000
Recreational golfers	11.2 million	27.8 million
Attendance at symphonies and orchestras	12.7 million	43.6 million
Americans taking cruises	0.5 million	3.6 million
Americans finishing high school	51.9%	77.7%
Americans finishing four years of college	13.5%	24.4%
Employee benefits as a share of payroll	29.3%	40.2%**
Life expectancy at birth (years)	70.8	75.4
Death rate by natural causes (per 100,000)	714.3	520.2
Accidental death rate	56.2	34.9
Index of pollution	100.0	34.1

*figures are for 1991
**figures are for 1992

pursuits. A job is one of them. Another is the pursuit of pleasure.

KILLING TIME

In the 1990s, Americans aren't just enjoying the plenty of bigger houses, better cars, and more electronics. As people get wealthier, they are likely to want more time off work, trading higher income for additional leisure. Today's lickety-split lifestyles leave many people breathless, but there's plenty of evidence that a typical American spends less time than ever at work—either at home or on the job. (*See Table 2.*)

Additional free time comes from the confluence of several trends. Americans

Table 2

Less Work, More Leisure

Activity	1870	1950	1973	1990
Age starting work (avg.)	13	17.6	18.5	19.1
Life expectancy (years)	43.5	67.2	70.6	75.0
Retirement age (avg.)	death	68.5	64.0	63.6
Years on job	30.5	49.6	45.5	44.5
Retirement (years)	0	0	6.6	11.4
Annual hours worked	3,069	1,903	1,743	1,562
Annual hours home work	1,825	1,544	1,391	1,278
Lifetime Hours				
Working at job	93,604	94,389	79,307	69,509
Working at home	61,594	81,474	67,151	59,800
Waking leisure	99,016	216,854	266,129	308,368

Today's workers may feel pressed for time, but as a nation, we start to work later in life and work fewer hours than earlier generations. In 1870, Americans could expect to spend 39 percent of their waking hours at leisure. Now, the time we spend in childhood vacations, evenings, holidays, and retirement adds up to 70 percent of our waking hours.

are starting work later in life. On average, the age of initial employment has been pushed back seven months in the past 20 years. Once at work, Americans are putting in fewer hours because of shorter weeks, more holidays, and longer vacations. In the past two decades, there's been a gain of the equivalent of 23 days off a year. At home, Americans on average are devoting 18 minutes less a day to chores. Over the course of a year, that adds up to an extra four days of leisure. Toward the end of life, Americans are retiring earlier and living longer. As a result, a typical retirement grew by four years since 1973.

When it's all added up, the results are mind-boggling: Workers have added the equivalent of nearly five years of waking leisure to their lives since 1973. The typical employee spends less than a third of all non-sleeping hours on the job—that's better than any generation in U.S. history.

There's indirect confirmation that Americans have more free time these days: We're participating in more recreational activities and spending more money on leisure activities. Ownership rates more than doubled for vacation homes and rose 50 percent for recreational boats. Pleasure trips per capita rose from 1.5 a year in 1980 to 1.8 in 1991. Americans took 4.4 million cruises in 1994, compared with 500,000 in 1970 and 1.4 million as recently as 1980.

Increased leisure has fueled a sports boom. Attendance at National Football League games rose from 10 million in 1970 to 15 million in 1994. A fan backlash over [1994's] strike is keeping baseball attendance down, but hockey, basketball, golf, car racing, and other sports are drawing bigger crowds—in person and on television.

Participatory sports are booming, too. From 1970 to 1991, Americans who play golf regularly doubled to 11 percent of the population. In 1970, a quarter of Americans bowled; now, a third of them do. Even after adjusting for population growth, the number of adult softball teams jumped sixfold in two decades. Growing up, few of us ever imagined rock climbing, bungee jumping, or Rollerblading. These are now regular activities for millions of Americans.

Cultural activities haven't been shortchanged. Per capita attendance at symphonies and operas doubled from 1970 to 1991. Movies, pop-music concerts, and television fare are proliferating. We're even buying more books: Annual sales rose from 6.6 per person in 1974 to 8.1 in 1991. The much-bemoaned overcrowding of national parks bespeaks the arrival of a great democracy in free time, with the masses enjoying what was once possible for only a privileged few.

Money tells the same story. Total recreational spending, adjusted for inflation, jumped from $91.3 billion in 1970 to $257.3 billion in 1990, an average annual gain of 9.1 percent that well outstrips population growth of 1 percent a year. During the 1980s alone, outlays rose from $1.2 billion to $4.1 billion for recreational vehicles, $2.7 billion to $7.6 billion for pleasure boats, and $17 billion to $44 billion for sporting goods. Over the past 20 years, money allocated to recreation increased from 5 percent of consumer spending to nearly 8 percent.

One of the advantages of statistics is they reduce subjectivity. In polls, Americans will swear life is more hectic than it used to be, that there's not enough time anymore. What's crowding their lives, though, isn't necessarily more work and more chores. It is the relentless chasing after the myriad leisure opportunities of a society that has more free time and more money to spend.

REAL INTANGIBLES

The preferences of richer countries extend beyond additional consumption and leisure. The better off a country is, the more citizens will value non-material aspects of living standards: better health and safety, more pleasant working conditions, a cleaner environment. All of us could add other considerations we regard as important.

Intangibles, by their very nature, aren't as easy to count as televisions sets or hours of work. Yet, there are some numbers that counter fears that the United States is losing ground in most of what might be loosely called the quality of life.

In fact, longevity may be the most important measure of well-being in a modern society. The data show that an average American's life expectancy at birth has risen decade after decade. As might be expected, the biggest gains came in the first half of the 20th century, but the upward trend continues into the 1990s. Over the past 10 years, the life expectancy increased by more than one year and eight months.

What's more, the populace reports that it feels healthier. Surveys by the U.S. Department of Health and Human Services show a steady drop in the proportion of Americans who rate their health as "fair or poor"—from 12.2 percent in 1975 to 9.3 percent in 1991. Infant mortality rates fell from 20 deaths per 1,000 live births in 1970 to fewer than nine in 1991. The death rate from natural causes fell by 27 percent from 1970 to 1990, with most of the progress coming in combatting diseases of the heart. The portion of the adult population with high cholesterol fell sharply over the past two decades. What once was fatal can in many cases now be treated. Heart, liver, and lung transplants, experimental to theoretical in the early 1970s, are increasingly common today.

But the country isn't just healthier; in many respects, it's also safer. Accidental deaths have declined in every category, especially since 1970. In 1991, 88,000

Americans died in accidents, the lowest figure since 1972. Highway deaths totaled 43,500 in 1991, the best since 1962. Even more encouraging, the death rate per 100 million miles traveled on the nation's roads fell from 3.0 in 1975 to 1.8 in 1990. The incidence of death from crashes of scheduled airliners is just a fraction of what it was 20 years ago. Safety at work is improving, too. Accidental deaths on the job have declined steadily since at least 1945. Job-related injuries are well below what they were in previous decades.

Americans are also making progress on improving the environment. Levels of such major air pollutants as particulate matter, sulfur oxides, volatile organic compounds, carbon monoxide, and lead hit their peaks in 1970 or before. Levels of nitrogen oxides have been declining since 1980. Overall, air quality is better now than at any time since data collection began in 1940. Water quality has improved since the 1960s, when authorities banned fishing in Lake Erie and fires erupted on the polluted Cuyahoga River as it passed through Cleveland. The U.S. Geological Survey, examining trends since 1980, found that fecal coliform bacteria and phosphorus have decreased substantially in many parts of the country. Other indicators of water quality—dissolved oxygen, dissolved solids, nitrate, and suspended sediments—haven't been getting any worse....

WAGE DISCRIMINATION

A wealth of data makes a case for rising U.S. living standards. Even so, there's the pesky problem of the falling real wages the declinists bring up so often. Common sense seems to dictate that smaller paychecks are simply incompatible with a society being better off.

The data on rising consumption, plus additional leisure, suggest that the decline in real wages isn't the best indicator of what's happening to the country's economic prospects.

And, it turns out, there are better ways to show how the typical American is doing. The most straightforward alternative to real hourly wages is per capita income. One of its virtues is simplicity: divide total output by the number of people. This computation isn't skewed by changes in the way we work, the way we live, how we're paid, or what we produce. When we look at per capita personal income, the historical trend shows no monumental sign of a decline during the post–World War II era. It rose by an annual average of 1.7 percent since 1974, compared with 2.0 percent in the 1950s and 1960s.

Statistics on average hourly wages suffer from one glaring omission—fringe benefits. Over the past two decades, as tax rates and income have risen, these non-wage benefits have surged. Workers have chosen to take more compensation in the form of additional health care, contributions to retirement savings, or employee assistance programs. Overall, non-monetary benefits as a percentage of payroll increased by a third since 1970. Compared with a generation ago, more employers are providing eye care, dental benefits, paid maternity leave, and stock-purchase plans. Today's more progressive companies are starting to offer day care and paternity leave— both unheard of in the early 1970s.

When fringe benefits are included, there is indeed a slowdown in the *rate* of growth for total compensation in the past 20 years. But even so, the average American worker is still better off than his counterpart in the early 1970s, with a total gain of almost 15 percent.

Part of this relates to a change in the distribution of wages throughout the economy. Since 1973, the gap has widened between income and compensation. This trend tells us that the share of income paid for production and nonsupervisory work is declining, while the share paid elsewhere—to professionals, supervisors, managers, and owners—is growing.

One explanation appears to be the rising return to human capital. In an increasingly information- and service-oriented economy, business capital has come to encompass not just plant and machinery, but, more and more, intellectual capital as well.... [T]he workers reaping most of the economic gains have been those at the higher end of the education spectrum. The income premium to education is substantial and has grown markedly over the past two decades. In 1992, college graduates made an average of 82 percent more than high school graduates, up from only 43 percent in 1972. The really big returns to education these days come with advanced degrees—Ph.D.s, M.D.s, J.D.s, M.B.A.s, etc. In 1972, people with advanced degrees made 72 percent more income than high school graduates. By 1992, they made 2.5 times more. Today, high school dropouts earn scarcely half as much as high school grads, and the split is growing....

Per capita income and total compensation don't exhibit the downturn that's so unsettling in the statistics for real wages. To the contrary, they maintain an upward thrust up through the most recent data. More to the point, these measures of earning power square with the other evidence showing that Americans are better off than they used to be....

* * *

There's plenty of good, hard data refuting the notion that American living standards are in decline. We're enjoying more of almost all material goods. We're taking more leisure. We're healthier. We're making gains on other measure of well-being. We're making daily life easier by paying others to do what we once did for ourselves. We've got no reason to be alarmed by the evolution of two-income households, or the faster growth rates of other countries....

To be sure, economic changes are coming fast and furious. Many of us grew up in an era where workers could take a job and expect to keep it until retirement. Those entering the labor force today might have as many as four different jobs during their lifetimes—and three of them haven't been invented yet. In addition, there's an unsettling shift from a national economy to an international one, and all the new Information Age technology that changes the way we live and work. Transitions are hard on humans. The arrival of the Industrial Revolution created similar upheavals, though. Over time, people will get used to the new environment, make the necessary adjustments, and look back to wonder how they could have lived in the previous age.

The United States has its economic problems, no doubt about it. Budget deficits are too big. Too many people are still poor. Workers need skills to match today's technology—and tomorrow's. So, with real problems at hand, we shouldn't spend our time on phony ones. Being distracted by the myth of declining living standards isn't getting us anywhere. The evidence is overwhelming. On average, Americans are better off than ever before.

NO

Beth A. Rubin

SHIFTS IN THE SOCIAL CONTRACT: UNDERSTANDING CHANGE IN AMERICAN SOCIETY

SOCIAL CHANGE IN THE TWENTIETH CENTURY

Workers who once felt relatively immune from unemployment are discovering that a college degree and a big paycheck are no guarantee against it. Consider the example of IBM, which has long offered many of its workers essentially lifetime employment. In April 1993, in response to declining business conditions, IBM laid off 7,700 workers. Many of these workers were well-paid professionals in their 50s who thought they were at the zenith of their careers. Unlike many blue-collar workers, none of them had ever had to cope with layoffs and employment insecurity. This security was, after all, why they have invested in good educations at colleges and universities. Now, these well-educated, highly skilled, and highly paid workers—who were accustomed to a high standard of living—meet in support/prayer group meetings to discuss their lost careers, provide emotional support for one another, and develop strategies for job hunting and survival. Such support is necessary. In Dutchess County, New York, where three huge IBM plants are located, social service workers report an increase in drinking and family violence (*New York Times* editorial (The Rise of the Losing Class, Louis Uchitelle, November 20, 1994) claimed that the changing economy was linking the white-collar, skilled, college-educated workers with blue-collar, unskilled, high school educated workers through a shared experience of "uncertainty, insecurity, and anxiety about their jobs and incomes."

Surprisingly, unemployment and layoffs were occurring in a period characterized by economic recovery. But this recovery was an unusual one. Despite economic growth in the early 1990s, economic inequality (the gap between the rich and poor) continued to grow. While inequality has been increasing since the late 1970s, for perhaps the first time in America's history economists were faced with the puzzle of falling *median income* (the income level that half the population is above and half below) at the time of increased economic growth (*New York Times*, October 9, 1994)....

Turmoil is not, of course, confined to the United States. Economic insecurity is so great internationally that the International Labor Organization calls it a "global crisis." One out of three workers in the world's labor force is either unemployed or earning insufficient wages to allow a decent standard of living (*Times-Picayune*, March 7, 1994). Persistent long-term joblessness affects both industrial countries like the United States and developing countries like Mexico.

Global economic hardship has a number of consequences. It can increase competition for resources, engender political conflicts, and foster immigration. Former Secretary of State Lawrence Eagleburger called the current period one of global revolution (*Los Angeles Times*, February 18, 1993). Unchecked, such instability can lead to massive economic depression and even war. In fact, the 1990s provide evidence of such. As the countries that once constituted the Soviet Union struggle to redefine themselves, hatred, ethnic conflict, and bloodshed have often filled the gap left by a once strong centralized government....

Clearly the United States, along with most other countries in the world, is undergoing massive social change. Such change is related to a systematic transformation in the basis of social relations and social institutions (such as the economy, the government, the family).... *[C]ontemporary American society is changing from a social world characterized by long-term, stable relationships to one characterized by short-term, temporary relationships.* This social change alters the *social contract* that underpins society....

This shift results from changes in the economy. Specifically, economic relationships are changing to emphasize flexibility rather than stability in the use of resources. In a larger context the relationships among countries are growing increasingly complex. The result is a kaleidoscope of economic and social changes....

For over 200 years, a central part of American culture has been the belief in the American Dream. When people talk about the American Dream, they are talking about a belief in a society characterized by political and religious freedom in which anyone, regardless of family background, ethnicity, or race, can "make it." By *making it*, we mean that people can—by virtue of education, hard work, luck, and motivation—have a good job, a home, a happy family, and leisure time. Moreover, they can have these in a social climate free from oppression....

This dream continues to motivate people from all over the world. Waves of immigrants continue to come to the United States seeking the same mobility and opportunity that earlier generations sought. Achieving these goals, however, has grown increasingly difficult since the paths to upward mobility have altered.

Accord in the Post–World War II Era

By the beginning of the twentieth century, America was on its way to becoming one of the richest, most successful countries in the world. During the two and half decades following World War II, America was, in many ways, at its zenith. No country appeared richer, more powerful, more sure of itself. The American Dream seemed a reality for unprecedented numbers of Americans. For both blue-collar industrial workers (such as assembly line workers in automobile or electronics plants) and white-collar businessman (such as managers of Dow chemical or Metropolitan Life), upward mobility, comfort, and security appeared to be the norm. Secure workers married, had children, and bought houses. Those who were excluded from this expanding middle class, particularly African-Americans, placed demands on the government for civil rights and equal opportunities. The government responded with a variety of social programs. American culture also reflected the optimism of this period of expansion and growth....

The expansion of the economy provided a certain lifestyle to thousands of American workers. My father-in-law left the army after World War II with a high school degree and got a job with the telephone company. He moved to Santa Barbara, California, and was able to buy a house for $12,000. That house today would cost at least 20 times as much, something a worker with only a high school education is unlikely to have. However, the postwar economy provided him (as it did so many Americans) with a welter of opportunities, such as to marry and raise a family in economic comfort....

Many women who had filled in for absent male workers during World War II returned home, and men filled the jobs in their stead. Those jobs, however, paid well enough to allow a single income to provide for a family. Thus, although later generations of white, middle-class women would fight for the right for equal employment, postwar affluence freed many working-class women from participating in the paid labor force. The breadwinner–homemaker model of families that had dominated the middle class was now a possibility for large portions of the working class as well. In 1940, 70% of families were male breadwinner–female homemaker families. For the next 25 years, more than half of all families conformed to this norm....

End of a Century, End of an Era

While not everyone's experience of life in America during the years 1947–1970 was upbeat, this period was generally one of economic growth, stable work, a liberal and interventionist state, and an increasingly exploratory culture. Once the stability and growth of the economy faltered, however, so too did stability and growth in other institutions. Clearly, the way social life was organized in the period after World War II is extremely different from the way social life is organized at the end of the twentieth century....

For a variety of reasons... the growth of the American economy slowed in the early 1970s. Increased international economic competition and failure to upgrade existing production techniques, among other factors, led to declining business success. As a result, employers experimented with a variety of strategies to maintain their prior economic dominance. All their efforts centered on decreasing the expenses involved in production and finding ways to compete more effectively. The less it costs to produce goods, the more profit businesses can make. Paying workers less, decreasing the number of workers hired, replacing workers with computers, robots, and automated assembly lines, moving to regions of the country and world where production was cheaper—all were ways in which American businesses tried to recoup declining profits.

Moreover, unlike in the decades following World War II, during the 1970s and 1980s other nations were competing successfully with the United States. Whereas American cars, for instance, used to dominate the automobile market, Japanese and German cars now outsold American cars. The increased economic strength of business in other countries also created more economic activity at a *global* level.

The efforts on the part of American business to succeed in the face of newly emerging international economic competitors have changed the national economy and workplace in a number of ways.

• Whereas our economic base previously came from manufacturing (e.g., cars, steel, electronics), it now comes increasingly from services (e.g., education, medical and financial services). This shift in the industrial base of the economy has, like other changes, had enormous consequences for workers and the workplace. Many service-sector jobs (such as restaurant and cleaning services) pay far less than manufacturing jobs. Those that pay well require *at least* a college education. Thus, this change results in fewer opportunities for the non-college-educated.

• Fewer and fewer workers are in jobs in which there is the possibility for continuous movement up a career ladder in a single firm. Like the IBM workers mentioned earlier, more and more workers are finding that jobs they thought they would have for a lifetime, or at least decades, are now part-time and temporary. In their efforts to create greater flexibility in the use of workers, technology, and resources, employers are replacing full-time jobs with temporary or part-time jobs, regardless of the skill or education associated with the occupation. Part-time workers are much cheaper since they receive not only lower wages but also few nonwage benefits such as health and disability insurance, paid vacations, and so forth.

• In manufacturing, roughly 75–80% of the workers used to be unionized (other industry groups such as trucking, mining, and construction had almost as many). Unions provide workers with high wages, benefits, and job security, and they provide employers with a well-disciplined work force. However, unions also create limitations for employers; they do not allow employers to fire workers when business conditions decline, for example. Thus, to increase the flexibility of the work force, employers have sought to rid their workplaces of unions, and so fewer and fewer workers have the economic and job stability that unions provide.

In summary, most of the changes in the economy and the workplace have resulted in far more insecurity and instability for workers. In addition, the paths to upward mobility have changed and have become unclear, and so many workers find themselves unsure of their future....

In addition to economic and political changes, major changes have occurred in another major institution—the family. The nuclear, breadwinner–homemaker family in which husband and wife raise their own biological offspring—once the dominant family form—is now a minority....

The increased divorce rate means that many families are now *blended*. That is, families are increasingly composed of biological parents, stepparents, children from multiple marriages, and so on. Similarly, more and more people in their 20s, instead of forming their own marriages and households, are "returning to the nest" (moving home to live with parents)....

As the question of responsibility has become more important in the context of the family, the same thing has happened in the context of government. Whereas in post–World War II years the government was actively involved in solving problems of poverty, inadequate housing and job and business regulation, in more recent decades it has withdrawn substantially from these commitments. Additionally, with the loss of the Vietnam War and the end of the cold war in the early 1990s, the American government has played an uncertain and vacillating role in international conflicts....

A second factor contributing to the withdrawal of the government from problem solving at home and intervention abroad is the reduction in resources available to the government to finance solutions. A combination of economic and demographic changes (more elderly and more young people, fewer people at high-paying jobs) has decreased the tax base. Moreover, the increasing national debt absorbs any economic surplus that could be used to finance social programs....

FROM INDUSTRIAL ECONOMY TO FLEXIBLE ECONOMY

When I graduated from high school in the Washington, D.C., area in 1972, I went to college, but my old boyfriend Ricky didn't. He looked for a good, unionized factory job. He knew he could make good money and maybe buy a little house in the same neighborhood his parents and sister Sara lived in. His sister didn't go to college, either. She had a job as a typist in a big office building outside the Beltway, in the Maryland suburbs. At the same time, my best friend's father was some sort of researcher. He worked in a big firm located in nearby Bethesda, Maryland, in which he had started out at the bottom and worked his way into one of the nice offices with huge windows. The occupants of those offices had expense accounts, three-martini lunches, and wives at home raising kids like us in well-heeled suburbs.

Now, the factory is gone, and Ricky is trying to figure out how he can keep paying his mortgage on one third of his old salary. The factory moved to Mexico and now employs young Mexican women. The home office is still in Bethesda, Maryland, but it employs only half the number of men it did 20 years ago. Most of the jobs have been taken over by computers or are done on a consulting basis. The only job Ricky could find was as a security guard for one of the new hotels that have opened up in the Washington, D.C. area.

The typewriter Sara used is also gone. When her office switched to computers, Sara had to learn how to use the new system. She thought that when she did, perhaps she could move into a better paying job, but that didn't happen. She still spends all her time typing, but now, instead of getting together with the other "girls in the pool" between typing letters, she sits alone all day in an office with a computer. During her breaks she sometimes logs into a computer bulletin board on the Internet. There, she pretends that she is a famous artist with an international reputation. Nobody knows differently; nobody will ever meet the face behind the computer identity.

My best friend's father doesn't work in Bethesda anymore, either. His office moved to Japan, and he travels back and forth now doing consulting work. He has also learned how to speak Japanese, German, and a little bit of Thai. He travels a lot and misses his family.

Neither Ricky nor his sister votes; they don't see what difference it makes. Sara is divorced and raising two children on her own. She isn't sure how to answer any of the questions her children ask; so they've stopped asking the questions. Ricky drinks too much and worries about losing his house; he blames his problems on welfare cheats and homosexuals. Neither brother nor sister really understands why nothing worked out the way they thought it would, the way it did for their parents.

The difficulty comes in seeing how large-scale social changes are affecting their day-to-day lives; but that's what is happening. From 1972, when they graduated from high school, to 1994 the *economy* —that is, the set of institutions and relationships that produces and distributes goods and services—has changed dramatically. . . .

Bad Jobs: Statically Flexible Workers

Evidence suggest that the majority of workers in the flexible workplace are not in the relatively stable core but are working in an expanded secondary labor market characterized by the *instability* of jobs (Mingione, 1991; Colclough and Tolbert, 1992). This expanded sector is characterized by strategies of static flexibility (or *numerical flexibility*) rather than a dynamically flexible production process. *Static flexibility* refers to the organization of employment around labor demand. Employers attempt to reorganize the labor process so that they have to pay workers only for specific jobs or for short periods of time. Consider the typical secretary, for example. She (about 99% of all clerical workers are female)

may be very busy at some times, but under the usual employment contract (8 hours a day, 5 days a week) she may also have long periods when there is very little work to do. Under these conditions, an employer will be paying a worker just to sit around. However, reorganizing the workplace around statically flexible workers might mean that an office does not have a full-time clerical worker but instead uses part-time or temporary clerical workers as needed. This scenario is most feasible where the skills of the statically flexible workers are minimal and interchangeable. In the labor–capital accord era, employers used this strategy only with relatively unskilled workers. In the flexible economy, however, skilled, well-educated workers are used in the same way (Colclough and Tolbert, 1992; Harvey, 1989). In fact, Belous finds that more than half of all temporary workers are employed in technical, sales, and administrative support occupations (1989, p. 28). His research also shows that "at least 17% of the temporary work force is employed in occupations that are managerial, professional, technical or skilled blue collar" (Belous, 1989, p. 29). Those occupations may well include accountants, architects, engineers, financial advisors, lawyers, and doctors, just to name a few. . . .

Displacement   At the extreme, computerization and automation eliminate jobs. More jobs have been lost to subcontracting than to technology; but technology —in combination with industrial shifts, mergers, and general downsizing—has led to a massive displacement of workers. *Displacement* is the loss of jobs for reasons that are completely independent of how well workers have worked. A worker who is habitually late and is subsequently fired leaves an opening that will probably be filled. But a worker who is out of a job because the factory moves to Mexico has been displaced.

Well-paid blue-collar workers who had benefited from the labor–capital accord constituted the majority of displaced workers in the 1970s. In the 1980s, white-collar financial, professional, and managerial workers were also displaced. Using a broad definition of displacement, evidence suggests that "displacement rates have increased by 20% to 40% since the early 1970s" (Doeringer, 1991, p. 49). Displaced workers suffer far more than the pain and economic costs of immediate job loss. Workers who cannot find equivalent jobs right away often experience permanent wage reductions and repeated job instability. Additional problems may include loss of houses, breakup of families, increased rates of alcoholism, illness, and even homelessness.

In the film *Roger and Me*, Michael Moore interviews a woman who has been displaced from her job in the auto industry. Since there were few alternative sources of employment, she resorted to selling rabbits "for pets or meat" (the title of his next movie). In one particularly chilling sequence she calmly skins a rabbit while talking about how General Motors hurt her by closing the plant, leaving her with no option but the one so gruesomely depicted in the film. While all workers do not end up selling bunnies as future stew meat, they do end up strapped for work. In their study of displaced electronics workers in Indiana, Perrucci, Perrucci, Targ, and Targ (1988) found that in addition to lost income, a diminished community tax base, and other economic indicators, the displaced workers evinced "high levels of alienation and distrust of the groups and institutions that comprise the social fabric in the community and at the national level" (p. 123).

The displacement process is one factor that has enabled the creation of a numerically flexible labor force. Workers who have been displaced from a job because of industrial restructuring or downsizing are in very vulnerable positions. When an automobile plant closes, what happens to the 50-year-old who worked in the autobody painting department for the last 30 years? There are no other automobile plants in town for him to get a comparable job. And the sector of the economy that is expanding—services—is unlikely to provide him with a job comparable to the one he's been displaced from. He doesn't have the skills or experience to obtain one of the better paid, more secure jobs in the expanding financial and business sector. The types of jobs to which he will have access (security guard, janitor) are likely to be far less lucrative. Displaced workers may be unable to find any job at all and thus join the ranks of the structurally unemployed.

Workers who are displaced have a variety of strategies for coping. Some of the more skilled and privileged displaced workers are able to start their own businesses. The local paper often has stories of people who have turned their labor market adversity into an opportunity. For example, one woman who had been displaced from an administrative position used the skills and contacts she had gained on the job to develop her own temporary employment agency, a business that has relatively low start-up costs. But not all displaced workers have these opportunities. Some fall back on behaviors that are particularly destructive (like alcoholism and substance abuse).

Contingent Work   One member of my family, Peter, worked in the banking industry for years, developing and using new computer software for the bank's information systems. Over the years Pete's job seemed to develop along the lines of flexibly specialized workers. He continually upgraded and used skills to improve the bank's communications network as part of an ongoing process, and he was rewarded handsomely for this work. When the bank merged with another bank, Pete played a central role in restructuring their communication network. Despite massive layoffs, his skills assured him of his position until his boss—and then he—were fired. For 3 years thereafter, despite an impressive array of skills and an equally impressive resume, he was unable to find another full-time job. Instead he has turned to temporary work. Corporations hire him to do a single job; when he completes the job, he has to look for more work.

Pete is not alone in this experience; he represents part of the new and expanding *contingent labor force*. The contingent labor force includes both part-time and temporary workers—some voluntarily contingent and some involuntarily so. Contingent workers receive lower pay, no fringe benefits, and little occupational protection. Their work is contingent on labor demand, and their security is up for grabs. Most would rather work full-time if they could. Research shows that since 1970, involuntary part-time work has grown 121% (Callaghan and Hartman, 1991, p. 4). It is no wonder that it is involuntary, given these conditions. Part-time workers are six times more likely to work for minimum wage than full-time workers. Additionally, the Internal Revenue Service has estimated that up to 38% of employers deliberately misclas-sify their workers as independent contractors rather than full-time workers to avoid paying unemployment compensation and social security tax (duRivage, 1992, p. 87). duRivage also finds that only one in six contingent workers is covered by a pension plan.

The involuntary, part-time work force is growing more rapidly than the full-time work force and is becoming a permanent part of the modern workplace (Callaghan and Hartman, 1991). Recent estimates suggest that contingent workers represent 25–30% of the work force and appear most often in the retail trades and in services, which are low-productivity, low-wage jobs (Callaghan and Hartman, 1991). Women make up roughly two thirds of the contingent work force. Black men in temporary, blue-collar manual work constitute the second largest category of contingent workers (duRivage, 1992). One report indicated that "displaced white-collar workers are told up front that any job they get in any company should not be expected to last longer than three to five years—if they are lucky and stay on their toes" (*Times-Picayune*, October 9, 1994).

In contrast to earlier periods, high levels of what economists call *human capital* (e.g., education, training, and skills) no longer ensure status as a primary worker as firms increasingly hire consultants, accountants, marketing researchers, lawyers and technical help on a temporary, as-needed basis. The firm of the future is likely to include very few permanent workers and to subcontract out for the rest of its workers, from the low-skill janitorial and cafeteria staff to the highly skilled workers.

Reliance on a contingent labor force has two major advantages for employers. First, it dramatically decreases labor costs. On average, part-time workers earn 60% of the hourly wages of full-time workers (Belous, 1989; duRivage, 1992, p. 87). Most receive neither pensions, health benefits, fringe benefits, nor unemployment insurance. When banks hire Peter on a contingent basis to do work similar to what he had been doing, they get the same work from him as they used to. Now, however, they do not have to pay for the generous benefits workers at his level usually receive.

Second, reliance on contingent workers also allows employers to use workers only as they need them, rather than maintain a stable work force during, for example, periods of slack demand. Ironically, though, there is evidence that employers are not using contingent workers solely in response to shifting demand conditions (i.e., hiring extra sales workers during the holiday season). Rather, they are using contingent workers on a permanent basis (Belous, 1989; Callaghan and Hartman, 1991; duRivage, 1992)....

Conclusions

Industrial transformation has eliminated many of the good—that is, stable and well-paid—jobs held by workers with only a high school diploma. Now, increasing numbers of jobs require a college education. Moreover, they require complex interpersonal skills and computer literacy, something that schools often fail to provide to all students. These differences pose dilemmas for young entrants into the labor market. Students in wealthy school districts have access to a quality of education, both in content and in resources, that can provide them with the human capital necessary to compete in the future workplace. For many more students, however, particularly those in in-

ner cities or economically depressed rural areas—in fact, all communities that lack sufficient tax monies to maintain and upgrade existing schools—the education is of a quality that leaves them increasingly unprepared for the twenty-first century. Those students who are unable to acquire the necessary skills are likely to fall into the secondary labor market. Unfortunately, given the increasingly rapid pace of knowledge growth, initial deficiencies will be even harder for those students to overcome than they were in earlier periods.

The nature of the flexible economy is such that many workers can no longer anticipate long-term employment relationships with a single employer or a small number of firms over the course of their working lives. Instead of anticipating a relatively predictable career path, more and more workers are becoming contingent workers or homeworkers. The shift to flexible employment threatens the well-being of workers in a number of ways. Workers lose access to stable health care, for instance. Correspondingly, low pay associated with the secondary labor market makes health benefits purchased from private providers harder to afford.

Flexible work arrangements also result in loss of access to retirement and other benefits. This problem is exacerbated by the anticipated increased burden on the social security system as the population ages and fewer labor-market entrants support it. Moreover, lower paid workers contribute less in taxes, reducing government's resources for providing health and retirement benefits.

The flexible workplace is less an actual place than ever before. Workers go to a job, but they are less and less likely to have a "place of work." Likewise, the job ladders they used to climb are broken. Now, they may be confronted with an endless effort to upgrade skills and hustle up jobs, just to pay the rent. Finally, work in modern society has been a major source of identity. Without a stable workplace, what will provide the bond that links people to society? What will replace the social contract that used to be formed within the workplace?

POSTSCRIPT

Are Standards of Living in the United States Improving?

Cox and Alm label as a myth the statement "U.S. living standards are falling, and Americans aren't as well off as they were 25 years ago." They are aware that many indicators seem to support this idea. They even acknowledge that wages have declined 0.8 percent per year on average since 1978. Nevertheless, they conclude that "Americans never had it so good." They support this conclusion by showing that Americans have more living space, more appliances, more leisure time, and almost five more years of life now than they did in 1970. However, Cox and Alm do not discuss the quality of family life and personal relations, which Rubin maintains are highly correlated with happiness, and they omit many other indicators, such as crime rates and measures of anxiety and stress. Rubin focuses on family life and job insecurity and denies that "Americans never had it so good."

The pessimists dominate the literature on the direction of change in the overall quality of life. America's economic difficulties are analyzed by Jeffrey Madrick in *The End of Affluence: The Causes and Consequences of America's Economic Dilemma* (Random House, 1996). Two works are extremely pessimistic about job opportunities: Jeremy Rifkin, in *The End of Work: The Decline of the Global Labor Force and the Dawn of the Post-Market Era* (Putnam, 1995), presents a picture that is more bleak than that of Rubin. Stanley Aronowitz and William DiFazio, in *The Jobless Future: Sci-Tech and the Dogma of Work* (University of Minnesota Press, 1994), focus on the relentless expansion of technology, which displaces workers. For a sensitive and astute description of the impacts of layoffs on men's identities and lives, see Kathryn Marie Dudley, *The End of the Line: Lost Jobs, New Lives in Postindustrial America* (University of Chicago Press, 1994). For a close-up look at the lives of America's suburban middle class today, see Katherine S. Newman's *Declining Fortunes: The Withering of the American Dream* (Basic Books, 1993). As her title suggests, she portrays the current generation of young adults as worse off than the previous generation. Barbara Ehrenreich also describes the hardships of the middle class in *Fear of Falling: The Inner Life of the Middle Class* (Harper Perennial, 1990). A very different interpretation of the American dream is provided by Robert J. Samuelson in *The Good Life and Its Discontents: The American Dream in the Age of Entitlements* (Times Books, 1996). He argues that the economy is doing quite well and life has improved but that Americans have exaggerated expectations so their dreams have failed and they feel that they are losing ground.

CONTRIBUTORS TO THIS VOLUME

EDITOR

KURT FINSTERBUSCH is a professor of sociology at the University of Maryland at College Park. He received a B.A. in history from Princeton University in 1957, a B.D. from Grace Theological Seminary in 1960, and a Ph.D. in sociology from Columbia University in 1969. He is the author of *Understanding Social Impacts* (Sage Publications, 1980), and he is the coauthor, with Annabelle Bender Motz, of *Social Research for Policy Decisions* (Wadsworth, 1980) and, with Jerald Hage, of *Organizational Change as a Development Strategy* (Lynne Rienner, 1987). He is the editor of *Annual Editions: Sociology* (Dushkin/McGraw-Hill) and of *Sources: Notable Selections in Sociology*, 3rd ed. (Dushkin/McGraw-Hill, 1999).

STAFF

David Dean   List Manager
David Brackley   Senior Developmental Editor
Juliana Poggio   Associate Developmental Editor
Rose Gleich   Administrative Assistant
Brenda S. Filley   Production Manager
Juliana Arbo   Typesetting Supervisor
Diane Barker   Proofreader
Lara Johnson   Design/Advertising Coordinator
Richard Tietjen   Publishing Systems Manager

AUTHORS

RICHARD ALM is a business writer for the *Dallas Morning News.*

MARCIA ANGELL is a physician, an author, and the executive editor of *The New England Journal of Medicine.* She is the author of *Science on Trial: The Clash of Medical Evidence and the Law in the Breast Implant Case* (W. W. Norton, 1996).

JEFFREY M. BERRY is a professor of political science at Tufts University in Medford, Massachusetts. He is the author of *The Interest Group Society,* 2d ed. (Scott, Foresman, 1989).

PETER BRIMELOW is a senior editor for *Forbes* and *National Review* magazines. He is also the author of *The Patriot Game* (Hoover Institution Press, 1986).

LESTER BROWN is the founder, president, and senior researcher at the Worldwatch Institute in Washington, D.C. His *State of the World* reports remain his most highly regarded and popular works.

DANIEL CASSE is senior director of the White House Writers Group, a public policy communications firm.

WILLIAM H. CHAFE is the Alice Mary Baldwin Professor at Duke University. He is the author of *The Unfinished Journey: America Since World War II,* 3rd ed. (Oxford University Press, 1995).

STEPHANIE COONTZ teaches history and family studies at the Evergreen State College in Olympia, Washington. A former Woodrow Wilson fellow, she has also taught at Kobe University in Japan and the University of Hawaii at Hilo. She is coeditor of *American Families: A Multicultural Reader* (Routledge, 1998).

W. MICHAEL COX is vice president and economic adviser at the Federal Reserve Bank of Dallas.

MARY CRAWFORD is a professor of psychology and women's studies at West Chester University of Pennsylvania.

CHRISTOPHER C. DeMUTH is president of the American Enterprise Institute for Public Policy Research.

JOHN J. DiIULIO, JR., is a professor of politics and public affairs at Princeton University in Princeton, New Jersey. His publications include *No Escape: The Future of American Corrections* (Basic Books, 1991).

G. WILLIAM DOMHOFF has been teaching psychology and sociology at the University of California, Santa Cruz, since 1965. His books on political sociology include *Diversity in the Power Elite* (Yale University Press, 1998).

NICHOLAS EBERSTADT is a researcher with the American Enterprise Institute and the Harvard University Center for Population and Development Studies. His articles have appeared in *The Public Interest, Commentary,* and *Society,* and his books include *The Tyranny of Numbers: Mismanagement and Misrule* (AEI Press, 1995).

D. STANLEY EITZEN is a professor emeritus of sociology at Colorado State University in Fort Collins, Colorado, where he has taught criminology, social problems, and the sociology of sport. His publications include *Society's Problems: Sources and Consequences* (Allyn & Bacon, 1989).

ERNEST ERBER is affiliated with the American Planning Association in Washington, D.C., which is involved in urban and rural development.

MILTON FRIEDMAN is a senior research fellow at the Stanford University Hoover Institution on War, Revolution, and Peace. He was the recipient of the 1976 Nobel Prize in economic science. He and his wife, **ROSE FRIEDMAN**, who also writes on economic topics, have coauthored several publications, including *Tyranny of the Status Quo* (Harcourt Brace Jovanovich, 1984).

The late **DAVID M. GORDON** (d. 1996) was the Dorothy H. Hirshon Professor of Economics at Manhattan's New School for Social Research. His publications include *After the Waste Land: A Democratic Economics for the Year 2000* (M. E. Sharpe, 1990).

GERTRUDE HIMMELFARB is a professor emeritus of history at the Graduate School of the City University of New York. She is the author of *Darwin and the Darwinian Revolution* (I. R. Dee, 1996).

CARL F. HOROWITZ is a policy analyst at the Heritage Foundation in Washington, D.C. He has also held an academic appointment at Virginia Polytechnic Institute and State University.

JAMES A. INCIARDI is director of the Center for Drug and Alcohol Studies at the University of Delaware, a professor in the Department of Sociology and Criminal Justice at Delaware, an adjunct professor in the Comprehensive Drug Research Center at the University of Miami School of Medicine, and a member of the South Florida AIDS Research Consortium. He has published about three dozen books and more than 180 articles and chapters in the areas of substance abuse, criminology, folklore, social policy, AIDS, medicine, and law.

JOHN ISBISTER is provost of Merrill College at the University of California, Santa Cruz, where he teaches courses on immigration, the economic development of low-income countries, and social change in the Third World. He is the author of *Promises Not Kept: The Betrayal of Social Change in the Third World*, 2d ed. (Kumarian Press, 1991)

PAUL KRUGMAN is a professor of economics at the Massachusetts Institute of Technology. He is the author of many books, including *The Accidental Theorist* (W. W. Norton, 1998).

EVERETT C. LADD is a professor of political science at the University of Connecticut and the president and executive director of the university's Roper Center for Public Opinion Research.

MARTIN A. LEE is cofounder of Fairness and Accuracy in Reporting (FAIR) in New York City and the publisher of FAIR's journal *Extra!*

H. JOACHIM MAITRE is a professor of journalism and of international relations at Boston University and director of the university's Center for Defense Journalism.

PAUL R. McHUGH is the Henry Phipps Professor and director of the Department of Psychiatry and Behavioral Sciences at Johns Hopkins University School of Medicine.

RICHARD D. MOHR is a professor of philosophy at the University of Illinois, Urbana. His publications include *A More Perfect Union: Why Straight Americans Must Stand Up for Gay Rights* (Beacon Press, 1994).

ETHAN A. NADELMANN is director of the Lindesmith Center, a New York drug policy research institute, and an assistant professor of politics and public affairs in the Woodrow Wilson School of Public and International Affairs at Princeton University in Princeton, New Jersey.

CLARENCE PAGE is a Pulitzer Prize–winning journalist for the *Chicago Tribune*.

DAVID POPENOE is a professor of sociology and an associate dean for the social sciences at Rutgers–The State University in New Brunswick, New Jersey. He is the author of *Disturbing the Nest* (Aldine de Gruyter, 1988).

JEFFREY REIMAN is the William Fraser McDowell Professor of Philosophy at American University in Washington, D.C. He is the author of *Justice and Modern Moral Philosophy* (Yale University Press, 1992).

MORGAN O. REYNOLDS is a professor of economics at Texas A&M University in College Station, Texas, and a senior fellow of the National Center for Policy Analysis in Dallas, Texas. He is the author of *Economics of Labor* (South-Western, 1994).

BETH A. RUBIN is an associate professor in the Department of Sociology at Tulane University.

CHRISTINE A. SAUM is a research associate in the Center for Drug and Alcohol Studies at the University of Delaware.

ALBERT SHANKER is president of the American Federation of Teachers in Washington, D.C. He is recognized as the first labor leader elected to the National Academy of Education, and he is the author of the Sunday *New York Times* column "Where We Stand."

ROBERT SHEAFFER is a consulting editor for *Skeptical Inquirer* and the author of *Resentment Against Achievement: Understanding the Assault Upon Ability* (Prometheus Books, 1988).

JULIAN L. SIMON is a professor of economics and business administration in the College of Business and Management at the University of Maryland at College Park. His publications include *The Ultimate Resource*, 2d ed. (Princeton University Press, 1994).

NORMAN SOLOMON is a media critic whose news analyses and articles have been published in numerous magazines and newspapers. His publications include *Killing Our Own* (Delacorte Press, 1982), coauthored with Harvey Wasserman.

DAVID STOESZ holds the Samuel S. Wurtzel Chair in Social Work at Virginia Commonwealth University in Richmond, Virginia, where he has also been a caseworker and welfare department director. He is coauthor, with Charles Guzzetta and Mark Lusk, of *International Development* (Allyn & Bacon, 1998).

DEBORAH TANNEN is a professor of sociolinguistics at Georgetown University in Washington, D.C. She is the author of *The Argument Culture: Moving from Debate to Dialogue* (Random House, 1998).

KEVIN WALTHERS teaches government at Mesquite High School in Dallas, Texas.

WALTER E. WILLIAMS is the John M. Olin Distinguished Professor of Economics at George Mason University.

INDEX

abortion, 4, 7, 198, 265, 267, 332; feminism and, 72, 73, 75, 77
academic standards, 249–250, 254–256, 257, 259
affirmative action, 47; controversy over, 170–183; women and, 178–183
African Americans: and controversy over affirmative action, 170–183; feminism and, 79; immigration and, 50, 51–53, 54
Agnew, Spiro, 31, 34
agriculture, 340–346, 349
Aid to Families with Dependent Children (AFDC), 144, 159, 161, 162, 227, 228, 230, 231, 233–241
AIDS, 33, 124, 265, 300, 302, 303, 347
alcohol, abuse of, 310–311, 313
Alm, Richard, on U.S. standards of living, 356–364
American Medical Association (AMA), 265, 268, 303
Angell, Marcia, on doctor-assisted suicide, 264–269
aquifers, 340, 342–343
Asia: drugs and, 301; economic growth in, 357
Asian Americans, affirmative action and, 171, 173, 174, 175, 178, 180–181
Asians, immigration and, 52, 53, 54–55
Australia, 146, 301, 302, 303, 306

baby boomers, 123
Bell Curve, The (Murray and Herrnstein), 147, 178
Bellah, Robert, 19
Berry, Jeffrey M., on influence of big business on government, 196–203
Bethell, Tom, 26
big business, controversy over influence of, on government, 190–203
bilingualism, 43–44, 47
block grants, 227, 233, 242, 252
boot camp, for young offenders, 324
Borker, Ruth, 88, 92, 94, 95
Brazil, 46, 212, 341
Brimelow, Peter, 51, 52, 53, 54; on immigration, 42–47
Britain, 4, 6, 8–11, 15, 51, 54, 209, 221, 256, 327
Brown, Lester, on population growth, 340–346
Buchanan, Patrick, 33
Bush, George, 31, 199, 201, 300, 303

California: affirmative action in, 171, 173–175, 177; drug policies in, 305; economic inequality in, 140; education in, 44, 254; homosexuals in, 104, 107, 108, 110–112; immigration and, 49; prisoners in, 323, 325; traditional families in, 126; welfare-to-work policy in, 235

Canada, 46, 212, 214, 302, 327
capitalism, 74, 76; controversy over role of government in, 208–222
Caplow, Theodore, 15
Carter, Jimmy, 37, 178
Casse, Daniel, on welfare reform, 226–232
Centers for Disease Control (CDC), 302, 303
Chafe, William H., on feminism, 69–79
child care, 73, 75
children: abuse and neglect of, 233; born out of wedlock, 4–6, 8, 126–127, 158; and controversy over traditional families, 118–134; and controversy over solving the ills of education, 248–259; declining mortality rate of, 348; poverty and, 154, 155, 330
China, 52, 218, 341, 343, 345, 348, 350
Chubb, John E., 249, 250
Chung, Connie, 25
cigarette smoking, health and, 295
citizen groups, influence of, on government, 196–203
civil rights: and controversy over affirmative action, 170–171, 173, 178–179, 181–183; feminism and, 65, 66, 70, 78; homosexuals and, 103–104, 107–108, 110–112; movement, 191, 196, 197, 198
Clinton, Bill, 24, 25, 26, 48, 144, 145, 146, 226, 233, 234, 235, 240, 243, 300, 303, 305
cocaine, 300, 301, 304, 306, 308, 309, 310, 311, 313
communitarian individualism, 120
Congress: and controversy over influence of big business on government, 190–203; and drug policies, 300, 302, 306; and economic inequality, 146; and immigration, 48; and physician-assisted suicide, 266; and welfare reform, 226, 227, 234, 240, 241, 243
consumption, as a measure of material welfare, 149
contingent labor force, 372–373
controlled legalization of drugs, 303–305, 306–307, 312
Coontz, Stephanie, on decline of the traditional family, 125–134
Council on Economic Advisors, President's, 226, 228
Cox, W. Michael, on U.S. standards of living, 356–364
Crawford, Mary, on gender gap, 91–98
crime: controversy over, 282–296; and controversy over effectiveness of prisons, 318–333; and controversy over legalizing drugs, 301, 303, 304, 306, 309–312; and controversy over moral

decline, 4–5, 6; immigration and, 43; inner-city street, 282–287; poverty and, 155, 159; violent street, 327–333; young males and, 123, 285, 328, 330; work-related or white-collar, 288–296
criminal justice system, reforms of, 331–332

date rape, 6
Declaration of Independence, 13–14, 20, 49
decriminalization of drugs, controversy over, 303–313
DeMuth, Christopher C., on economic inequality, 146–150
deviancy, definition of, 6–7
Dilulio, John J., Jr., on street crime versus white-collar crime, 282–287
discipline, in schools. *See* academic standards
divorce, 5, 6, 20, 67, 105, 108, 110, 119, 123, 128, 157, 159, 368
Domhoff, G. William, on influence of big business on government, 190–195
drugs, 332; controversy over decriminalization of, 300–313
D'Souza, Dinesh, 27, 179, 181, 182

early release, of older prisoners, 324
Earned Income Tax Credit, 145, 227
Eberstadt, Nicholas, on poverty, 154–160
economic growth: controversy over environmental issues and, 340–352; controversy over improving, 356–374; feminism and, 64, 66, 77–78; immigration and, 46, 47, 49–51
economic inequality, 211, 213, 218; controversy over, 140–150
economic theory of crime, 318–319
editor, news, as ideological gatekeeper, 27
education: affirmative action and, 170–176, 179; controversy over vouchers as solution to the ills of, 248–259; crime and, 332–333; economic inequality and, 144, 147–148; immigration and, 43–44, 47; poverty and, 163; single-sex, 65; and standards of living, 372, 373
Educational Alternatives, Inc. (EAI), 257–258
Eisenhower, Dwight, 16, 37
Eitzen, D. Stanley, on violent street crime, 327–333
electronic monitoring, of parolees, 324
England. *See* Britain
environmental issues, 363; and economic growth, controversy over, 340–352; health and, 295, 347, 348, 350–351
Environmental Protection Agency (EPA), 219, 295
Epstein, Richard, 181, 182
Equal Rights Amendment (ERA), 72, 73, 76, 77, 79, 108, 198
Erber, Ernest, on role of government in a capitalist economy, 208–214
Etzioni, Amitai, 126
Europe: drug policies in, 301, 302, 303, 306, 307; economic inequality in, 146; immigration from, 51, 52

euthanasia, doctor-assisted suicide and, 265, 266, 267, 271, 274
expressive individualism, 120

Families First, 228–229, 232
Federal Register, 218, 219
Federal Reserve, 210
Feminine Mystique, The (Friedan), 70, 71
feminism, controversy over, 62–79
flexible economy, 370–374
Fogel, Robert, 147, 148, 149
food: additives, health and, 295; scarcity of, and population growth, 340–346, 349
Ford, Gerald, 37
France, 15, 54, 146, 210
Frankel, Max, 27
Friedan, Betty, 70, 71, 73
Friedman, Milton, 25, 249–252; on role of government in a capitalist economy, 215–222
Friedman, Rose, on role of government in a capitalist economy, 215–222

Gans, Herbert, 32
Geiger, Keith, National Education Association and, 252
gender gap: controversy over, 84–98; experiential aspects of, 88–89, 92–93; two-cultures approach to, 92–98
Germany, 15, 51, 54, 216, 221, 302, 327
global energy economy, and controversy over population growth, 340–352
Goodwin, Marjorie Harness, 89
Gordon, David M., on poverty, 161–166
government: controversy over influence of big business on, 190–203; controversy over role of, in capitalist economy, 208–222; policy-making process of, 199–203; role of, in white-collar crime, 293–296
Gray, John, 91, 93
Great Depression, 155, 156, 157, 191, 282
gun control, 331

harm reduction, drug policies using, 301–307
health: drug policies and, 306; economic issues and, 146, 147, 150, 362; environmental issues and, 295, 347, 348, 350–351
heroin, 301, 302, 303, 304, 305, 307, 308, 309, 311, 313
Herrnstein, Richard J., 147, 148, 178
Hersh, Seymour, 34–35
Hertsgaard, Mary, 32
Himmelfarb, Gertrude, on moral decline, 4–11
Hispanics: affirmative action and, 171, 173, 175, 181; feminism and, 79; social progress and, 121
HIV, drugs and, 300, 302, 303, 307
Holland. *See* Netherlands
homelessness, 6, 154
homosexuality: controversy over, 102–114; decriminalization of, 107; employment and, 133

Horowitz, Carl F., on societal acceptance of homosexuality, 109–114
human capital, 147–148, 372, 373
hunger. *See* food

immigration: controversy over, 42–55; impact of, on economics, 46–47, 49–51; impact of, on education, 43–44
Inciardi, James A., on decriminalization of drugs, 308–313
India, 45, 212, 218, 343, 349, 351
individualism: moral conduct and, 10–11, 18–20; traditional families and, 120–121
Industrial Revolution, 209
Iran, 45, 216
Iran-contra scandal, media and, 35, 36
Ireland, 45–46, 51, 52, 54
Isbister, John, on immigration, 48–55
issue network politics, 199–203
Italy, 51, 52, 54, 210

Japan, 54, 146, 209, 212, 214, 216, 221, 321, 344, 345, 369
Job Training Partnership Act (JTPA), 230
jobs, standard of living and, 365–374
Johnson, Lyndon, 37, 121
Josephson, Michael, 13

Karp, Walter, 36
Kennedy, John F., 36, 143
Kevorkian, Jack, 264, 268, 270, 272–274, 275, 276
Keynes, John Maynard (Keynesianism/Keynesian Revolution), 210, 212
Kidder, Rushworth M., 12
Kinsley, Michael, 29, 30, 33
Krauthammer, Charles, 6, 33
Krugman, Paul, on economic inequality, 140–145

Ladd, Everett C., on moral decline, 12–20
laissez-faire policies, 213, 214
land, for agricultural use. *See* food
Latin America, drugs and, 301
Latinos: affirmative action and, 171, 173, 175, 181; immigration and, 49, 50, 51–53, 54; poverty in U.S. and, 166, 330
LEAP (Learning, Earning, and Parenting), 239
Lee, Martin A., on bias in the news media, 31–37
lesbians. *See* feminism; homosexuality
Levin, Michael, 64, 65
liberal bias, controversy over, in the media, 24–37
liberal feminism, 72–74, 79
Lipset, Seymour Martin, 14, 170

Magnet, Myron, 7
Maitre, H. Joachim, on bias in the news media, 24–30
Maltz, Daniel, 88, 92, 94, 95
marijuana, 301, 305–306, 308

marriage, 119, 121–122, 124, 127–132, 157–158; homosexual, 108, 110
Marsden, George, 16
Marxism, 64, 68, 76, 157, 209, 210
McHugh, Paul R., on doctor-assisted suicide, 270–276
media: bias in, 14; controversy over liberal bias in, 24–37; distortion of reality by, 328; suppression of information by, 26–27, 34–37
Medicaid, 162, 217, 227
Medicare, 146, 217
melting pot, metaphor of, 51–53
Men Are from Mars, Women Are from Venus (Gray). *See* gender gap; Gray, John
methadone, 303–304, 307
Meyerson, Adam, 33–34
Mexico, 52, 116, 212, 369, 371
Michigan, and controversy over doctor-assisted suicide, 264, 270, 272–276
Moe, Terry M., 249, 250
Mohr, Richard D., on societal acceptance of homosexuality, 102–108
moral decline, controversy over, 4–20
Moynihan, Daniel Patrick, 5, 6, 52, 158, 234
multiculturalism, 44–46, 47, 51–55
Murray, Charles, 6, 147, 148, 178

Nadelmann, Ethan A., on decriminalization of drugs, 300–307
Nader, Ralph, 198, 221, 294
Nation at Risk, A (National Commission on Excellence in Education), 248–249
National Gay and Lesbian Task Force, 103, 110
National Organization for Women (NOW), 72, 73, 76
Netherlands: crime in, 327–328; drug policies in, 302; doctor-assisted suicide in, 267, 272, 275
Neuhaus, Richard John, 14, 28
New Chance, 230
New Deal, 27, 154, 155, 156, 160, 217, 218, 231
new familism, 123, 124, 127
New York Times, 12, 27–28, 30, 32, 37, 146, 288, 289, 293, 365, 366
Nietzsche, Friedrich, 67–68
Nixon, Richard, 31, 34–37, 180, 305
nuclear families, 119, 121–124, 132, 368

objectivity, lack of, in news media, 24–30
Occupational Safety and Health Administration (OSHA), 293

Page, Clarence, on affirmative action, 177–183
Parent's Fair Share (PFS), 240
Pavetti, LaDonna, 241
Personal Responsibility and Work Opportunity Act (PRWOA), 233, 234, 240–243
pluralism, 53, 193, 259
political scandals, media and, 34–36
politicians and the media, 31–37

pollution, environmental, 219–220, 344, 350–351, 363
Popenoe, David, 127, 130; on decline of the traditional family, 118–124
population, controversy over environmental effects from growth of, 340–352
poverty: and controversy over economic inequality, 140–150; and controversy over welfare reform, 226–243; and crime, 155, 159, 283, 295–296, 332; "culture" of, 161, 163, 234
power, dynamics of, in cross-gender relations, 94–95, 98
power elite, influence of, on Congress, 191–192, 194–195
premarital sex, 4, 5, 6, 17
prisons, 295; controversy over effectiveness of, 318–333; drug policies in, 302; alien population in, 43
privatization: of parolee monitoring, 324; of prisons and prisoner employment, 324; of public schools, 254–259
public assistance, means-tested forms of, 155, 159. See also Aid to Families with Dependent Children
public schools, and controversy over vouchers as the solution to the ills of public education, 248–259

Quayle, Dan, and family values, 9, 125, 130; and affirmative action, 179
queerbashing, 103–104
quotas: and immigration, 48; racial and gender, and controversy over affirmative action, 172–173, 175–176, 179–183

radical feminism, 72, 74–76, 79
Ranney, Austin, 14
rape, 6, 319, 320, 322, 324, 327
Raspberry, William, 9, 239
Rather, Dan, 24, 25, 30
Reagan, Ronald, 25, 26, 31, 33, 35–37, 140, 143, 198, 199, 209, 300, 330
Reiman, Jeffrey, on street crime versus white-collar crime, 288–296
religion: homosexuality and, 105–106; moral decline and, 8, 10, 11, 14–18
Reynolds, Morgan O., on prisons, 318–326
Robinson, Michael, 14
Roosevelt, Franklin D., 36, 218, 227. See also New Deal
Rossi, Alice, 70, 71
Rothman, Stanley, 16
Rubin, Beth A., on U.S. standards of living, 365–374
Russia, 52, 209, 214, 218

Saum, Christine A., on decriminalization of drugs, 308–313

school: choice, 251–253, 256; vouchers, 248–253, 254, 255, 256, 257
sexual harassment, 97
sexual revolution, 7, 17, 124
Shanker, Albert, on school vouchers, 254–259
Sheaffer, Robert, on feminism, 62–68
Simon, Julian L., on population growth, 347–352
single-parent families, 5, 6, 9, 20, 67, 119, 122, 123, 126–127, 133, 154, 159, 322; and crime, 159–160, 284
Smith, Adam, 10, 209, 210, 215, 216, 221
Smith, Ted, 25–26
social change, and standards of living, 365–374
social feminism, 72, 76–77, 79
Social Security, 146, 217
social variables linked to criminal behavior, 328–329
Solomon, Norman, on bias in the news media, 31–37
South Korea, 147, 212
standards of living: controversy over improving, 356–374; and controversy over population growth, 340–352; and income inequality, 140–150
standards-based system of education, 256
Steinfels, Peter, 28–29
stepfamilies, 122
stereotypes: of crime, 290–291; of criminals, 289–291; of homosexuals, 102–103; as power dynamics, 94
Stoesz, David, on welfare reform, 233–243
suicide, doctor-assisted, controversy over, 264–276
Supplemental Security Income, 227
Supreme Court, 28; affirmative action and, 170, 172; doctor-assisted suicide and, 264, 266, 269; rights of criminal defendants and, 322, 325
Sweden, 15, 52, 211, 214
Switzerland, 302, 304–305

Tannen, Deborah, 93–98; on gender gap, 84–90
taxpayers, and education, 248, 250, 252, 253, 258
technology, and economic inequality, 142; standards of living and, 351–352, 358–359, 370
Temporary Assistance for Needy Families (TANF), 227, 233
Third World: and economic inequality, 142; and immigration, 44–46
Tocqueville, Alexis de, 18, 20
Troemol-Ploetz, Senta, 94–95

underclass: affirmative action and, 178, 180, 183; and controversy over moral decline, 5, 6, 9; and economic inequality, 140–142, 145; employment and wages of, 50; and poverty, 163, 164, 234, 239

unions: labor, decline of, 143–144, 145, 192, 368; teacher, 249, 252, 253, 259

values: and controversy over moral decline, 7–11, 18; and inequality of wealth, 141, 142, 145; the traditional family and, 123–124, 127, 130
Vietnam War: and feminist movement, 69, 74; impact of, on foreign policy, 369
violence: and controversy over legalizing drugs, 304, 308–312, 313; threat of, regarding homosexuals, 103–104, 113–114

Walthers, Kevin, on school vouchers, 248–253
War on Poverty, 154, 217
Warren, Earl, 322, 325
Washington Post, 29, 30, 31, 33, 35, 36
water, and controversy over effects of population growth on environment, 340–352
Watergate scandal, Nixon and, 34–36
welfare, 5, 8, 9, 144, 155, 161, 164, 217, 284

welfare reform, controversy over benefits of, 226–243
welfare-to-work programs, 235–238
white-collar crime, 288–296
Whitehead, Barbara Dafoe, 9, 159
Williams, Walter E., on affirmative action, 170–176
Wilson, William J., 283, 328
women: and controversy over feminism, 62–79; and work, 69–71, 78, 79, 129–134, 148, 161–163, 178–183
Women's Equity Action League (WEAL), 72, 73, 74
work: declining opportunities for, 147, 163–165; prisoners and, 324; and standards of living, 332, 359–361; voluntary reduction of, 148–149, 150, 360; welfare and, 144, 161–163, 164; women and, 69–71, 78, 79, 129–134, 148, 161–163, 178–183
work ethic: decline of, 212; egalitarian, 142–144
workplace, occupational health and safety and, 288–296